Domestic Violence Risk Assessment

Domestic Violence Risk Assessment

Tools for Effective Prediction and Management

SECOND EDITION

N. ZOE HILTON

AMERICAN PSYCHOLOGICAL ASSOCIATION

Published by
American Psychological Association
750 First Street, NE
Washington, DC 20002
https://www.apa.org

Order Department
https://www.apa.org/pubs/books
order@apa.org

In the U.K., Europe, Africa, and the Middle East, copies may be ordered from Eurospan
https://www.eurospanbookstore.com/apa
info@eurospangroup.com

Typeset in Charter and Interstate by Circle Graphics, Inc., Reisterstown, MD

Printer: Gasch Printing, Odenton, MD
Cover Designer: Beth Schlenoff Design, Bethesda, MD

Library of Congress Cataloging-in-Publication Data

Names: Hilton, N. Zoe, author.
Title: Domestic violence risk assessment : tools for effective prediction and management / N. Zoe Hilton.
Other titles: Risk assessment for domestically violent men.
Description: Second Edition. | Washington : American Psychological Association, 2020. | Revised edition of Risk assessment for domestically violent men, c2010. | Includes bibliographical references and index.
Identifiers: LCCN 2020023542 (print) | LCCN 2020023543 (ebook) | ISBN 9781433832918 (paperback) | ISBN 9781433833229 (ebook)
Subjects: LCSH: Abusive men. | Wife abuse.
Classification: LCC HV6626 .H47 2020 (print) | LCC HV6626 (ebook) | DDC 362.82/922—dc23
LC record available at https://lccn.loc.gov/2020023542
LC ebook record available at https://lccn.loc.gov/2020023543

https://doi.org/10.1037/0000223-000

Printed in the United States of America

10 9 8 7 6 5 4 3 2

Contents

Acknowledgments

Here I have reproduced the acknowledgments from the first edition, written by Grant Harris, Marnie Rice, and myself, with small updates, as thanks to everyone whose contributions have carried forward to this second edition. Then, I present additional acknowledgments for contributions that have been made since the publication of the first edition.

ACKNOWLEDGMENTS FROM THE FIRST EDITION

We are indebted to Detective Chief Superintendent Kathryn J. Lines, Bureau Commander of the Ontario Provincial Police (OPP) Investigation Support Bureau, for her contribution to the development of the Ontario Domestic Assault Risk Assessment and the collaborative research of the OPP and the Mental Health Centre Penetanguishene (MHCP), now Waypoint Centre for Mental Health Care (Waypoint). We owe a great deal of gratitude and appreciation to our respected friends and colleagues, Catherine Cormier, Sonja Dey, Angela Wyatt Eke, and Carol Lang, for their contribution to the ideas and work contained in this book.

The Ontario Ministry of Community Safety and Correctional Services (MCSCS), Peel Regional Police, and York Regional Police permitted and facilitated access to offender information. In particular, we thank Kathy Underhill, Tina Gaspardy, Gregory Brown, Ed Gale, Al Cleewer, Karen Noakes, C. Daunt, staff of MCSCS Archives, Probation and Parole offices throughout Ontario, and the OPP Behavioural Sciences and Analysis Section data entry, information technology and Eric Silk Library staff. We also thank Norah Holder and Mary Metcalfe of the Orillia Soldiers Memorial Hospital, Sarah Kaplan and Maureen Hartle of the Cornwall Hospital, Nancy Stirling of Muskoka Interval House, and Natalie Seltzer of Rosewood Shelter, and their clients, for sharing information pertaining to clinical interviews.

Several of our colleagues reviewed drafts of the first edition of this book. Michael Seto read large parts of the manuscript and provided insightful suggestions. Carol Lang consulted on the scoring of the practice cases and painstakingly edited the scoring criteria in the Appendices. We also thank Catherine Cormier, Angela Wyatt Eke, Martin Lalumière, Shari McKee, and Vern Quinsey for their comments on draft chapters. Sonja Dey and Amilynn Sharpe carefully examined the entire manuscript for consistency. For the final content of the first edition, we thank an anonymous scholar who reviewed the book for the American Psychological Association, and Emily Leonard, our cheerful and encouraging production editor.

Many people have been directly involved in our research into domestic violence, and we thank Craig Beach, Stacey Beckles, Leslie Belchamber, Skye Berry, Andrea Boyd, Tamara Burke, Joseph Camilleri, Ashley Caputo, Amanda Cocclioni, Jennifer Ellis, Marnie Foster, Michelle Green, Kelly Grubb, Elke Ham, Ruth Houghton, Angela Knowlton, Tracey Lowe-Wetmore, Carolyn Lucarillo, Sarah McGuire, Julie McKay, Andrew Parker, Alyssa Quesnelle, Rob Rawn, Kelly Rawson, and Amilynn Sharpe. We have also enjoyed a productive collaboration with Suzanne Popham, Chief Psychologist of the Algoma Treatment and Remand Centre, Sault Ste. Marie, Ontario.

Throughout our research careers, we have benefited from the support of senior administrators at the Mental Health Centre Penetanguishene and, more recently, Waypoint. We would like to thank Waypoint staff, particularly Pat Reid and Jolene Wintermute, upon whose excellent librarian services we have depended; Trent Maracle, who has given tireless support to the ODARA training program; and Barb Desroches who provided pleasant and efficient confidential access to clinical files over many years, followed more recently by Amanda Macy and other Clinical Information Services staff.

The research reported in this book was supported by operating funds of Waypoint and of the OPP, the Social Sciences and Humanities Research Council of Canada, and more recently by Justice Canada, Public Safety Canada, the Ontario Mental Health Foundation, and the Ontario Ministry of Community Safety and Correctional Services. The opinions expressed herein do not necessarily reflect the opinions of these funders.

We express our gratitude to our spouses, Brad Fisher, the late Emily Harris, and Greg Rice, for their support, and to Janice Leadbetter for providing loving and reliable childcare during the years of the research described in the first edition this book.

ACKNOWLEDGMENTS FOR THE SECOND EDITION

Grant Harris and Marnie Rice did not have the opportunity to contribute to this second edition. Yet this book is largely a product of the years in which Grant and Marnie were my teachers, mentors, and friends. All the ODARA and DVRAG construction and cross-validation research, as well as many other studies that I describe in the book, was done together with Grant, Marnie, and other members of their research team.

I am deeply grateful to family, friends, and colleagues who stood with me through the sudden and complicated losses of 2014 and 2015. I am thankful for opportunities to work with new research partners for the first time. At Waypoint, Elke Ham and Shari McKee gave me courage to continue through dark times, and the endeavors we undertook together have flourished thanks to their creativity, intelligence, and remarkable work ethic. Sandy Jung, Liam Ennis, and Kevin Nunes invited me to join their proposal on Optimizing Risk Assessment for Domestic Violence, and we have ventured into threat assessment research, built new alliances, and laughed a lot together. Being part of the Communication of Risk Assessment project with Maaike Helmus brought me the renewed delight of conducting experimental studies and many moments of statistical excitement. Meeting and working with early-career researcher Dana Radatz has been a pleasant surprise, and our harmonious working and writing styles have proven productive.

I thank the professionals who shared their experiences of implementing the ODARA across the United States and Canada: Mary Ann Campbell, Delaney Dixon, Crystal Giesbrecht, Kate Faragher Houghton, Becky Kinnamon, Chris Lowenkamp, Sherie Luevano, Faye Luppi, Hayley Maddeaux-Young, David River, Doris Schnell, Rachel Zimmermann Smith, Stephanie Stanford, Scott Stevens, Johnnie Trujillo, and Avis Vallis.

I am indebted to colleagues who provided thoughtful and constructive feedback on draft chapters or statistical advice on analyses conducted or verified for this edition: Angela Book, Catherine Cormier, Angela Wyatt Eke, Liam Ennis, Anne Harris, Barna Konkoly-Thege, Karl Hanson, Maaike Helmus, Olivia Humphreys, Sandy Jung, Shari McKee, Kevin Nunes, Anna Pham, Vern Quinsey, and Michael Seto. Dana Radatz gave helpful feedback on several original and revised chapters. Elke Ham independently scored the practice cases and consulted on the scoring criteria, and she and Della Saunders generously read all chapters and gave feedback on content, style, and consistency. Finally, I thank the three anonymous reviewers and David Becker, APA Books Development Editor, for their thoughtful and constructive suggestions.

I dedicate this second edition to Grant Harris and Marnie Rice, in sorrow and remembrance.

Domestic Violence Risk Assessment

INTRODUCTION

Domestic Violence Risk Assessment and Management

Randy Iles was in his third marriage when he began an intimate relationship with Arlene May. His previous marriages had ended with episodes of child abduction, stalking, and threats with a weapon. He had amassed criminal convictions for harassment, possession of stolen property, breach of probation, and a weapons offense. Witnesses later recalled that Iles's violence toward May began when she became pregnant. Soon after, May went to a shelter for abused women and contacted the police to report an assault. Iles was arrested and attended a bail hearing, but the court was unaware of an outstanding arrest warrant in the neighboring jurisdiction. He was granted bail, ordered to leave the jurisdiction and not to have contact with May, and forbidden to acquire firearms. But he continued to contact May with death threats, and the license enabling him to purchase firearms was never confiscated.

There was a warrant for Iles's arrest for breaching bail conditions when he purchased a gun and ammunition and waited at May's home. When she and her children arrived, he took them hostage. He later released the children but shot and killed May and himself. This case summary was drawn

https://doi.org/10.1037/0000223-001
Domestic Violence Risk Assessment: Tools for Effective Prediction and Management, Second Edition, by N. Z. Hilton

from information that is publicly available (e.g., Ontario Office of the Chief Coroner, 1998) and sufficient to score the Ontario Domestic Assault Risk Assessment (ODARA; Hilton et al., 2004), one of the risk assessment tools in this book. Had the ODARA then existed, it would have been possible in about 10 minutes to ascertain that Iles was, at the time of his prior court appearances, in the highest category of risk for repeated domestic assault. Research with the ODARA also suggests that had this score been presented, the court would have been more likely to hold Iles in pretrial custody.

RISK ASSESSMENT TOOLS IN THIS BOOK

The ODARA is a 13-item actuarial risk assessment that was developed and cross-validated on samples of several hundred men with a police record for assault on a female domestic partner. Actuarial tools are used to predict outcomes using data from measured variables that are combined using mechanical formulas derived from the variables' statistical associations with the outcome. For example, insurance companies use actuarial tools to identify individuals' risk of accidents, illness, or death within the time period of their insurance coverage. The ODARA was designed to predict the likelihood of domestic violence recidivism. Higher ODARA scores are related to greater risk of a new domestic assaults, to shorter time until the first new assault, and to more frequent and severe future assaults. ODARA scores are divided into risk categories. Each category is associated with a likelihood of recidivism (within a specified definition and time frame) and a percentile rank, so that assessed men can be compared with others in terms of risk for domestic violence recidivism. There is evidence that the ODARA is also a valid predictor of domestic violence recidivism by women. The ODARA is easy to score and interpret and has shown excellent interrater agreement, especially after brief training, making it an important part of efforts to promote a coordinated, cross-sector response to domestic violence.

The Domestic Violence Risk Appraisal Guide (DVRAG; Hilton, Harris, Rice, et al., 2008) is a related actuarial tool with a similar development and purpose. It offers a way to combine the ODARA items with the Psychopathy Checklist–Revised (PCL-R; Hare, 2003). The PCL-R was created to help understand the personality characteristics and behavior patterns associated with psychopathy, and it has become well known for its ability to identify individuals in correctional and forensic settings who are most at risk for reoffending. The DVRAG requires more resources to score than the ODARA does, and it uses weighted scores for most of its items rather than simply scoring yes or no for each item. The DVRAG was created to improve prediction of domestic violence recidivism in relatively high-risk samples, in which detecting differences among individuals can be more challenging.

The ODARA and DVRAG are considered "static" tools to the extent that their items concern events occurring up to and including the most recent domestic assault (see Chapter 8 for a discussion of definitions and limitations of static vs. dynamic risk assessment). It is not recommended that scores are adjusted to reflect subsequent events, with the exception that assessors may opt to reassess individuals after a new domestic assault.

Like actuarial approaches in general, the ODARA and DVRAG are largely atheoretical. Causal theories have been important in generating tests of domestic violence risk factors at the individual, interpersonal, and sociocultural level, as I describe in Chapter 1. In contrast, there has been limited theory development in the field of risk assessment generally, and domestic violence risk assessment especially. The perspective I adopt in this book is largely influenced by the Risk–Need–Responsivity (RNR) principles of effective correctional service (e.g., Bonta & Andrews, 2017). The RNR principles are derived from the general personality and cognitive social learning theory of criminal conduct, and I recommend Bonta and Andrews's work for its balance of theory, research, and practical wisdom. Readers interested in explanations of domestic violence could begin with Ali and Naylor's (2013) overview of the most influential theories. However, assessors do not need to be conversant with theory to use the ODARA and DVRAG.

NEED FOR DOMESTIC VIOLENCE RISK ASSESSMENT

Violence in intimate relationships has a long criminal justice history (e.g., Hilton, 1989), but views and understandings of this behavior have changed dramatically over our lifetimes. Indeed, in the 2 decades since the May–Iles tragedy that spurred the Ontario government into action, there has been progress in identifying those men at greatest risk for committing severe violence in intimate relationships and in building more effective responses to this problem.

A pivotal influence on the decision my colleagues and I took to study men who assault their female partners was a call by the Government of Ontario for such research in response to the May–Iles tragedy. A high-profile inquiry identified poor communication across jurisdictions, and failure to share records, as causes of the criminal justice system's failure in this case. It recommended that the Ontario Provincial Police "in consultation with representatives from shelters, victim services and other authorities in the field of domestic violence, develop a risk assessment instrument" (Ontario Office of the Chief Coroner, 1998, Recommendation H6). The inquiry also recommended policies directing police officers to assess risk during routine domestic violence investigations (Recommendation C4). A government committee subsequently made 11 recommendations for the development and implementation of risk assessments by police, community services, probation, parole, and correctional facilities (Baldwin, 1999).

This work led directly to our research collaboration with Kate Lines, then a detective inspector managing the Ontario Provincial Police's Behavioural Sciences and Analysis Section and a member of that government committee. The research team at first included me, Marnie Rice, Grant Harris, Catherine Cormier, and Carol Lang from the Research Department at the Mental Health Centre Penetanguishene (now Waypoint Centre for Mental Health Care; I describe the team and our work in more detail in Chapter 3 of this volume). With expertise in investigation and records management from the Behavioural Sciences and Analysis Section, and research and statistical expertise from the research team—plus several months developing proposals, submitting grant applications, and ensuring confidential and secure handling of information—a productive and enduring partnership began. As a result of this partnership, the ODARA was developed and validated over the next few years (Hilton et al., 2004) and was admitted as evidence in court soon after its publication.

The ODARA proved useful in a subsequent case for which our research team provided expert testimony and is summarized here with names and several other details changed. On an unusually warm November morning, James crouched between the garbage cans outside the shelter where he stayed after a breakup with his girlfriend Angie. She was coming to bring him some belongings, and as he waited, she approached on the back of a motorbike driven by a mutual friend. When Angie went to the shelter's front door, James sprang out and ran toward the friend, an iron bar in one hand and a paper bag with eye holes over his head. He clubbed the friend on the neck and back with the bar. Angie ran to stop James, but he pushed her to the ground. In the struggle, the paper bag was torn off, revealing James's identity. James ran off but was soon arrested and charged with assault, mischief, and using a disguise while committing an indictable offense. At a bail hearing, the prosecutor submitted James's score on the new ODARA risk assessment tool. The arresting police officer testified that James's score placed him in the highest category: Fewer than 10% of men with a police report of violence against a domestic partner in the ODARA construction and cross-validation research scored in this range. The court admitted the ODARA score into evidence and detained James in custody to await trial.

SCOPE OF THIS BOOK

This book is about measuring and communicating the risk of domestic assault recidivism. I describe the work that my colleagues and I, our collaborators, and other researchers have done to study this problem and develop tools to aid service provision in criminal justice, offender treatment, and victim safety. I present a risk assessment system comprising the ODARA and DVRAG so that others can learn to score, interpret, and communicate the results of these assessments and to incorporate their results into public policy. These tools were cross-validated before initial publication, and validation research has continued since then. It is important to test risk assessment tools in different populations, to examine modifications that may be necessary before they are applied, and to search for improvements to the tools and to the risk assessment and management process. Since the first edition of this book, the ODARA has become one of the most widely tested and used domestic violence risk assessment tools. In this second edition, I describe all the published and unpublished studies testing the ODARA and DVRAG's discriminative accuracy that I am aware of at the time of writing (Chapters 3–5). Risk assessment research has taken some new and important directions, and domestic violence risk assessment researchers in particular have begun to look beyond assaults perpetrated by men against female partners. I describe this research as it concerns domestic violence risk assessment broadly (in Part I); the ODARA and DVRAG specifically (in Part II); and other considerations, such as risk communication and controversial issues in risk assessment (Part III).

One thing that has not changed in the second edition is how the ODARA and DVRAG are scored and interpreted. I have modified some of the item names and clarified other details to improve understanding and optimize scoring accuracy on the basis of feedback from 15 years of training professionals on these tools. I have also aimed for gender-neutral language in the ODARA scoring criteria on the basis of initial evidence of the ODARA's predictive validity for domestic violence recidivism for women (such research has not yet been conducted for the DVRAG). The DVRAG-4, an alternative scoring method that uses only a subset of PCL-R items, has been added. There has not yet been sufficient research to support other substantial changes such as adding new items or removing others, although this might happen in the future.

Audience

The work described in this book has been published in journals and presented at training sessions for academics, child protection workers, clinicians, lawyers, nurses, physicians, police officers, policymakers, probation and corrections officers, and shelter workers. Here, I bring this work together in a comprehensive volume and in a format accessible to readers outside of any specialized discipline yet suitable for those who want to delve into more detail. I show how the ODARA and DVRAG can function as one system of risk assessment across the criminal justice, offender treatment, and community victim service sectors and how sharing a common risk assessment method can aid communication and promote an integrated community response to violence against intimate partners. The full scoring criteria and various interpretation materials (verbal, numeric, and graphic) provided in Chapters 6 and 7 can be used by all those who need to identify the individuals most at risk of recidivism, decide on release conditions, determine priority for intervention, or assist a client who has been assaulted. Thus, this book is written with a view to supporting assessors, policy analysts, and others undertaking professional training.

The book will also appeal to academic faculty teaching graduate courses in applied risk assessment in the context of policing, corrections, social work, or mental health or to those in graduate programs offering specialized training in domestic violence research and counseling that have expanded in recent years. The second edition responds to this growing audience by engaging students with a variety of new features. "Researcher Profiles" provide insight into the career paths of emerging and established researchers in the domestic violence and risk assessment fields, including their thoughts on future directions for research and practice. Chapter summaries have been streamlined and styled as "Points to Remember" to aid student note-taking and individual study. "Questions to Consider" suggest five questions on the details and implications of each chapter to aid classroom discussion, self-study, or course assignment.

Terminology

I use the word *assault* to refer to specific acts of physical violence (listed in Chapter 6) involving physical contact with the person being assaulted or the use of a weapon to cause or threaten physical harm. I also refer to assaults and other physically violent acts as *violence*. In the first edition, my coauthors and I referred to assaults perpetrated by a man against a woman with whom he had lived at any time as *wife assault*, as distinct from violence against a stranger, acquaintance, or dating partner. The body of research on domestic violence risk assessment, including the ODARA, has since expanded to include violence by women and encompass violence in dating relationships; therefore, I refer to such violence as *domestic violence,* especially when referring to the wider literature, but take care to refer to the gender by which sample cases are identified wherever possible.

Throughout the book, I use the word *risk* to indicate the chance, probability, or likelihood that an event will occur. Most often, I mean the risk of *recidivism* (the reoccurrence of crime), or of being an individual who *recidivates* (commits another offense after the assessment, also sometimes referred to as being a *recidivist*), by means of a new act of assault. *Risk assessment,* then, is the process or method of evaluating or estimating the likelihood of recidivism. The primary outcome is usually whether such recidivism occurred, but my colleagues and I also measured the severity and frequency of recidivism and how soon it occurred. The ODARA and DVRAG also *rank-order* assessed individuals or place them in order from the least to greatest risk of recidivism. I aim to use terms such as *individuals who have committed domestic offenses* in place of *offenders* or *perpetrators* in keeping with current standards for person-first language in preference to convenient, but potentially dehumanizing, shorthand labels.

I acknowledge that many terms are in current use to describe violence against domestic and intimate partners and that readers may use different terms from (or even object to) those used in this book. Many professionals now prefer the term *intimate partner violence* (IPV), and in this edition, I use IPV when describing research studies and samples that included (or possibly included) partners who were not married or living together. The original ODARA and DVRAG research, however, included only men who were or had been married or living with the women they assaulted. Moreover, *domestic* was the preferred term for this type of violence among the ODARA/DVRAG research team and our partners at the time the tools were created, and domestic assault and domestic violence became part of the names by which they are now widely known. Some authors define violence as encompassing not only physical violence, but also verbal aggression, psychological and emotional abuse, and other forms of harm. In contrast, I use violence to mean assault (defined at the beginning of this section); I aim to specify the definitions of IPV used in studies that I review in this book.

Appropriate terminology changes over time. What remains most important for effective communication is that the results of risk assessment be reported in terms with a shared understanding. In the actuarial approach, assessments are reported as numerical scores and percentile ranks with objective interpretations and are also expressed in words or graphs (Chapters 6 and 7). Communicating risk in this way is possible because of the data obtained in follow-up studies used to construct actuarial instruments.

Applicability

Although the ODARA and DVRAG research was conducted in one Canadian province, my colleagues and I took steps to enhance the generalizability of our findings to similar populations. For example, the research was conducted in a diverse population, and no cases were excluded on the basis of individuals' race, ethnicity, religion, or socioeconomic status. Furthermore, casting our research nets province-wide meant including both multicultural urban areas and less populated regions, including Indigenous communities. Finally, we validated the ODARA and DVRAG in the Greater Toronto Area, Canada's largest and most ethnically diverse metropolis. Extensive research indicates that the strongest predictors of violent recidivism are the same across cultures. The methods we used to develop the ODARA/DVRAG system were the same as those used to develop actuarial systems that have proven to be valid predictors of recidivism by violent offenders and sex offenders in Canada, the United States, Australia, Asia, and Europe (Harris, Rice, et al., 2015; http://www.vrag-r.org/). I hope these tools will help prevent the kinds of serious miscalculation and poor communication that resulted in the May–Iles tragedy. More generally, valid risk assessment is essential to a system that cannot allocate all services equally to all cases but must apportion resources in accordance with risk.

Risk Management

I take the position in this book, as in related works on violence risk assessment (e.g., Harris, Rice, et al., 2015), that accurate assessment of risk is essential to effective risk management. There is growing consideration of the need to adhere to the RNR principles when identifying characteristics or circumstances that require intervention to reduce domestic violence recidivism. Research has not yet established which levels of supervision, treatment, or safety planning reduce domestic violence recidivism, but RNR provides a strong empirical evidence base for risk management decisions. The risk management process begins with the principle that cases at greatest risk of recidivism receive the most comprehensive interventions (e.g., Bonta & Andrews, 2017). Valid risk assessment is, therefore, indispensable to evidence-based risk management. The ODARA and DVRAG are validated tools that support this first essential step.

PLAN FOR THIS BOOK

This edition is divided into three parts. Part I, Overview of Domestic Violence Risk Assessment, includes two chapters that survey the state of the field. Chapter 1 is new for this second edition. It outlines the leading theories of risk for domestic violence and gives an overview of the research literature that is at least partly influenced by theory, from tests of individual risk factors for assaulting a partner through to typologies and multi-item risk assessment tools and guides. Chapter 2 describes how and why the ODARA and DVRAG development research was focused on the criminal justice system, with men's physical violence against female domestic partners as a priority, and explains the rationale for developing assessments to quantify risk. Readers will also find brief explanations of the statistics used in evaluating the accuracy of risk assessment tools, the principles of effective correctional service, and how actuarial risk assessment works within criminal justice, offender intervention, and victim support services. Students and others seeking a review of the literature and methodological context into which the ODARA and DVRAG fits will find it in Part I.

Part II, Understanding and Applying the ODARA and the DVRAG, delves into the how and why of these tools. Chapter 3 describes the construction and testing of the ODARA in samples of men drawn from police reports of domestic violence in Ontario, Canada. A new Chapter 4 chronicles studies that have validated and applied the ODARA in different populations, relationships, and jurisdictions and for various outcomes, mostly conducted since the first edition. Chapter 5 sets out the construction and validations of the DVRAG and considers the explanatory power of general antisociality, which makes a large contribution to the statistical prediction of domestic violence. Chapter 6 comprises the ODARA scoring manual and provides the newly clarified eligibility and scoring criteria, frequently asked questions, interpretation tables and figures, and a sample report. Chapter 7 does the same for the DVRAG. Readers already versed in domestic violence risk assessment research and methods can dive into Part II.

Part III examines additional considerations for risk assessment and management. Chapter 8 reviews current controversies in domestic violence risk assessment that have important implications for choosing risk assessment tools, interpreting their results, and applying them to risk management and policy decisions. In this new chapter, I critically examine the evidence for clinical judgment, dynamic risk, prediction models, and individual-level interpretations. Chapter 9 attends to the importance of effectively communicating risk to practitioners, decision makers, and individuals affected by domestic violence. Risk communication is an integral part of the risk assessment and risk management process. This chapter shows the pitfalls of avoiding numbers and how verbal terms or categories such as "low risk" or "high risk" show poor agreement and can be inappropriately influenced by contextual factors having nothing to do with individuals' risk of recidivism. The chapter is substantially updated with research conducted in the past few years, including promising practices to improve risk communication. Chapter 10 shows how actuarial assessments can be used to develop criminal justice policy intended to reduce violent recidivism and recounts the experience of working with the police and bail courts in Ontario. New for this edition, I share lessons learned from ODARA implementation experiences in the United States and Canada that I have been privileged to assist with over the past 10 to 15 years. Finally, Chapter 11 poses and answers some of the most frequently asked questions about using the ODARA/DVRAG system.

A new Afterword considers the future of domestic violence risk assessment research and practice. The Appendix includes four all-new fictional materials for scoring practice and reliability testing for the ODARA and DVRAG.

In sum, this book is a substantially revised edition, with new chapters on domestic violence risk research, controversial issues in risk assessment, and ODARA validation studies. Other updates include emerging research directions, such as assessing risk among women who offend or individuals who assault same-sex partners, advances in risk communication, and the application of risk assessment to threat assessment and to other forms of family violence. Detailed exhibits on side issues or analyses have been reduced in favor of adding researcher profiles, points to remember, and questions to consider at the end of several chapters to facilitate academic study and continuing education. ODARA and DVRAG scoring manuals are incorporated into the body of the book. I hope this edition will be a learning resource for students and professionals, as well as a reference source for the ODARA and DVRAG.

PART I OVERVIEW OF DOMESTIC VIOLENCE RISK ASSESSMENT

1 DOMESTIC VIOLENCE RISK ASSESSMENT RESEARCH AND THEORY

Domestic occurrences comprise the largest category of calls to police in the United States (e.g., Klein, 2009), and violence against intimate partners accounts for more than one in four victims of violent offending reported to police in Canada (Burczycka & Conroy, 2017). After a long history with criminal justice systems that overlooked, limited, or failed to enforce criminal sanctions against assaults on intimate partners, domestic violence now commands substantial attention from law enforcement (for reviews, see Hilton & Ennis, 2020; Hilton & Harris, 2009a; Maxwell & Garner, 2012). This extraordinary change is partly due to the battered women's movement (e.g., Hilton, 1989). It also results from strategies within policing agencies to increase arrests and evaluate their effectiveness. These endeavors have not been without their challenges, and reaction to some aspects of traditional policing approaches (including unanticipated consequences of gender-neutral policies; e.g., Fraehlich & Ursel, 2014) led to further efforts such as increased prosecution (e.g., Maxwell & Garner, 2012) and specialized domestic violence courts (e.g., Collins et al., 2019; Tutty & Koshan, 2013). To better manage the criminal justice burden of domestic violence, and

https://doi.org/10.1037/0000223-002
Domestic Violence Risk Assessment: Tools for Effective Prediction and Management, Second Edition, by N. Z. Hilton

protect victims assaulted by their intimate partners, police and courts began implementing risk assessment procedures in the 1990s, following a longer tradition in correctional services (e.g., Hilton & Ennis, 2020).

WHAT IS RISK ASSESSMENT?

Risk assessment is a prognostic task (i.e., estimating the likelihood of an offense) rather than a diagnostic task (determining whether a person is "dangerous" or not; e.g., Helmus & Babchishin, 2017). The essential purpose of violence risk assessment is to enable the differential handling of cases. Detaining accused persons, rather than releasing them with a notice to appear in court, is an instance in which a distinction is made at least partly on the perceived likelihood of violent recidivism—that is, a subsequent act of violence. Other examples are applying conditions to release on bail, sentencing a convicted individual to custody rather than probation, prioritizing some individuals over others for the most comprehensive domestic violence treatment program available in a community, and assigning individuals to more or less intense supervision protocols. Considerable research demonstrates that the effects of criminal justice and therapeutic interventions are maximized when their intensity is determined by the level of risk (e.g., Bonta & Andrews, 2017). Incarceration and community supervision are two broad tools the criminal justice system has to impede violent offending, and risk assessment can help identify persons who are most in need of such restrictions. The principles of effective practice, however, involve an array of interventions designed to help individuals change their behavior. The extent to which correctional services address characteristics that are most strongly related to offending behavior significantly affects their success (e.g., Bonta & Andrews, 2017).

Risk assessment, therefore, is a necessary first step in risk management: the process of identifying and intervening with individuals deemed likely to commit a new offense. Structured methods to aid the assessment of risk of domestic violence, or violence against a current or past marital, cohabiting or dating partner (intimate partner violence [IPV]) first emerged in the late 1990s, and reviews remain limited to a handful of studies per tool (e.g., Graham et al., 2019; Messing & Thaller, 2013). The field still faces substantial limitations, not least being that the vast majority of validation studies are restricted to men who assault women. Much of this research has been an atheoretical search for factors that increase the likelihood that domestic violence will occur, but the choice of variables to investigate, at least initially, was driven by theory. I begin by briefly tracing these approaches.

THEORIES OF RISK FOR DOMESTIC VIOLENCE

Theoretical foci in this field can be broadly described as ranging from the predisposing, psychological characteristics of individuals to predetermining, political aspects of society as a whole. There has been substantial tension between these two extremes, some strong debate (e.g., Dutton, 2012), and attempts to move from broad strokes to complex, multilevel explanations.

Individual Level

A focus on intrapersonal risk factors derives from the theoretical notion that, regardless of the sociopolitical environment, some individuals are more likely to perceive and respond to environmental cues with violence. Further, these individuals can be distinguished from others, who are less likely to assault their partners. In theory at least, these distinctive features are causal contributors to violence and, therefore, promising targets for therapies to reduce risk.

The first explanations of domestic violence focused on individual psychology. This perspective remains the largest in terms of accumulated empirical support, as observed by Corvo and Johnson (2013), who described it as the most parsimonious and thorough explanation. In one of the earliest accounts, Gayford's (1975) article on 66 "battered wives" assumed that identifying risk factors in individual case histories would be valuable for prevention. The women described their physically violent husbands' problematic drinking, gambling, and "pathological jealousy." Research has since identified a range of psychological characteristics, such as anger, depression, lack of assertiveness, and violence-supportive attitudes that appear more common among men who perpetrate domestic violence than comparison samples, across community and institution-based studies (e.g., Birkley & Eckhardt, 2015; Hanson et al., 1997; Holtzworth-Munroe et al., 1997). There is a well-established link between frequent or problematic alcohol or drug use and domestic violence, as illustrated in a meta-analysis of 285 studies (Cafferky et al., 2018).

Psychopathology was prevalent in foundational studies of men in domestic violence treatment (e.g., Hamberger & Hastings, 1989). These findings continue to be confirmed in more recent research, with evidence of psychiatric disorders (e.g., depression, anxiety, and personality disorder) in men's and women's self-reports and clinical interviews (e.g., Askeland & Heir, 2014; Shorey, Elmquist, et al., 2012; Shorey, Febres, et al., 2012). Psychological tests also suggest poorer self-regulation and cognitive functioning among men convicted of domestic violence than nonoffenders (e.g., Becerra-García, 2015). Impaired interpersonal functioning, along with hostility and impulsivity, are diagnostic criteria for borderline personality disorder (BPD; American Psychiatric Association, 2013). BPD has attracted a good deal of attention from researchers seeking to understand individual-level contributors to domestic violence. For example, borderline personality features contribute six items to the Propensity for Abusiveness Scale (PAS), a 29-item self-report assessment derived from a study of 140 men in domestic violence treatment and their female partners (Clift et al., 2005). Other items measure anger, attachment, trauma symptoms, and childhood treatment by parents. There is evidence in clinical and community settings that higher PAS scores relate to men's threats and physical aggression against partners (e.g., Dutton et al., 2001). Women in community treatment for domestic violence have scored higher than their male counterparts (Allen et al., 2015).

BPD may encapsulate the outward expression of emotional dysregulation, empathy deficits, and impulsivity that are thought to mediate the relation between borderline and antisocial personality features and perpetration of domestic violence (e.g., Jackson et al., 2015; Romero-Martínez et al., 2016). Measures of antisocial personality have been consistently related to the occurrence, frequency, and severity of domestic violence among men and women (e.g., Cunha et al., 2018; Fernández Suárez et al., 2018), although the association appears to be stronger for men (e.g., Kelley & Braitman, 2016; Mager et al., 2014). My colleagues and I contributed to this body of work (Hilton et al., 2001; Hilton, Harris, Rice, et al., 2008), and I say more about implications of psychopathy for domestic violence theory in Chapter 6.

Individual-level theories of domestic violence have begun to draw on the extensive literature on the biological bases of violent behavior (e.g., Barnes et al., 2013; Pinto et al., 2010). One study of same-sex twins (87% female) found that self-reported domestic violence was more similar between identical than fraternal twins, which is evidence that genetic factors account for some of the variation in violence perpetration (Hines & Saudino, 2004). Scientists can now analyze genes relatively easily from saliva samples, and there is growing research showing that men who have certain gene variations are more likely to commit repeated assault or injure their partner (e.g., Stuart et al., 2016).

Interpersonal and Family Level

Interpersonal-level perspectives hold that factors related to the interaction of dyads or groups (in the case of domestic violence, the intimate relationship or the family) are necessary to understand domestic violence fully. An example is family systems theory, which describes domestic violence as occurring in the context of a host of stressors within the relationship (e.g., financial stress) and other aspects of family life, such as parenting (e.g., Holt et al., 2008). There is a well-established association of marital discord or dissatisfaction with physical aggression by either partner, and especially by men (e.g., Stith et al., 2008). Conflict with parents-in-law has also been associated with self-reported perpetration by men (Chan, 2014). Family systems theory has produced fruitful research on the intergenerational transmission of violence.

The intergenerational transmission hypothesis is that domestic violence seen and learned in childhood is later expressed in one's adolescent and adult relationships. Self-report research with community, treatment, and custodial samples provides consistent support for childhood abuse or domestic violence exposure being a risk factor for later perpetration (e.g., Chan, 2014; Costa et al., 2015; Godbout et al., 2019; Hilton, Ham, & Green, 2019; Milaniak & Widom, 2015). However, the effect is small and possibly stronger for men than women (Cubellis et al., 2018; O'Leary et al., 2014).

Intergenerational transmission is often interpreted from a broad social learning perspective, whereby aggression is learned through processes of modeling and positive reinforcement. Social learning theory has garnered some empirical support (e.g., Wareham et al., 2009). However, there is relatively little work on the mechanisms of intergenerational transmission, and genetic factors cannot be ruled out. There is evidence that attachment anxiety mediates the link between childhood exposure and later domestic violence perpetration in both male and female young adults (e.g., Godbout et al., 2017). Other studies point to abused men having a more negative communication style (hostile, dominant, coercive; e.g., Nguyen et al., 2017). Childhood abuse and exposure to domestic violence are related to changes in the brain, and such changes may be expressed in posttraumatic stress disorder (PTSD) and other mental disorders (Teicher & Samson, 2016).

Sociocultural Level

Sociocultural level explanations set violent behavior within the broader context of social and political influence. There is empirical support for sociocultural risk factors for domestic violence, such as unemployment, lower income, common-law marriage, and cultural minority status (see review by Capaldi et al., 2012). Nested ecological theories set individual and interpersonal factors within the context of broader social structures (e.g., Beyer et al., 2015).

Feminist theories, in particular, view violence against women as men's expression of power and control within a culture of patriarchy that perpetuates gender inequality in social, economic, and political spheres. Feminist theories of domestic violence emerged with classic exposés of the problem (e.g., Dobash & Dobash, 1979). Ellen L. Pence and Michael Paymar's "power and control" wheel influenced a generation of "batterer intervention" programs (Gondolf, 2010). Feminist thinking has become more nuanced with the application of intersectionality theory that accounts for individuals' experience across gender, sexual, ability, racial, class, age, religious, and other identities (e.g., Chavis & Hill, 2008). Feminist scholars are critical of research methods that focus on individual or interpersonal factors (e.g., Hamby, 2016; M. P. Johnson, 2011) and have been criticized in return for relying on ideological concepts and limited empirical evidence (e.g., Corvo & Johnson, 2013; Winstok, 2017).

Limits of Domestic Violence Theory and an Alternative From General Offending

Attempts to explain why men assault their female partners remain polarized, with no good empirical studies testing one theory against each other and limited parallel work on other gendered relationships. Another limitation is that there is very little theory in most current work on domestic violence recidivism. Explanations of why people commit domestic violence in the first place do not necessarily help identify those who will do it again or help explain domestic violence recidivism (e.g., adverse childhood experiences; see Exhibit 1.1). In fact, domestic violence theory has been noted for its failure to produce predictive models (Bell & Naugle, 2008).

In the past few years, I and other domestic violence researchers (e.g., Hilton & Radatz, 2018; Radatz & Wright, 2016) have drawn upon an influential and well-supported theoretical framework for assessing and intervening with general criminal offending. This model is the general personality and cognitive social learning (GPCSL) approach, and the related Risk–Need–Responsivity (RNR) principles of effective correctional intervention (e.g., Bonta & Andrews, 2017; Bonta et al., 2014). GPCSL theory incorporates individual, interpersonal, and sociocultural factors, plus situational factors, that contribute to the balance of rewards and costs of crime and the decision to engage in criminal conduct. From the GPCSL, Bonta and Andrews identify the "central eight" empirically supported risk factors: criminal history, procriminal attitudes, procriminal associates, antisocial personality pattern, family or marital problems, school or work problems, substance use, and low levels of leisure and recreation.

EXHIBIT 1.1. Adverse Childhood Experiences

Adverse childhood experiences (ACEs) include physical, sexual, or verbal abuse and neglect, witnessing domestic violence, or parents' substance use, mental illness, or criminal behavior. ACEs increase the risk of a host of serious physical and mental health problems in adults (e.g., Felitti et al., 1998). Several studies report that individuals who commit offenses against their intimate partners are more likely than comparison groups to have had ACEs (e.g., Chan, 2014; Crane et al., 2013; Cunha & Gonçalves, 2013; Henrichs et al., 2015; Milaniak & Widom, 2015; Watt & Scrandis, 2013) or exposure to intimate partner violence specifically (Kimber et al., 2018). Child abuse is related to violence perpetration among men and women in same-sex relationships (Kimmes et al., 2019). The robustness of this finding raises some important questions: Do ACEs predict domestic violence recidivism? And are ACEs a suitable target for intervention?

Childhood abuse was related to some facets of psychopathy in a study of men under pretrial supervision after domestic or nondomestic charges (Swogger et al., 2012), but not to criminal history among men in domestic violence treatment (Henrichs et al., 2015). In one study of 228 men on probation for domestic violence, men who had a documented history of abuse recidivated more, and sooner, than those who only witnessed domestic violence or who neither witnessed nor experienced abuse (Fowler et al., 2016).

My colleagues and I examined reports of abuse and other ACEs in the psychosocial records of men admitted to a psychiatric hospital for forensic assessment (Hilton, Ham, & Green, 2019) and found that ACEs were common among the 99 men who had a history of domestic violence. However, they did not have significantly more ACEs than men with histories of general, nondomestic violence, except for one small difference: They were more likely to have witnessed domestic violence (13%) than other violent men (8%). There remains no clear answer to whether ACEs predict domestic violence recidivism and insufficient evidence for treating ACEs as a criminogenic need in domestic violence treatment programs.

RNR principles identify not only individual characteristics but also features of service provision that must be addressed for optimal outcomes. The risk principle states that the first step is to identify risk of recidivism and to exert risk management efforts in accordance with the level of risk. Seven of the central eight factors (all except criminal history) are potentially changeable and are referred to as criminogenic treatment needs. The need principle asserts that correctional services should focus on criminogenic needs. The responsivity principle involves ensuring that treatments use the most effective strategies and are delivered in a manner consistent with individuals' abilities and learning styles. Other principles in the RNR model pertain to basing interventions on empirically supported theories, delivering services in humane and professional ways, using effective staff and management approaches, and so on. In Chapter 2, I say more about applying the RNR principles in a section titled Risk Assessment for Domestic Violence Treatment.

Causal theories of criminal offending are not mere academic exercises; theoretical explanations point to the mechanisms of criminal conduct and, when empirically supported, provide a rational basis for delivering treatment and other interventions to change or interrupt those mechanisms. Elsewhere, I have elucidated the ways the RNR model can inform an understanding of not only domestic violence risk but also treatment needs and individual responsivity to domestic violence treatment (Hilton & Ennis, 2020). I will come back to the RNR principles several times throughout this book. For now, let us turn to factors that help identify risk of domestic violence recidivism.

RISK FACTORS FOR DOMESTIC VIOLENCE RECIDIVISM

Empirical research on risk factors for domestic violence recidivism has so far hinged on individual characteristics of the person who offended, or the person offended against, that increase the likelihood that another domestic assault will occur at a point in time after risk was or could have been measured. Although this research, as mentioned, has not been explicitly theory-driven, I review them here through the GPCSL lens where possible.

Single Risk Factors

Some predictors of domestic violence recidivism are similar to the individual-level characteristics I already described in this chapter. However, not all of the distinguishing features of people who have assaulted their partner help identify those most likely to repeat their violence. For example, childhood abuse and witnessing domestic violence are more common among those who commit domestic offenses than some comparison groups, but they are not clearly related to recidivism (see Exhibit 1.1). Instead, many of the most consistent predictors of domestic violence recidivism are similar to predictors of general violence and other offending risk factors identified in the GPCSL, such as younger age, lower education or socioeconomic status, relationship conflict, previous verbal abuse, and threats (e.g., Hilton & Harris, 2005; Lauch et al., 2017; O'Leary et al., 2014; Richards et al., 2013; Yakubovich et al., 2018).

Antisocial personality pattern is one of the central eight criminogenic risk factors. Antisociality is often associated with diagnostic measures of antisocial personality disorder or psychopathy such as the Psychopathy Checklist–Revised (PCL-R; Hare, 2003), a widely used measure with 20 items comprising two factors and four facets (Hare, 2016). Scores from the full or screening versions of PCL-R have predicted domestic violence recidivism among men and women and in clinical and community samples (e.g., Cunha et al., 2018; Hilton, Harris, Rice, et al., 2008; Okano et al., 2016). This finding is consistent with the broader field of criminal recidivism, in which the PCL-R rivals structured risk assessment instruments for predictive validity (e.g., M. A. Campbell et al., 2009; K. M. Williams et al., 2017). As I show in Chapter 5, PCL-R score improves the prediction of domestic violence recidivism, and a theory of domestic violence centered on antisociality can enhance risk assessment and management.

Another of the central eight risk factors is substance use. Substance use has been found to be especially prevalent or severe among men with a domestic offense history compared with others in correctional and forensic samples (Hilton & Radatz, 2018; Stewart & Power, 2014). In one study, men who used alcohol or illegal drugs when assaulting or intimidating their female partner were more likely to be arrested and convicted and also to reoffend within 5 years (Hirschel et al., 2010). Substance use predicted recidivism among both men and women arrested for domestic assaults, despite women's lesser history of drug use (Ménard et al., 2009).

Gender itself is a risk factor for domestic violence recidivism. Women who assault their partners are less likely to reoffend than their male counterparts (see review by Larsen & Hamberger, 2015). At the highest levels of antisociality or assessed risk, though, gender differences are less influential (e.g., Stansfield & Williams, 2014; Walsh et al., 2010). There is evidence of gender differences in how some factors relate to recidivism, such as criminal history being more influential for men and relationship factors (relationship terminated, nature of the assault) being more relevant for women (Ménard et al., 2009). Gender is a recognized risk factor for criminal conduct in the GPCSL and, importantly, a responsivity factor that could shape the appropriateness of the content and delivery of domestic violence treatment.

Vulnerability Factors Among Women Who Are Assaulted

Women who commit violence against their partners are themselves more likely to be assaulted (e.g., Richards et al., 2017). Although this finding is especially true in community-based self-report surveys of what has been called "common" or "situational couple violence" (M. P. Johnson et al., 2014), there is also support for recent domestic violence perpetration being predictive of revictimization in a short-term follow-up of women using victim support services (Kuijpers et al., 2012). Foa et al. (2000) proposed models of women's vulnerability that included both mental health problems, such as posttraumatic stress, and resiliency factors, such as self-esteem and resources. There is consistent support for PTSD and substance use being related to women's domestic violence victimization (e.g., Cafferky et al., 2018; McKee & Hilton, 2019), and some evidence that childhood victimization, neglect, or exposure to domestic violence increases the risk of revictimization among women, especially from multiple abusive partners in their lifetime (e.g., Ørke et al., 2018).

Other research has validated women's ability to assess their own risk of domestic violence revictimization (e.g., Cattaneo et al., 2007). Scores on risk assessment tools are associated with women's sense of danger (e.g., Connor-Smith et al., 2011; Messing et al., 2015). Furthermore, women at higher risk take more self-protective actions that have the potential to reduce their revictimization (Messing et al., 2015, 2017). However, intuitive risk assessments may not protect women from assault; many women who experienced potentially lethal violence did not think their partner was capable of killing them (e.g., J. C. Campbell et al., 2009; Nicolaidis et al., 2003).

Typologies

Typologies classify men who assault their female partners into different types according to their attributes and the circumstances in which they are violent. Typology researchers often use analyses that find clusters of individuals who are similar on measures that themselves are dimensional rather than categorical (e.g., antisociality, substance use). Types have not yet been subject to taxometric analysis that can examine the structure of underlying (*latent*) concepts to determine whether they represent a nonarbitrary class or *taxon* (as has been attempted for the concept of psychopathy; e.g., Harris, Rice, et al., 2007). Typologies may simply be heuristics that capture variation among individuals and reflect theories regarding characteristics important to domestic violence prediction and risk management. I discuss them in this section because typologies draw us closer to multifactor risk assessment by identifying clusters of individual factors and their association with the likelihood of reoffending.

Holtzworth-Munroe and Stuart (1994) proposed three subtypes by drawing on characteristics studied in the literature on domestically violent men: psychopathology, violence severity, and violence generality. First, a *family-only* type is expected to commit the least severe violence against partners and have the least psychopathology or antisocial behavior outside the home. Second, a *dysphoric/borderline* type is expected to commit more severe physical and sexual violence, not necessarily exclusively against their partner, and to experience emotional dysphoria, characteristics of borderline personality disorder, or other psychological problems. Third, a *generally violent/antisocial* type is expected to show the most severe and persistent domestic violence and other antisocial behavior. Typology research revealed that many men who assault their partners do not specialize in domestic offending, a finding later confirmed in studies of official criminal records and self-reports (e.g., Hilton & Eke, 2016; Piquero et al., 2014; Richards et al., 2017).

Several empirical studies with community, clinical, or correctional samples support the Holtzworth-Munroe–Stuart model or variations on the three-type system (e.g., Cunha & Gonçalves, 2013; Fowler & Westen, 2011; Walsh et al., 2010) or a four-type system that adds a low-level antisocial type (e.g., Holtzworth-Munroe et al., 2003; Serie et al., 2017; Thijssen & de Ruiter, 2011). These typologies commonly include a generally violent, antisocial group that commits more severe domestic violence, has more criminogenic factors, or has higher measured risk than other types. Generally antisocial men are more likely than other types to have personality disorders and substance use problems (e.g., Petersson et al., 2019), to drop out of treatment (e.g., Cantos et al., 2015), and to reoffend (e.g., Goldstein et al., 2016; Huss & Ralston, 2008; Loinaz, 2014). This type seems to capture what has been called *intimate terrorism* (e.g., Johnson et al., 2014), in contrast to more common but relatively minor *situational couple violence* that is typical of the family-only domestic offender type. The generally violent type is perhaps like the "Type 1" individuals whose heart rate lowers during conflict (Stare & Fernando, 2014) or perhaps responsible for the "random" violence pattern that is more frequent yet less predictable to victims than "periodic" or "chaotic" patterns (Burge et al., 2016). This group may be indistinguishable from men who commit nondomestic violence in such risk factors (Juarros-Basterretxea et al., 2018).

Typologies might have implications for the kinds of treatment offered for domestic violence, but its application to domestic violence risk assessment is less clear. Classifying men into types can be challenging and unreliable (e.g., Huss & Ralston, 2008), and studies do not always clearly distinguish generally violent, antisocial individuals as the riskiest group (e.g., Chiffriller & Hennessy, 2009). Moreover, in a study of men convicted of violence and other offenses against intimate partners in Spain after release from prison, a two-category typology (family-only and antisocial) was less sensitive than a police-scored risk assessment tool at detecting criminal recidivism

(Loinaz, 2014). These findings may not be a surprise, considering that continuous measures, such as scores on a personality test or the total number of risk factors present, retain more information than a two- or three-category typology. As a result, risk assessment scores have more power and can be more useful than typologies when it comes to assessing risk for reoffending.

DOMESTIC VIOLENCE RECIDIVISM ASSESSMENT TOOLS AND GUIDES

A 2014 survey of mental health professionals found that more than 400 tools are used to assess violence risk around the world (Singh et al., 2014). Hundreds of locally developed or commercially available tools undergo little or no empirical validation. Assessors who use tools that give a valid estimate of the risk of recidivism can help ensure that the highest risk individuals receive the best treatment available, the most intense supervision, or the most secure custody when needed. Fortunately, in domestic violence, there are a few widely used and well-validated instruments. Validated instruments help evaluators assess risk of domestic violence recidivism through victim interview, mechanical assessment, case formulation, clinical judgment, or a combination of these methods. My review concentrates on these tools and guides. For a more systematic review, see Graham and colleagues (2019).

Validity and Reliability in Brief

The degree to which an assessment measures what it is supposed to measure is central to validity. There are several kinds of validity. The validity that matters most in risk assessment is predictive validity (or criterion-related validity): the degree to which actual outcomes match predicted outcomes. In this section, I describe research that uses a predictive validity statistic called the receiver operator characteristic area under the curve (AUC), so I offer a brief explanation here (see Chapter 8 for more detailed discussion of ways to assess the accuracy of risk assessment tools).

Predictive validity is usually assessed by scoring the assessment tool based on information at the time of one offense and following up cases to see who recidivates (i.e., commits another offense later). The AUC is interpreted as the probability that a randomly selected person who recidivates scored higher on the risk assessment tool than a randomly selected person who does not recidivate. AUCs between .56 and .64 are equivalent to a small predictive effect, those from .64 to .71 are medium effects, and those greater than .71 are large effects (Rice & Harris, 2005). Actuarial violence risk assessment tools typically yield medium or large effect sizes; for example, meta-analyses of the Violence Risk Appraisal Guide report mean AUCs of .68 to .75 (Harris, Rice, et al., 2015). Structured assessment tools generally perform significantly better than unstructured clinical judgment in the prediction of violence (e.g., Hanson & Morton-Bourgon, 2009), including domestic violence recidivism (Seewald et al., 2017).

Another essential aspect of risk assessment is reliability: the consistency with which the measurement produces scores. In violence risk assessment, reliability is usually tested by comparing the scores that two or more assessors obtain when independently evaluating the same people. This property is known as *interrater reliability* and is usually expressed as a *correlation:* the extent to which two variables are associated with each other so that, as one increases, the other one also increases (positive correlation; e.g., height and weight) or the other one decreases (negative correlation; e.g., truancy and school grades). The correlation is given as a coefficient between −1.0 and +1.0. Positive values are interpreted as the extent to which different assessors come up with similar scores.

Danger Assessment

The Danger Assessment (DA) was first published by J. C. Campbell (1986; Profile 1.1). The DA is unique among the tools I discuss here in that it assesses women's risk of domestic homicide (also known as femicide) regardless of their partner's involvement with the criminal justice system. It involves interviewing an assaulted woman to review the past year's assaults on a calendar, then asking a series of questions. Half of the 20 questions concern the abuse (violence escalation, weapon use, threats to kill, forced sex, choking, controlling behavior, violent jealousy, beaten when pregnant, threatened her children, surveillance). Other questions concern the partner's other behavior (gun ownership, unemployment, avoided arrest for domestic violence, illegal drugs, alcohol problem, threatened suicide) and the woman's situation (tried to leave, believes he could kill her, has a child who is not his). The women's suicidal history is queried but does not contribute to the risk score. The full DA includes weighted item scoring, accessible upon training at https://www.dangerassessment.org/DA.aspx. Risk is interpreted in one of four categories that are tied to the score and range from "Variable Danger" to "Extreme Danger." These categories derive from empirical studies of women in violent relationships and women who were killed by their partner.

Reviews of the DA's predictive accuracy across different versions and various outcomes report average AUCs of .61 to .62, with substantial variability across studies (Helmus & Bourgon, 2011; Messing & Thaller, 2013). Interrater reliability has not been reported. However, scores are interpreted based on information provided by the woman during the interview, and test–retest among 30 women at two interviews 1 week apart was .97 (E. P. Stuart & Campbell, 1989).

The 20-question format of the DA uses the strongest risk factors found in an 11-city study that compared 220 femicide victims with 343 women who were abused but survived (J. C. Campbell et al., 2003). In case-control research, DA scores distinguished between attempted femicide victims and surviving women with a large effect size (AUC = .92; J. C. Campbell et al., 2009). A five-item version was developed from research into the most sensitive predictors of severe and potentially fatal assaults in a 9-month follow-up of 400 women recruited from courts, hospitals, shelters, and other agencies serving domestic violence victims (AUC = .79; Snider et al., 2009). A 7-month follow-up of near-lethal violence among 619 women validated this version, called the DA-5 (AUC = .68; Messing, Campbell, & Snider, 2017). The Lethality Screen uses 11 DA items that identified the women who experienced severe violence at a 6-month follow-up interview, among 440 women interviewed after police involvement (Messing, Campbell, Sullivan Wilson, et al., 2017). These highly sensitive tools may have high false-positive rates but likely identify all the risky cases, making them useful for screening and prioritizing cases for further assessment. A version of the DA for immigrant women was created using items that best predicted severe assaults in a 9-month follow-up (AUC = .77; Messing et al., 2013). Another was created for women abused by female partners, using items related to new assaults or threats in a 1-month follow-up (Glass et al., 2008). It will be important to confirm the predictive validity of each of these modifications of the DA.

The DA has been tested in cases of nonlethal domestic violence in studies that interviewed women at two time points. Higher scores significantly increased the odds of new assaults and threats in a 3-month follow-up of 92 women whose partners were arrested for domestic violence, even when controlling for extent of prior violence (Goodman et al., 2000). In a 15-month follow-up of 499 cases of men in treatment, DA scores obtained through partner interviews predicted multiple repeat assaults (AUC = .70; Heckert & Gondolf, 2004). However, scores were not associated with new assaults or serious threats in a smaller study with a shorter, 4-month follow-up, when controlling for the women's predictions of violence (Weisz et al., 2000). In a study that my colleagues and I conducted, we scored the unweighted DA using police and criminal records among 589 men with a police record for domestic assault, and total scores predicted recidivism with a medium effect (AUC = .64, Hilton et al., 2004).

Spousal Assault Risk Assessment Guide and Related Guides

The Spousal Assault Risk Assessment Guide (SARA) combines information gathered from interviews with both parties involved in the domestic assault, other informants, and police reports and criminal records, including statements by the accused person and alleged victim that the official records may contain (e.g., Kropp & Hart, 2000, 2015). Randall Kropp (Profile 1.2) and others developed the SARA as an alternative to both unstructured clinical judgment, which is not based on empirical evidence and has poor validity, and actuarial risk assessment, which uses empirical evidence to calculate risk mechanically (for an overview of the mechanical–clinical distinction, see Grove & Meehl, 1996; Hilton, Harris, & Rice, 2006). The SARA uses the structured professional judgment approach that allows assessors to use their clinical judgment to select some risk factors and to summarize overall risk.

The SARA authors drew risk factors from an empirical literature review and considered clinical and other issues in their final selection of 20 items (Kropp et al., 1999; Kropp & Hart, 2000). The items cover criminal history (assaults on family members, assaults on strangers, and conditional release violations), spousal assault history (physical assault, sexual assault or jealousy, use of weapons or death threats, recent escalation, no-contact order violations, minimization, and attitudes that support spousal assault), most recent offense (severe or sexual assault, use of weapons or death threats, and no contact order violation) and psychosocial adjustment (relationship problems, employment problems, victim or witness of family violence, substance abuse, suicidal or homicidal ideation, psychotic or manic symptoms, and personality disorder). The assessor codes all items as 0 = *absent*, 1 = *possible or partial*, or 2 = *present*, and identifies any items thought to be critical risk factors for spousal violence. The assessor then weighs this information, and any other considerations, before making a summary judgment of low, moderate, or high risk of violence toward a partner or other person.

Published studies of the SARA show that the total score predicts domestic violence recidivism. Reviews by Helmus and Bourgon (2011) and Messing and Thaller (2013) reported an average AUC of .63. This result includes my research with colleagues in which we scored the SARA items from police reports and other official records and found AUCs of .64 among men with a police record for domestic violence (Hilton et al., 2004) and .59 in cases with relatively in-depth correctional records (Hilton, Harris, Rice, et al., 2008). More recent work by Jung and Buro (2017) found AUCs of .74 for domestic violence convictions and .68 for charges, among 198 men with criminal charges for violence or threatened violence against an intimate partner.

Fewer studies have evaluated the predictive validity of the SARA summary risk ratings, and the results have been more varied. Helmus and Bourgon (2011) reported AUCs ranging from .56 to .84 and averaging .67 (.64 after removing an outlier). A subsequent study of 429 men who assaulted or threatened their female partner found that the police-scored SARA judgment predicted later police contacts for the same behaviors with an AUC of .57 (Belfrage et al., 2012).

Two studies reported large interrater reliability coefficients for SARA total scores, with correlations of .84 (Kropp & Hart, 2000) to .85 (Grann & Wedin, 2002). The coefficient was .70 for SARA total scores by research coders in a sample of 32 cases referred by police to a specialist threat assessment service (Hilton et al., 2020). Kropp and Hart (2000) reported reliability for the summary risk ratings, which was .63. Individual item reliability has ranged from .30 to 1.00, with medium-sized correlations on average (.58, Grann & Wedin, 2002; .65, Kropp & Hart, 2000). Training can improve SARA assessments by increasing the number of risk factors and critical factors correctly identified (Storey et al., 2011).

Spousal Assault Risk Assessment Guide Version 3

Over time, the SARA has evolved from a tool created for "forecasting future behavior" (Kropp & Hart, 2000, p. 109) to a set of guidelines for case formulation and scenario-planning to aid risk management for each assessed person (e.g., Kropp & Hart, 2015). As with the previous version, the third version (SARA-V3) encourages evaluation of preselected items as well as any other risk factors the assessor believes to be potentially relevant to the individual. The 24 preselected items cover three domains. Two are similar to the SARA: the nature of intimate partner violence (intimidation, threats, physical harm, sexual harm, severe violence, chronic violence, escalating violence, and IPV-related supervision violations) and individual characteristics (intimate relationship problems or conflict, nonintimate relationship problems, employment/financial problems, trauma/victimization, antisocial conduct, mental disorder, personality disorder, substance use, violent/suicidal ideation, and distorted thinking about IPV). A new section pertaining to "victim vulnerability" includes barriers to security, barriers to independence, interpersonal resources, community resources, attitudes or behavior, and mental health. Using the SARA-V3 does not involve coding the items but instead evaluating their past and recent influence (prior to vs. within a year of the evaluation) and formulating risk scenarios in which these factors could lead to future violence, whether the best or worst case scenarios, repetition of past patterns, or possible new twists. These scenarios inform risk management strategies and conclusory opinions about case prioritization, risk for serious IPV, and imminence of IPV.

At the time of writing, there are no published tests of the SARA-V3's predictive accuracy. In her doctoral research, Ryan (2016) tested interrater reliability on 30 cases scored from case files and reported coefficients for total scores (.85), risk ratings (from .40 for case prioritization to .68 for serious physical harm), and individual item scores, which ranged from .10 to .92. In 32 threat assessment cases scored by two research coders, the coefficient for total scores was .83, and item score reliability ranged from .01 to 1.00 (Hilton et al., 2020).

Brief Spousal Assault Form for the Evaluation of Risk

Kropp and Hart (2004) developed the Brief Spousal Assault Form for the Evaluation of Risk (B-SAFER) as a checklist and structured interview guide for police and other criminal justice professionals during routine investigations. They removed redundant SARA items identified in a factor analysis of 2,796 known or suspected domestic violence cases. They kept the items most closely related to the professional judgment of risk in these cases, most of which were also related to domestic violence recidivism in a subsample of 102 cases (Kropp & Hart, 2004). Scores on the original 10-item version distinguished between men with and without a history of domestic violence (Au et al., 2008). A second version (Kropp et al., 2010) expanded the B-SAFER to 15 items in three domains. Intimate partner violence includes violent acts, violent threats or thoughts, escalation, court-order violations, and violent attitudes. Psychosocial adjustment includes general criminality, intimate relationship problems, employment problems, substance use problems, and mental health problems. Victim vulnerability factors include inconsistent attitudes or behavior, extreme fear, inadequate support or resources, unsafe living situation, and health problems.

Evidence for the B-SAFER's predictive validity is mixed. Among 40 men released from prison in Spain, B-SAFER total scores predicted recidivism (return to prison) with a large effect (AUC = .76, Loinaz, 2014). Total scores and risk ratings both predicted subsequent police contacts for domestic violence among 249 men with police contact for domestic violence in Sweden

(AUCs = .70 and .69, respectively; Storey et al., 2014). However, another Swedish study of 216 assessments conducted by police found an inverse effect for B-SAFER summary risk judgments—men judged to be high risk were less likely to commit a new offense than those judged to be low risk (Belfrage & Strand, 2012), and a third with 301 cases (11 female) reported no effect (Svalin et al., 2018). B-SAFER scores had a small and nonsignificant association with new domestic violence charges among 158 men in a U.S. court-ordered treatment program following domestic violence or stalking an intimate partner (AUC = .55, Gerbrandij et al., 2018).

Interrater reliability for the B-SAFER has also varied. Thijssen and de Ruiter (2011) reported that interrater reliability for four B-SAFER items was .57 on average but better for criminal history items and poorer for mental health problems. Hilton and colleagues (2020) found a similar pattern in threat assessment cases: Item reliability coefficient was .54 on average and better for criminal history items than mental health; reliability for the total score was .70. In contrast, Gerbrandij and colleagues (2018) reported excellent reliability for the total score (.96).

Research with the B-SAFER and other SARA tools sheds light on how police officers conduct risk assessment and management. Officers' summary risk ratings are related to most individual items, but less so to court-order violations, employment problems, and some vulnerability factors (e.g., Belfrage & Strand, 2012; Storey & Strand, 2017). When officers rate someone as high risk, they recommend more risk management strategies, such as consulting with a prosecutor or crime registry or discussing a safety plan with the person who was assaulted (e.g., Belfrage et al., 2012). Thus, although not created with the RNR model in mind, the SARA tools have helped show how risk assessment can facilitate needs identification and intervention.

Domestic Violence Screening Instrument-Revised

The Domestic Violence Screening Instrument–Revised (DVSI-R) was developed and tested by Kirk Williams and colleagues in Colorado and Connecticut to help assign individuals who perpetrate family violence offenses to services and supervision according to risk (Williams, 2012; Williams & Grant, 2006). Assessors use all information available after an arrest, including interviews with the involved persons, police reports, criminal history, and other official sources.

The original DVSI had 12 items chosen through a literature review, criminal justice and community focus groups, and a large-sample statistical analysis of variables that distinguished individuals on probation who did and did not repeat their domestic offenses (Williams & Houghton, 2004). The authors later responded to assessors' feedback by adding a professional judgment of low, moderate, or high risk for imminent violence (Williams & Grant, 2006). They also clarified and consolidated the scoring, resulting in the 11-item DVSI-R. Most items concern the assessed person's history: family assaults, nonfamily assaults, prior family violence interventions, community supervision or protection-order violations, verbal or emotional abuse, recent violence frequency, and recent violence escalation. Others concern their employment, substance use, and weapon use and whether children were present during a violent offense. DVSI score predicted domestic violence recidivism in an 18-month follow-up of 1,465 men arrested for domestic violence (AUC = .61, Williams & Houghton, 2004). It also predicted severe threats and severe violence reported by their partners in 125 cases (AUCs = .68 and .65) but not less serious physical assault (AUC = .49).

DVSI and DVSI-R scores have since been validated for domestic and general family violence recidivism in large samples of men and women (e.g., AUC = .62, Williams, 2012; AUC = .71, Williams & Grant, 2006; AUC = .63, Wong & Hisashima, 2008). Most notably, Stansfield and Williams (2014) conducted an 18-month follow-up through state criminal records of 29,317 arrested individuals (30% were female). The DVSI-R was scored by family relations counselors and predicted new family violence offenses (AUC = .65) and protection-order violations (AUC = .69). In research in Canada involving men with a police report of domestic assault, DVSI score predicted subsequent police reports of domestic violence (AUC = .61, Hilton, Harris, Rice, et al., 2008). Tests of the DVSI-R summary risk rating have yielded AUCs of .61 to .64 for new domestic violence offenses (Williams, 2012; Williams & Grant, 2006; Wong & Hisashima, 2008).

DVSI-R research has highlighted variables that moderate or mediate domestic violence risk. Moderators are variables that interact with the main variables and affect the strength of the main effect. In this case, the main independent variable is the risk assessment score and the main dependent variable is recidivism. Stansfield and Williams (2014) found that gender moderated the association between DVSI-R and new family violence arrests, whereby women reoffend less often and less quickly than men except for women in the highest risk category. Similarly, persons identified as non-minority reoffended less than minority individuals except at the highest risk level. Mediators are variables that are independently associated with both of the main variables and statistically explain some of the main effect. Williams and Stansfield (2017) found that time men and women spent in jail or on probation substantially mediated the association between their risk and domestic violence recidivism. Furthermore, longer sentences were more likely to lead to domestic violence recidivism among individuals initially assessed as lower risk (just as would be predicted by the RNR risk principle). This research shows the importance of using valid risk assessment to help guide risk management decisions.

Ontario Domestic Assault Risk Assessment and Domestic Violence Risk Assessment Guide

The Ontario Domestic Assault Risk Assessment (ODARA) and its sister tool, the Domestic Violence Risk Assessment Guide (DVRAG), are both actuarial instruments. That is, they were developed through empirical research and are interpreted using statistical data. They were created to fill the gap in empirically driven domestic violence risk assessment in the late 1990s, although theory did influence the choice of potential predictors studied, and the RNR principles serve as the underlying theoretic framework. At the time, there was no tool suited to use by first-line responders such as police officers, and none had been tested in this context. When risk assessment is implemented in the absence of empirical testing, it can lead to disappointing results (e.g., Turner et al., 2019). My colleagues and I believed it was important to demonstrate the validity of domestic violence risk assessment tools before promoting their use. As the development, validations, and applications of the ODARA and DVRAG are the primary subject matter of Part II of this book, I summarize them only briefly here.

To create the ODARA, we used statistical analysis to identify the strongest, unique predictors of men's domestic violence recidivism, using information available to law enforcement officers throughout the Province of Ontario, Canada, at the time of a police occurrence report (Hilton et al., 2004). The ODARA was later validated for domestic violence recidivism on similar samples drawn from police records databases in Ontario (AUCs = .65–.80, Hilton & Harris, 2009b; Hilton, Harris, Rice, et al., 2008; Hilton et al., 2004), elsewhere in Canada (e.g., AUCs = .66–.70, Jung & Buro, 2017), Switzerland (AUC = .63, Gerth et al., 2014), and Australia (AUC = .68, Lauria et al., 2017). ODARA scores also predicted domestic violence recidivism among men who served custodial sentences in Ontario (AUC = .64, Hilton et al., 2010) and Austria (AUC = .71, Rettenberger & Eher, 2013). Some of these studies included men who assaulted intimate partners they had never lived with. In a small prospective follow-up study, we found that the ODARA predicted domestic violence recidivism by women (AUC = .72, Hilton et al., 2014).

The DVRAG was developed through a study my colleagues and I conducted to improve on the ODARA for the prediction of several domestic violence outcomes: likelihood of recidivism, number of assaults and severe assaults, victim injury, seriousness of charges, and time until recidivism (Hilton, Harris, Rice, et al., 2008). The DVRAG combines the ODARA items with the PCL-R (Hare, 2003) and is appropriate to use when more time and resources are available so that more in-depth information can be gathered. In our validation research, the DVRAG provided improved assessment for individuals scoring in all but the two lowest risk categories on the ODARA. In Rettenberger and Eher's (2013) study, which included 66 prisoners who had committed sexual assault against an intimate partner, the DVRAG did not improve prediction over the ODARA, and they had a similar medium effect size.

Machine Learning Models

All the risk assessment tools I have described so far rely on a more or less fixed list of risk factors that assessors consider and interpret. Researchers can analyze a set of variables to find which work best in combination. Validity of these models is determined by how well they fit a given dataset, and there may be several models that fit the same dataset (e.g., Breiman, 2001). In contrast, machine learning is a process that uses all currently available information to maximize predictive accuracy. Machine-learning programs take advantage of big datasets and can incorporate new cases, always changing and improving predictions. Machine learning can forecast an outcome without the need for a score requiring interpretation (e.g., Berk & Hyatt, 2015). Whereas data modeling seeks a solution that explains or "models" the relation between predictors and outcomes, machine learning treats the relation as unknown and seeks an algorithm that provides the best prediction of the outcome (Breiman, 2001).

Berk et al. (2016) applied this approach to a data set of 28,646 adults charged with domestic violence in one U.S. city. Most were men (81%), and gender was one of the 36 variables input into the machine learning algorithm using information easily downloaded from the official records. The researchers aimed for an algorithm that best predicted cases with no new domestic violence arrests within 2 years, which would allow the remaining cases to receive more pretrial custody or supervision. This outcome was accurately predicted 89% of the time. This success could be an artifact of the high base rate of nonrecidivism (81%); further domestic violence with or without injury or threats occurred in 19% of cases, and prediction was accurate only 10% to 21% of the time. General violent and criminal history were among the strongest contributors to the model. In real-time forecasting, however, machine learning models can lack transparency in how the risk factors contribute to the outcome. Machine learning can inform basic risk management decisions, but it requires big data sets and specialized software.

IMPORTANCE OF EVALUATION IN DOMESTIC VIOLENCE RISK ASSESSMENT

I have selectively described only the most widely used and validated risk assessment tools here. The DA, SARA guides, DVSI-R, and the ODARA and DVRAG were all developed in the United States and Canada, but others have been reported internationally (see the review by Graham et al., 2019). Some tools have initial evidence of predictive accuracy, such as the Victoria Police screening Assessment for Family Violence Risk (McEwan et al., 2019). Many tools are created with the good intentions of being suited to a local population and supported by involved agencies but do not perform as well as empirically developed tools (e.g., Gerth et al., 2015; Hilton et al., 2004; Jung & Buro, 2017). Future research might show that existing tools can be improved, replaced with newer tools, or even superseded by other methods.

CONCLUSION

In this chapter, I have considered individual risk factors and combinations of factors that are suggested by different theoretical perspectives, in a broad sense, and surveyed the evidence for them. Later in this book, I explore in more detail the tension between hypothesis and evidence in current issues in domestic violence risk assessment (Chapter 8). The ODARA and DVRAG were shared only after a rigorous sequence of data collection and statistical analysis. In the next chapter, I describe the methodological premises and decisions made in constructing actuarial risk assessments for domestic violence.

POINTS TO REMEMBER

- There is a large literature on theoretically motivated risk factors for domestic violence but little empirical research testing one theory against each other and limited parallel work on other offender–victim gender relationships.

- A central point of domestic violence risk assessment research is to discover how best to support the RNR principles of effective intervention.
- A large number of violence risk assessment instruments have been created, of which four tools (or families of tools) have been widely researched and validated.
- Actuarial and structured professional judgment approaches produce medium to large predictive effects for domestic violence risk assessment.

QUESTIONS TO CONSIDER

1. Name three levels of risk factors identified through different theoretical lenses.
2. Identify three emerging issues in domestic violence risk assessment research.
3. How is the risk of domestic violence recidivism different from the risk of the onset of domestic violence?
4. What might be the advantages (e.g., empirical, practical, legal, economic) of machine learning over fixed risk assessment tools? What might be some disadvantages to implementing machine learning approaches?
5. How might theory improve domestic violence risk assessment? What theoretical lens would you apply, and what impact would it have on the risk factors, assessment methods, or interpretation approach chosen?

RESEARCHER PROFILE 1.1
JACQUELYN C. CAMPBELL, MSN, PhD

For my entire career, I have been incredibly interested in the health outcomes of domestic violence. I see health care, criminal justice, and domestic violence advocacy as a three-legged stool in the prevention of and response to domestic violence. As part of my master's degree in nursing at Wright State University, I did a small study of homicide in Dayton, Ohio. I found that the number one cause of death among young African American women was domestic homicide. I can remember all the women from that study.

One woman who was killed already had a cast on her arm from a fracture of the ulna, a symptom of attempting to protect herself from a previous assault. I realized that she had been treated by the health care system, but nobody had asked about domestic violence. I saw a significant preventive role for nursing, and I wanted to fix the health care system (J. C. Campbell, 1981).

As I continued my graduate studies, I volunteered with support groups in women's shelters. Occasionally, a woman's story would remind me of the homicide study. I realized that I was scared that these women would be killed, but they were not scared. Without trying to alarm the women, I talked to them about risk factors from the homicide study and other research. I asked how they would turn these factors into a question for other women, and that became the wording for the Danger Assessment (DA) items. The DA still uses women's wording. An important example is the item about choking. When I asked the women whether there was anything not included on the DA that scares them, they said, "When he chokes me." When asked to describe choking, the most common response is the perpetrator holding the woman up against a wall with his forearm across her throat. However, they don't see this act as strangulation and would say "no" if they were asked if they have been strangled. The DA asks about "forced sex" for the same reason; women abused by their partners do not perceive it as "rape."

My research concerns both validations of the DA and health outcomes for abused women. At Johns Hopkins University, my colleague Daniel Webster had previous experience with case-control research and helped design the 11-city femicide case-control study (J. C. Campbell et al., 2003). I am currently working on a replication of this study that will include both men and women affected by domestic violence and homicide and will include groups that are underrepresented in domestic homicide research, especially Native American nations and LGBT2Q communities. I also hope to study the effects of traumatic brain injury from repeated strangulation or blows to the head, face, and neck and to understand how cumulative violence (from adverse childhood experiences, to domestic and community violence, structural racism, etc.) affects overall health, including susceptibility to HIV.

I am worried about the overincarceration of Black men and how risk assessment that relies on custodial history contributes to this systemic racism. Black women know that their partners are more likely than other men to do jail time for domestic violence, so they think twice about reporting abuse. I want to help find effective domestic violence interventions suitable for men who are not reported to the criminal justice system to help these women.

About the Researcher

Dr. Campbell is Anna D. Wolf Chair at the Johns Hopkins University School of Nursing and National Director of the Robert Wood Johnson Foundation Nurse Faculty Scholars.

RESEARCHER PROFILE 1.2
P. RANDALL KROPP, PhD

I am a clinical and forensic psychologist specializing in the assessment and management of violent offenders. I frequently consult with provincial, state, and federal government ministries on matters related to violence against women and children, and the assessment and treatment of violent offenders. I have published numerous journal articles, book chapters, and research reports on interpersonal violence, and I am coauthor of several violence risk assessment guidelines employing the structured professional judgment (SPJ) approach.

Although I have researched many forms of violence, my primary interest has been in the assessment and management of intimate partner violence (IPV) perpetrators and victims. I was drawn to the field after graduate school when I was employed as research director for the British Columbia Institute of Family Violence in the early 1990s. Around that time, proactive arrest policies regarding IPV resulted in a dramatic increase in IPV referrals to my forensic psychology practice. However, at that time no procedures for IPV risk assessment and management existed. So, along with Drs. Stephen Hart and Chris Webster at Simon Fraser University, and Dr. Derek Eaves of the Forensic Psychiatric Services Commission of British Columbia, I drafted the first version of the Spousal Assault Risk Assessment Guide (SARA). The SARA proved to be a popular tool for those working with families affected by IPV. Now in its third edition, the SARA has been translated into at least 10 languages and is used on six continents. A shorter version of the SARA, the Brief Spousal Assault Form for the Evaluation of Risk (B-SAFER) is also used internationally.

The SARA was the first published SPJ risk assessment tool. The SPJ method reflects the scientist-practitioner training of its authors; thus, the SARA (and B-SAFER) are meant to be grounded in the empirical and professional literatures on violence risk assessment so that they are defensible (from a scientific perspective) and practical, flexible, and useful (on a professional level). My professional experience, which has involved working with hundreds of IPV perpetrators and victims, has always informed my approach to IPV risk assessment. I have found it gratifying that others around the world have also found the tools I cofounded to be helpful in their own work.

I have been pleased to see to the practice of IPV risk assessment vastly expand in the past 25 years. My own research and professional interests have evolved from simple risk assessment to a focus on risk management and the implications of risk assessment to victim safety planning. The latest version of the SARA-V3, for example, employs risk formulation and scenario planning techniques to assist users in developing management plans. I have also worked closely with communities to build partnerships, and although there is plenty of work to be done, I believe this is the key to preventing IPV moving forward. I recommend multiagency (e.g., victim services, law enforcement, corrections, health care, faith-based organizations, child protection services) approaches to risk assessment and management using structured risk assessment tools to guide their interventions.

About the Researcher

Dr. Kropp is a psychologist at the Forensic Psychiatric Services Commission of British Columbia, a threat assessment specialist with Protect International, Inc., and an adjunct professor of psychology at Simon Fraser University.

2 RISK ASSESSMENT FOR CRIMINAL JUSTICE, DOMESTIC VIOLENCE TREATMENT, AND VICTIM SERVICES

When my colleagues and I began the research described in this book, no actuarial method existed to assess the risk of domestic violence recidivism. Our review of the literature (Hilton & Harris, 2005) found some consistent predictors of domestic violence recidivism in follow-up studies: younger age, lower socioeconomic status, history of marital conflict, verbal aggression or psychological abuse, prior domestic assault severity, and previous arrest for domestic violence. Readers may recall from Chapter 1 that substance use and prior antisocial conduct are central criminogenic risk factors for both domestic violence and general criminal recidivism. An emerging literature sees the potential for psychopathy to explain the serious, generally antisocial subgroup found in domestic violence typologies (e.g., Huss & Langhinrichsen-Rohling, 2006).

Psychopathy is one of the strongest predictors of general violent recidivism (e.g., Harris et al., 2001). The Psychopathy Checklist–Revised score (PCL-R; Hare, 2003) is an item on the Violence Risk Appraisal Guide (VRAG; Harris, Rice, et al., 2015). The PCL-R score predicted violent recidivism among 88 men who committed serious domestic assaults, drawn from more than

https://doi.org/10.1037/0000223-003
Domestic Violence Risk Assessment: Tools for Effective Prediction and Management, Second Edition, by N. Z. Hilton

500 men in the original VRAG development and cross-validation samples (Hilton et al., 2001). Even though the 88 men had lower VRAG scores than the other men and were less likely to exhibit the core features of psychopathy (superficial charm, need for stimulation, callousness and manipulation, and antisocial history including early behavior problems, irresponsibility, impulsivity, and criminal versatility), the PCL-R predicted their violent recidivism, and the VRAG improved prediction (Hilton et al., 2001). Grann and Wedin (2002) also reported that the VRAG predicted domestic assault recidivism and no-contact violations. The question then arose as to why not simply advise the use of this existing actuarial violence risk assessment tool in cases of domestic violence. Although predicting domestic violence recidivism specifically, and distinctly from general violence, was of practical and theoretical interest, in 2001, my colleagues and I wondered whether it would be necessary or even feasible.

THE NEED FOR A TWO-PART RISK ASSESSMENT SYSTEM

We soon realized, however, that some VRAG items (e.g., psychiatric diagnoses, characteristics of psychopathy) could not be scored by police officers. Others, such as early childhood problems and criminal behavior before the age of 16, were simply not available to community-based treatment providers. Additional VRAG items (e.g., having a female victim, ever married) would not be as useful for distinguishing between individuals who recidivate and those who do not when it comes to violence against female partners. A further concern was that general risk assessment tools had no items pertaining to variables that pervaded the existing literature on predictors of domestic violence recidivism, such as domestic-specific assault history, relationship characteristics, or predictions made by individuals who have been assaulted (Hilton & Harris, 2005). For these reasons, we set out to create domestic violence risk assessment tools from scratch, using official criminal records and narrative police occurrence reports.

In the remainder of this chapter, I describe why men's physical violence against female domestic partners was a priority for us and describe how we made other methodological decisions. I explain the rationale for developing tools to identify individuals in greatest need of intervention, rather than concentrating on causes and potential treatments, and outline how the principles of correctional practice are receiving growing attention in domestic violence intervention. I outline the statistics used to evaluate violence risk assessment tools. Finally, I turn to services for people victimized by domestic violence, and the motivation to make risk assessment accessible to them.

METHODOLOGICAL CONSIDERATIONS

The decision to focus, at first, on the criminal justice system was a natural outcome of the positions my colleagues and I held as researchers at a secure psychiatric facility for justice-involved men and our collaboration with the Ontario Provincial Police Behavioural Sciences and Analysis Services. We looked to existing research to guide us in other decisions.

Focusing on Men's Violence Against Women Rather Than Violence by Either Partner

Although we included violence in dating relationships and women who assaulted their partners in our later studies, our original research to construct risk assessment focused on partner violence by men, and on current or former marital and cohabiting relationships in particular. Official police reports and criminal records indicate that the vast majority of domestic assaults, especially severe violence and homicide, are committed by men (e.g., Beattie et al., 2018; Fox & Fridel, 2017; Thornton, 2017). Using official records of 3,216 cases of IPV reported to police across four U.S. states, Hirschel and Buzawa (2013) found that women were less likely to be identified as offenders (22% of cases); however, once identified, women were more likely to be arrested than men (77% vs. 64%). Familicide, in which the partner and children are killed, is almost exclusively committed by men (e.g., Liem et al., 2013) and in a context of domestic violence (e.g., Harris, Hilton, et al., 2007). Men are more likely to recidivate than women after arrest for intimate partner violence (e.g., Gerstenberger & Williams, 2013). Hospital statistics (e.g., Buzawa et al., 2017) and economic estimates (e.g., Peterson et al., 2018) both show the greater cost of violence for women.

In our research using police reports from the mid-1990s of domestic assaults by men against women, we found that the woman also assaulted the man in about one third of cases. In fewer than 10%, the records indicated the woman assaulted the man first; in 2%, she was arrested or charged. Our limited information about these women indicated that they were less likely than other victims to have been severely assaulted or to be concerned about future assaults. We tried sampling cases of women who perpetrated domestic violence from more recent (2004–2005) police records; however, after identifying 200 reports, we found only a handful where the woman was the primary aggressor. In almost all cases, the police were called because of the man's conduct, and when women did initiate violence, it was usually considered innocuous by both parties. We also examined all intimate partner homicides reported in a federal police archive and found that 85% were committed by men (Eke, Hilton, Harris, et al., 2011).

Next, we and Suzanne Popham, chief psychologist of the Algoma Treatment and Remand Centre (ATRC), a correctional treatment facility, identified the ATRC's entire female population in a 10-year period (Hilton et al., 2014). Women's files indicated extensive histories of criminal behavior and substance abuse and childhoods of relentless and sometimes horrific physical, sexual, and psychological abuse. Among the 180 women, though, only 15% had been charged with offenses related to domestic violence. I describe a validation of the ODARA with these women in Chapter 4 (see "Women Who Assault Their Partners"). I do not dispute that women engage in domestic violence and that it can be severe, nor do I condone or minimize it. Indeed, observational studies of couples in violent marriages or at-risk cohorts also found that women were as likely as men to be physically aggressive (e.g., Capaldi et al., 2007). However, we were unable to find a large enough cohort of women who perpetrated domestic violence to construct and cross-validate domestic assault recidivism tools.

Using Official Data Rather Than Self-Report

Official criminal records are essential to accurate prediction of criminal recidivism. Decades of research have shown official criminal history data to be a very strong predictor (e.g., Harris, Rice, et al., 2015). Official data are far from being a complete measure of all the domestic violence. Estimates of unreported violence far exceed officially reported violence (e.g., Farrington & Ttofi, 2014). Official records, however, are likely to be an excellent measure of the violence that comes to the attention of the criminal justice system. Police officers are obliged to submit a report on every incident they respond to, and reports begin with the record of the complainant's call to the dispatch center. They include verbatim statements, so they are not completely influenced by officers' perceptions of severity (contrary to arrests and charges; see the section on Mandatory Arrest, Chapter 10, this volume) and record whether an act occurred. Police reports are created very close in time to the actual event, so they are unlikely to be subject to memory problems.

In contrast, studies of self-reported violence give the consistent impression that, in the population as a whole, men and women are equally likely to assault their partners. This finding is observed especially in Western countries and in general health or social surveys rather than crime or victimization surveys (see review by Archer, 2013), although it has been debated (e.g., Hamberger et al., 2016; Winstok, 2017). Shedding some empirical light on this debate, Graham-Kevan and Archer (2003) compared patterns of domestic violence among students, women in shelters, and men in prison. They found variation in the prevalence of domestic violence reported by men and women as a function of the sample and concluded (as have we; Hilton et al., 2000) that men underreport their violence perpetration. Although self-reports of lifetime prevalence of violence have yielded valid and meaningful results (e.g., Payne & Piquero, 2016), they are less suited to risk assessment research that requires a follow-up time frame (i.e., the time elapsed since a particular "index" event such as the first domestic assault). This issue amplifies the normal limitations of human memory. For example, people victimized by crime sometimes fail to report or recall incidents (e.g., Goldfarb et al., 2018), and *telescoping*, or recalling events as occurring at a different time than they actually occurred, can inflate self-reported prevalence (e.g., Averdijk & Elffers, 2012).

My colleagues and I observed this problem directly when we varied the time frame we used to solicit adolescents' reports about their experiences of aggression (Hilton et al., 1998). At first, we used short time frames (1 month or 6 months) on questionnaires, but then we compared these responses with those from longer time frames (up to 12 months) to evaluate whether extrapolation would be valid. In fact, participants generally reported the same amount of violence regardless of the time frames, except in the case of the most serious forms of aggression In this study, prorating to 12 months would have produced vastly different estimated annual rates of aggression depending on the time frame in the questionnaire. Short time-frame estimates could not be considered more reliable than longer ones. In sum, although self-reports are of theoretical interest—in large part because they are clearly influenced by things other than just whether the behavior occurred—they cannot be considered sufficiently valid for research in which the rate of occurrence of violence in a given follow-up time is an important concern.

Criminal Convictions

Criminal justice professionals working in courts often asked why criminal convictions were not used as the recidivism measure, rather than criminal charges or a police occurrence report alone. A conviction means that the accused person has admitted the behavior or it has been proven beyond reasonable doubt. On the other hand, criminal conviction is not a guarantee of guilt. Some innocent people are convicted, but most judicial systems are deliberately designed to accept some wrongful acquittals to minimize the number of wrongful convictions. Indeed, the concern for victim service providers is sometimes the opposite: Why rely on criminal justice records at all, given that only a fraction of domestic assaults come to the attention of police?

My colleagues and I took the position that criminal conviction is neither intended nor believed to be an accurate measure of criminal conduct. In designing a tool to assess domestic violence risk, we strove for a more behavioral criterion: We ensured that all the available information about any incident was only declared to be domestic assault if it was quite clear that behaviors meeting our definition of violence had occurred, whether or not the person who perpetrated the acts was charged or convicted. This definition yielded good interrater agreement in our research. It is also valid, to the extent that the people who commit the most undetected offenses are the same people who commit the most detected offenses (Farrington & Ttofi, 2014), and couples with domestic violence arrests also self-report the most undetected violence (Capaldi et al., 2009). This approach is also conservative because the frequency of reoffending estimated from criminal justice records underestimates actual behavior (e.g., Farrington et al., 2014).

Although our approach was the best of the available options, it inevitably entails some measurement error. Error in the measurement of outcome can, of course, plague all research on violent recidivism and, in turn, places an upper limit on the accuracy that one can reasonably expect to observe for any form of risk assessment (Harris & Rice, 2003).

Implications for Risk Assessment

Despite some limitations, official records are a robust measure of criminal behavior. Although they do not capture all violence, they are likely to be especially representative of the most serious. Research indicates that individuals who self-report the most crime, including domestic violence, are also those with the most extensive criminal history (e.g., Piquero et al., 2014). The pattern of results is similar for predicting official recidivism and self-reported recidivism (including domestic violence; Murphy et al., 2003), with a tendency for stronger results in the long run when using official recidivism rather than self-report (e.g., Farrington, 1985; Monahan et al., 2001; Pollock et al., 2015). Thus, an individual's rank order with respect to risk is expected to be similar whether based on official data or self-report, although estimated likelihoods of recidivism would obviously differ. The false negatives that can result from basing prediction only on official data (i.e., failure to identify individuals who commit new, unreported acts of domestic violence) are much less likely to affect the rank ordering of all individuals with respect to risk. Rank order is usually reported on the basis of 100 cases, or percentile. Percentile rank is especially useful for decisions about managing risks.

Official data can also be obtained for a follow-up of many years, without the problem of participant dropout that can limit self-report. Official data can be gathered with no intrusion and regardless of the perpetrator's current involvement with a domestic partner. Attrition can occur from official follow-up through death or moving to different jurisdictions, and even records in the Canadian national police archive of charges, convictions, and dispositions are not completely comprehensive or up to date. This source of data, however, has yielded excellent predictive accuracy in follow-ups of up to 49 years in studies of generally violent men (Rice et al., 2013). All these considerations weighed heavily in our decision to use federal records and police occurrence reports in our domestic violence research.

Selecting Potential Predictors

In the absence of data to develop an actuarial tool, the easiest way to compile a risk assessment tool would be to ask experts in the field—police, researchers, therapists, and so on—what they think ought to be included. Items nominated by the most experts would be compiled in a list that comprises the assessment. As long as all the items were expressed similarly (e.g., "has a history of domestic violence," "has a drinking problem," "partner fears future assaults"), the list could be a checklist of risk factors. The more items that were true in a particular case, the greater one could suppose the risk to be. This approach was used to make the first domestic violence risk assessment tools, such as a checklist created by the Ontario Provincial Police that our research showed predicted domestic recidivism with reasonable success (Hilton et al., 2004). Victim advocates, too, might be able to identify valid correlates of domestic violence recidivism (Cattaneo, 2007), and assaulted women themselves can sometimes predict reassault consistent with or better than risk assessment tools (e.g., Connor-Smith et al., 2011; Messing, Campbell, Sullivan Wilson, et al., 2017).

The most obvious drawback to this approach is that accuracy (or predictive validity) cannot be assumed and requires a follow-up study. That is, researchers must score the list for a sample of individuals and then check their outcomes to evaluate the list's level of accuracy in assessing the risk of subsequent recidivism. Because follow-up research is required anyway, using a simple checklist does not really offer much savings in effort over actuarial methods.

A second drawback is that the experts might miss some risk factors that they were unaware of or include items that they erroneously believe are risk factors. For example, many professionals overestimate the role of suicidality in domestic violence risk (e.g., Ward-Lasher et al., 2017). Suicide is a factor highlighted by domestic homicide inquests (e.g., Ontario Office of the Chief Coroner, 2017), and any suicide threat merits further assessment. However, few studies have examined whether suicidality predicts domestic violence recidivism. We found no association (e.g., Hilton et al., 2004), but others found a significant positive effect (e.g., López-Ossorio et al., 2017). Still others report that suicide threats do not significantly distinguish fatal and nonfatal cases after controlling for other risk factors such as gun access, marital separation, victim sex, and perpetrator age, sex, and criminal history (J. C. Campbell et al., 2003; Jung & Stewart, 2019). Perhaps no predictive relationship between suicidality and risk of subsequent domestic violence exists, or some individuals make insincere threats of suicide to control their partner's behavior. I hope that future research will investigate this distinction because it is both theoretically intriguing and intensely important to individuals faced with a partner's threat of suicide.

In the search for risk factors for recidivism, the best research designs follow a group of individuals who have committed violent offenses to determine who later recidivates or does not recidivate. Some research, especially in the early years of attempts to identify correlates of domestic violence, compared men with histories of violence to men without such histories (see Chapter 1, this volume). The main weakness of this approach is that it only shows what distinguishes men who do or do not have a violent history, which is quite different from predicting who will be violent again. Early studies of domestic violence risk assessment compared cases in which recidivism or nonrecidivism was already known (e.g., Kropp & Hart, 2000). Kropp and Hart's (2000) group comparison study helped advance understanding of domestic violence risk assessment while awaiting the time and other resources to conduct follow-up research, which they later did, such as the study led by Jennifer Storey (Storey et al., 2014; see also Researcher Profile 2.2). However, this design might exclude ambiguous cases or involve some sort of preselection that could restrict the variability of actual recidivism predictors in the sample (e.g., should individuals who commit nondomestic violent recidivism be excluded?) with the result that some important risk factors might not be discovered. It also turns out that this approach can inflate apparent predictive accuracy (Hilton & Harris, 2009b). A follow-up study without prior selection of cases with and without recidivism is required to empirically identify valid predictors of recidivism.

Conducting Follow-Up Research

A follow-up study begins with selecting a group of individuals who share a common set of relevant characteristics (called a sample) and then assessing one or more outcomes. In studies my colleagues and I have conducted of domestic and other violent recidivism, our samples are usually men who have all committed an act of violence, and we examine whether they do so again. We measure several (sometimes many) potential risk factors for each man in the sample, then compare those who recidivate with those who do not on each potential risk factor. The main advantage of this approach to selecting items for a risk assessment is that it asks the right question: Which things that could be known at the time of an earlier violent offense are actually informative about the likelihood of recidivism? Because the individuals are not preselected for recidivism and nonrecidivism, the effect on recidivism of anything that could be measured at the earlier time can be studied, so there is ample opportunity to discover previously unknown predictors. The size of the effect can be compared for each predictor; some variables will show only small predictive effects and might exhibit very large effects. A tool comprising the factors with the largest measurable differences would be the most accurate risk assessment system.

A more subtle advantage to a follow-up study is that it can eliminate redundant risk factors. It is possible for two or more variables to convey the same information. For example, in research with the VRAG, men with and without violent recidivism differed in their histories of nonviolent crime as well as their histories of violent crime; therefore, knowing a man's history of violent offending did not help assess the risk of violent recidivism after his nonviolent offending history was already known (e.g., Harris, Rice, et al., 2015). Some degree of redundancy among risk factors can help protect against missing information or measurement error, but when two risk factors convey essentially the same information, assessing them both increases the time and cost of risk assessment (and the faulty perception that there is more evidence of risk). A follow-up study allows developers to discover redundancy and to drop one of the fully redundant factors. In this way, items can be selected on the basis that they convey at least some unique information. This, in turn, means that a risk assessment tool does not need to include every known risk factor; it only needs to include nonredundant risk factors. An assessment system that used massive amounts of mostly irrelevant information might perform more poorly than the intuition of an experienced expert (Gladwell, 2005, provides some unusual examples; and Kahneman, 2011, compelling arguments). Thus, follow-up studies allow risk assessment to be much more efficient.

Choosing the Statistical Approach

My colleagues and I developed the ODARA/DVRAG system using the same approach that was used to develop the VRAG family of tools (e.g., Harris, Rice, et al., 2015; Rice et al., 2013). We measured every item on the ODARA and DVRAG from one point in time and showed that they were correlated with subsequent assaults. The weighting of items on the DVRAG was determined by each item's association with recidivism.

The statistical method we have described for developing a risk assessment tool identifies only simple additive relationships between the set of risk factors and the outcome variable. Thus, we could not detect whether two factors multiplied together would have had a larger predictive effect. Some actuarial risk assessments for general violent recidivism use methods based on a classification tree (e.g., Monahan et al., 2005). In this approach, risk factors are dealt with in order, and whether any particular risk factor is considered depends on the results for previously considered risk factors. This approach can be captured as the multiplication of many risk factors altogether and has been called *predictive attribute analysis* (e.g., Pritchard, 1977). It contrasts with the linear regression approach we used, in that the linear approach always considers the same factors, and the answers are added together to get a final score.

The classification tree has some appeal (e.g., easily interpreted results combined with the ability to incorporate powerful multiplicative predictive relationships) but also has large drawbacks. Predictive attribute methods tend to produce large predictive accuracy when developed but fail to replicate or predict much less well in subsequent samples (e.g., Bokhari & Hubert, 2018; Monahan et al., 2005; Pritchard, 1977). The interactions create a complicated structure, and a tree assessment often requires special software. Thus, the additional accuracy that can be captured by complex higher order relationships comes at a relatively high cost.

Classification trees are rarely used in domestic violence. Wijenayake et al. (2018) identified a simplified model using prior convictions, custody, and conditional releases that achieved an AUC of .65. However, they needed much more complex models to achieve the same predictive accuracy as linear models using the same data. For frontline police and criminal justice work, it is much easier to implement a simple tool that adds points based on evidence obtained in a routine investigation. Although simple linear systems cannot reflect complex interactions among variables, for most purposes, they can predict violent recidivism very well.

EVALUATING VIOLENCE RISK ASSESSMENT

Over time, actuarial risk assessment has had an increasing influence on forensic decisions and sentencing (e.g., Hilton, Simpson, & Ham, 2016; Monahan et al., 2020). I believe this shift is partly due to accumulating evidence supporting the reliability and validity of actuarial risk assessment.

Reliability and Accuracy in Risk Assessment

Two essential characteristics of every measurement are its reliability and its accuracy. Reliability is the consistency with which scores are produced using the measurement. For example, if I climb onto a bathroom scale and it reads 92 kg, and I get off then back on again and it reads 86 kg, then 98 kg, the scale is not measuring reliably. In violence risk assessment, reliability is important to ensure a tool can be scored consistently and is not affected by assessor bias (e.g., being especially inclined to view offender risk conservatively or leniently). Interrater reliability is usually assessed by comparing scores from two or more assessors (e.g., clinicians or research assistants) evaluating the same individuals independently. This property is known as interrater reliability, and as I mentioned in Chapter 1, is usually expressed as a correlation coefficient between −1.0 and +1.0. The intraclass correlation (ICC) is the commonly preferred measure of interrater reliability and permits choice over the modeling of such parameters as the random effect of raters (e.g., Mehta et al., 2018; Shrout & Fleiss, 1979). Sometimes poor reliability is due to not doing the measurement correctly—for example, leaning against the wall while standing on the bathroom scale. Sometimes poor reliability is an inherent problem with the measurement device itself, such as a broken spring inside a bathroom scale. In the case of a risk assessment tool, training its users and providing clear scoring instructions can enhance reliability by ensuring the measurement is used correctly, in accordance with its design. However, instructions to insert an unspecified amount of personal intuition would likely worsen reliability, according to the evidence for clinical judgment and override described in Chapter 8.

Reliability is a necessary but not sufficient condition for accuracy. Reliability places an upper limit on accuracy. Put another way, a reliable measure can be inaccurate, but an unreliable assessment cannot be accurate. If that bathroom scale gave a different reading every time, it could not be considered an accurate tool, even if one of those readings happened to be correct. Establishing accuracy is a separate and more complicated step, however.

The degree to which an assessment measures what it is supposed to measure is central to validity. Psychologists attend to several measures of validity. The validity that matters most in risk assessment is predictive validity (or criterion-related validity), the degree to which actual outcomes match predicted outcomes. There are many ways to assess the accuracy of a risk assessment tool, but the most useful are those that allow comparison from one study or application to another, using a common metric. The receiver operating characteristic *area under the curve* (AUC) allows for such comparisons and is a popular metric for the predictive effect size of violence risk assessments (Helmus & Babchishin, 2017; Rice & Harris, 2005). To explain the information captured by this accuracy statistic, see the illustration in Figure 2.1.

AUC and Related Accuracy Statistics

Figure 2.1 shows the scores obtained for two groups: men who committed domestic violent recidivism during a follow-up period (scores shown in the black bars) and men who did not (gray bars). The two groups overlap, but the mean (i.e., average) score for the recidivism group is different from

FIGURE 2.1. Number of Men With and Without Recidivism Obtaining Each Score on an Actuarial Risk Assessment Tool

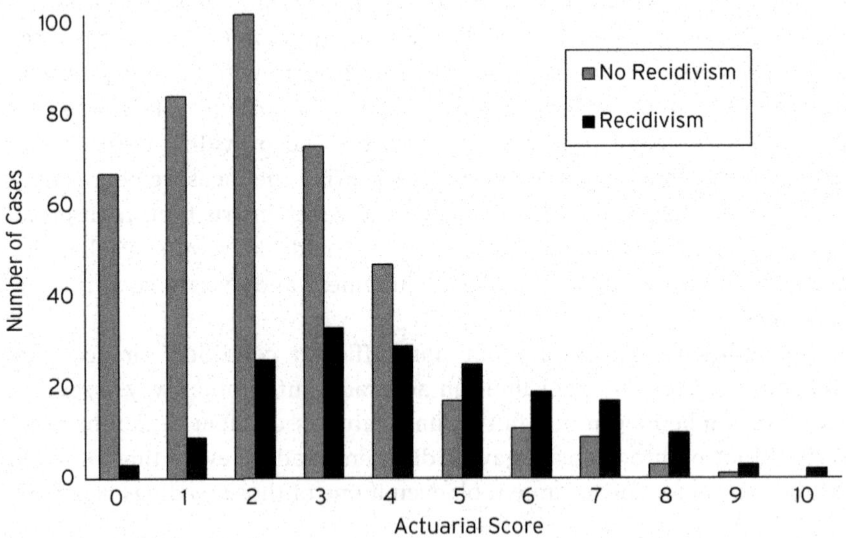

the mean score for the nonrecidivism group. A simple *t* test, described in any undergraduate statistics textbook, can tell us whether this difference is statistically significant according to an arbitrarily selected statistical cut-off point. So too can the 95% confidence intervals (CIs) around each group's average score; the CI shows the level of precision with which a point estimate is made and can be used to infer a difference between two point estimates that fall outside each other's CIs (e.g., Cumming & Finch, 2005; see Exhibit 2.1).

Cohen's *d* (Cohen, 1992; Rice & Harris, 2005) tells us how big the difference is. This measure of effect size uses standard units that relate to how spread out the groups' scores are proportionate to the number of cases in each group, or the *standard deviations.* In Figure 2.1, each group has a standard deviation of approximately 2, and the means are approximately 2 points apart; thus, $d = 1$. A *d* of .8 is considered "large" (Rice & Harris, 2005).

Base rate is shown in Figure 2.1 by the number of cases in the recidivist group as a percentage of the total number in both groups. In this case, about 30% of the total sample recidivated, so the base rate is 30%. The simplest measures of accuracy, such as true positives, false positives, and false negatives, are quite dependent on the base rate, the effect size, or both,

EXHIBIT 2.1. Confidence Intervals

"Thirty-six percent of 1,000 Canadians randomly polled said that they supported the government's current approach to reducing carbon emissions. This proportion is expected to be accurate to plus or minus 3%, 19 times out of 20." The statement of a plausible range of values for the finding is called a *confidence interval.* A confidence interval is an estimate of a range of values capturing the precision of measurement, usually with respect to the "true" value in the population. It shows the level of precision with which the point estimate is made. In general, confidence intervals are smaller (and precision greater) when more measurements are taken (or more people are sampled) and when measurement devices are better (e.g., using a stopwatch instead of a grandfather clock).

Confidence intervals also help in drawing conclusions about differences. For example, if the survey were conducted a month later and the result was "Thirty-eight percent of a thousand Canadians randomly polled . . .," the government should not conclude there has been a real increase in the Canadian population's support for its approach to reducing carbon emissions. It is common practice in psychological research to accept a 95% confidence interval as the statistical standard; however, it is incorrect to equate this interval with an alpha level for the rejection of null hypotheses when comparing two results. Actually, the practice of using "nonoverlapping" 95% confidence intervals as a test of group differences is very conservative (e.g., Cumming & Finch, 2005). Nonoverlapping 83% or 84% confidence intervals more closely approximate a statistical test with a significance level of 0.05 (Payton et al., 2003). Confidence intervals give information about measurement and results that are accessible and comprehensible.

so they are not useful for comparing across studies of recidivism. They also assume a single cutoff score, whereas risk assessment measures risk as a continuum (e.g., Helmus & Babchishin, 2017). Correlations indicate the degree to which two variables (e.g., predictor and outcome) are positively or negatively related to each other across the continuum but are also base-rate dependent.

The AUC expresses the trade-off between sensitivity and specificity (i.e., giving up sensitivity to avoid false positives vs. identifying all individuals who recidivate at the expense of false positives) across all possible scores. The trade-off is much less determined by the base rate than are their individual values (Rice & Harris, 1995). The trade-off can be plotted as in Figure 2.2, which uses the data in Figure 2.1. If there were no overlap between the two groups, the means in Figure 2.1 would be further apart, *d* would be >5.0, and everyone who recidivated would have a higher score than everyone who did not. Sensitivity would be 1.0, and specificity would also be 1.0. The plot would show a "curve" traveling up the vertical axis and

FIGURE 2.2. The Sensitivity-Specificity Trade-Off Illustrated in a Receiver Operating Characteristic Curve for the Data in Figure 2.1, Compared With the Line of No Discrimination

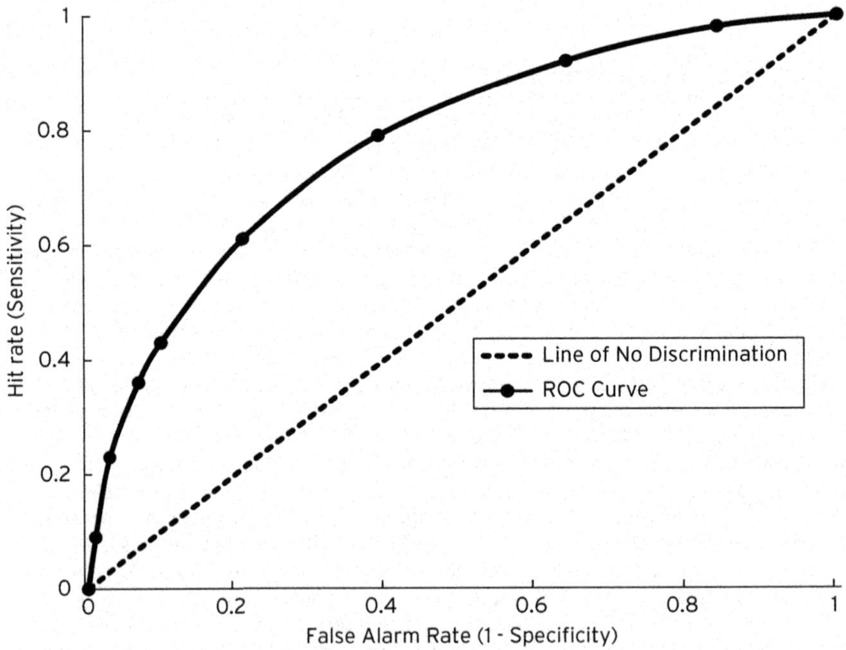

Note. ROC = receiver operating characteristic. The line of no discrimination is equivalent to an AUC (area under the curve) of .50.

then extending parallel to the horizontal axis. The AUC would equal 1.0, which is the entire area available under the curve and equals the probability that a randomly chosen person who recidivated had a higher risk assessment score than a randomly chosen person who did not.

The accuracy of a risk assessment with an AUC of 0.5 would be plotted exactly on the diagonal. It would carry a 50% chance of a recidivating individual having a higher score than a nonrecidivating individual—no useful prediction at all. The curve actually plotted in Figure 2.2 indicates an AUC of .77; that is, there is a 77% probability that the tool used to assess these cases gives a randomly chosen person from the recidivism group a higher score than a randomly chosen person from the nonrecidivism group. This AUC value corresponds to a *d* (effect size) of 1.03, or a large effect (Rice & Harris, 2005), suggesting a tool with great practical value. In fact, these data came from the sample used to construct the ODARA.[1]

The AUC is a generally accepted statistic for measuring the predictive accuracy of a risk assessment tool. It is relatively easy to interpret and suitable for comparisons across studies, provided the studies use similar methodology and terms (e.g., K. M. Williams et al., 2017). Because it is nonparametric, the AUC can be used to characterize the predictive value of either continuous predictors (e.g., risk assessment tool scores) or ordinal predictors (e.g., categories of increasing risk). AUCs can help decision-makers choose optimal cut-off points depending on the costs and benefits of different outcomes (as illustrated by Harris & Rice, 2007). A disadvantage is that AUCs can be affected by different follow-up durations within the sample. For this circumstance, some favor a statistic that groups cases according to time at risk, Harrell's C (e.g., Harrell et al., 1996), although AUC and C produce similar results in sufficiently large samples (e.g., Flores et al., 2017).

Not all researchers prefer the AUC, and there are other statistics suited to discrimination analyses (see review by Helmus & Babchishin, 2017). The primary disadvantage of AUCs is that they are affected by the range of the predictor variables. This means that testing a tool in unusually high or low risk samples will yield lower AUC values than the same tool tested in a more typical sample (e.g., Helmus & Babchishin, 2017). Basing sample selection on a specific type of offense history, or predicting specific offense types, also limits the AUC (e.g., Howard, 2017), leading to the expectation

[1]Of the two cases scoring 11 in the ODARA construction sample, one had been misassigned as a nonrecidivist (not shown in Figure 2.1) after a charge of assault that appeared ambiguous because of an incident involving both his partner and a neighbor. We discovered this later and removed the case from further analyses.

that AUCs for domestic recidivism in samples selected for domestic violence will be lower than in samples selected for any violence or general offending.

Regression coefficients from Cox regression or logistic regression coefficients are less sensitive than AUCs to a restricted range of scores (e.g., Helmus & Babchishin, 2017). Regression coefficients indicate how much the rate of recidivism increases with each 1-point increase in the score. Regression can incorporate multiple independent variables, so they are often used to test incremental validity—that is, whether one potential predictor adds information about risk beyond that afforded by all other predictors in the model. These methods, however, are best suited to continuous measures and should only be used to compare accuracy of risk factors or assessment tools with a similar range of scores (e.g., Helmus & Babchishin, 2017).

Calibration

The statistics we have just described characterize a tool's *discriminative accuracy*; that is, the extent to which it discriminates, in a given sample, between individuals who will and will not recidivate. Calibration statistics measure the correspondence in recidivism rates between two samples, especially between rates predicted from a construction sample and those observed in a validation sample. Calibration has not been widely adopted in violence risk assessment, although Harrell and colleagues (1996) argued that it should be measured before applying a tool to new cases. The statistics are fairly easy to calculate and interpret, such as the chi-square or the E/O index of expected divided by observed numbers of recidivists (e.g., Hanson, 2017; Helmus & Babchishin, 2017). A statistically nonsignificant chi-square value (which depends on the number of cases and risk categories) indicates good calibration. An E/O index of approximately 1 also indicates good calibration. The E/O index is the ratio of the expected number of cases with recidivism divided by the observed number of cases with recidivism. Thus, the E/O index is a measure of the extent to which the prediction tool overestimates or underestimates recidivism rates. If a tool predicts that 75 individuals will recidivate and 100 do, then the E/O index will be .75. An E/O index greater than 1 indicates overprediction of recidivism (Helmus & Babchishin, 2017).

Meta-Analytic Studies

Meta-analytic studies are important for determining overall effect sizes in the body of research. In the most recent meta-analysis of violence risk assessment tools, for example, Whittington and colleagues (2013) reported 51 studies of the VRAG and a mean AUC of .72 among those they included. However, not all meta-analyses are of equal quality. Some fail to include eligible studies, misclassify the outcomes used in original research, inappropriately dichotomize assessment scores, and even misidentify authors or omit statistical procedures that may produce different conclusions (e.g., Harris et al., 2010; K. M. Williams et al., 2017; for more details, see Harris, Rice, et al., 2015, pp. 164–166). It is important, therefore, to examine the quality of meta-analyses as well as the quality of the studies they include.

Jill Messing conducted a meta-analysis of domestic violence risk assessment tools drawn from 10 published studies, finding that the ODARA had the largest mean effect size (AUC = .666; Messing & Thaller, 2013; see also Research Profile 2.1). Later, van der Put et al. (2019) found an AUC of .690 for the ODARA and reported that actuarial tools performed better than other methods. Other reviews, though, have reported little statistical difference between mean AUCs across tools in published and unpublished validation studies (Graham et al., 2019; Helmus & Bourgon, 2011).

Measuring Bias

Bias can enter into any decision-making system, including risk assessment and risk management decisions. Well-designed, replicable research studies can keep some methodological biases in check. Actuarial assessment, if implemented systematically and appropriately, can help limit biases that are inherent in all human decision-making. Even so, domestic violence risk assessment is biased toward research with men who assault their female partners, which can result in overestimation of the risk of recidivism by women in instruments designed for men (e.g., Hilton, Popham, et al., 2014). Cultural, ethnic, and socioeconomic bias has been a growing concern among risk assessment researchers and practitioners (as I describe in the Chapter 8 section titled Individual Risk and Bias) and remains an important area for future research in domestic violence risk assessment.

RISK ASSESSMENT FOR CRIMINAL JUSTICE

Risk assessment in the criminal justice context is the evaluation of the risk that an individual will recidivate (commit another offense). Most risk assessment research has taken place in the context of criminal justice, although laws limiting domestic violence are a historically recent phenomenon (e.g., Hilton & Harris, 2009a). As recently as the late 20th century, there was a policing bias against making arrests that often overrode even strong victim preferences for arrest, which could deter future reporting (Buzawa et al., 2017).

Now, in the 21st century, physical or sexual violence against intimate partners is a crime in all industrialized nations, and most police services have presumptive or mandatory arrest policies for domestic violence. There are efforts to filter in the highest risk domestic cases for the most intensive police response, including threat assessment (e.g., Ennis et al., 2015). Still, there is variation in the use of, and factors contributing to, arrest (Buzawa et al., 2017; see the section Mandatory Arrest in Chapter 10, this volume). Police officers make the first of many decisions throughout the criminal justice process as to whether an individual should be arrested and held in custody. Risk assessment tools are increasingly considered valuable aids to such decisions.

RISK ASSESSMENT FOR DOMESTIC VIOLENCE TREATMENT

Proarrest policies led to court-mandated treatment and increased attendance at community-based treatment services, often known as batterer intervention programs (Radatz & Wright, 2016). Research on interventions for general offending has suggested three principles of effective correctional practice: risk, need, and responsivity (RNR; e.g., Bonta & Andrews, 2017; see the description in the section titled Limits of Domestic Violence Theory and an Alternative From General Offending in Chapter 1, this volume). The first step in planning intervention is to identify the individuals for whom it will be most beneficial. Those who have little likelihood of reoffending at the outset will have little to gain from any intervention. Dollars spent on the least risky individuals will be least cost-effective and might increase the likelihood of offending, whereas treatment programs for the riskiest individuals are likely to reduce both costs and recidivism (e.g., Taxman et al., 2014). Radatz and Wright (2016) observed that domestic violence treatment providers have begun using risk assessment but do not consistently base treatment decisions on their results and that treatment programs lack clear guidelines for using risk assessment to its full potential. To adhere to the risk principle, the highest risk individuals should receive the most intensive intervention (including custody, where appropriate) and have the highest priority for intake if there is a waiting list.

The second principle of effective correctional practice is to target the causes of crime referred to as *criminogenic needs*. Although the causes of crime have generally yet to be determined, it is certain that they are among the correlates of crime. Thus, effective practice requires, at the very least, targeting personal characteristics that are empirically associated with recidivism and usually not intervening with characteristics unrelated to recidivism. For example, attitudes and beliefs about gender roles and domestic abuse, although popular domestic violence treatment targets (e.g., Radatz & Wright, 2016), lack rigorous evidence showing their association with domestic recidivism. Some evidence points to an influence of more implicit cognitions about violence and gender on treatment compliance and criminal recidivism (e.g., Eckhardt & Crane, 2014), but more research is needed to translate this finding into effective intervention. Thus, popular treatment targets are not necessarily criminogenic needs. Fortunately, many treatment providers are familiar with criminogenic needs such as substance use, although more work is needed to consistently assess these needs and target them in treatment (Radatz & Wright, 2016).

Dana Radatz and I studied criminogenic needs in a cohort of men admitted to the forensic assessment unit at one hospital between 2009 and 2012 (Hilton & Radatz, 2018). Of the 638 men, 99 had a previous or current criminal charge for a violent offense against an intimate partner, 233 had violent charges but no domestic offense history, and 103 had only a nonviolent criminal history. We identified six of the "central eight" criminogenic needs in the men's criminal, medical, and psychosocial records: antisocial personality traits, procriminal attitudes, social supports for crime, substance use, poor marital or family relationships, and work or school problems (omitting antisocial history because it is not considered a treatment target and leisure or recreation problems due to data limitations). Men with a domestic offense history had all of these criminogenic needs, especially work or school problems, poor marital and family relationships, and substance use. They were more likely than either the violent or nonviolent group to have every need except work or school problems. There was no significant difference between groups in their noncriminogenic needs, including mental health or physical health problems. In another study, we examined criminogenic needs identified through police and correctional records of men with a police report of domestic violence, and found they were related to domestic violence recidivism (Hilton & Radatz, in press). This research shows that criminogenic needs are at least as important to managing the risk of domestic violence as for general offending risk management. It underscores the need to apply the need principle in domestic violence treatment programs and opens up a field of established evidence-based practice to draw from.

The third principle of effective correctional practice is responsivity. Some interventions work better than others and individuals vary in their response to interventions. Cognitive-behavioral, social learning approaches are generally more effective than insight-oriented counseling or punitive sanctions (Bonta & Andrews, 2017). Thus, interventions adhere to the *general responsivity* principle if they go beyond psychoeducational "talk therapy" and instead teach prosocial cognitive and behavioral skills. Meta-analytic research to date shows positive but nonsignificant effects of treatment on domestic violence recidivism (e.g., Arias et al., 2013). In Chapter 1, in the section on typologies, I described research showing that men who have committed domestic violence differ in risk and other characteristics that might result in them responding differently to treatment. *Specific responsivity* involves providing treatment in a context or method that is sensitive to these characteristics. It is unclear whether domestic violence treatment programs currently address this principle (Radatz & Wright, 2016).

One responsivity characteristic might be general antisociality—or at its extreme, psychopathy. Individuals with strong psychopathic characteristics likely contribute to the "generally violent" type found in domestic violence typologies (e.g., Huss & Langhinrichsen-Rohling, 2006; Swogger et al., 2007; see also Chapter 1, this volume). Psychopathic traits have been associated with domestic violence treatment dropout and recidivism (e.g., Rock et al., 2013). When a small minority of a sample exhibits extreme and correlated scores on two variables (e.g., substance abuse and violence), modest correlations can be found in the entire large sample even when there is no correlation between the two variables in the great majority (Harris & Hilton, 2001). This phenomenon suggests that modest correlations of variables with domestic violence could spur attempts to identify subgroups that might be responsible for the correlation. Furthermore, the search for treatment responsivity characteristics within domestic violence subtypes might lead to more effective treatment.

A final lesson from the general literature on effective intervention, where effective treatments have been demonstrated, is that it is difficult to change criminal behavior. Standardized treatment implemented with high integrity by skilled staff is required (Bonta & Andrews, 2017; Harris, Rice, et al., 2015). All these requirements mean that a one-size-fits-all approach that provides the same intervention to all individuals can be justified by neither fiscal responsibility nor the need to maximize public safety. A valid risk assessment system is essential to the efficacy of domestic violence treatment.

RISK ASSESSMENT FOR COMMUNITY VICTIM SERVICES

A common theme in assaulted women's experience of the criminal justice system is the feeling of revictimization through disempowerment, lack of information about court procedures, and even public humiliation (e.g., Cubells & Calsamiglia, 2018; Hilton & Harris, 2009a). Mandatory charging and no-drop prosecution policies, originally intended to increase action against domestic violence, carry bureaucratic and professional implications that can disempower victims and overshadow their needs and preferred processes (e.g., Buzawa et al., 2017; Holder & Daly, 2018). Lack of psychosocial support can lead to assaulted women dropping out of justice proceedings (e.g., Cala et al., 2016). Risk assessments conducted in the criminal justice system may not have victims in mind. Some tools require information that is not available to those who work in the victim service sector, or results are simply not accessible to the people they support.

The ODARA offers victim service providers a valid and accessible risk assessment that uses the same information used by the criminal justice system in a way that is both practical in a client interview and sensitive to clients' needs for immediate information about risk. The finding that self-reports of domestic violence can be predicted with similar accuracy, and by the same variables, as criminal record statistics (Murphy et al., 2003), further supports making tools constructed with official records available to individuals victimized by domestic violence. Thus, although the normative data provided in this book likely underestimate the occurrence of violence, the highest scoring individuals are the most likely to commit domestic violence recidivism, whether scored from official data or from a victim interview.

Women assaulted by their partners can predict reassault reasonably well (as I described in the section Vulnerability Factors in Chapter 1, this volume). Those who notify police or access victim support services are less likely to be revictimized, perhaps because they become more informed of risk assessment and safety planning options (e.g., Xie & Lynch, 2017). Some women, however, underestimate the seriousness of their situation or cannot mobilize the protection and support they need (e.g., J. C. Campbell, 2004; J. C. Campbell et al., 2009). In my research with women who were assaulted, I found that having children to care for meant that women stayed with their partners longer than they would have otherwise (Hilton, 1992). One woman said that she could not leave because of the disruption to school-age children, and another reconciled with her husband because he had temporary custody. Several others stayed because their partner threatened to harm the children if she left. I was struck by the finding that most women suffered much physical violence and psychological abuse before eventually leaving their partner only when they realized that their children were also at risk of violence, directly or indirectly.

CONCLUSION

Actuarial risk assessment for domestic violence is designed to provide an objective, realistic appraisal of the danger posed by an individual. It not only helps women make crucial decisions about themselves and their children but also provides evidence to support their need for protection by the criminal justice system, such as increased police patrols and emergency cell phones directly linked to the police. Without a shared understanding of the risks of violence in a given case, the criminal justice and victim service sectors—and their clients—can often be at odds as to the need for intervention. A shared, empirically supported risk assessment system can improve both risk assessment and risk communication.

With this vision, my colleagues and I began work on the ODARA/DVRAG system, a brief tool to assess the likelihood that an individual who has assaulted their intimate partner will do so again.

POINTS TO REMEMBER

- The work to develop an actuarial domestic violence risk assessment tool was influenced by earlier work with the VRAG, an actuarial instrument shown to predict violent recidivism over many follow-up times, outcome measures, and populations.
- Official records, although they underestimate the rate of undetected violence, are most appropriate for developing risk assessment tools for the criminal justice system and are not subject to memory problems and other biases associated with self-report.
- The predictive validity of risk assessment tools is most often assessed by measuring discrimination between individuals who recidivate and those who do not recidivate, using the AUC, a statistic that indicates the effect size.
- Domestic violence intervention should be based on the risk, need, and responsivity (RNR) principles of effective intervention; valid risk assessment is an essential starting point.

- Community victim service providers having access to a valid risk assessment tool that is shared with criminal justice can improve risk communication and promote the coordination of all services responding to domestic violence.

QUESTIONS TO CONSIDER

1. Summarize the three key principles of effective correctional intervention.
2. State four reasons why risk assessment tools designed for general violence were insufficient or impractical for domestic violence risk assessment.
3. Why are follow-up studies necessary for developing a risk assessment tool?
4. What are the advantages of using official data for developing risk assessment tools rather than self-report data? What are the limitations? In what circumstances would it be preferable to use self-reports?
5. How might you create a child abuse risk assessment tool? How would you select the items, and what validation methods (sample, design, statistical approach) would you use?

RESEARCHER PROFILE 2.1
JILL MESSING, MSW, PhD

My undergraduate thesis at California State University, San Bernardino, examined multiple murder in the domestic context. I was struck by the pervasiveness of intimate partner violence (IPV) in the stories of men who killed. In graduate school at the University of California, Berkeley, I focused on IPV and, in particular, the trajectory from nonlethal IPV to homicide. My interest in predicting intimate partner homicide led to a postdoctoral research fellowship with Dr. Jacquelyn Campbell at Johns Hopkins University.

As a feminist, I understand IPV as the manifestation of structural inequalities played out in the lives of individuals. As a social worker, I am interested in how risk assessment can be used to stop IPV and prevent severe violence and homicide. As such, I study protective factors and dynamic risk items—that is, women's particular strengths as well as risks that can be mitigated through intervention. I also use an evidence-based practice framework, whereby risk assessment is only one piece of the intervention puzzle. Risk assessment is the best evidence of future IPV or homicide and should be integrated with practitioner expertise and IPV survivor self-determination to build the best intervention for each person.

I primarily conduct experimental and quasi-experimental field trials. Ideally, risk assessments are used in interventions; in a research study, I combine a test of predictive validity with an evaluation of the intervention's effectiveness. A good example is my study of the Lethality Assessment Program (LAP), a risk-informed collaborative intervention developed by the Maryland Network Against Domestic Violence. Police officers assess risk at the scene of an IPV incident and place high-risk survivors in telephone contact with domestic violence advocates. In a study funded by the U.S. National Institute of Justice, I examined the predictive validity of the risk assessment within a comparison group. I then compared the LAP intervention group with the comparison group to look at the effectiveness of the intervention. For high-risk victims who spoke to the advocate at the scene of the domestic violence incident, the LAP increased help-seeking and reduced violent victimization.

Given emerging policy trends, IPV risk assessments that are primarily used to connect survivors with domestic violence services need to be adapted for use in pretrial settings. I would like to conduct a study that combines pretrial risk assessment items with IPV risk assessment items to develop tools that are flexible enough to inform collaborative interventions for survivors and to assist with pretrial decisions for offenders. Once I understand the predictive power of these combined risk assessments, I would like to examine their effectiveness to inform pretrial decision-making. Technology is also at the cutting edge of risk assessment implementation. Risk assessments need to be more flexible (e.g., with items scored differently depending on the setting or goal); automation would reduce scoring errors and enhance risk-informed communication across collaborating agencies. I am on the research team that developed and tested myPlan (http://www.myplanapp.org), an app or internet-based intervention that provides users immediate feedback on their Danger Assessment score and allows survivors a safe, private space to weigh their priorities and determine the best path forward. On the basis of the survivor's risk assessment score and priorities, myPlan provides an interactive safety plan with links to resources. We are in an exciting time with regard to the science and technology of IPV risk assessment; the research being conducted has the potential to influence both policy and practice, ultimately bringing us one step closer to ending IPV.

About the Researcher

Dr. Messing is an associate professor in the School of Social Work at Arizona State University.

RESEARCHER PROFILE 2.2
JENNIFER E. STOREY, PHD

My focus on interpersonal violence can be traced back to a 4th-year undergraduate presentation at Carleton University, where stalking was one of many topics suggested by my professor, Dr. Craig Bennell. I came across a literature review by Dr. Barry Rosenfeld on the risk factors for stalking, which narrowed my focus to risk assessment. A second article by Kropp et al. (2002) drew me in further and influenced my choice of graduate study. Drs. Hart and Kropp became my graduate supervisors for my master's and PhD in forensic psychology at Simon Fraser University (SFU), and Dr. Rosenfeld was an external examiner for my master's. I then completed a postdoctoral fellowship jointly between SFU and Mid Sweden University. Drs. Hart, Kropp, and Rosenfeld have provided continued advice and support throughout my career. Thus, the initial presentation and the decision to reach out to those who inspired me had a highly influential impact on my career.

In graduate school, my focus broadened from stalking to intimate partner violence (IPV) and later elder abuse, always maintaining its roots in violence risk assessment. A key influence for me was a placement at the Vancouver Police Department. What was meant to be two semesters turned into 7 years with the Domestic Violence and Criminal Harassment unit because I enjoyed it so much! There, I saw the development of an elder abuse team and learned about the true nature of IPV and the application of the work on risk assessment that we do. The unit's officers often asked me what the practical application of this research was. This is the lens through which I now conduct my research.

My most influential study to date is Belfrage et al. (2012) because it identified the ability of a violence risk assessment tool not only to predict but also to help prevent violence. Specifically, the SARA as completed by police predicted new police contacts for IPV and threats against their female partners. In high-risk cases, police officers recommended higher levels of intervention, which was associated with decreased recidivism for these cases. The management of violence risk is an area in which I continue to work and feel is an important direction for the field.

Elder abuse is a second understudied area in which I am excited to be working. More study is needed in two aspects. First, there are cases in which couples who have had continued violence in their relationship have grown old. Much of the victim assistance available is for younger women. Older women with care needs can be turned away from shelters who cannot meet their needs and turned away from care homes who cannot take on clients with a risk of violence. More awareness and study of these victims is needed to support them in staying safe. Second, there are cases in which couples only become violent in their old age. These cases, I argue, have different risk factors for IPV (e.g., cognitive problems, dependency) than those involving younger couples. Research on risk assessment and management in this area is limited and hindered by several factors, including underreporting, a lack of criminal justice system involvement, and the heightened risk of mortality for the victims. Further to these circumstances, the aging population means that both of these situations will occur with more frequency in the future. Therefore, issues related to elder abuse are increasingly urgent areas for research that is highly applicable to practice.

About the Researcher

Dr. Storey is a forensic psychologist working as a lecturer in the School of Law at Royal Holloway, University of London.

PART II UNDERSTANDING AND APPLYING THE ODARA AND THE DVRAG

3 CREATING A FRONTLINE RISK ASSESSMENT

The Ontario Domestic Assault Risk Assessment

In this chapter, I describe the work I did with my colleagues, Grant Harris, Marnie Rice, and others I introduce in what follows, to develop a frontline actuarial risk assessment tool for domestic violence recidivism. This work necessitated many decisions about the research procedure, what cases would be eligible, how we would measure predictors and outcomes, what resources could be allocated to the research, and so on. We chose at the outset to create a tool for assessing risk, rather than a scheme to classify types of individuals who commit domestic violence, such as those I describe in the Typologies section in Chapter 1. Later research by Ismael Loinaz (see Researcher Profile 3.1), who reported that a risk assessment tool predicted domestic violence recidivism better than a typology did, suggested this choice was wise. For reasons I outlined in Part I, we decided that the risk assessment system would be actuarial, which required a follow-up study. We would have to locate a large number of instances of violent behavior meeting a consistent definition of domestic violence and also have the capacity to find out whether the behavior recurred. In this chapter, I describe how we accomplished this task, resulting in the Ontario Domestic Assault Risk

https://doi.org/10.1037/0000223-004
Domestic Violence Risk Assessment: Tools for Effective Prediction and Management, Second Edition, by N. Z. Hilton

Assessment (ODARA; Hilton et al., 2004). I also demonstrate how strongly ODARA scores were associated with subsequent recidivism (i.e., predictive accuracy), how well users agreed with each other on individual ODARA scores (i.e., inter-rater reliability), and how the ODARA fared in new tests in similar samples (i.e., cross-validation).

A second fundamental decision was that the risk assessment tool was to be for use on the "front line." That is, although we would use methods of statistical analyses and psychological assessment construction, we did not expect that the principal users of the new tool would themselves be psychologists or actuaries. Rather, the idea was that police officers investigating occurrences of domestic violence would use the tool to inform decisions about whether to detain men accused of assaulting their partners and whether to offer additional protection to the partners. There was some expectation that the risk assessment would assist the courts (including prosecutors and the defense) in dealing with men accused of domestic violence, especially for decisions about the applicability of bail, conditions of release, and sentencing. We hoped, too, that women who had been assaulted would benefit from objective information about their partner's likelihood of recidivism when making their own safety decisions or when seeking assistance from the criminal justice system. In Chapter 6, I describe risk assessment for later stages in the criminal justice process and, in Chapter 9, the value of being able to communicate risk using a common metric.

A FOLLOW-UP STUDY OF DOMESTIC VIOLENCE RECIDIVISM

The primary purpose in developing an actuarial risk assessment tool was to design a way to help frontline assessors make decisions that are more informed about domestic violence risk. This section describes the decisions that shaped the research study used to create this tool.

Finding Representative Cases

Deciding to use a follow-up study required a suitably large sample that could be tracked over time. Fortunately, a partnership was formed between with the Ontario Provincial Police (OPP), including requisite legal, ethical, and security procedures. The OPP is the second largest police service in Canada and is the only police service for a large part of the Province of Ontario, Canada's most populous jurisdiction. At the time, the OPP used an electronic archive to record all police contacts, a system that housed reports written by frontline officers, including those of the OPP, First Nations Police Services, and approximately 50 municipal police services. A few large metropolitan police services did not subscribe to this archive, so we also partnered with police services in the dense urban area of greater Toronto, Canada's largest and most ethnically diverse city, to supplement the OPP by deliberately sampling from these different archives.

Except for the urban areas for cross-validation sample, we allowed no selection of cases on the basis of region, neighborhood, police service, language, or completeness of the report. Ethnicity and racial data were not available to us, so we cannot compare the racial makeup of our research samples with census data. Nevertheless, we were confident that our selection of cases yielded as representative a sample as was feasible, with respect to sociodemographic, ethnic, and geographic characteristics of the population of Ontario men with a police record for domestic assault during the study period. Although such characteristics might affect whether an assault came to the attention of the police in the first place, the best predictors of violence have shown validity across ethnic and socioeconomic groups (e.g., Olver, Neumann, et al., 2018; Skeem & Lowenkamp, 2016), including in large-sample research by Kirk Williams (see Research Profile 3.2) and others with his risk assessment tool, the Domestic Violence Screening Instrument–Revised (Stansfield & Williams, 2014).

Using Available Data

The electronic archives contained anecdotal reports of every reportable instance in which police officers had contact with members of the public in the conduct of their duties. The anecdotal accounts identified all the people involved by full names and other identifiers (those who perpetrated assaults, who were assaulted, or who witnessed incidents), time of day, location, statements by involved persons, officers' observations, and the actions they took (cautioned, arrested, laid criminal charges, etc.). Even more valuable was the ability to link and collate all reports pertaining to any police contact with a single alleged perpetrator, so it was easy to ascertain whether there were prior or subsequent reports of police contact. We were also able to use the national database of criminal charges and convictions maintained by the Royal Canadian Mounted Police, the criminal record database that is readily accessible to frontline and investigating officers across Canada (Government of Canada, 2018). Professionals working in hospitals, shelters, and even domestic violence treatment programs do not normally have access to these data, but it is possible for them to use the

ODARA (examples described in Chapters 4 and 10). I encourage different sectors to share information to promote accurate assessment and effective risk management (see the Cooperation and Coordination Among Agencies section and the Challenges to Effective Implementation section, Chapter 10, this volume).

We also collaborated with the provincial probation and parole service. About half the cases we identified for research had some kind of record compiled by these correctional agencies, and we included information gleaned from these records if it would be reasonably available to frontline personnel. An example was whether the man was unemployed; although not always addressed in the police reports, unemployment is something that frontline officers can find out, and therefore we considered it in the research even if the actual data came from correctional files (that are not routinely available to frontline officers). Another example was whether the individual had an alcohol use problem. Not all police reports addressed substance use, but this information could be reasonably available to investigating officers, and therefore we included it in the research even if it actually came from the correctional files.

The result of these decisions was that our research considered all information that would reasonably be available to police officers investigating and making decisions about domestic violence cases. This approach also meant that professionals who respond to domestic violence in other contexts, such as hospital, shelters, and transition houses, could apply the research in their settings because the information could be accessible to them—with the important exception of police and criminal records. A police record check is usually required, although the ODARA may be scored from an interview with a woman seeking victim support services when there is no criminal or civil procedure.

Case Eligibility

From these extensive electronic records, we selected every report classified as a domestic incident. Then each report was individually examined to ensure that the officers' accounts clearly reported that forcible physical contact had occurred in which a man had assaulted his female domestic partner—that is, a woman with whom he lived or had previously lived. In our jurisdiction, a person may be charged with assault if they threaten to commit a forcible assault, regardless of the effect on others; however, we did not use this definition. We only included such a case if a credible threat of death was made to the partner with a weapon in hand in the presence of the partner; as it turned out, there were few of these cases in our sample.

We confined our study to men's violence against women, by far the most common form in the police records. Similarly, we limited cases to couples with a marital or cohabiting history because the nature of the relationship (e.g., dating, friends, or unrequited interest) was difficult to determine otherwise. These early decisions meant that we could only be certain that our eventual risk assessment system was applicable to what we called *wife assault* recidivism. Not all domestic violence comes to the attention of the police, and thus we could not necessarily be certain that our resulting tool would apply to the risk of recidivism among cases without police involvement. However, because our primary purpose was to aid risk assessment in the criminal justice system, we decided this definition was acceptable. We would study the tool's applicability to other cases in later research.

Because of our eligibility criteria and the general approach entailed in the actuarial method (see Methodological Considerations in Chapter 2, this volume), we knew from the outset that until we validated the resulting tool in other populations, we could only be certain that it would apply to the population from which we drew our cases: men who were or had been living with the victim and who had at least one police report of violence towards the victim. We were wary of unsubstantiated applications but cautiously optimistic regarding the generalizability of the resulting actuarial tool, based on our experience with VRAG tools described in Chapter 2. Our later research that included dating violence and women who assaulted their partners was consistent this expectation (see the sections Women Who Assault Their Partners, and Dating and Same-Sex Relationships in Chapter 4).

Although the original intended users of our research were criminal justice professionals, we did not require that the police had laid criminal charges. At first glance, this might seem odd; evidence of a charge of assault might increase our confidence that violence had indeed occurred. But consider our purpose in conducting this research. That is, we expected that police officers would use the resulting tool to make decisions during their investigation of domestic violence occurrences, to prioritize cases for interventions such as detaining in a police cell, issuing a warrant for arrest, or transporting affected individuals to a shelter—decisions that can be made before deciding the final charges. We also expected that bail courts would use the tool to determine whether bail should be granted, the level of supervision, and the conditions applied; therefore, we could not require that the index assault resulted in a conviction. This reasoning is similar to our argument against predicting criminal convictions for assault (see Criminal Convictions in Chapter 2): Had we restricted our initial research to men who were criminally charged for or convicted of the index assault, the resulting risk assessment tool could only be applied with confidence to perpetrators who would be charged with or convicted of the index assault.

We decided to include all cases in which the police reports clearly and reliably indicated that violence had occurred. Information that gave such indications included formal charges of assault and also written statements by the investigating officers describing violent behavior, eyewitness statements, documentation of injury of alleged victims, and recorded statements by alleged perpetrators admitting to violent behavior. We rejected cases in which it was unclear whether violence had occurred and the many "domestic disturbances" in which it clearly had not. Interrater reliability among our research assistants exceeded .90 (Hilton et al., 2004).

Getting the Work Done

The next step was to write a coding manual specifying exactly how each useable piece of information was to be turned into a number or precise descriptive verbal terms (see Exhibit 3.1). Our entire research team pored over police occurrence reports and correctional files and determined what information they contained and how, in precise detail, the information could be extracted. Practice and testing with drafts of the coding manual had to follow before it was finalized, and formal tests of interrater reliability were conducted. Three students spent a summer coding with our research team, producing data that we used to explore initially promising variables. Due to the months of training required for accurate coding, we replaced summer positions with a full-time research assistant, Ruth Houghton, who became a principal coder, along with our colleagues Carol Lang and Catherine Cormier.

Meanwhile, research students read every police occurrence report and screened it for eligibility. Requests for correctional files were processed by many parole and probation offices as well as staff members at the provincial archives, with the assistance of Ontario Ministry of Corrections officials. We combed through electronic records with much assistance from the OPP Behavioural Sciences and Analysis Section research manager, Angela Wyatt Eke, and support from OPP information technology staff. Finally, we had to carefully code more than 1,400 cases and then enter them into a computerized database for analysis. Our colleague, Sonja Dey, entered about 3 million data points into dozens of files. This is meticulous work, and I gratefully acknowledge these colleagues.

EXHIBIT 3.1. Example Portions of the Research Coding Manual

Demographic Information for the Index

A *domestic* incident is one in which the offender is the perpetrator against his current or previous cohabiting partner and/or her children. The *index* incident is the domestic incident which occurred prior to and closest to January 1, 1997, and which involved the use of physical violence by the offender against his current or previous cohabiting partner. *Physical violence* includes physical contact with the victim or a credible threat of death with a weapon in hand in the presence of the victim. A *nondomestic* incident is one which does not involve the offender's current or previous cohabiting partner and/or her children. Include a nondomestic incident only if the offender physically or sexually assaulted the victim, used weapons during the incident, or was stalking the victim.

OMPPAC (police database) incident report number. Specify the OMPPAC identification number from the OMPPAC incident report (do not include the dash). Code "999" for the first incident report which is not an OMPPAC report, "888" for the second, "777" for the third, etc.

Organization Identification (ORG ID). Specify the Organization Identification (numbers and/or letters) from the OMPPAC report.

Date of index. Code the date the index occurred, not the date that it was reported.

The Victims of the Incident

Relationship of the victims to the offender. Specify the number of victims in each category.

1. Index partner (victim of the index incident)
2. Previous partner (previous to the index partner)
3. New partner (after the index partner)
4. Offender's biological child
5. Child of the index partner (but not offender's child)
6. Offender's biological family (e.g., mother, father, sister, etc.)
7. Biological family of the index partner
8. Offender's friend, acquaintance or neighbour
9. Stranger
10. Other: (specify)

Physical Injury to the Most Seriously Injured Victim of the Index

VRAG Injury Scale. "Weapon" refers to any object used by the offender to injure the victim, other than his hands or feet.

1 = no injury
2 = slight injury, no weapon
3 = slight injury, weapon
4 = treated in clinic and released
5 = victim hospitalized at least 1 night
6 = death
7 = death and postdeath mutilation

(*continues*)

EXHIBIT 3.1. Example Portions of the Research Coding Manual (*Continued*)

DA Injury Scale

Code "." (NA) if the victim died as a result of her injuries.

1 = no injuries and/or lasting pain
2 = bruises, cuts, and/or continuing pain
3 = severe contusions, burns, broken bones (include cuts requiring stitches)
4 = head injury, internal injury, permanent injury
5 = wounds from weapon

The Offender's Use of Physical and Sexual Violence during the Index

Offender used physical and/or sexual violence against the victims of the index (y/n).
If "yes," code below:

Minor violence (y/n). Minor violence includes: held the victim down, threw something at the victim that could hurt, twisted the victim's arm or hair, pushed or shoved the victim, grabbed the victim (include "pulled" and "dragged"), slapped the victim ("slapped" includes any hitting other than punching; include "striking"), other minor violence (include "shaking").

Severe violence (y/n). Severe violence includes: used a knife or gun on the victim (*used* implies actual or attempted contact with the victim's body; include discharging a gun while pointing it at the victim), punched the victim with his fist or hit the victim with something that could hurt, hoked the victim (include "grabbed by the neck or throat" or "headlock"), slammed the victim against a wall, "beat up" the victim, burned or scalded the victim on purpose, kicked the victim, other severe violence (include "picked up and threw," "head-butting," "pushed down the stairs," biting).

Sexual violence (y/n). Sexual violence includes any use of force (by any means) to coerce the victim into having sexual contact when he or she does not want to. Include any sexual contact with children whether or not force is used.

Identifying Potential Predictors

The next task was to identify and measure the potential risk factors. We cast our nets broadly, including all the recommendations of experts embodied in existing rationally derived systems and previous follow-up studies (see the review by Hilton & Harris, 2005), and established risk factors from the research literature on the prediction of violent recidivism in general, including the VRAG. This approach meant coding variables about childhood adjustment, early aggression, and exposure to family violence, as well as symptoms associated with several psychiatric diagnoses and a few variables that reflected our own theoretical perspectives about the causes of domestic violence (e.g., aspects of sexual jealousy). However, we confined our analyses for the frontline tool to information that police officers could reasonably be expected to access, such as offense details, victim statements, and perpetrators' police records. All the other potential risk factors (e.g., pertaining to psychiatric symptoms and childhood history), were set aside for a study of in-depth predictors (discussed in Chapter 5).

Measuring Recidivism

The next step was to define the outcome. The research cohort was selected from a list of cases that were in the police record system several years before we began gathering data. For each individual who was identified by the police as a suspect in a domestic occurrence, the domestic assault that occasioned a police report closest to but no later than a specified date (the end of 1996) was declared to be his index offense; thus, by definition, every case had at least one instance of domestic assault. After we identified men with an eligible index assault, we followed them through subsequent records and found that about one third (30%) reappeared in police records with at least one subsequent instance of domestic assault, which we defined as *recidivism*. Thus, we used a follow-up method; we did not select recidivists a priori.

For the recidivistic offenses, we coded several related outcome measures: a dichotomous variable indicating the occurrence of at least one subsequent instance of domestic assault in the police or criminal record, the total number of such offenses, the total amount of injury caused in these offenses based on two scales (J. C. Campbell, Messing, & Williams, 2017; Harris, Rice, et al., 2015), and the seriousness of the reoffending based on a standard definition of the severity of violent acts (Straus et al., 1996) and the Cormier–Lang weighted score for each criminal charge (Harris et al., 1993, 2015). Finally, we derived a measure of the time between the index assault and the resolution of subsequent criminal charges for recidivism. We decided that the primary outcome measure would be dichotomous: A man either committed a subsequent domestic assault or he did not. In previous research with the VRAG, this measure was the simplest to obtain, and it correlated highly with other outcome measures (e.g., number of recidivist offenses, severity of recidivism, time until recidivism; Harris, Rice, et al., 2015).

All the incidents pertaining to an individual were linked to each other on the police records system, which meant that the people who coded the outcome were not masked to the measurement of the potential risk factors (and vice versa), which is a possible source of methodological bias. We decided against attempting a masked coding procedure for all cases because a fully trained researcher would have had to read through all the material to identify the index and then separate information about potential predictors from recidivism—a tricky task because police reports at every incident usually referred to previous incidents. It would have required one of our research coders to be dedicated from this task at the outset, adding months or years to the project. Instead, we conducted a test of interrater reliability on 24 masked cases, with excellent results (Hilton et al., 2004) to help ensure that the accuracy we reported for the resulting risk assessment tool did not benefit from any such threat to internal validity. In fact, the ODARA predicted recidivism with the same accuracy in these masked cases as it did in the unmasked test (Hilton et al., 2004).

To be counted as recidivism, there had to be clear evidence in the police records of a later assault by the man against a female domestic partner, using the same definition as that for case eligibility. We did not contact anybody involved in the incidents, police officers, or anyone else to find out about any subsequent domestic violence that did not appear in the criminal justice or police records. Thus, our recorded rates of repetition of domestic violence almost certainly underestimate the actual rates (even granting that some men subsequently charged or convicted were innocent of any recidivism). At one level, this limitation is serious and of indeterminate magnitude. The ODARA's norms could not be used to make statements such as "This man is a member of a group of men with a police record of domestic assault who had a 22% likelihood of subsequent domestic assault" without the qualification "that came to the attention of police." At another level, however, the problem of undetected recidivism is much less serious because there is good reason to believe that the individuals who commit the most officially detected crime are the same as those who engage in the most undetected crime (e.g., Farrington & Ttofi, 2014; see also Chapter 2, this volume). Furthermore, had we included incidents of recidivism that were not reported to police, the resulting tool would have less ready application to the criminal justice system. Our later research has examined the utility of the ODARA to community victim services and their clients who do not normally have access to the databases we used to develop the ODARA (see Victim Services in Chapter 4).

Detecting Actual Predictors

The next task was to select the most efficient list of valid predictors of recidivism using multivariate statistical analyses. All these analyses used our dichotomous "wife assault" recidivism measure as the dependent variable. We selected predictors from among the variables that pertained to the time up to and including the index assault, before subsequent recidivism. Thus, we used a prediction method. We did not examine which variables were correlated with prior violence (i.e., "postdiction"). More than 30 independent variables were significantly correlated with the outcome, and we used several steps to identify the best of these predictors.

First, we subdivided them into sets of similar variables: index assault details (e.g., injury, a weapon used), domestic violence history (e.g., number and severity of preindex assaults), other criminal history (e.g., correctional sentences, parole violations), sociodemographic variables (e.g., age, employment), relationship characteristics (e.g., duration, separations), and the partner's circumstances (e.g., social support, having young children at home). We tested each set of potential predictors in repeated random samples of two thirds of the 589 cases. From each set, we discarded variables (even variables significantly related to the outcome) unless they made a statistically significant incremental contribution in most subsample tests. This test of incremental contribution used multiple logistic regression, a statistical technique that uses many repeated calculations to hold one or more variables constant while examining the additional effect of another in their combined association with the outcome variable. Finally, we tested all the variables that survived this analysis together and retained only the 13 items that made a significant independent contribution in the total sample (see Chapter 6, this volume).

Assault Severity

Index assault severity and use of weapons, perhaps surprisingly, did not survive the selection process. We measured injury at the index assault, preindex injury to the partner at the index assault or other domestic partners, and preindex injury in nondomestic assaults. We also coded whether the frequency or severity of the man's assaults or threats against his partner had increased in the days or weeks before the index assault. But none of these measures survived the analyses that selected unique predictors of domestic violence recidivism. In fact, they bore little or no correlation with recidivism (e.g., correlation between recidivism and injury to the partner at the index = .06; Hilton et al., 2004). Similarly, we measured weapon use, and threatened use of weapons, in a variety of ways and found no association between weapons at the index assault and subsequent violence (correlation coefficient = .03; Hilton et al., 2004). Gun access was not common (8%), and although men who had gun access did commit more severe index assaults, they largely used a weapon other than a firearm (Folkes et al., 2013). There was a small effect whereby men who had gun access or used a weapon at the index assault had higher ODARA scores, but these items were not related to either the occurrence of recidivism or the severity of new assaults.

Of course, our research was based in Ontario, Canada, and gun laws and firearm access may be different elsewhere. For example, firearm access is common among individuals who perpetrate domestic offenses in the United States, and firearms restrictions may reduce domestic homicides (e.g., Díez et al., 2017). Even so, gun use in nonlethal assaults is comparably rare (e.g., Sorenson & Schut, 2018). No study has yet shown that firearms can improve risk assessment of domestic violence recidivism. A related matter is that escalation of violence was not selected for the ODARA. More recently, Bland and Ariel (2015) studied 36,000 domestic incidents in police records and found no evidence of escalating harm and no increase in frequency of assaults in relatively severe cases. Therefore, despite widespread belief that injury, escalation of violence, and weapon use are important domestic violence risk factors (e.g., Robinson et al., 2018), there is insufficient evidence to include them in the ODARA.

In one of our cross-validations of the ODARA, we found that 21 men (8%) committed an assault of a sexual nature on their partner at the index assault. These men scored higher on the ODARA and were more likely to recidivate than a random sample of 21 men who had not sexually assaulted their partner. However, this small study did not show that sexual assault could improve prediction over and above the ODARA. In contrast, making threats of physical harm at the index assault was a surviving item in the ODARA construction research.

Equal Item Weights

In our analyses, some valid risk factors that passed all our tests had stronger relationships with the outcome than others. For example, the man's substance use was twice as strong a predictor than whether he threatened to physically harm or kill anyone in the index offense. We could have given each item a weighting that reflected the strength of this relationship in construction. However, previous research showed that whereas simple linear relationships are remarkably robust (i.e., replicate in repeated retesting), weightings are much less robust (e.g., Grann & Långström, 2007). Making each item weight binary (dichotomous or yes/no) tends to produce only a small loss in accuracy (e.g., Grove & Meehl, 1996) and can improve generalizability (e.g., Helmus & D. Thornton, 2015). Thus, to make the final risk assessment as easy as possible to implement, we decided to forgo the small increment in predictive accuracy that we could have achieved using more complex scoring procedures and instead make each item weight the same and each item have only two possible answers: 0 or 1.

FIGURE 3.1. Receiver Operating Characteristic Area Under the Curve Showing the Sensitivity and Specificity of the Ontario Domestic Assault Risk Assessment at Each Cutoff Score

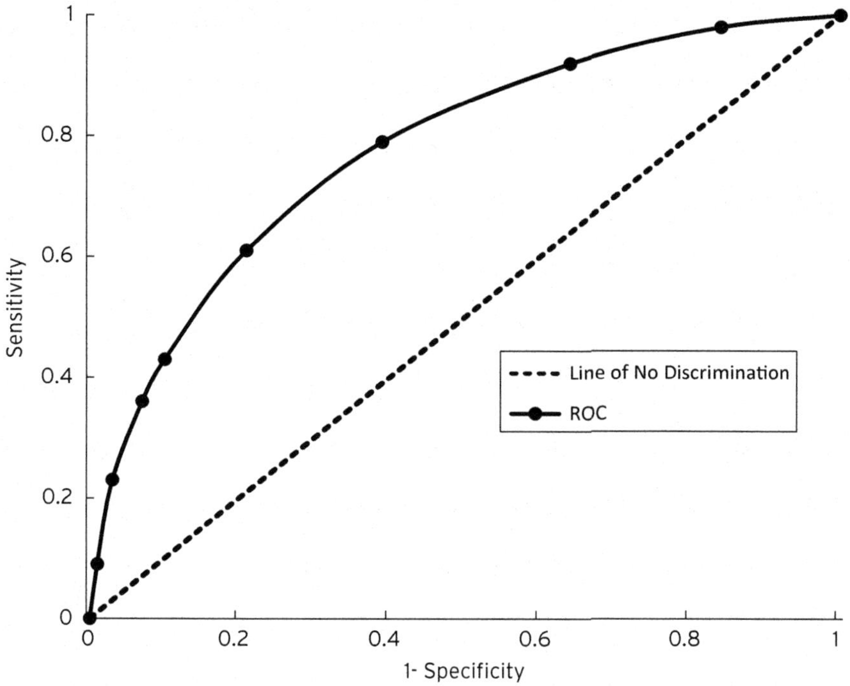

Note. ROC = receiver operating characteristic. Data from Hilton et al. (2004). See Exhibit 3.2 for explanation.

The result was the 13-item ODARA, which has a total possible score ranging from 0 to 13. ODARA score yielded a large effect in discriminating domestic violence recidivists from nonrecidivists in the construction sample of 589 offenders. Figure 3.1 illustrates the ODARA's predictive accuracy in the construction sample, and Exhibit 3.2 provides further explanation.

ONTARIO DOMESTIC ASSAULT RISK ASSESSMENT

Taking an actuarial approach to designing a risk assessment and identifying individual items revealed some surprising findings. First, some variables expected to be good predictors were not, in fact, significantly related to recidivism. An example was injury to the partner at the index assault. Another was whether the man threatened suicide or appeared to be suicidal

EXHIBIT 3.2. Further Psychometric Properties of the ODARA in the Construction Sample

Figure 3.3 illustrates the linear relationship between ODARA category and the probability of domestic assault recidivism. As illustrated in Chapter 2 of this volume, adopting different cutoff scores would yield different true positives and false alarm rates. For example, if every case scoring above 3 were predicted to recidivate while all below 4 were predicted not to recidivate, there would be a hit rate (sensitivity) of .63 and a false alarm rate (1–specificity) of .22. Sensitivity-specificity pairs can be derived for all possible ODARA cutoff scores and then plotted to reveal a symmetrical area under the curve (AUC) subtending a proportional area of .77.

By customary standards, this AUC falls in the range of a large effect size (Rice & Harris, 2005). Recall that this AUC can be interpreted as a probability of .77 that a randomly selected individual who recidivates would have a higher score than a randomly selected individual who does not recidivate.

There are other ways to capture predictive relationships. For example, computing the average difference in ODARA score between those who recidivated and those who did not yields a Cohen's $d = 1.1$ in the ODARA construction sample. The Pearson product-moment correlation coefficient for the association between the seven ODARA categories and dichotomous recidivism in the ODARA construction sample was .44, $p < 001$. Or a cutoff above which all cases are expected to recidivate could be adopted to calculate how often that expectation is correct. This statistic is the positive predictive power (PPP). Similarly, negative predictive power (NPP) characterizes the accuracy of the expectation that all individuals at or below the selected cutoff will not recidivate. For details on PPP and NPP in the ODARA construction sample, see Hilton and colleagues (2004). Unlike the AUC, PPP and NPP depend on the overall base rate; therefore, they do a generally poorer job of characterizing predictive accuracy. Readers may wish to refer back to the Chapter 2 section AUC and Related Accuracy Statistics. For more detail, I recommend the primer on risk assessment and statistics for its evaluation by Helmus and Babchishin (2017).

at the time of the index assault. Other variables were related to recidivism but did not improve the risk assessment after the 13 selected items were included. Unemployment and sexual jealousy are examples. Both were positively correlated with recidivism in our study but neither assisted with the assessment of risk over and above the ODARA items.

Characteristics of the ODARA

After the final instrument was developed, the average ODARA score was 2.89 with a standard deviation of 2.14. We tested its interrater reliability (again, by getting two people to code a set of cases independently then comparing their answers) both for research assistants and for experienced police officers. In all tests, the items and the total scores on the final risk assessment system met stringent standards for reliability (Hilton et al., 2004). The interrater reliability achieved both by research assistants (.90) and by police officers (.95) was very good and far above the minimum level expected for a useful assessment.

The second, and more difficult, aspect of evaluating an assessment's value is accuracy, or the extent to which it measures what it purports to measure. It is common for test designers to establish what is known as concurrent validity by showing that the new test is correlated with existing tests designed to assess the same thing. We showed that the ODARA yielded statistically significant correlations with other, rationally constructed domestic violence risk assessments, including our own jurisdiction's Domestic Violence Supplementary Report checklist for police (DVSR; Ontario Ministry of the Solicitor General, 2000), the Danger Assessment (DA; J. C. Campbell, 1986), and the Spousal Assault Risk Assessment (SARA; Kropp et al., 1999; see also Chapter 1, this volume). We scored these schemes as closely as we could to their instructions, although we conducted no victim interviews for the study. We used correctional records for items that required more than frontline information (e.g., evidence of mental health problems, psychopathy), although these items were not considered for the ODARA.

Concurrent validity was not sufficient evidence of accuracy. The form of validity most relevant to a risk assessment is predictive accuracy: the extent to which the assessment predicts the outcome it was designed to predict. It turned out that each of the other assessments we tested predicted domestic violence recidivism, but the ODARA was significantly more accurate. Figure 3.2 compares the ODARA scores of men who recidivated and men who did not. Readers will see that few cases scored 5 or above, which meant that these scores had to be collapsed into two categories (5–6 and 7–13) to yield reliable estimates of recidivism. This figure is similar to the example given in Figure 2.1 in which the black bars represent those cases who recidivated. A slightly different way to present the same results is with only one bar instead of two for each category. In this case, the height of each bar shows the proportion of all cases in each category that met the criteria for domestic violence recidivism. Figure 3.3 shows the proportion of men who recidivated in each ODARA category for two samples: the 589 construction cases (in black bars) and the remaining cases in our research (in cross-hatched bars).

Individuals in the different ODARA categories also differed in our measure of time at risk—that is, the duration of time between their index assault and either the date we last checked their police and criminal record (if they did not reoffend) or their recidivism (if they did reoffend; 80% of the sample spent no intervening time in custody). For this test, we used a Cox regression analysis, which is useful for showing the relation between

FIGURE 3.2. Ontario Domestic Assault Risk Assessment (ODARA) Scores of Men With and Without Recidivism in the ODARA Construction Sample

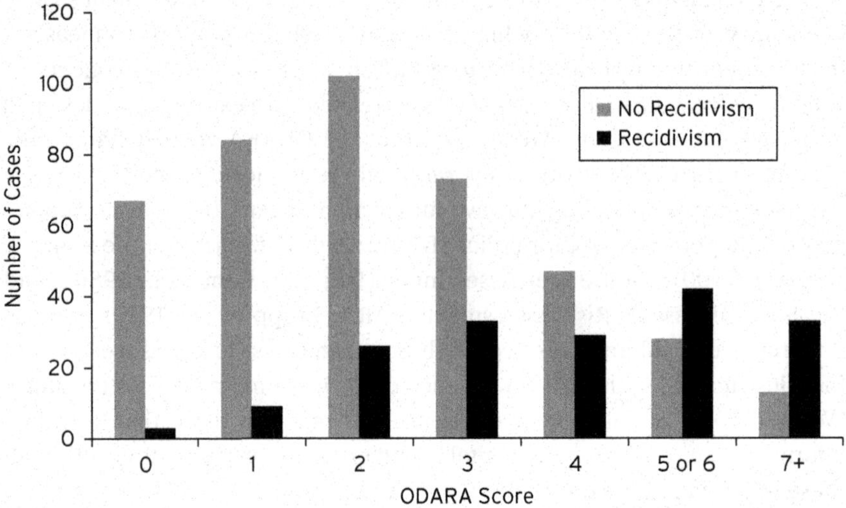

Note. Data from Hilton et al. (2004).

FIGURE 3.3. Percentage of Men Who Recidivated as a Function of Ontario Domestic Assault Risk Assessment (ODARA) Scores in the Construction Sample and Cross-Validation Samples

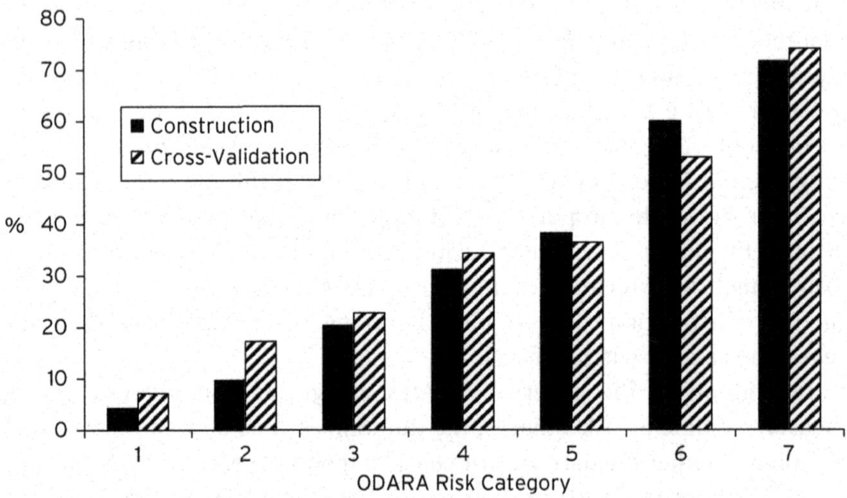

Note. Construction data from Hilton et al. (2004); cross-validation data from Hilton et al. (2004), Hilton, Harris, Rice, et al. (2008), and Hilton and Harris (2009b).

the predictor and a time-dependent outcome when the follow-up time varies in the sample. The Cox regression hazard ratio showed that the likelihood of recidivism increased by 1.75 for every increase in ODARA category, with a 95% confidence interval of 1.51 to 1.95.

Cross-Validations

Next, we tested the ODARA's validity in the sample of 100 cases we had earlier set aside for cross-validation. The ODARA significantly predicted recidivism in this sample too, with an AUC of .72, a large effect (Hilton et al., 2004). Two more tests, using entirely new cases, reconfirmed the ODARA's predictive validity. We were able to conduct one cross-validation when we tested the relative accuracy of our in-depth assessment (Hilton, Harris, Rice, et al., 2008). In that study, we found further evidence for the tool's statistical association with the frequency and severity of domestic violence recidivism in a sample of 346 new cases (see the section Definition and Cross-Validation of the In-Depth Assessment in Chapter 5, this volume). The third cross-validation involved 391 cases that had no in-depth assessment information available (Hilton & Harris, 2009b). This time, we experimented with different research designs and found that the ODARA yielded AUCs of up to .80 when we compared equal-sized groups of known domestic violence recidivists and nonrecidivists (who had no known subsequent violence). This result represents a large effect size (see AUC and Related Accuracy Statistics in Chapter 2). These studies all measured discrimination accuracy and confirmed the ODARA's ability to rank order domestic offenders, identifying those at highest risk of recidivism and those with comparably lower risk.

The total number of cases in the construction sample and all three cross-validation studies was more than 1,420. Across all the samples, 32% of men recidivated, and the ODARA yielded an AUC of .71, corresponding to a large effect size and a correlation of r =.36. ODARA category yielded smaller but statistically significant ($p < .001$) correlations with the total number of recidivistic offenses, the total amount of injury caused, the severity of new assaults, and the seriousness of criminal charges at recidivism (rs = .26, .22, .30, and .20, respectively). As well, the available data pertaining to time at risk indicated that, among men who reoffended, those with higher ODARA scores reoffended sooner ($r = .26$; Hilton et al., 2004).

The precision of measurement (i.e., how close, on average, a single obtained score is to the "true" score) is calculated using interrater reliability and the standard error of measurement (SEM, which is equal to the standard deviation multiplied by the square root of 1 minus reliability). The interrater reliability coefficient for the ODARA was .90, and the SEM for ODARA category across all cases was .54. The 95% confidence interval (see Exhibit 2.1) around an obtained score was 1.06. That is, an individual result would be expected to be misclassified (i.e., deviate from the true score) by more than one category in only 5% of cases.

Another aspect of validation is calibration, or the extent to which the recidivism rates from the construction data provide a good estimate of recidivism rates in the new samples. Calibration can be determined by examining the ratio of the observed number of recidivists (O) to the expected number (E; Hanson, 2017; Helmus & Babchishin, 2017). The resulting E/O index will be 1 if the tool is perfectly calibrated, and the 95% confidence interval will include 1 when recidivism rates are not significantly different between samples. Readers can surmise from Figure 3.3 that the number of observed cases with recidivism was lower than expected in two categories (i.e., scores of 5–6 or 7+) and higher than expected in the remaining categories. The calculated E/O indexes for each ODARA category in our combined cross-validation samples showed that differences were nonsignificant for all but two categories: Men who scored 0 or 1 recidivated at about twice the expected rate. So far, calibration of the ODARA has only been tested in this cross-validation sample, a small sample of women (Hilton et al., 2014), and one independent study (Gerth et al., 2017; see the sections Studies in Europe and Australia and Women Who Assault Their Partners in Chapter 4, this volume). It is important to assess calibration in samples drawn from different populations before applying the recidivism rates from the original ODARA research to the new populations.

USING THE ONTARIO DOMESTIC ASSAULT RISK ASSESSMENT

The next step was to create a manual describing the eligibility criteria for scoring the ODARA and how to score each item as closely as possible to the way in which it was coded in the research. As simple as this might sound, the process went through many drafts required to respond to users' questions and to correct for misinterpretations. One version of the manual was a booklet designed by our OPP colleague Tracy Lowe-Wetmore that expressed the research coding criteria in language familiar to frontline police officers. The booklet had a prorating table to allow scoring when some information is ambiguous. Another important feature was an experience table, a tabulated version of Figure 3.2 that permits statements about an individual's risk of domestic violence recidivism in both absolute and relative terms. We also included an example risk assessment report summary. The booklet improved scoring accuracy among police officers (Hilton, Harris, Rice, Eke, & Lowe-Wetmore, 2007; see the section Training Users to Score the ODARA Reliably in Chapter 10, this volume). Chapter 6 provides a complete ODARA scoring manual.

Adjustment

A more subtle issue pertained to whether we would recommend any factors to be added to ODARA scores to determine risk. However, in the absence of more in-depth information that can be incorporated into the actuarial assessment (e.g., psychological characteristics; see Chapter 5), the ODARA can stand alone as an index of domestic violence recidivism risk.

In practice, police officers and other frontline assessors will likely take additional information into consideration when forming a risk management plan. Professionals may feel that additional factors cause concern about the risk posed by some individuals, perhaps taking their cues from those affected by the domestic violence. Full details of the ODARA items are provided in Chapter 6. I note here that the partner's expression of fear or concern about future assaults is an ODARA item, and in our research, it was most strongly correlated with another ODARA item, Threat to Physically Harm or Kill at the Index Assault ($r = .26$, $p < .001$). When specific threats of physical harm have been made, a policy incorporating the duty to protect can be invoked regardless of the ODARA score, without the need for adjusting the items or scoring.

A related point is that some assessors feel uncomfortable including certain items, such as prior offenses that did not result in criminal conviction, or substance use by the partner (which can reduce access to crisis services; e.g., Macy & Goodbourn, 2012; Mason et al., 2017). Assessors sometimes want to use their professional discretion to omit or substitute items. I will discuss the role and limits of clinical assessment in Chapter 8 (under Hypothesis 1). However, the research needed to validate such adjustment has yet to be conducted, and any advantage for domestic violence risk assessment has not yet been demonstrated. Future research could explore the effects of altering the ODARA item scoring criteria, incorporation of other variables to enhance prediction in new populations, or novel combinations of ODARA scores and professional judgment. The ODARA could be revamped or replaced with a new tool or process that captures change over time shown to optimize risk assessment. Researchers have begun to explore the ODARA's validity for different jurisdictions, outcomes, and populations (see Chapter 4) but have not yet addressed these other crucial questions. Until they do, modifying the ODARA items, adjusting the score (other than for prorating, see Chapter 6, Table 6.1), or consulting the score but setting it aside to make a final judgment of risk, would introduce an unknown degree of error. Thus, I advise against blending the ODARA score with professional judgment in these ways.

Interpretation

When the ODARA is scored as specified, the experience table can be used to make individual assessments of the risk of domestic violence recidivism (see Chapter 6, Table 6.2). The norms are from the combined construction and validation cases. The second column indicates the proportion of men obtaining each ODARA score who met the research definition of domestic violence recidivism in an average follow-up of nearly 5 years. The other columns indicate the rank order applicable to individuals with the obtained score, independent of time. That is, the highest scoring individuals who have committed domestic violence are the same individuals regardless of the time period of interest. The proportion scoring lower, sometimes with the addition of the proportion obtaining the same score, is called the percentile rank.

As an example of how this relative information can be used to make decisions, consider the police chief of a hypothetical small city whose officers handle hundreds of domestic occurrences each year. The police cells can hold four men accused of domestic assault at any one time, and the bail court takes an average of 2 days to deal with an accused (i.e., to release on bail or remand to the county jail). The police chief can instruct the city's police officers that all men who are charged with domestic assault and who score 3 or greater on the ODARA will, as a matter of departmental policy, be detained for a bail hearing. Under normal circumstances, those scoring two or lower shall be released with a summons or promise to appear. The police chief can also inform the city council that an estimated two more cells would allow the ODARA cut-off score to be reduced by 1 point, providing an additional estimated amount of public protection. Similar decisions could potentially be made about women apprehended for domestic violence, although the available evidence indicates that women recidivate at a lower rate than men (this finding might not apply to women who assault female partners; Gerstenberger et al., 2019), and an experience table is not yet developed for this population.

CONCLUSION

In this chapter, I have described evidence of the ODARA's discrimination and calibration, two aspects of predictive accuracy, in the construction and validation samples drawn from police records management systems in Ontario, Canada. Subsequent studies have validated the ODARA in different populations and investigated ways in which actuarial risk assessment can be applied to different research questions. The next chapter describes this research.

POINTS TO REMEMBER

- The ODARA was developed on a representative sample of men who had a police record for "wife assault" (i.e., forceful physical contact with their female domestic partner, or credible threat of death with weapon in hand in the victim's presence) before 1997.
- The ODARA was designed to predict a subsequent instance of domestic assault.
- The ODARA contains 13 items, each of which is scored dichotomously and which adds incrementally to predictive accuracy.
- Our research showed that the ODARA can be scored reliably by police officers with a scoring manual.
- ODARA scores were correlated with other domestic violence risk assessment tools but are more strongly related to domestic violence recidivism.
- In data from construction and three cross-validations, the ODARA yielded a large effect size for predicting dichotomous recidivism and also predicted number of recidivistic offenses, time until first recidivism, total amount of injury caused, and severity of new assaults.

QUESTIONS TO CONSIDER

1. What were the interrater reliability coefficients for the ODARA scored by researchers and police officers?
2. State five outcome measures for which the ODARA was cross-validated.

3. Describe the pattern of findings for the ODARA and domestic violence recidivism in the construction and cross-validation samples.
4. Why is a scoring manual important for the ODARA? What might be the consequences of conducting a risk assessment without referring to the scoring manual?
5. Imagine you are developing a study of injuries to intimate partners and their children during domestic incidents reported to the police. Create a short coding form, specifying how each variable is defined and quantified.

RESEARCHER PROFILE 3.1
ISMAEL LOINAZ, PhD

Some of my first readings on intimate partner violence (IPV) were Donald Dutton's books *The Batterer* (Dutton & Golant, 1995) and *The Abusive Personality* (Dutton, 2007). At that time, I learned about batterer typologies, and I started to work in a prison in Barcelona, Spain, for my PhD, using Holtzworth-Munroe and Stuart's (1994) classification. Around 2010, while working on a revised version of an actuarial risk assessment tool (Escala de Predicción del Riesgo de Violencia Grave Contra la Pareja–Revisada; Echeburúa et al., 2010) used by the Basque Country Police (Ertzaintza), I followed ideas from the ODARA and the first edition of *Risk Assessment for Domestically Violent Men* for this review. I also had the opportunity to do a research stay with Dutton at the University of British Columbia while working on my doctorate and attended seminars at Simon Fraser University with researchers including Stephen Hart and Kevin Douglas, improving my violence risk assessment training.

I am a psychologist and criminologist, so I have two lenses. The therapeutic lens relates to specific psychological risk factors linked to the development of IPV and violent recidivism; the criminological lens relates to crime prediction and risk management—from the police perspective, for example. This background makes me consider risk factors and objective facts more than theoretical or ideological perspectives. My main question is why some people commit such violent acts and whether we can find specific risk factors for predicting violence and improving psychological treatment. My main research question concerns the idea that "one size doesn't fit all." I started replicating typologies to help design different types of treatments for different batterers and then extended the idea into risk assessment and recidivism. Now we are looking at different profiles in both prison and police recidivism samples.

A highlight of this work is my study of on typologies, risk and recidivism, published in *Psychology, Crime & Law* (Loinaz, 2014). Although it was a pilot study, it encompassed all my main ideas in a single study: batterer typologies, their different psychological profiles and different risks, and how they can be used to develop cut-off scores that are associated with recidivism after release from prison. This was the last paper on typologies from my PhD work, with which I introduced the analysis of batterer typologies to Spain (the first paper on the topic was published in 2010, in *Psicothema*).

I am currently collaborating on two interesting projects on IPV. One is related to research and development of revised versions of VioGen, the national tool used by Spain's state police and most local police services to predict IPV recidivism. This work includes new prediction algorithms as well as the differentiation of severe recidivism and homicide. Another involves the training of legal system professionals who will be working in specialized comprehensive forensic assessment units in different regions across Spain to assess violence risk in the forensic context. The professionals include forensic doctors, psychologists, and social workers who will inform judges about offender risk and management.

I think IPV research in the near future will develop procedures to manage the risk related to children inside a violent relationship (going beyond just the partner) as well as tools for violence in dating relationships, a problem that is increasingly prevalent (in Spain at least) and in many ways different from IPV among adults. Prediction is important, but there is greater interest in specific management procedures to reduce risk.

About the Researcher

Dr. Loinaz is an associate professor of criminology at the University of Barcelona.

RESEARCHER PROFILE 3.2
KIRK R. WILLIAMS, PhD

My engagement in research on intimate partner violence (IPV) commenced with my faculty affiliation with the Family Research Laboratory (FRL) at the University of New Hampshire. I was already empirically studying how violence manifests in many forms and contexts, but the affiliation with the FRL yielded collaborations with colleagues that ignited my keen interest. Murray Straus, director of the FRL, became an unselfish mentor, teaching me how to craft fundable proposals (we collaborated on two grants) and to highlight both the theoretical and translational significance of my research. Angela Browne, a postdoctoral fellow in the FRL at the time, was working on her landmark book, *When Battered Women Kill.* I found her work truly inspirational. We subsequently wrote together about IPV homicides and collaborated on grant-supported research on homicide trends over time and across U.S. cities. I collaborated with Richard Hawkins, another senior postdoctoral fellow in the FRL, on applying social control and deterrence theory to the empirical study of IPV. That research began my work focused on IPV desistence. I learned so much about conducting IPV research from these colleagues and many others (including my students). They also fostered my understanding of how IPV ultimately shreds the social fabric, having destructive consequences for everyone involved.

My interest in risk assessment commenced when I was the founding associate director of the Center for the Study and Prevention of Violence (CSPV) at the University of Colorado at Boulder. Probation Services in Colorado was given a judicial mandate to shift to risk-based decision making in managing IPV perpetrators. They contacted CSPV for research support in developing a risk assessment instrument. The inquiry was timely because I was shifting my professional commitments to the translational significance of research; at the time, we referred to it as "bridging the gap between research and practice." This collaboration produced the original Domestic Violence Screening Instrument (DVSI), a tool that was successfully validated.

When I was conducting the validation research, I was contacted by Family Services, part of the Court Support Services Division (CSSD) of the Judicial Branch in Connecticut. They were reassessing their own risk assessment protocol for managing multiple forms of domestic violence, including IPV. I worked with Family Services assessors and other staff to pilot a substantial modification of the DVSI based on their input and quality assurance data. That collaborative effort produced the Revised Domestic Violence Screening Instrument (DVSI-R), with CSSD owning the copyright.

Numerous empirical studies were published on the DVSI-R's predictive validity and other issues bearing on IPV (e.g., dual arrest, the gendered nature of IPV, assessing risk and recidivism across categories of race, ethnicity, and gender). Research continues to identify evidence of disparities by gender, race, ethnicity, and relationship type, including LGBTQ couples, in IPV risk assessment and recidivism. In collaboration with Jackie Campbell, we incorporated potential lethality items into the risk assessment protocol and began validating the outcome in 2018. Other issues will be addressed as the DVSI-R moves into new contexts involving the assessment of risk, such as its application to the process of obtaining restraining orders in family (civil) courts in Connecticut. Like my broader research interest in IPV, I owe much to my collaborators over the years at CSSD, especially Kathy Ceruti, Joe DiTunno, Steve Grant, Deb Kulak, Brian Hill, and Bryan Sperry, and students working with me on this project, especially Caryn Bell Gerstenberger and Richard Stansfield.

About the Researcher

Dr. Williams is a professor of criminology, law and society at the University of Arizona, Tucson.

4 VALIDATIONS AND APPLICATIONS OF THE ONTARIO DOMESTIC ASSAULT RISK ASSESSMENT

The construction of the Ontario Domestic Assault Risk Assessment (ODARA) was only the beginning of research with the new actuarial instrument. Cross-validation in new cases drawn from the same databases showed that the results were reproducible, but it was important to demonstrate replicability by validating it in other samples. Generalizability to different populations, such as those in legal jurisdictions outside of Ontario or Canada, those drawn from correctional institutions rather than the community, or women who have assaulted their partners rather than only men, had to be demonstrated before the ODARA could be used with confidence in these new contexts. Studies by independent researchers not connected with the ODARA team are especially desirable because the investigators are perceived to be less invested in obtaining certain results. Risk assessment validation studies by the assessment tools' authors have yielded larger effect sizes than studies by other researchers, an "allegiance effect" that may be partly explained by authors' greater fidelity to the scoring procedures (Harris et al., 2010). The effect might also be attributable (whether conscious or inadvertent) to potential counterallegiance to other tools, a bias toward

https://doi.org/10.1037/0000223-005
Domestic Violence Risk Assessment: Tools for Effective Prediction and Management, Second Edition, by N. Z. Hilton

publishing successful studies, or even misclassification of tools and their authors (Harris et al., 2010).

In this chapter, I review the current body of ODARA research. I describe study characteristics and effect sizes in terms of the area under the curve (AUC; see AUC and Related Accuracy Statistics in Chapter 2, this volume) to permit comparisons across validation studies (summarized in Table 4.1). Many of the studies I refer to have other interesting features and analyses that space does not allow me to describe here. I recommend reading the full articles for a more complete picture.

REPLICATION IN POLICE SAMPLES

Most risk assessment takes place at decision points within the criminal justice system, so it is not surprising that most risk assessment validation research has also occurred in this domain. The original work developing the ODARA used samples drawn from police records across the Province of Ontario, and I begin this review with the most similar studies.

Studies in Canada

In 2004, I began a prospective study with my colleague Angela Eke by gathering police reports in "real time." That is, we checked police records every 2 weeks for any cases of assault on a marital, cohabiting, or dating partner, or former intimate partner that had occurred since our last check. Over the course of 4 months, we identified 93 men who physically assaulted their female partners. When we followed up their police and criminal records 7.5 years later, 24% had committed a new assault on any intimate partner. The ODARA predicted this recidivism with a medium effect size (AUC = .67). ODARA scores that were prorated as needed for ambiguous information produced a similar effect (AUC = .66). A large predictive effect was found for any recidivism relating to an intimate partner, including violence, stalking, harassment, and conditional release failures (AUC = .71; Hilton & Eke, 2016).

In her University of New Brunswick master's thesis, Angela Moser studied men and women who committed violence and other acts against intimate partners identified in police reports of domestic disputes (Moser, 2012; Moser & Campbell, 2012). The 174 men in the sample were or had been married to or cohabiting with their partner. In an average prospective follow-up of 3.5 years, 45% reoffended, and the ODARA predicted recidivism

TABLE 4.1. Summary of ODARA Validation Studies

Population	Sample size	Follow-up average	Recidivism		Predictive effect (AUC)	95% CI
			Type	Base rate		
Policing						
Gerth et al. (2017)[a]	185 (male)	5 years	DV	32%	.63	[.55, .71]
Hilton & Eke (2016)	93 (male)	7.5 years	DV	24%	.67	[.55, .79]
			Any IP	40%	.71	[.61, .82]
Jung & Buro (2017); Olver & Jung (2017)	289 (full sample)[b]	3.3 years	DV	9%	.72	[.83, .82]
			V	16%	.73	[.65, .81]
			G	47%	.75	[.69, .81]
	226 (male)[c]		DV	16%	.66	[.57, .76]
			V	25%	.67	[.59, .76]
			G	62%	.73	[.66, .79]
	41 (female)		G	20%	.70	[.45, .94]
Lauria et al. (2017)	200 (male)	16 weeks	DV	10%	.68	[.55, .81]
			Nonviolent IP	23%	.72	[.61, .82]
McTague (2018)[d]	209 (male)	1 year	DV	34%	.64	[.56, .72]
	100 (female)	1 year	DV	18%	.52	[.36, .68]

(continues)

TABLE 4.1. Summary of ODARA Validation Studies (*Continued*)

Population	Sample size	Follow-up average	Recidivism		Predictive effect (AUC)	95% CI
Moser (2012); Moser & Campbell (2012)[d]	200 (full sample)	6 years	DV	44%	.70	[.63, .77]
	174 (male)		DV	45%	.70	[.63, .78]
	26 (female)		DV	36%	.67	[.46, .88]
	48 (nonviolent index incident)		DV	48%[e]	.70	[.54, .85]
Nazarewicz (2020)	99 (female)[d]	1 year	DV	6%	.53	[.31, .75]
			Nonviolent IP	9%	.56	[.33, .80]
	20 (subsample with DV index)		DV	20%	.40	[.06, .66]
			Nonviolent IP	15%	.63	[.37, .88]
Sentürk et al. (2016)[f]	186 (male)	5 years	DV	18%	.58	–
			G	27%	.60	–
	44 (female)		DV	9%	.61	–
			G	16%	.60	–
Ulmer (2015)	281 (male)	2 years	V	–	.57	–
			G	50%	.54	–
Corrections						
Buchanan (2009)	99 (male)	2 years	DV	19%	.72	–
Gray (2012)	94 (male)	3.6 years	DV	13%	.71	[.61, .80]
			V	23%	.62	[.51, .72]
			G	44%	.54	[.43, .66]

Hilton et al. (2010)	150 (male)	8 years	DV	27%	.64	[.54, .73]
			V	61%	.56	[.47, .66]
			G	90%	.69	[.55, .82]
Hilton et al. (2014)	30 (female)	9 years	DV	23%	.72	[.50, .94]
Rettenberger & Eher (2013)[b]	66 (male)	4.6 years	DV conviction (including sexual)	21%	.71	[.58, .84]
			V	24%	.69	[.57, .82]
			G	35%	.66	[.53, .79]
Forensic						
Seewald et al. (2017)	30 (male)[d]	8 years	V	20%	.78	[.62, .94]
Community treatment						
Schafers (2019)	88 (male)	15 months	V	14%	.63	–
			G	26%	.72	–

Note. DV = domestic (intimate partner) violence or related offenses; G = general criminal offense; IP = offense against an intimate partner; – = indicates information not provided; ODARA = Ontario Domestic Assault Risk Assessment; V = any violent offense.

[a]Gerth et al. (2017) used a fixed follow-up time, included both violent and nonviolent acts (threats, coercion) at index and recidivism, and report AUC for ODARA risk category. [b]Olver and Jung (2017) and Rettenberger and Eher (2013) based recidivism on convictions. [c]Jung and Buro (2017) also provided results for recidivism convictions in the male sample, not reported here. Recidivism reported for all studies is based on charges (or new police reports) unless noted. [d]Moser (2012), Moser and Campbell (2012), and McTague (2018) included both violent and nonviolent acts (e.g., threats, breaches, property offenses) at index and recidivism; Nazarewicz (2020) included violent and nonviolent incidents at index in the full sample and also reports on nonviolent outcomes; in Seewald et al. (2017), most individuals committed threats rather than assault at the index event;. [e]Personal communication, M. A. Campbell, 22 August 2019. [f]Sentürk et al. (2016) used an exact follow-up time. Variation in the characteristics of the samples, measures, methods, and quality of studies could account for some variation in measured predictive accuracy. See the text for other study details.

with a medium effect size (AUCs = .70). Jessica McTague (2018) scored the ODARA for men and women identified in domestic disputes from the same New Brunswick population, about 85% of whom had assaulted their partner. The 209 men scored 6.0 on average, 34% had a new domestic dispute in police reports in a maximum follow-up of 12 months, and the ODARA predicted this outcome with a medium effect size (AUC = .64).

Another Canadian province, Alberta, was the site of research by Sandy Jung and her colleagues (Jung & Buro, 2017; see also Researcher Profile 4.1). They obtained a sample of 300 men and women who were charged for actual or threatened violence against their current or former intimate partner. Few (15%) were female, and only one woman reoffended, so the study focused on the 246 men. The researchers coded ODARA items from police records, and coded recidivism from both police and criminal records. Among 226 men with sufficient information on item scores and recidivism, the average ODARA score was 5.7; 16% recidivated in a retrospective follow-up averaging 3 years. The ODARA had medium predictive effects for charges (AUC = .66) and convictions (AUC = .70).

Studies in Europe and Australia

Gerth and her colleagues (2014) evaluated a German translation of the ODARA among men arrested for assaulting or seriously threatening their female partner in Zurich, Switzerland. I helped verify the translation, with much help from my colleague Elke Ham, and the researchers achieved good inter-rater reliability with us when they used the German version. In an initial 3-month retrospective follow-up, the ODARA risk category had a large predictive effect (AUC = .73; Gerth et al., 2015). After 5 years, 32% of the 185 men who assaulted or threatened their intimate partner had a new police report of such offenses. ODARA scores averaged 5.1 and were skewed toward higher scores, where calibration was poorest with the published norms (Chapter 6, this volume). The AUC for the ODARA risk category was .63 (.639 is considered a medium effect; Gerth et al., 2017). Also using a German version, Sentürk et al. (2016) studied men and women documented as perpetrating domestic violence by police in Germany. They reported an interrater reliability coefficient of .86. All cases were followed for 5 years. The 186 men had an average ODARA score of 3.85, 18% had a new police report for domestic violence, and the ODARA had a small effect size (AUC = .58, a nonsignificant result). The AUC was .64 among the 128 men who had lived with their partners.

The first test of police officers' ability to identify risk of domestic violence recidivism using the ODARA was conducted in Australia by Lauria and colleagues (2017). Incidents involving intimate partners comprised more than two thirds of their family violence cases. The study included only the 200 men who assaulted a female current or former cohabiting partner (or made a threat with weapon in hand). Excluded were 86 women, 64 dating relationships, 16 same-sex relationships, four incidents perpetrated by minors, and 211 nonviolent incidents. In a follow-up averaging 16 weeks, 10% of men had a new police report of violence against the same partner. The ODARA discriminated between men with and without recidivism with a medium effect size (AUC = .68). Of the ODARA items, the strongest predictors were Preindex Custodial Sentence and Preindex Nondomestic Assault. Nonviolent domestic recidivism was more prevalent (23%) and was predicted with an AUC of .72. Lauria and colleagues noted that the police officers were not trained in the ODARA. Research is still needed to determine whether training, which can increase scoring accuracy and may be key to successful implementation (see Training Users to Score the ODARA Reliably in Chapter 10, this volume) can improve the ODARA's predictive validity in field tests.

GENERALIZATION ACROSS POPULATIONS

Risk assessment was common in custodial institutions, community corrections, and forensic hospitals for decades before police services began using structured assessment tools. The ODARA is the most commonly used domestic violence risk assessment tool in Canadian correctional settings (Bourgon et al., 2018). Three studies to date tested the ODARA among persons who had been adjudicated for domestic violence.

Buchanan's (2009) University of Regina doctoral thesis tested the ODARA among 99 men convicted of an assault, threat, or forcible entry offense against their current or former married or common-law female partner in Saskatchewan. In a 2-year average follow-up, 19% committed a subsequent assault against a female domestic partner, which the ODARA predicted with a large effect size (AUC = .72). The study included 54 men identified as Indigenous, for whom the ODARA had a medium effect size (AUC = .64) compared with the larger effect for men identified as Caucasian (AUC = .77; Buchanan, 2009). A similar result was reported by Gray (2012) in his master's thesis at Carleton University. He retrospectively followed

94 men with a history of assaulting their marital, cohabiting, or dating partner, for an average of more than 5 years after release from federal corrections. In this time, 13% were charged for another domestic assault, and the ODARA predicted domestic violence recidivism with an AUC of .71 (and its severity, $r = .23$). Gray also reported an interrater reliability coefficient of .90.

My colleagues and I tested the ODARA among 150 men in custody at a correctional treatment center in Ontario (Hilton et al., 2010). All the men had been admitted to a domestic violence program because they had a police record or self-report of assaulting a current or former marital, cohabiting, or dating partner (all the victims were female). We coded the ODARA from information available in the men's institutional files and then examined federal criminal records and provincial offender tracking reports for any criminal charges after release to the community. In an average 8-year prospective follow-up, 27% of the men were charged for a new assault against a partner (all female), and the ODARA had a medium predictive effect size (AUC = .64).

A challenge in this study was finding enough information from the available records to score all the ODARA items. We rejected 10 other cases where there was insufficient information to score any items, and another 27 who were missing information for more than five items. The ODARA can be prorated for up to five items with ambiguous information (see Chapter 6, this volume), so we used this procedure on the remaining 150 cases where needed. Predictive accuracy of the prorated score was reduced, but not significantly so, compared with the raw score (AUC = .61). As the average raw score was over 5, we also tried to create an extra risk category for scores over 7, 8, or 9, but these attempts did not improve predictive accuracy (AUC = .61).

We did have good information about release dates and time spent in custody for other offenses during the follow-up. The average follow-up time was 8 years, but men spent an average of just over 5 years at risk of recidivism in the community. We conducted survival analyses, splitting the sample into two groups at the median ODARA score (0–6 vs. 7–13). Men with higher ODARA scores were more likely to recidivate, and did so sooner, than men with lower scores. These data also gave us the opportunity to look at how the ODARA performed over different follow-up times, from 6 months to 8 years postrelease. We found AUCs ranging from .64 to .66 (and over .85 for the 6-month follow-up, considered an outlier).

Another follow-up of men released from custody was conducted in Austria by Rettenberger and Eher (2013). As part of a study on men convicted of sex offenses, the researchers identified 66 men who had sexually assaulted their current or former intimate partner. They scored the ODARA from comprehensive forensic evaluation records and gathered details of violent reoffenses from criminal courts. They used a German-language version of the ODARA, which they used to established interrater reliability with us on 10 cases from our standard test for ODARA trainees (see Online Training: "ODARA 101," in Chapter 10, this volume). The single-measures ICC was .95. In an average follow-up of 4.6 years, 21% men were convicted of a new sexual or violent offense against an intimate partner. The ODARA predicted domestic violence recidivism with a large effect (AUC = .71).

WOMEN WHO ASSAULT THEIR PARTNERS

In Chapter 2, I described the challenges faced in identifying a sample of women who commit domestic violence (see the section Focusing on Men's Violence Against Women). Moser's (2012) thesis study found 26 women identified as perpetrators in 200 randomly selected domestic occurrence reports. Women scored nearly 1 point lower than their male counterparts on average (4.46 vs. 5.28) and reoffended at a lower rate than men (36% vs. 45%). The ODARA's predictive effect for women was in the medium range (AUC = .67), although the lower bound of the 95% confidence interval fell below .50, indicating a statistically nonsignificant result. McTague (2018) drew a similar conclusion from her sample of 100 women, 18% of whom had a repeat occurrence within 12 months. McTague reported a nonsignificant AUC of .52. Again, women scored lower than men (4.35 vs. 6.01). In her doctoral thesis at the Swinburne University of Technology, Julia Nazarewicz (2020) studied 99 women identified as perpetrators of an incident against an intimate partner in Australia. In a 12-month follow-up, six (6%) women had a police report for perpetrating a physical assault against the same partner (including four, or 20%, of the 20 women who had physically assaulted their partner at the index incident). There was no significant predictive effect for the ODARA (AUC = .53). I note that the incidents in these three studies included but were not limited to domestic violence at index, recidivism, or both. Sentürk and colleagues (2016) studied 44 women who had committed domestic violence, with an average ODARA score of 2.07. Within 5 years, 9% had a new police report of domestic violence (half the men's rate). The predictive effect was small (AUC = .61, a nonsignificant result).

A search of correctional treatment center files, in collaboration with Suzanne Popham, resulted in a sample of 31 women with domestic violence charges, 30 for whom recidivism data were available. We scored the ODARA from their files, then followed them an average of 9 years after release from custody (Hilton et al., 2014). Most women identified as Indigenous (68%), 20% assaulted a dating partner, and 7% assaulted a female partner. In the 9-year average prospective follow-up, women were at risk for an average of 2 years, and 23% were charged for new assaults on an intimate partner. The ODARA had a large predictive effect (AUC = .72) and a small, positive, although not statistically significant, association with the severity of recidivism (correlation coefficient = .34).

The average ODARA score was just under 6, placing the sample in the second highest category for domestic violence recidivism, according to the norms derived from samples of men (Chapter 6, this volume). However, only 23% recidivated. Calibration analysis showed that women recidivated at a significantly lower rate than expected from the normative data for men. It is difficult to draw firm conclusions from such a small study, but other studies of women who commit domestic offenses concur that they recidivate less than men (e.g., Gerstenberger & Williams, 2013; Ménard et al., 2009; although this finding may apply only to women who assault male partners; Gerstenberger et al., 2019). Sample sizes in the hundreds are needed to recalibrate the ODARA actuarial tables for women.

In the 2014 study, we tested modified versions of seven items: whether the individual being assessed had been assaulted by a domestic partner preindex, had been assaulted by a nondomestic partner preindex, had committed a domestic assault when she was pregnant, had a child with a previous partner, or faced barriers to support, and whether her partner threatened to physically harm anyone at the index or had committed a preindex, nondomestic assault. Substituting these items for the original ones also produced a large predictive effect (AUC = .73) but not sufficiently different to recommend replacing the existing ODARA items. I hope to see more research in the future on how the prediction of women's domestic recidivism can be improved.

DATING AND SAME-SEX RELATIONSHIPS

Although there is no published validation of the ODARA in a sample consisting only of dating violence cases, several studies included dating violence at the index assault or recidivism, or at least did not expressly exclude cases on grounds that the partners had never lived together (e.g., Gerth et al., 2015, 2017; Hilton & Eke, 2016; Hilton et al., 2010; Jung & Buro, 2017; Rettenberger & Eher, 2013; Sentürk et al., 2016). I know of no theoretical or empirical grounds to expect the predictors of violent recidivism to act differently depending on the current relationship status of the person being assessed.

In contrast, there is limited work on domestic violence risk assessment for individuals with partners of the same sex. Moser (2012) identified five same-sex (female) relationships in her thesis sample of 200 domestic occurrences, and there were two in my study of women (Hilton et al., 2014). These samples are too small to test predictive accuracy of the ODARA for this population. Violence in same-sex relationships comprised less than 1% of family violence occurrences reported to police in Victoria, Australia (262 of more than 44,000 occurrences), and recurrence of any family violence within 12 months was predicted by a family violence risk assessment tool with a small effect size (AUC = .57, compared with .65 for all intimate partner cases; McEwan et al., 2019). Most recently, Gerstenberger, Stansfield, and Williams (2019) identified 332 male and female individuals in same-sex relationships in a sample of 6,711 people arrested for partner violence in Connecticut. In an 18-month follow-up, rearrest for IPV was observed among 30% of the men (not statistically different from recidivism by men with female partners) and 35% of the women—a significantly higher rate of recidivism than among women with male partners. This different recidivism rate between women with male and female partners was observed despite a similar average score on the Domestic Violence Screening Instrument–Revised (DVSI-R). The DVSI-R predicted recidivism with AUCs of .61 to .63 for all groups except women in same-sex relationships (AUC = .56, a nonsignificant result). These findings suggest some commonality of risk factors for domestic violence recidivism among men and women but raise concerns about the validity of applying existing approaches to women who assault their female partners. Research testing the ODARA's predictive accuracy in same-sex relationships is needed and could show modifications that are necessary for optimal prediction in these cases.

GENERALIZATION ACROSS OUTCOMES

When researchers determine recidivism from criminal records and a full description of the offense is not available, it is not always possible to know whether the victim of the new offense is an intimate partner. In one of the ODARA cross-validation studies, one in four cases that were counted as having no domestic recidivism did show some postindex violence for which the relationship could not be ascertained. Eliminating those men from the study raised the domestic violence recidivism base rate and improved the ODARA's AUC from .67 to .74. (Hilton & Harris, 2009b). It also drew our attention to the prevalence of nondomestic violence committed by men known for domestic violence.

In our research with a correctional sample, most of the men had at least one new charge for any criminal offense after release from custody (90%), and at least one charge for a violent offense (61%; Hilton et al., 2010). The ODARA predicted both these outcomes (AUCs = .69 and .56, respectively). We compared the ODARA with a measure of general criminal risk that was routinely scored by the correctional staff, the Level of Service Inventory (LSI; Andrews & Bonta, 2001). We expected the LSI to identify men at risk of general criminal recidivism, which it did (AUC = .70), but it was not associated with domestic violence recidivism (AUC = .50). Rettenberger and Eher's (2013) follow-up study of men convicted of domestic sex offenses also included nondomestic outcomes. Reconviction rates were 45% for general recidivism and 24% for violent recidivism (including sexual offenses). The ODARA was associated with both outcomes (AUCs = .66 and .69, respectively). Sentürk and colleagues (2016) found that the ODARA predicted new police reports of general recidivism among 186 men (27%, AUC = .60) but not significantly so among 44 women (16%, AUC = .60).

Another study tested the ODARA in a forensic psychiatric sample. Seewald and her colleagues followed up 30 men after a court-mandated assessment in Switzerland for assaulting (27%), threatening (77%), or sexually assaulting (7%) an intimate partner (Seewald et al., 2017). Coders scored the ODARA from forensic experts' evaluation reports (average interrater reliability coefficient = .62). In an average follow-up of 8 years, 20% were charged with a new violent offense. ODARA category predicted violent recidivism with a large effect size (AUC = .78), significantly better than the experts' clinical judgment (AUC = .35).

In Jung and Buro's (2017) study with a policing sample, the ODARA was also related to charges and convictions for other outcomes. Effect sizes were in the medium range for any violent offenses (AUCs = .67–.71) and large for general recidivism (AUCs = .73–.75). Olver and Jung (2017) further analyzed these data in the total sample of male and female cases (289 had recidivism data). They tried combining the ODARA with the SARA, and with subsets of SARA items related to spousal assault history, psychosocial adjustment, index offense, and criminal history. Overall, the SARA significantly improved prediction of domestic violence recidivism over the ODARA, and the strongest unique predictor was the SARA's psychosocial adjustment domain. For any violent recidivism, in contrast, the ODARA provided unique prediction over the SARA. Both tools incrementally predicted general recidivism; that is, when both the ODARA and the SARA were included in the statistical analysis, both made a significant contribution to the model predicting any criminal recidivism overall.

In her doctoral thesis at George Fox University, Ulmer (2015) studied the ODARA's use by police officers in Oregon. Among 281 men who assaulted their female partner, 50% were rearrested for any general offense in a 2-year follow-up. The ODARA did not significantly predict general recidivism (AUC = .54) but had a small predictive effect for violent recidivism, including rape, assault, and coercion (AUC = .57). Ulmer cited training problems, limited information gathering and time constraints as possible contributors to the ODARA's limited predictive validity in this study. Schafers's (2019) doctoral dissertation at the University of Saskatchewan examined general and violent recidivism by 88 men who attended a community-based domestic violence treatment group, with an average pretreatment ODARA score of 5.5. Treatment completers had significantly lower scores than noncompleters. In an average follow-up of 15 months from the last group treatment session, the ODARA significantly predicted general recidivism with a large effect size (AUC = .72) and had a moderate, but not significant, predictive effect for violent recidivism (AUC = .63).

With regard to individuals' criminal careers, criminologists have studied different criminal career paths, including one characterized by chronic and high rates of more than one kind of offending. Chronic criminal offending was associated with the highest rates of self-reported domestic violence in one longitudinal cohort study (Theobald et al., 2016). I have already argued that the individuals who commit the most severe and persistent domestic violence are those with a general antisocial history (see the Typologies section in Chapter 1, this volume) and that criminal history increases the risk of domestic violence recidivism, as evidenced in the ODARA construction research (see Chapter 3).

Angela Eke and I further explored the diversity of criminal careers among men charged with domestic violence in our "real-time" study (Hilton & Eke, 2016). We found that the men were charged with all types of criminal offenses in the 8 years preindex: sex offenses, 2%; stalking, 9%; conditional release failures, 34%; domestic violence, 36%; any violent offense, 53%; and any nonviolent offense, 62%. We found the same pattern in our prospective follow-up 8 years postindex. Moreover, the ODARA predicted every type of domestic and nondomestic recidivism, with medium effect sizes for some (e.g., any violent offense or sexual assault, AUC = .67) and large effects for others (e.g., conditional release failures, threatening, stalking, or any nonviolent offense, AUCs = .72 to .78). These findings add to evidence of the nonspecialization of criminal careers, at least among individuals who have contact with the criminal justice system for domestic violence.

APPLICATIONS OF DOMESTIC RISK ASSESSMENT

I now turn to ways in which the ODARA has been applied to the assessment context. I also show how the ODARA can help inform service provision for individuals who perpetrate or are affected by domestic violence.

Threat Assessment

The profession of threat assessment has grown in response to the justice system's need for specialized services to assess risk in especially concerning cases. The movement reflects increased efforts to assess and potentially avert violence that would overstretch routine police resources. Police-based services that are integrated with forensic psychologists and psychiatrists can go beyond assessing risk, to identifying avenues for intervention and linking individuals with services to improve outcomes (e.g., Ennis et al., 2015; Guldimann et al., 2016). The typical case referred for threat assessment involves an identified person who has been the target of violence, threats, stalking, or other unwarranted contact (e.g., Eke, Meloy, Brooks, Jean, & Hilton, 2014). Targets often include public figures and acquaintances, but intimate partner violence dominates the threat assessment caseload (e.g., Eke, Hilton, Meloy, et al., 2011; Ennis et al., 2015). Threat assessors gather as much information as they can from reports and consultations with law enforcement, child protection, and other agencies and try to take all information into consideration as they identify risk factors, potential scenarios of violence, and possible interventions for each individual case.

Threat assessors usually use actuarial tools or other structured risk assessment as part of their information gathering, including the ODARA (e.g., Guldimann et al., 2016). In emerging research with domestic cases referred for threat assessment, ODARA scores were higher among individuals whose violence was rated as instrumental and planned rather than reactive and emotional (Ennis et al., 2017).

Cook et al. (2014) described how structured professional judgment guides were used in the threat assessment of a man who assaulted and stalked several women. Cook and colleagues scored the B-SAFER and a similar guide for assessing stalking risk. They gathered information from interviews, publications, and public records and evaluated each potential risk factor, then developed a case formulation, ultimately judging the individual to be high risk for intimate partner violence and stalking. They also proposed risk management strategies: custody, curfews, no-contact orders, frequent supervision interviews, therapy for interpersonal relationship problems, and intensive correctional treatment for domestic or general violence, as well as victim advocacy, counseling, and security procedures. A key part of the assessment was an analysis of the individual's personality and the effects of having been raised by a single mother on his possible emasculation and need for dominance. I reviewed the case information published by Cook and colleagues and found that the ODARA and DVRAG placed the man in the highest category at the time he was assessed and would have done so at the time of earlier offenses had it been possible to assess him (Hilton, 2014).

Case Prioritization

No amount of analyzing and planning will prevent violence if risk management is not implemented effectively. In their review of 73 studies evaluating risk management and recidivism after use of a risk assessment tool, Viljoen and colleagues (2018) noted that careful implementation of risk management guidelines and staff training may optimize the benefits of risk assessment. Most forensic and threat assessment risk management recommendations appear to be implemented, especially further assessment, enforcing court orders, and discussing safety plans with victims (Ennis et al., 2015; Levin et al., 2019). Unfortunately, police officers, probation officers, psychologists, and other professionals do not consistently adhere to the Risk–Need–Responsivity (RNR) principles even after conducting a structured risk assessment (e.g., Dyck et al., 2018; Viljoen et al., 2018; see the description of RNR in the section on Limits of Domestic Violence Theory in Chapter 1, this volume). Despite using valid risk assessment to inform risk management plans, practitioners do not always intervene effectively, and individuals do not receive services matched to their needs (e.g., Peterson-Badali et al., 2015; Viljoen et al., 2018). Notably, some needs tend to be overserviced, suggesting that greater adherence to the RNR principles could increase cost effectiveness (e.g., Drawbridge et al., 2019).

Domestic violence treatment programs (often called *batterer intervention programs*) bear much of the burden of efforts to reduce risk of domestic violence recidivism. Yet research has revealed limited benefits of domestic violence treatment (see Exhibit 4.1). To be successful, and avoid adverse effects, they must adhere to the RNR principles of effective correctional

EXHIBIT 4.1. The Quandary of Domestic Violence Treatment

Readers might notice an apparent contradiction in my position on domestic violence treatment. I advocate assigning people to treatment based on their actuarial risk but make no suggestion that treatment reduces recidivism. In fact, in the original Ontario Domestic Assault Risk Assessment research, individuals who received treatment were significantly more likely to recidivate (Hilton & Harris, 2005), a finding paralleled by the Domestic Violence Screening Instrument-Revised (e.g., Williams, 2012) in which treatment raises the assessed risk. Why, then, recommend treatment for managing any level of risk?

Does being assigned to domestic violence treatment result in lower recidivism than the routine criminal justice processes alone? Unfortunately, despite thousands of domestic violence treatment programs across the United States, few conduct any evaluation research (e.g., Babcock et al., 2016). Random assignment of eligible cases to treatment or a comparison group is the most informative evaluation design but strikes fear into the hearts of some policy makers: What if someone assigned to the control group later commits a serious assault? That is exactly what treatment is intended to avoid, so a deliberate decision to allow it seems hard to defend. Indeed, reports of experimental evaluation designs indicate that police or judges do sometimes override random assignment (e.g., Babcock et al., 2004). One consequence is that quasi-experimental studies that compare individuals who complete treatment to those who drop out outnumber studies with experimental designs (e.g., Arias et al., 2013; Cheng et al., 2019).

Other methodological problems pertain to who should count as a treated case: individuals assigned to treatment; those who begin it; those who attend all sessions; or those who, in the opinion of the therapists, are successful? What should the outcome be: therapists' ratings of successful completion, official recidivism, or partner reports of subsequent violence? Because the highest risk individuals are most likely to avoid treatment, quit, or be ejected (e.g., Hilton & Harris, 2005) and because therapist ratings have little or no association with recidivism (Gondolf & Wernik, 2009), intent-to-treat designs, in which everyone assigned to treatment is counted in the treatment group, whether or not they attend, are the most informative. A good evaluation would also track outcomes for noncompleters and gather both police and victim reports to counter the biases of each outcome measure. Important decisions must be made about what counts as nonrecidivism (Hilton & Harris, 2009b). The technical and political difficulties of evaluating treatment may explain why there are so few scientifically informative studies.

Regarding the evidence, the bad news is that meta-analyses show small overall effects at best, precluding the conclusion of an overall treatment effect (e.g., Arias et al., 2013; Cheng et al., 2019), even for cognitive behavior therapy (e.g., Nesset et al., 2019). Domestic violence treatment providers are being encouraged to move toward evidence-based approaches (e.g., Babcock et al., 2016; Crane & Easton, 2017; Radatz & Wright, 2016). There is some evidence that treatment works better for some people than others, such as those who exhibit general antisociality (e.g., Cantos et al., 2019), consistent with risk, need, and responsivity principles. Perhaps current treatment programs, most of which aim to change attitudes toward gender roles and power in control in intimate relationships (e.g., Cannon et al., 2016), are simply targeting the wrong things. Treatment essentially puts a theory into practice, and the causal theories underpinning current domestic violence treatments are, at best, incomplete and limited (see Chapter 1, this volume). I am more optimistic about the future direction of interventions that focus on criminogenic needs, and strongly recommend that priority for treatment participation be in accordance with actuarially determined risk (e.g., Radatz & Hilton, 2019).

service. Treatment providers struggle to assess risk based on treatment participants' self-reports, without access to criminal histories or partner reports (e.g., Weisz et al., 2012). Canadian correctional researchers have led the field in RNR-informed domestic violence treatment by assigning individuals to different levels of custodial treatment intensity using structured risk assessment and providing more sessions and additional content for the high-intensity groups (Connors et al., 2012, 2013), with beneficial effects on recidivism (Stewart et al., 2014).

Along with Dr. Dana Radatz (see Researcher Profile 4.2), I illustrated how the ODARA can be used to identify high, medium, and low treatment-intensity groups (Radatz & Hilton, 2019). We reanalyzed data from the ODARA construction and cross-validation studies, selecting only the 970 cases with criminal charges at the index assault, to best reflect the population of individuals who are directed to attend domestic violence treatment after adjudication or diversion in the criminal justice system. We divided the sample according to *percentiles*, or how individuals are ranked among others with respect to risk. Our aim was to show how treatment agencies could choose their own treatment-intensity categories based on the ODARA scores they routinely obtain at their intake assessments or when referrals are made by police who have already scored the ODARA. For example, if an agency receives twice as many referrals for treatment as it has resources to serve, then at most, the highest scoring 50% of referred individuals could be offered treatment. These referrals could be further divided so that the highest scoring individuals receive the longest, most intensive, evidence-based treatment on offer, in proportion with the number of places that are available. Instead of accepting all referrals and having an ever-increasing waiting list, taking this RNR-adherent approach to apportioning treatment services could not only improve the impact of treatment but also take the pressure off treatment agencies to provide the same resource-intensive treatment to every referred individual.

We designated ODARA scores of 0 to 2 as the "low" treatment-intensity category, which represented the lowest scoring 42% of our sample. The "medium'" category comprised scores 3 and 4, or 35% of our sample. Our "high" treatment-intensity category included scores 5 to 13, the remaining 24% of the sample (Radatz & Hilton, 2019). We later found that men in higher treatment-intensity categories did have more criminogenic needs (Hilton & Radatz, in press).

Victim Services

My ideal is that the ODARA/DVRAG system should be accessible to everyone involved in the community response to domestic violence. Sharing a risk assessment tool could promote effective risk communication (the subject of Chapter 9, this volume), contributing to improved coordination of responses across sectors. I hope that women may be empowered by having information about their partner's risk as they make choices for themselves and their children, and I seek to support victim service workers who advocate with police and others for their clients' safety. For these reasons, my colleagues and I have endeavored to make the ODARA accessible to assaulted women, primarily through agencies that provide services for women, children, and families. As soon as the ODARA was developed, we worked with the Ontario Network of Sexual Assault/Domestic Violence Treatment Centres (SADVTCs) and our local women's shelters to provide ODARA training, receive feedback on how to report ODARA scores (see Chapter 6, this volume), and study the ODARA within their services.

In particular, we partnered with Norah Holder, then director of the Orillia Solders' Memorial Hospital SADVTC, to transform our research variables into a series of questions to be used as an interview with a female client (Hilton, Harris, & Holder, 2008). Shelter staff piloted the interview with 25 women and SADVTC nurses began offering the ODARA interview as a service option. SADVTCs are hospital-based clinics supported by the Ontario government to provide emergency medical and nursing care and assessment, crisis counseling, forensic evidence collection, and assessment and referral services for women and children who have been recently assaulted, including risk assessment and safety planning with adults assaulted by their partners. From 111 women who participated in our study at these clinics, we gained valuable information about characteristics of the ODARA victim interview. Statistically, ODARA scores were more or less normally distributed, and the items were correlated with each other, giving evidence of internal consistency, as in the construction research. Also, the scores were associated with other variables in ways similar to our original research; for example, higher scores were observed in cases with stalking or preindex injury. These results provided some validation of the ODARA interview in terms of consistent psychometric properties and concurrent validity.

More than half the women in our study rated the risk of violence by their partner in the next year as 10 on a scale of 0 (*no chance*) to 10 (*sure to happen*). This rating is the highest reported in related research (cf. Cattaneo & Goodman, 2003; Dichter & Gelles, 2012; Harding & Helweg-Larsen, 2009; Weisz et al., 2000). Women's ratings were correlated with the ODARA, but not when we removed the item Victim Concern. Despite their perceived risk, only a small minority of the women had involved the police (13%) or gone to a shelter (5%) for the index assault, and those who had were not necessarily those with worse injuries or greater risk of assault (according to ODARA scores). The uncommon use of other services suggested that the clinics served a unique clientele. Most women relied on informal supports, primarily their female friends (60%) and female biological relatives (55%). Participants were significantly more likely to consider calling professionals such as therapists, clergy, or lawyers (32%) than police (21%), providing further grounds for making the ODARA accessible outside of law enforcement.

Connor-Smith and colleagues (2011) interviewed 728 women and asked whether they thought their partner would be violent with them in the next year. The researchers also compared women's perceived risk with a 10-item modification of the ODARA, omitting Victim Concern and two other items. Splitting participants into two groups based on ODARA scores in the highest risk category (scores of 7 or higher) versus lower scores, the researchers found that women's perceived risk agreed with these two categories in 67% of cases. Women more often disagreed with a higher risk score than a lower risk score, suggesting that women are good judges of their partners' risk on average, but when they disagree with the actuarial data, they tend to underestimate risk.

Domestic Homicide

Attempts have been made to develop lethality risk assessments or to discover distinguishing characteristics of people who kill their partners (see Controversies in Inferring Individual Risk in Chapter 8). In research with Angela Eke, we had sufficient data from police case files to score the ODARA retrospectively for 30 men who killed their female partner. Their average ODARA score was in the second highest category of risk for domestic violence recidivism and in the highest risk category among those with a prior assault known to police (average score = 9) or other agencies (average score = 7; Eke, Hilton, Harris, et al., 2011).

Jaffe and colleagues (2014) reported on another retrospective review of 40 domestic homicide cases. They noted that ODARA scores did not differ between individuals who perpetrated domestic homicide with or without child victims in addition to the domestic partner.

Child Abuse

It is noteworthy that children figure prominently in the appraisal of domestic violence risk; that is, the number of children that the individual or their partner have, the partner having a biological child from a previous relationship, and the partner having a minor child in the home to care for all indicate greater risk of another assault. These items are on the ODARA (and DVRAG) because they predicted domestic violence, although it is not well understood whether or how they might cause it. Possible reasons include parenting stress, jealousy aroused by the presence of children from a previous relationship, the association of antisociality with both violence and number of offspring, and the peak of violence propensity at an age coinciding with childbearing years. Being responsible for children may make a woman more dependent on financial support and more afraid of a custody dispute and, therefore, less able to leave home than she would be without children. Each of these hypothesized pathways could contribute to the violence, or each could be wrong. Further theory-driven research is needed to investigate why the existence of children is empirically related to recidivism.

Men with higher ODARA scores are more likely to have physically assaulted their children as well as their partner, and stepchildren are especially at risk. In a study my colleagues and I did of 118 men who had both a genetically related child and a stepchild who were minors when the index assault occurred, these men were more likely to assault their stepchildren, regardless of their level of antisociality (Hilton, Harris, & Rice, 2015). These findings attest to the value of domestic violence risk assessment in child protection. Child protection workers may interpret exposure to violence between adults in the home as child maltreatment or neglect, although increased service does not necessarily result (e.g., Henry, 2018; Lawson, 2019). In their review of domestic homicides, Jaffe and colleagues (2014) noted that the 13 cases involving a child victim did, in fact, have more agencies involved with the family; sadly, this did not result in enhanced risk assessment or safety planning. One of the first agencies to adopt the ODARA in Ontario was a child protection service that integrated the tool into their rigorous assessment protocol. This practice may reflect a growth in actuarial assessment of child abuse risk (e.g., Schwartz et al., 2017). Child abuse allegations could be the first opportunity for professional attention and criminal justice intervention for domestic violence.

Pets and Other Animals

There is growing evidence of the link between animal abuse and domestic violence (e.g., Monsalve et al., 2017). The ODARA construction research did not find much evidence of cruelty toward pets or other animals, nor was this behavior related to domestic violence recidivism. However, the simple presence of animals creates complex logistic, financial, and emotional scenarios for partners seeking to leave an abusive relationship (e.g., Wuerch et al., 2017). The hardship is heightened when an individual has harmed the animals or threatened them in an effort to control the partner (e.g., Hardesty et al., 2013). These challenges can perhaps be fully understood only by those who have loved a pet or been responsible for farm animals. Awareness of the link between domestic violence and animal maltreatment is prompting women's shelters to consider pet safety services (e.g., Stevenson et al., 2018).

CONCLUSION

In this chapter, I have presented all the empirical evidence of the ODARA's ability to discriminate between cases of recidivism and nonrecidivism in various populations, along with its utility in threat assessment, domestic violence treatment, victim services, and child protection. The ODARA has performed well in these studies and when compared with other approaches. Researchers have been able to improve on the ODARA only when using more detailed information than is normally available in frontline police and victim service work. The next chapter describes this research.

POINTS TO REMEMBER

- The ODARA is a validated tool for assessing the risk of domestic violence recidivism from police reports and criminal records. It also predicts any violent or nonviolent incident involving intimate partners, as well as other violent and general criminal recidivism.
- Emerging evidence supports use of the ODARA for women who assault their partners and in cases of dating violence.
- The ODARA is a brief and easy-to-use tool that offers precise information for threat assessment or for classifying individuals into treatment intensity categories.
- Abused women's perceptions of risk generally align with ODARA-based estimates, but they may over- or underestimate risk relative to actuarial data.
- The severity of a domestic assault is not a strong or consistent indicator of the severity of future violence.

QUESTIONS TO CONSIDER

1. For what range of follow-up periods has the ODARA been tested in the studies reported in this chapter?
2. Identify three circumstances other than male-to-female physical violence in cohabiting relationships for which the ODARA has been validated.
3. How does actuarial risk assessment differ from the case formulation approach?
4. Could the ODARA be useful for identifying families in need of child protection services? What are some of the research, ethical, or practical considerations of this application?
5. Choose an area in which there is relatively limited ODARA research. Write a research question for this area of research and outline a study to answer it.

RESEARCHER PROFILE 4.1
SANDY JUNG, PhD, RPSYCH

My interest in forensic psychology grew after taking undergraduate classes with Drs. Robert Hare and John Yuille at the University of British Columbia. I found it fascinating learning about correctional offenders and the decisions that needed to be made to keep the public safe. My interest in risk assessment started when I learned about the Psychopathy Checklist (Hare, 2003). Initially, I worked with youth probation services and helped evaluate the predictive validity of a precursor to the Youth Level of Service Inventory (Hoge & Andrews, 2002). What I learned from the experience guided my next decisions. First, I did not enjoy working with youth, but I later found my niche during my doctoral studies with adult violent and sexual offenders. Second, I really enjoyed psychometric evaluation, and I expanded my knowledge working as a clinician in Edmonton, where risk assessment was instrumental in formulating my conclusions and making decisions about treatment for each offender.

Only when I moved to MacEwan and began working with the Edmonton Police Service was I exposed to the complex issues associated with intimate partner violence (IPV). The number of domestic calls was daunting (about 8,000 annually), and my risk assessment lens allowed me to focus on questions that would increase efficiency. From then I was hooked. I wanted to contribute something useful to the police that would lead to important changes in reducing those numbers, or at least influence how police effectively dealt with these events.

My research applies the risk, need, and responsivity principle (see Limits of Domestic Violence Theory in Chapter 1, this volume) in law enforcement. For example, is risk assessment of accused perpetrators valid when conducted by police officers? Can risk assessment help with efficient allocation of resources to reduce breaches of recognizance and further IPV? The police have many roles, and assessing risk, although inherent in what they do, is almost never made explicit; thus, the breadth of our evidence-based forensic psychology is rarely taught to officers.

My most important study so far examined the predictive accuracy of risk assessment measures in the context of police investigations of IPV (Jung & Buro, 2017). We found that the Family Violence Investigative Report (FVIR), a tool mandated for police in Alberta, Canada, did not predict violent or IPV reoffending among IPV perpetrators. Instead, the ODARA and SARA were effective. This study led to Edmonton Police Service's adopting the ODARA, and I received further funds to examine the effective allocation of resources for IPV perpetrators using this tool.

I primarily conduct archival research that involves review of police files and criminal records. This is particularly suited for my role as an undergraduate mentor, and the students I supervise can quickly learn about this research method and gain specific knowledge in this area of forensic psychology. In 2015, I began partnering with the Integrated Threat and Risk Assessment Centre in Alberta and collaborating with an excellent team of researchers, Drs. Liam Ennis, Zoe Hilton, and Kevin Nunes and doctoral candidate Anna Pham, on a seminal study of risk assessment conducted by police: the Optimizing Risk Assessment for Domestic Violence project. I think the continuing collaboration of researchers with police and other frontline professionals is absolutely necessary to bring evidence-based practice to law enforcement and also to teach academic researchers how to do good, useful research that actually helps prevent violence.

About the Researcher

Dr. Jung is a Board of Governors Research Chair and an associate professor in the Department of Psychology, MacEwan University, Edmonton, Alberta, Canada.

RESEARCHER PROFILE 4.2
DANA L. RADATZ, PhD

While working on my undergraduate degree in psychology at Eastern Michigan University (EMU), I decided to take a criminology class because I had a strong interest in understanding criminal behavior. That one criminology course led to several others, and upon graduation, I pursued a master's degree in criminology and criminal justice from EMU. In my second year of graduate education, I enrolled in a domestic violence course. It was then that my interest in domestic violence research was sparked. In addition to understanding the plight of victims, I also learned of the challenges that criminal justice system agencies and related organizations had in addressing domestic violence. Each class developed and fueled my newly discovered passion for victim advocacy, and also ignited my desire to find plausible solutions to violence and victimization. Ultimately, this led to my decision to pursue a doctorate in criminology and criminal justice at the University of Nebraska at Omaha.

My goal of obtaining a doctorate degree was to bridge the gap between the practical and academic realms of domestic violence work—to learn from both realms and work together to find effective solutions. To do this, I volunteered and collaborated with multiple nonprofit agencies and organizations working to address domestic violence. I also worked with Dr. Lisa Sample throughout my graduate career to conduct process and program evaluations for a grant-funded organization in Nebraska. These experiences provided me with a better understanding of practical realm work and helped me to develop the skillset of conducting evaluations. It was also during this time that I began working with my mentor, Dr. Emily Wright. As a victimologist interested in domestic violence and correctional programming, Dr. Wright helped me to further develop my desire to find plausible, effective solutions to domestic violence. She introduced me to effective correctional programming, namely, the principles of effective intervention (PEI). She and I both viewed the PEI, an evidence-based approach to the rehabilitation of criminal offenders, as a plausible solution to the minimally effective domestic violence programming used by the criminal justice system.

It was during this time that our collaborative article in *Trauma, Violence, & Abuse*, "Integrating the Principles of Effective Intervention Into Batterer Intervention Programming: The Case for Moving Towards More Evidence-Based Programming," was written (Radatz & Wright, 2016). This article was a call to begin exploring the integration of evidence-based practices into domestic violence programming. A substantial amount of my subsequent work, including my dissertation, has explored the principles outlined in that article. My research agenda uses well-known domestic offender datasets to examine domestic violence offenders through a PEI lens (e.g., Hilton & Radatz, 2018; Radatz, 2015; Radatz & Hilton, 2019), while simultaneously designing research projects and collecting data specifically created to examine the PEI among domestic violence offenders and within domestic violence programming. My work and that of others working to improve the effectiveness of domestic violence programming through the PEI has been well received and has garnered positive attention from both the practical and the research realms. This work has afforded me the opportunity to work with others, many in different disciplines from my own, and has contributed to my belief that the solution to effective domestic violence programming is an evidence-based, interdisciplinary approach. And although I am in the early stages of my career, my hope is that my work as a whole continues to contribute to the goal of finding a plausible and effective solution to domestic violence.

About the Researcher

Dr. Radatz is an assistant professor of criminology at Niagara University, New York.

5 CREATING AN IN-DEPTH RISK ASSESSMENT

The Domestic Violence Risk Appraisal Guide

The Ontario Domestic Assault Risk Assessment (ODARA; Hilton et al., 2004) was developed for frontline police officers or victim advocates, rather than for forensic clinicians and criminal justice professionals who usually have access to detailed case information. As I show in this chapter, certain in-depth information can substantially improve the identification of men at risk of domestic violence recidivism. In this chapter, I make a case for adding measures of habitual antisociality to domestic violence risk assessment, where possible, to increase the accuracy, replicability, and utility of the assessment. I describe steps my colleagues and I took (and the directions we abandoned) as we developed the Domestic Violence Risk Appraisal Guide (DVRAG; Hilton, Harris, Rice, et al., 2008). I review validations of the DVRAG and a modified version, the DVRAG-4. I also answer some practical questions about when and how to use the DVRAG. Then I explore the implications of this work for domestic violence theory. This research paints a picture very similar to what is known about violent offending in general.

https://doi.org/10.1037/0000223-006
Domestic Violence Risk Assessment: Tools for Effective Prediction and Management, Second Edition, by N. Z. Hilton

THE VALUE OF IN-DEPTH INFORMATION

Clinicians often think that they can do the best job of predicting whether individuals will reoffend if they have as much information about the individuals as possible. Characteristics clinicians especially want to know include mental health status and psychiatric symptoms, insight, life stressors, self-esteem, parent–child attachment, and childhood exposure to abuse. Many of these details, however, have turned out to be unrelated to violent recidivism—or related in the direction opposite to that believed. Certain other kinds of clinical information, though, can increase the accuracy of risk assessments.

When we constructed the ODARA, we considered only information that would normally be available to a police officer conducting a domestic investigation; therefore, we did not include robust predictors such as the Violence Risk Appraisal Guide (VRAG; Harris et al., 1993; Harris, Rice, et al., 2015), or childhood experiences and behavior. Furthermore, we considered items from existing domestic violence risk assessment tools only if a frontline police officer could reasonably score them. In some circumstances, the opportunity might arise to score more information. A particularly promising tool was the Psychopathy Checklist–Revised (PCL-R; Hare, 2003; see the section Single Risk Factors in Chapter 1), widely used in forensic and correctional assessment because of its implications for understanding offending behavior and for treatment planning. The PCL-R's association with violence risk is well established (e.g., Williams et al., 2017). Emerging studies by Adelle Forth and others suggest that women's preferences for and behavior toward male potential partners are positively related to the men's psychopathic personality (Brazil & Forth, 2020), but this attraction may have adverse consequences for the women (see Researcher Profile 5.1). Research on domestic violence types (see Typologies in Chapter 1) suggests that incorporating more theory-driven concepts such as psychopathy could improve domestic violence risk assessment. So we set about the task of identifying men for whom in-depth information would be available and began the search for improvements to the ODARA.

DEVELOPING AN IN-DEPTH RISK ASSESSMENT

In this section, I describe the methods used to develop the DVRAG. Because we wanted to create an actuarial instrument, we relied on a follow-up study, as we did when developing the ODARA (Hilton et al., 2004; see also

Chapter 3, this volume). However, we took a different approach to selecting the sample and choosing potential predictors.

Selection of a Sample for Study

We started our search for instruments or variables to improve upon the ODARA by examining predictors in the original construction sample of 589 men plus the 100 men in the first cross-validation sample, for a total of 689 cases (from Hilton et al., 2004). Several nonactuarial tools—scores on the Spousal Assault Risk Assessment (SARA; Kropp et al., 1999), the Danger Assessment (DA; Campbell, 1986), and the Domestic Violence Supplementary Report (DVSR; Ontario Ministry of the Solicitor General, 2000)—predicted domestic recidivism, and each was correlated with the ODARA (Hilton et al., 2004; see Characteristics of the Ontario Domestic Assault Risk Assessment, Chapter 3, this volume). Many, but not all, of the 689 men had an extensive correctional file that contained enough information to score existing in-depth tools completely. The SARA, in particular, includes personality disorder, attitudes, and childhood exposure to violence. When we had this information (which we usually found in presentence reports containing detailed background history and assessment results), we relied on it (rather than only the police reports) to score these other assessments. To be confident that we had adequate information, and consequently to give each tool the best chance of predicting the outcome, we chose only the 303 of the original 689 men for whom we had this information. This decision meant that there were 303 individuals in the DVRAG development sample and that the resulting in-depth risk assessment would apply to cases in which there had been the opportunity for a professional forensic or correctional assessment.

Restricting the sample this way had some effects on the expected predictive accuracy of all the tools we tested. It tended to limit the number of individuals with relatively low ODARA scores and thus the men least likely to recidivate, which we expected to reduce the correlation between all assessments and recidivism. To illustrate this effect, imagine computing the correlation between height and weight. In the adult population, this correlation is positive: as height increases, so does weight. The relationship is imperfect—there are people who are 5 feet 7 inches (1.7 meters) and weigh more than people who are 6 feet 0 inches (1.8 meters) tall, and so on—but across the population of all shapes and sizes, height is a good predictor of weight. If we eliminated anyone under 5 feet 2 inches (1.6 meters) from consideration, an adequate sample size would still likely yield an association between height and weight but, without the shortest (and usually the lightest) adults contributing data, the correlation would be reduced.

So it was with the correlations among the assessments and recidivism when we limited our sample to men who had a correctional assessment on file. The percentage of men scoring in the lowest two ODARA categories was cut to about a third of what we saw in the ODARA construction sample, and the percentage in the highest two categories doubled. Not surprisingly, the 303 individuals had higher scores on average (e.g., the mean ODARA score was now 4.1 compared with 2.9, and there were similar increases in the SARA and DA scores) and a higher recidivism rate (i.e., nearly 50% compared with 30%). As a result, the correlations between risk assessment scores and outcomes and the area under the curve statistics (AUCs; see the AUC and Related Accuracy Statistics section in Chapter 2) were lower in this sample of 303 men than in the ODARA construction sample.

This lower accuracy of the ODARA in the correctional sample reflects the fact that the police and other criminal justice professionals are more likely to detain individuals who are more likely to recidivate (e.g., Hilton, Harris, & Rice, 2007). Our goal when we developed the DVRAG was to find an instrument that would improve upon the accuracy of the ODARA in the limited sample of men for whom in-depth information was available. The sample had proportionately more men scoring relatively high on the risk measures than did the original ODARA construction sample and, therefore, had the potential to yield an instrument that would permit greater discrimination at the higher end of risk. But this advantage came at the cost of reduced utility at the lower end.

Selection of Predictors and Outcomes

When deciding which variables to consider, we could have started from scratch and thrown every variable from our dataset into the mix. However, we already knew that the ODARA items optimized prediction in the absence of in-depth information. Our approach, then, was to see what made an incremental contribution to the prediction of domestic recidivism once the ODARA was already part of the assessment system. This task set a high bar, given that the ODARA was constructed using the best predictors in a very similar sample, and the power to detect additional contributions to prediction would be limited by the sample size. On the other hand, adopting this strategy meant we could avoid creating an entirely new tool and could take advantage of existing assessments that were likely to be in routine use in correctional and forensic assessment. We considered the DA, the SARA, and what was then a new tool, the Domestic Violence Screening Instrument (DVSI; Williams & Houghton, 2004). We also considered the Hare PCL-R because we were aware of its already well-established association with violent recidivism (e.g., Harris, Skilling, & Rice, 2001).

The VRAG (Harris, Rice, et al., 2015) was another obvious choice. We had already found the VRAG to be a good predictor of violent recidivism among men with a record of serious domestic assault (Hilton et al., 2001). The VRAG's ability to distinguish between individuals with and without recidivism has proven robust, with replications now spanning several outcomes and populations and decades of follow-up (http://www.vrag-r.org). Assessment is optimal when no VRAG items are deleted or replaced (Harris & Rice, 2003). Unfortunately, two of its items could not vary in our sample of men who assaulted their female marital or cohabiting partners: index offense perpetrated against a female person and having never been in a marital or equivalent relationship. The DVRAG development sample raised a further challenge because we had insufficient evidence to indicate that any individual met the criteria for a diagnosis of schizophrenia. A revision of the VRAG that does not require coding psychiatric diagnostic criteria had not yet been created (VRAG-R; Rice et al., 2013). The result is that we tested a nine-item modification of the VRAG.

Next, we decided to select the best predictors of not only whether recidivism would occur but also the frequency and severity of recidivism (defined in the next paragraph). A risk assessment tool that predicted whether an offense would occur but did not also predict the number and severity of such offenses could be confusing and difficult to apply in the context of the risk, needs, and responsivity (RNR) principles of correctional service (e.g., Bonta & Andrews, 2017; see Limits of Domestic Violence Theory in Chapter 1, this volume). These other outcomes might be just as important to sentencing decisions, parole and supervision, or a partner making safety planning decisions. In general, our actuarial risk assessments that were constructed with dichotomous (yes–no) recidivism as an outcome have turned out to be positively correlated with the severity of violence and how soon a new offense occurred (see Cross-Validations in Chapter 3 for details on these statistics for the ODARA). When we developed the DVRAG, we took steps to ensure the selection of components associated with these other outcomes.

There were also empirical reasons to consider other outcomes. In the correctional sample, we anticipated a greater likelihood of recidivism, so examining other aspects of recidivism would help us discriminate among men who did and did not recidivate. Continuous measures, such as a severity scale or the number of recidivistic incidents, can also afford greater precision of measurement than a yes–no dichotomy of recidivism. When we developed the DVRAG, we tested whether assessments improved prediction of several aspects of recidivism. These five outcome measures all showed moderate to large correlations with each other (Hilton, Harris, Rice, et al., 2008):

1. Any new incident of assault on a female domestic partner (a dichotomous measure)
2. The number of incidents meeting the criteria for domestic assault recidivism (a continuous measure)
3. The number of recidivistic incidents involving severe violence—that is, incidents meeting the criteria for domestic assault recidivism in which the man committed acts ranging from punching or kicking through to using a knife or gun (a continuous measure)
4. The total score on an injury scale, from 1 (*no injury*) through 5 (*wounds from a weapon*), summed across all the postindex incidents of domestic violence (a continuous measure)
5. The total score on the Cormier–Lang Criminal History scale, which assigns a numeric value to the severity and frequency of criminal charges (Harris, Rice, et al., 2015), summed across all the postindex incidents of domestic violence (a continuous measure)

Another outcome that interests the criminal justice system is how soon an individual might commit a new offense (e.g., will someone reoffend during a period of conditional release?). Our actuarial risk tools, although constructed with dichotomous recidivism as an outcome, have turned out to be positively correlated with time until a new offense. In Chapter 3, I described these statistics for the ODARA, as well as the limitations of the original measure of men's time at risk to recidivate. When my colleagues and I developed the DVRAG, we created an improved estimate of opportunity to reoffend by manually checking all our available records on time spent in custody and deducting this from the follow-up period. We also examined the number of recidivistic incidents within this time at risk.

What Improves Prediction Over and Above the ODARA?

In the study of 303 men with in-depth file information available, 49% committed domestic assault recidivism, and the ODARA was correlated with dichotomous recidivism (r = .27; Hilton, Harris, Rice, et al., 2008;

for explanations of correlation, accuracy statistics, and effect sizes see the section on AUC and Related Accuracy Statistics in Chapter 2 of this volume). Scores on all the other assessments we tested were also associated with domestic assault recidivism in the sample of 303 men; correlations ranged from .18 (DVSI) to .25 (PCL-R). None, however, passed the (admittedly challenging) test of making an incremental contribution to prediction of dichotomous recidivism once the ODARA was already considered. Using linear regression techniques, we found that PCL-R score significantly improved predictive accuracy for the number of recidivistic incidents, the number involving severe violence, and the total victim injury resulting from recidivism. PCL-R score did not improve the prediction of the Cormier–Lang score for recidivism; DVSI score did (even though it had the smallest correlation with dichotomous recidivism) perhaps because several of its items pertain to offenses incurring charges and convictions. From this procedure, we picked the PCL-R to add to the ODARA because it was the most highly correlated with domestic assault recidivism and the most consistent contributor to improved prediction of the remaining outcome measures. The PCL-R score was also correlated with the item Victim Concern ($r = .21, p < .01$).

As I described earlier, we based all scoring on correctional and criminal justice records. We did not interview individuals involved in the domestic assaults or other informants, but these records themselves often contained material from such interviews. This file-based method was previously used to study interrater reliability and predictive accuracy even for tools that recommend interviews in practice (e.g., Kropp & Hart, 2000). This research method indicates the predictive accuracy of these instruments when scored from file only; it leaves unexplored the question of whether the addition of interviews improves or worsens predictive accuracy.

Definition and Cross-Validation of the In-Depth Assessment

We considered several ways to combine the ODARA and the PCL-R to create a new instrument. We wanted something that would be easy for assessors to fit in with their normal assessment, so we tried simply adding the two scores together. The combined score, however, gave undue weight to the PCL-R, whose potential scores run from 0 to 40, compared with the ODARA, whose maximum possible score is 13. We also considered a decision-tree approach in which the ODARA score would be calculated first and the PCL-R scores within each ODARA category would be associated with a particular rate of recidivism. The tree, however, would have required so many potential

ODARA/PCL-R categories as to be unwieldy to use and impossible to construct reliably without a sample size in the thousands.

Our search for a valid and parsimonious combination of assessments led us back to a system that weights each item, with a positive or negative score, based on how much the item's presence changes the observed likelihood of recidivism, compared with the base rate (the Nuffield weighting system as used in Harris et al., 1993). That is, we calculated weights (+ or –) for each ODARA item and for the PCL-R score, according to the contribution (and direction) of each item to the prediction of dichotomous recidivism in the DVRAG development sample of 303 men. For each item, values that resulted in no change from the base rate of recidivism were assigned a weight of zero.

We did not base the item weights on the other outcomes (e.g., frequency, severity), but our choice of the PCL-R on the basis of its ability to improve prediction of these outcomes ensured that the eventual in-depth assessment would predict those outcomes too. Indeed, the DVRAG was a significant improvement over the ODARA for every outcome measure in the development sample (Hilton, Harris, Rice, et al., 2008). The AUC for dichotomous recidivism was .71 (95% confidence interval [CI] [.67, .75], $d = .78$), compared with .67 (95% CI [.61, .73], $d = .62$) for the ODARA in this sample. The DVRAG's correlations with the continuous outcome measures ranged from the Cormier–Lang score for postindex domestic assaults ($r = .33$) to the number of postindex domestic assaults ($r = .40$), and all were significantly larger than those for the ODARA in one-tailed tests. The DVRAG was also associated with shorter time at risk ($r = -.23$), similar to the ODARA in this sample ($r = -.21$).

In a new sample of 346 men, all with in-depth assessment information from a corrections file, the DVRAG had an AUC of .70 (95% CI [.64, .75], $d = .75$), a medium effect size, and a marginal improvement over the ODARA, AUC = .65 (95% CI [.59, .71], $d = .55$). In this cross-validation sample, the correlations for the continuous outcome measures ranged from the Cormier–Lang score ($r = .29$) to the number of postindex assaults and victim injury (both *rs* = .40), all medium effect sizes (Rice & Harris, 2005). That is, the cross-validation showed that DVRAG score is related not only to how likely it is that a man will assault his partner again but also to how many assaults will be known to police within a given time frame, how many will involve severe violence, how much injury will occur, and how serious the resulting criminal charges will be.

Possible scores on the DVRAG range from –10 to +41. I provide the scoring instructions, and a scoring sheet that compares the scoring of the

ODARA and DVRAG, in Chapter 7. The Appendix includes a DVRAG scoring practice case.

The next task was to define the DVRAG categories. The DVRAG has a wide range of scores compared with the ODARA. Each ODARA score could easily be considered a category, except for higher scores, which were too uncommon to yield stable risk estimates without some collapsing across scores. The DVRAG is more like the VRAG family of tools (Harris, Rice, et al., 2015), in which scores are divided into categories on the basis of an equal range of scores, except for the highest DVRAG risk category containing a range of scores at which 100% of individuals who reoffended. We observed that the 3% of men in our combined sample of 649 individuals with the highest DVRAG scores all reoffended, leading us to place these scores into the top category and an equivalent number of cases into the lowest category. Remaining categories were created to each capture about 20% of the sample.

Figure 5.1 shows the proportion of men who recidivated within each DVRAG category. As with the ODARA (see Figure 3.3), recidivism increases with each increase in DVRAG category. The norms in the actuarial experience

FIGURE 5.1. Percentage of Men Recidivating as a Function of Domestic Violence Risk Appraisal Guide (DVRAG) Score in the Combined DVRAG Construction and Cross-Validation Samples

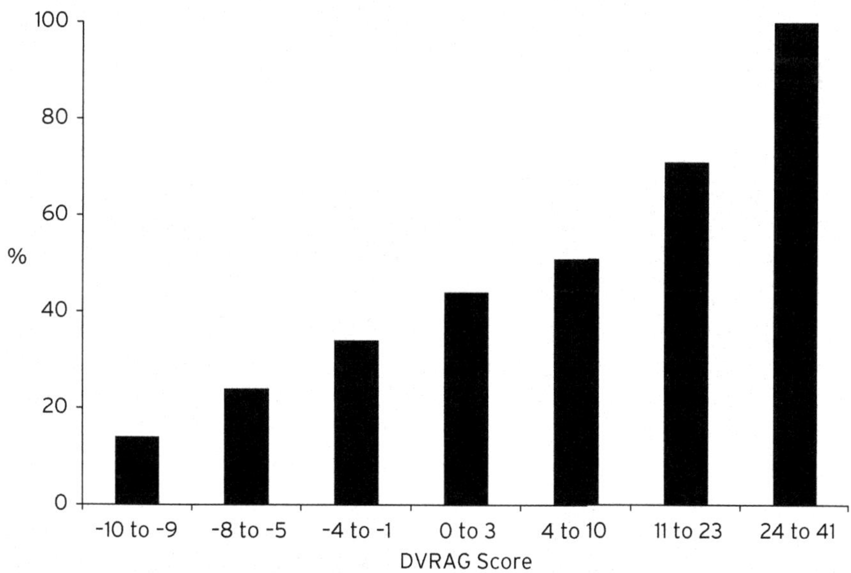

Note. Data from Hilton, Harris, Rice, Houghton, and Eke (2008).

table (Chapter 7, Table 7.2, this volume) show that the lowest DVRAG category comes with an expected recidivism rate of 14% compared with 7% for the lowest category on the ODARA. Thus, the DVRAG may be a poorer tool than the ODARA for relatively low-risk samples. Its intended advantage is to afford more discrimination than the ODARA among the highest risk men. Whereas the ODARA's highest risk category is associated with a large range of scores because of a limited number of cases at this level of risk in the community-based construction sample, the DVRAG has two risk categories that correspond to recidivism rates more than 70%.

In sum, we examined the ability of several risk assessment tools to improve upon the ODARA, but the PCL-R, a diagnostic tool for psychopathy, was superior because of its ability to predict both the occurrence and continuous measures of domestic assault recidivism. A linear combination of the ODARA items and PCL-R score significantly improved prediction over the ODARA score alone. The result was an actuarial risk assessment tool suitable for use when in-depth file information is available, especially when discrimination among relatively high-risk individuals is desired. We named the in-depth risk assessment the Domestic Violence Risk Assessment Guide not only because of its connection to the VRAG family of instruments but also to reflect its similar empirical development, including statistical selection of the strongest unique predictors. Of both practical and theoretical interest, all include measures of criminal history and the PCL-R.

Scoring and Using the DVRAG

The DVRAG is an actuarial instrument and should be scored with close attention to the item criteria and interpreted with reference to the experience table (see Chapter 7, Table 7.2, this volume). Using these scoring criteria, excellent interrater reliability was achieved between research coders and a forensic clinician on 16 individuals (correlation coefficient = .83; Hilton, Harris, Rice, et al., 2008). The standard error of measurement (SEM), which is the average relationship between an observed and true score and is a function of reliability and variability, was 2.2. Thus, on average, an individual would have a less than .05 probability of misclassification by more than one category.

The ODARA and DVRAG together form a system of risk assessment. The ODARA is usually scored at the time of the individual's first contact with the criminal justice system, during or shortly after police contact. During a subsequent presentence or forensic assessment, a probation officer or mental health professional could build on the information in the ODARA by scoring the DVRAG using available in-depth information. The additional discrimination among higher scores that the DVRAG affords can aid correctional and forensic decisions about sentencing, security, release, intervention, and so on. The DVRAG can also be used in these contexts to allocate resources according to risk: broader and more intense interventions for higher risk individuals, less secure and intense supervision for lower risk individuals, and so on. I cover recommendations for implementing a policy of assessment, communication, and forensic decision-making using the ODARA and DVRAG systematically in more detail in Chapter 10.

The DVRAG does require more time and professional resources than the ODARA. Assessors could weigh the costs and benefits of obtaining a reliable PCL-R score on the basis of the initial ODARA score. In the combined DVRAG construction and cross-validation samples of 649 men, more than 50% of individuals who scored in the lowest or second lowest ODARA categories (i.e., scores of 0 or 1) remained in the lowest or second lowest categories, respectively, when scored on the DVRAG. At ODARA scores of 2 or more, there was more dispersion of DVRAG scores, indicating that adding PCL-R conferred relatively more information about risk of recidivism. For ODARA scores of 7 or more, few individuals (14%) were identified as being lower risk by the DVRAG, but a quarter were distinguished as being in the DVRAG's highest risk category. We suggest that assessors score the ODARA first and, whenever the ODARA indicates a score of 2 or more, consider whether their services can be optimized by obtaining a reliable PCL-R score to enable scoring the DVRAG.

VALIDATIONS AND MODIFICATION OF THE DOMESTIC VIOLENCE RISK APPRAISAL GUIDE

The DVRAG requires more resources to score than the ODARA, and perhaps for that reason there have been fewer validation studies to date. In a doctoral dissertation at Alliant International University in 2010, Trinh examined domestic violence recidivism among 64 men attending domestic violence treatment in California. The DVRAG was coded from existing files, and had an average score of 1.67, with observed scores from −10 to +24. The DVRAG predicted domestic violence recidivism after treatment completion, with a large effect size (AUC = .77).

Gray (2012), in a Carleton University master's thesis, retrospectively followed 94 men with a history of assaulting their female marital, cohabiting, or dating partner. In an average 3.6 years after release from a federal

Canadian correctional institution, 13% of men were charged for another domestic assault. The DVRAG was scored independently by two researchers with an inter-rater reliability (intraclass correlation coefficient [ICC], absolute agreement) of .81 and had an average score of 25.59. The DVRAG predicted recidivism with an AUC of .71. This effect was the same as that found for the ODARA; that is, the PCL-R did not improve on the ODARA's predictive validity. Similarly, Rettenberger and Eher (2013) found that the PCL-R did not achieve significant incremental prediction over the ODARA, in a sample of 66 men convicted of domestic sexual offenses and subsequently released from prison in Austria. ODARA and DVRAG risk categories both predicted domestic violence recidivism with an AUC of .71. The DVRAG also predicted violent and general recidivism with AUCs of .70 and .71, respectively.

The lack of studies with sufficiently large samples makes it difficult to ascertain whether the DVRAG's advantage over the ODARA for predicting domestic violence recidivism in relatively high-risk samples will be shown to replicate. Another consideration is that in the Gray (2012) and Rettenberger and Eher (2013) studies, researchers scored the ODARA items, whereas the PCL-R score was extracted from the file as documented by the institutional assessors. In contrast, Moser (2012) scored both the ODARA and a measure of psychopathic traits from files in a master's thesis studying men and women arrested for domestic incidents in New Brunswick, Canada (Moser, 2012). Psychopathic traits significantly added to the ODARA's predictive validity (a combination of psychopathic and borderline personality traits did not; McTague, 2018). Perhaps predictive accuracy is affected by fidelity to scoring protocols, and researchers may adhere more closely to scoring instructions than clinicians do.

I hope that future research will evaluate the predictive accuracy of the DVRAG as scored entirely by either researchers or clinicians. As a psychological assessment, the PCL-R can be used by a qualified professional to diagnose psychopathy (Hare, 2003). As a risk assessment item, the PCL-R, scored from either an interview and file information or file information alone, predicts violent recidivism, including domestic assault recidivism (Harris, Rice, et al., 2015). The DVRAG research team had a well-established record of demonstrating that using file information alone to score the PCL-R produces good predictive accuracy. To use PCL-R score as a DVRAG item (and bearing in mind reservations about scoring fidelity), it should be scored by assessors who can demonstrate good interrater reliability (i.e., correlation coefficients of at least ICC = .80).

Scoring the DVRAG With PCL-R Facet 4

Studies of the PCL-R factors and facets have helped simplify violence risk assessment, including in the VRAG-R. For example, the VRAG-R uses just the five PCL-R items representing Facet 4, Antisociality: poor behavior controls, early behavior problems, juvenile delinquency, revocation of conditional release, and criminal versatility (Rice et al., 2013).

Together with Vern Quinsey, I tested a similar approach for the DVRAG, substituting the PCL-R score with the Facet 4 score. We called the modified tool the DVRAG-4 (Hilton & Quinsey, 2017). Each Facet 4 item is scored from 0 to 2, according to the PCL-R criteria (Hare, 2003). The average Facet 4 score in the DVRAG construction sample of 303 men was 3.06, with a range of 0 to 9. We gave a weight of plus or minus 1 point for each (rounded) 5% difference from the sample base rate observed for Facet 4 scores. The DVRAG-4 predicted domestic violence recidivism in this construction sample (AUC = .71). Then we tested the DVRAG-4 in the cross-validation sample of 346 men, where it had a large predictive effect (AUC = .73). This result represented a statistically significant improvement over the ODARA. I hope that the DVRAG-4, being easier to score, will encourage wider use and validation research.

Calibration

No tests of the DVRAG's calibration in a new sample have yet been conducted. Future research should pay particular attention to the reproducibility of the extreme risk categories, which were defined on the basis of containing only 3% of the sample each and could be unstable across samples.

DOMESTIC-SPECIFIC PREDICTION AND EXPLANATION

One might expect that domestic-specific variables would be most helpful to discerning domestic-specific recidivism. However, the research my colleagues and I conducted found that this was not so. When we first ventured into the field of domestic violence risk assessment, we wondered whether a risk assessment specifically for this outcome was needed at all. We had just found that the VRAG had a large effect size for the prediction of violent recidivism by men who seriously assaulted their female domestic partner (Hilton et al., 2001). We later found that the VRAG and PCL-R predicted domestic assault well in the DVRAG development and construction samples.

Their predictive accuracy was better than the domestic violence assessment tools (DA, SARA, and DVSI) that had AUCs of .56 to .61 and smaller correlations with the continuous outcomes (.14 to .27).

We were not the first to discover the relatively modest ability of domestic-specific risk assessment tools to distinguish between individuals with and without recidivism in a sample of men with a history of domestic offenses. In a 1-year follow up of men convicted of domestic violence or homicide, Grann and Wedin (2002) found that SARA total score predicted subsequent convictions for violence, sexual assault, threats, or no-contact violations against an intimate partner, with an AUC of .59. In the same time frame, however, the PCL-R achieved an AUC of .71, and the VRAG, .75, both significantly more accurate than the domestic-specific assessment (i.e., falling above the upper 95% confidence limit). Then a meta-analysis of 19 studies examining predictive accuracy of domestic violence or general violence risk assessment tools found that the latter yielded higher effect sizes than the former (Hanson, Helmus, & Bourgon, 2007), raising the question as to whether domestic-specific assessments offer any value above general violence risk assessments.

When we developed the DVRAG, we wanted to be sure that we gave domestic-specific variables every chance to be selected as predictors. So we also examined, in addition to total scores on the DA, SARA, and DVSI, individual items from these assessments that were not already covered by DVRAG items. Many of the items we tested concerned prior assaults, conditional releases or no contact orders, substance abuse, threats, victim fear, or assault during pregnancy, all of which are DVRAG items. Others measured aspects of jealousy, stalking, psychological abuse, sexual abuse, escalation of violence, violence toward pets or property, weapon use in prior domestic incidents, suicidal history, separation from the partner, and the partner's support network. We tested nearly 50 other variables from these assessments or elsewhere in our coding manual because we or other professionals had thought them promising. Some had been considered in the ODARA construction research but failed to meet the statistical selection criterion. This time, we tested whether any of these variables were correlated with dichotomous domestic assault recidivism in the combined samples of 649 men used to develop and cross-validate the DVRAG. Three SARA items did predict recidivism: recent employment problems, extreme minimization or denial of assault history, and personality disorder with anger, impulsivity, or behavioral instability. However, they were highly correlated with PCL-R score and did not improve prediction over the DVRAG.

Only one other variable—stalking the index partner by following her—had a small, significant correlation with recidivism ($r = .08$); however, once all the DVRAG items were accounted for, stalking did not add any predictive accuracy. There is evidence from studies led by Angela Eke that stalking is a risky circumstance in itself (e.g., Eke, Hilton, Meloy, et al., 2011; Eke et al., 2014; see Researcher Profile 5.2). To date, though, we have not been able to conclude that stalking contributes uniquely to the risk of domestic violence recidivism over the ODARA or DVRAG. Not all the characteristics typical of men who commit domestic violence predict their recidivism. Childhood variables are commonly thought to be associated with domestic violence, and the research literature does indicate that men who report childhood exposure to violence or other abuse are also more likely to assault their partners, but there is little evidence so far that they predict recidivism (e.g., Fowler et al., 2016; see Exhibit 1.1 in Chapter 1). These variables were present in at least 200 cases in the DVRAG samples, but they were not related to domestic assault recidivism.

THE PREDICTIVE POWER OF GENERAL ANTISOCIALITY

Could there be some worthwhile variables that we had overlooked, pertaining either to the domestic relationship or to victim characteristics that were not measured on our coding form? After developing the DVRAG, we were so impressed with the performance of the PCL-R and VRAG that we explored further tests of the predictive power of general antisociality.

A Search for Additional Predictive Power

First, we examined any remaining variables that were coded as present for at least 200 men and associated with domestic violence recidivism. The few such variables predicted general violent recidivism in previous research: procriminal attitudes, attitudes unfavorable to convention, and suspension or expulsion from elementary school. Only one improved upon the DVRAG; that is, having been arrested before the age of 16 predicted recidivism in three of 15 tests (total injury, in both the cross-validation and combined samples, and the Cormier-Lang score for recidivism in the cross-validation sample only; Hilton, Harris, Rice, et al., 2008).

General Criminal Recidivism

Our next step was to explore the ability of the Level of Service Inventory (LSI; Andrews & Bonta, 2001) to predict domestic assault recidivism. The LSI is used to assess factors relating to an individual's offending behavior as well as to identify individuals at risk for criminal recidivism in general. There is abundant evidence that the LSI is associated with general criminal recidivism (Bonta & Andrews, 2017), and some evidence already showed it was associated with domestic violence (Hendricks et al., 2006). Men in our in-depth samples almost always had a version of the LSI on file because it is used routinely in the Ontario correctional system. Every LSI had been scored in the field, usually by probation officers with access to the case file, criminal records, the individual being assessed, and sometimes an interview with the partner. In contrast, other assessments in our research were scored item-by-item by research assistants using only archival information. Because the LSI was obtained in a systematically different way from the rest of our measures, we did not include it in our search for assessments to improve prediction over the ODARA.

In the whole sample of 649 men, we used the first LSI scores recorded in the correctional files if (for recidivists) it was recorded before the calendar year of the first recidivistic incident. The mean LSI score in the resulting sample of 406 men was 9.88 ($SD = 6.61$), and it had a medium predictive effect for domestic assault recidivism, AUC = .67. LSI score was also strongly positively correlated with the ODARA, PCL-R, and DVRAG with large correlation coefficients of .54 to .58, and it had smaller correlations (up to .34) with the remaining domestic violence risk assessment tools. In regression analyses, the LSI did not significantly improve upon the predictive validity of the ODARA, DVRAG, PCL-R, or VRAG, but it did improve upon the SARA, DVSI, and DA (according to Wald statistics that ranged from 8.24 to 14.19). Thus, it appeared that the nonactuarial domestic risk assessment tools could be improved by adding an established assessment of the risk of general criminal recidivism.

We later tested a version of the LSI in a study of incarcerated men with a history of domestic offending (Hilton et al., 2010). Again, the LSI did not significantly improve the ODARA. It was, however, a comparable predictor of postrelease violent and general recidivism.

The corollary to this conclusion is that a risk assessment that predicts domestic violence recidivism well should also be able to predict general recidivism. In Chapter 4 and earlier in this chapter, I showed how the ODARA and DVRAG are, in fact, associated with nondomestic recidivism. In the DVRAG construction and validation samples, the best predictor of charges for any violent recidivism was the nine-item modified VRAG, $r = .30$; the ODARA was comparable, $r = .27$. The best predictor of general recidivism, defined by criminal charges of any kind, was also the VRAG, $r = .37$, and the ODARA had a small predictive effect, $r = .20$, $p < .001$.

Individual Antisociality Versus Neighborhood-Level Explanation

In the Chapter 2 section on Risk Assessment for Domestic Violence Treatment, I argued that domestic violence interventions must identify and target criminogenic needs; that is, they must attempt to change characteristics or behaviors that are statistically, and potentially causally, related to violent behavior. Identifying the causes of domestic violence is, therefore, key to designing and evaluating interventions. As I described in Chapter 1, no one (including me) has fully articulated a causal theory of domestic violence with adequate explanatory power. The results I have described in this chapter, however, show how strong general antisociality variables are at predicting men's domestic assault recidivism. I hypothesize that a complete explanation of the most frequent and severe domestic violence, particularly that by men against women, will have to include general tendencies toward antisocial behavior, and psychopathy in particular. The strong association between PCL-R score (measured up to and including the time of the index assault) and violent outcome (occurring after the index) supports this hypothesis.

My colleagues and I tested this hypothesis in the DVRAG construction and cross-validation samples. We omitted 102 men whose index assault did not take place in their home or for whom we were otherwise unable to match to a residence in a school catchment area. This match was needed because we used Canadian census data aggregated to the level of elementary school catchment area (D. Johnson, 2005) to measure neighborhood characteristics theoretically related to domestic violence (Harris, Hilton, & Rice, 2011). Neighborhood poverty or socioeconomic disadvantage has been associated with higher rates of domestic violence, at both the individual and sociocultural level (e.g., Fox & Benson, 2006; Wright, 2015). Neighborhood disadvantage could help explain domestic violence through its effects on lower social cohesion, unemployment, lower education, and housing instability. The census information we linked to each individual's neighborhood included: percentage born outside of Canada, the United States, or the United Kingdom; percentage speaking English or French as a first language; percentage with a high school diploma or some college education; percentage of single-parent families with children; percentage unemployed; percentage moving home in the past 5 years; average household income; average school enrollment; and proportion of school enrollment that is male. This level of information offers an alternative theoretical perspective on domestic violence in contrast to individual-level characteristics.

In this study, we compared neighborhood disadvantage with general antisociality measured at the individual level by PCL-R score, number of antisocial personality diagnostic criteria present, having been suspended or expelled from elementary school, having been sentenced to custody for 30 days or more, and total injury caused in nondomestic violent offenses, using our data coded from police and correctional files. We also tested individual attitudes and values, including these variables coded from files: antisocial attitudes or values, attitudes unfavorable to convention, sexual jealousy, minimization of domestic violence, and having had domestic violence treatment. A fourth domain came from relationship variables: length of relationship, age difference, cohabitation, number of children, partner's children from a previous relationship, and socioeconomic status.

We analyzed the data using regression methods similar to those used to construct the ODARA and DVRAG, only in this study we were attempting to statistically explain the frequency of domestic violence committed by individual men. Our outcome measure was the total number of domestic assaults committed at index, preindex, or postindex incidents. Variables from each of the four domains (neighborhood disadvantage, general antisociality, attitudes and values, and relationships) made a statistically significant contribution to the model of total domestic violence. General antisociality had the strongest independent and incremental association. In addition, the interaction of antisociality and neighborhood variables made a significant contribution. That is, the effect of antisociality was greater in higher risk neighborhoods. We concluded that although neighborhood, relationship, and other variables may help explain the context of violent behavior, general antisociality carries much of the explanatory variance in men's domestic violence (Harris et al., 2011).

Implications for Intervention

It would be wise to reserve the most intensive interventions for individuals who score relatively high on the PCL-R and, by extension, the DVRAG. Community treatment programs appear unlikely to recruit men with psychopathic traits, leading some observers to comment that routine measurement of psychopathy is hard to justify in such settings (e.g., Huss & Langhinrichsen-Rohling, 2006). Others prefer psychopathy scales on omnibus psychological assessments that have broader clinical utility (e.g., Rock et al., 2013).

Psychopathic traits raise the possibility that the highest risk individuals will charm their way out of treatment or even be excluded from community-based treatment programs (e.g., Rock et al., 2013) without further intervention. For these reasons, I recommend routine assessment of risk in domestic violence treatment programs using the DVRAG or DVRAG-4 where possible.

CONCLUSION

In this chapter, I have reviewed all the empirical evidence of the DVRAG's ability to discriminate between cases of domestic violence recidivism and nonrecidivism, its intended purpose of improving prediction in relatively high-risk samples, and its contribution to the understanding of men's domestic violence by the incorporation of more in-depth and theory-driven information. More research is always needed to replicate existing findings, and this need is particularly present for calibration studies of the DVRAG, validation of the DVRAG-4, and the continual search for new predictors, or new ways to measure a construct that captures unique predictive power.

I know that publishing research articles alone will do little to improve the lives of individuals affected by domestic violence. In the next two chapters, I provide the entire scoring instructions and interpretation materials for the ODARA (Chapter 6) and DVRAG (Chapter 7). Then in Part III, I look at other considerations for integrating domestic violence risk assessment into effective risk management, including the importance of research evidence (Chapter 8), how to communicate risk assessment results in a way that optimizes their chances of being understood and influencing vital decisions (Chapter 9), and the need to integrate research into criminal justice policies and community victim services (Chapter 10).

POINTS TO REMEMBER

- Several other assessments of violence risk and general antisociality were tested in the ODARA construction sample of men with in-depth information, and the PCL-R (a well-established measure of psychopathy) produced the most consistent improvement in prediction.
- The Domestic Violence Risk Appraisal Guide (DVRAG) provides an algorithm for combining the ODARA items with the PCL-R score, using weights based on the DVRAG construction sample.
- The DVRAG was designed to assess risk of injury and severity of assaults, not just the likelihood of recidivism, and yields a moderate effect size for all these outcomes.
- Assessors who can obtain a reliable PCL-R score should consider using the DVRAG or DVRAG-4 for individuals who score 2 or higher on the ODARA.
- This research adds to existing evidence that general antisociality influences and explains a wide range of antisocial and violent behavior.

QUESTIONS TO CONSIDER

1. Name the two assessment tools that are combined in the DVRAG.
2. State the five outcomes used in the DVRAG development research.
3. In what circumstances is the ODARA a suitable tool to use? When would it be more appropriate to use the DVRAG?
4. What steps were taken to explore the contribution of general antisociality to domestic violence? Why do you think antisociality increases the risk of domestic violence recidivism?
5. How would you incorporate the DVRAG into the intake, assessment, and case prioritization of a domestic violence treatment program? What would be your greatest challenge in doing so, and how might you overcome it?

RESEARCHER PROFILE 5.1
ADELLE FORTH, PHD

I am not directly involved in intimate partner violence research, but I study individuals who engage in a substantial amount of intimate partner violence (IPV), and these are individuals with psychopathic traits. I got involved in this as a third-year psychology undergraduate at the University of British Columbia. I was on track to go to law school and become a lawyer (I have a twin sister and our plan was to become lawyers and open our own law firm). But my interests changed when I took a forensic psychology class with Robert Hare. On the first day, Bob stated, "I don't know that much about forensic psychology, but what I do know a lot about are psychopaths." The more Bob described what psychopathy was and the research he was doing, the more fascinated I became. I dropped the lawyer idea and went to graduate school to get an MA in biopsychology and PhD in forensic psychology with Bob as my supervisor. These programs had a large emphasis on experimental design and statistics. Having this background influenced me to design methodologically rigorous studies to answer questions about psychopathy.

My specific focus has changed over time, and depending on the interests of my graduate students. Initially, I was interested in the manifestation of psychopathic traits in youth and community samples and examined the reliability and validity of both self-report and rater measures of psychopathy.

My methods have ranged from experimental tasks to online surveys using longitudinal and cross-sectional designs. My varied research questions have included cognitive and affective processing deficits, motivations for violence, reoffending rates in psychopathic youth, stability of psychopathic traits, and their association with perceptions of victim vulnerability.

My most influential work has been the Hare Psychopathy Checklist: Youth Version (PCL: YV), an assessment measure published in 2003 with my coauthors David Kasson and Robert Hare. The goal was to develop a measure of psychopathic traits to provide researchers with a common matrix and to encourage systematic research on the construct of psychopathy in youth. The PCL: YV is an expert-rater format that uses a multidomain and multisource approach to assess psychopathic traits. It has been used by researchers around the world to help identify casual mechanisms, delineate psychobiological correlates, and develop effective early intervention programs.

I think we are on the cusp of understanding how both genetics and environmental factors impact the development of psychopathic traits, and this understanding will aid efforts to prevent the development of psychopathy. There are now numerous labs around the world with many outstanding young researchers, and international and multidisciplinary collaborations are emerging that will provide a more diverse understanding of psychopathy.

Currently, I do research with individuals whose lives have been affected by psychopaths. Their voices have been neglected in previous research about psychopathy. These individuals can provide a rich source of information. An important example is the high rate of IPV reported by those in an intimate relationship with a psychopath, and the many mental and physical health consequences. We are now conducting interviews with women who were in an intimate partner relationship with a psychopathic individual to further examine the experiences of abuse and its impact and identify better ways to address the needs of the survivor at both the individual and societal level. I'm also part of Carleton University's dog therapy program that provides support to students who are stressed, along with my friendly flat-coated retriever, Zak. Zak's office hours at the university are much more popular than mine!

About the Researcher

Dr. Forth is an associate professor in the Department of Psychology at Carleton University.

RESEARCHER PROFILE 5.2
ANGELA WYATT EKE, PhD

I've always had an interest in both psychology and law. I focused on psychology as well as criminology during my bachelor of science degree at the University of Toronto. While there, I attended a volunteer fair and signed up to work in corrections. It was such a valuable experience! I learned about the practical side of psychology and participated in group work and individual therapy. I went on to complete my master's and PhD in psychology at York University. I volunteered many hours during my undergraduate and graduate days, later completing a graduate research practicum in corrections. Throughout this time, my interest in applied research developed. It was exciting to incorporate research into practice while also developing research ideas based on real-life settings. This led to my focus on operational research such as risk assessment and case management in stalking, intimate partner violence (IPV), and child sexual exploitation.

Through my undergraduate research supervisor, Professor Lester Krames, I met an Ontario Provincial Police (OPP) officer named Kate Lines. She was one of the first police criminal profilers in Canada, and she led the development of the Behavioural Sciences Section within the OPP (now called the Behavioural Sciences and Analysis Section). Kate hired me during my master's studies as an analytical assistant and research assistant within the Provincial Violent Crime Linkage and Analysis Section. I've worked with the OPP ever since and was appointed as a Member of the Order of Merit of the Police Forces in 2017.

The first research I conducted in the area of IPV related to stalking (criminal harassment in Canadian law). Although not all stalking victims are harassed by someone they know, a majority do involve current or prior intimate partners. My master's thesis examined the characteristics of these offenses as well as the psychological and social impact of being stalked. During this research, I worked directly with individuals who had been stalked. I learned so much from each of them, both professionally and personally. This work lay the foundation for my continued interest in stalking and IPV.

Although I work within a police environment, I'm in daily contact with colleagues from clinical settings, academia, and other government agencies. I have the good fortune of collaborating on research with great colleagues. When you bring together individuals from multiple environments, you can build projects that have direct relevance across areas; in addition, you're working with a range of expertise and experience, which adds substantially to the quality of the work.

In 2000, I had the opportunity to work on a collaborative project between the OPP and the Mental Health Centre Penetanguishene (now the Waypoint Centre for Mental Health Care) examining IPV risk assessment. The goal of this project was to develop a risk measure for use by frontline police officers; this led to the development of the ODARA, a tool widely used today. Individuals involved in this study, including Drs. Zoe Hilton, Marnie Rice and Grant Harris, became close colleagues. Across the years, we extended our research to child abuse within families, stalking, and other aspects of IPV. I miss our colleagues Drs. Harris and Rice. Their work in the area of violence and risk assessment has been the cornerstone to innumerable additional projects and developments in our field, and their kindness and openness as mentors had a significant impact on so many researchers and practitioners.

About the Researcher

Dr. Eke is the research coordinator for the Criminal Behaviour Analysis Unit, Ontario Provincial Police, and an adjunct faculty member at Laurentian University.

6 SCORING MANUAL FOR THE ONTARIO DOMESTIC ASSAULT RISK ASSESSMENT

This chapter provides instructions on how to decide whether to use the Ontario Domestic Assault Risk Assessment (ODARA), how to score the items, and how to adjust scores when information for one or more items is ambiguous. It also answers some common questions about item scoring. I include a sample ODARA report, an interpretation table of ODARA scores for men being assessed, and graphs to aid interpretation (see Figures 6.1 & 6.2). I encourage readers to refer to other chapters in this volume for details of the rationale and method of the ODARA's development (Chapters 2 and 3), validation studies across varied populations (Chapter 4), controversial issues in risk assessment with implications for the ODARA (Chapter 8), how the ODARA is used in cross-sector communication and implementation (Chapters 9 and 10), and other questions and answers about the ODARA's use (Chapter 11). I use person-first language where appropriate. For clarity in the scoring criteria, however,

---

Portions of this chapter have been adapted from *Ontario Domestic Assault Risk Assessment General Scoring Criteria*, by Mental Health Centre Penetanguishene Research Department, 2005. Copyright 2005 by Mental Health Centre Penetanguishene Research Department.

https://doi.org/10.1037/0000223-007
Domestic Violence Risk Assessment: Tools for Effective Prediction and Management, Second Edition, by N. Z. Hilton

FIGURE 6.1. How Does the Individual Being Assessed Rank Among Men With a Police Record of Domestic Violence?

ODARA score = 0: According to the client's responses and the information available in the police and criminal records, the individual being assessed scores 0 on the ODARA. This score represents the lowest of seven risk categories. One out of 10 men with a police record of domestic violence scores 0.

ODARA score = 1: According to the client's responses and the information available in the police and criminal records, the individual being assessed scores 1 on the ODARA. This score represents the second lowest of seven risk categories. One quarter of men with a police record of domestic violence scores 1 or lower.

ODARA score = 2: According to the client's responses and the information available in the police and criminal records, the individual being assessed scores 2 on the ODARA. Half of men with a police record of domestic violence score 2 or lower.

ODARA score = 3: According to the client's responses and the information available in the police and criminal records, the individual being assessed scores 3 on the ODARA. This score represents the second lowest of seven risk categories. Seven out of 10 men with a police record of domestic violence score 3 or lower.

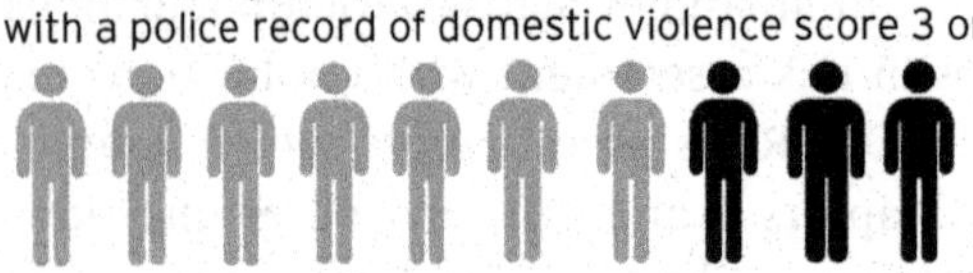

ODARA score = 4: According to the client's responses and the information available in the police and criminal records, the individual being assessed scores 4 on the ODARA. This score represents the second lowest of seven risk categories. Eight out of 10 men with a police record of domestic violence score 4 or lower.

FIGURE 6.1. How Does the Individual Being Assessed Rank Among Men With a Police Record of Domestic Violence? (*Continued*)

ODARA score = 5–6: According to the client's responses and the information available in the police and criminal records, the individual being assessed scores 5 (or 6) on the ODARA. This score represents the second highest of seven risk categories. Nine out of 10 men with a police record of domestic violence score 6 or lower.

ODARA score = 7–13: According to the client's responses and the information available in the police and criminal records, the individual being assessed scores 7 (or higher) on the ODARA. This score represents the highest of seven risk categories. Fewer than one out of 10 men with a police record of domestic violence score in this category.

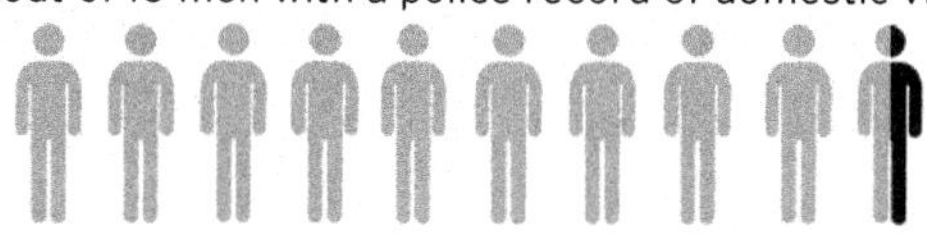

Note. Reprinted from *Risk Assessment for Domestically Violent Men: Tools for Criminal Justice, Offender Intervention, and Victim Services* (p. 206), by N. Z. Hilton, G. T. Harris, & M. E. Rice, 2010, American Psychological Association (https://doi.org/10.1037/12066-000). Copyright 2010 by the American Psychological Association.

I use *perpetrator* to refer to the individual who has assaulted a partner and whose risk is being assessed and either *partner* or *victim* to refer to the partner who has been assaulted. The person being assessed is the perpetrator.

IDENTIFYING THE INDEX ASSAULT

The *index assault* is the most recent incident known to the police in which the individual engaged in violence against a domestic or dating partner. The index assault requires physical contact with the partner or a credible threat of death with a weapon in hand in the partner's presence. Criminal charges do not have to be laid for a domestic incident to qualify as the index assault. In the ODARA development research, however, research coders had to be confident, on the basis of evidence in the police report, that an act of physical contact with the partner had been committed or a credible threat of death with a weapon in hand in the presence of the partner. Incidents that research coders did not agree on were excluded; often, an earlier incident that clearly met the eligibility criteria could be found. In practice, therefore, if the most recent incident does not clearly meet the eligibility criteria, an

FIGURE 6.2. How Likely Is the Individual Being Assessed to Commit Domestic Violence Recidivism?

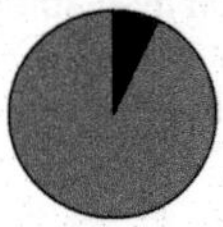

ODARA score = 0: 7% of such men with a police record of domestic violence commit another assault against their partner (or, in some cases, a future partner) that comes to the attention of the police, within an average of about 5 years.

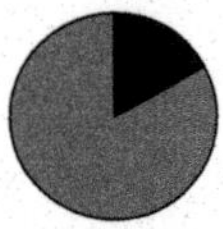

ODARA score = 1: 17% of such men with a police record of domestic violence commit another assault against their partner (or, in some cases, a future partner) that comes to the attention of the police, within an average of about 5 years.

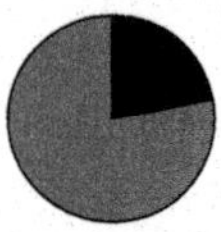

ODARA score = 2: 22% of such men with a police record of domestic violence commit another assault against their partner (or, in some cases, a future partner) that comes to the attention of the police, within an average of about 5 years.

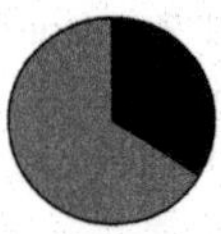

ODARA score = 3: 34% of such men with a police record of domestic violence commit another assault against their partner (or, in some cases, a future partner) that comes to the attention of the police, within an average of about 5 years.

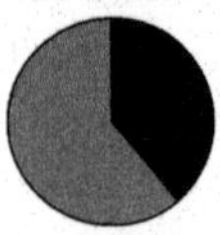

ODARA score = 4: 39% of such men with a police record of domestic violence commit another assault against their partner (or, in some cases, a future partner) that comes to the attention of the police, within an average of about 5 years.

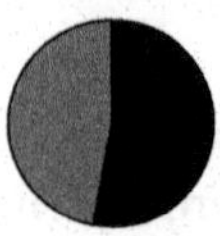

ODARA score = 5–6: 53% of such men with a police record of domestic violence commit another assault against their partner (or, in some cases, a future partner) that comes to the attention of the police, within an average of about 5 years.

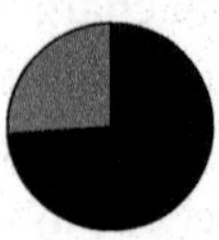

ODARA score = 7–13: 74% of such men with a police record of domestic violence commit another assault against their partner (or, in some cases, a future partner) that comes to the attention of the police, within an average of about 5 years.

Note. ODARA = Ontario Domestic Assault Risk Assessment. Reprinted from *Risk Assessment for Domestically Violent Men: Tools for Criminal Justice, Offender Intervention, and Victim Services* (p. 207), by N. Z. Hilton, G. T. Harris, & M. E. Rice, 2010, American Psychological Association (https://doi.org/10.1037/12066-000). Copyright 2010 by the American Psychological Association.

earlier incident meeting the criteria can be used as the index assault. All ODARA items are scored based on events up to and including the identified index assault.

The index assault typically includes one police occurrence report. For a cluster of assaults reported at one time to the police, the most recent eligible assault and all other eligible assaults against the same partner that occurred in the 23 hours 59 minutes preceding it count as the index assault. Any assault occurring at least 24 hours before the most recent assault should be counted as a preindex assault. This cluster rule also applies to identifying preindex domestic and nondomestic incidents.

DEFINING RECIDIVISM

During the research, only postindex occurrences of violence against a domestic partner met our definition of domestic violence recidivism. In a few cases, the criminal record indicated a charge of assault against a partner, but the research coders did not have the police occurrence report that described the acts of violence; these charges met the definition of domestic violence recidivism. The criteria we used to code postindex acts of violence were broadly based on the physical violence subscale of the Conflict Tactics Scales (Straus et al., 1996). Any of the following acts were included as violence: held the partner down; threw something at the partner that could hurt; twisted the partner's arm or hair; pushed or shoved the partner; grabbed the partner (includes pulled and dragged); slapped the partner (includes struck the partner); other minor violence (e.g., shook the partner); punched the partner with a fist or hit the partner with something that could hurt; choked the partner (includes grabbed by neck or throat, put into a headlock); slammed the partner against wall; "beat up"; burned or scalded the partner on purpose; kicked the partner; used a knife or gun on the partner (i.e., actual or attempted contact with the partner's body; includes discharging a gun while pointing it at the partner, threat of physical harm with weapon in hand); and other severe violence (e.g., picked up and threw the partner, head-butted, pushed down the stairs, bit). In addition, any use of force (by any means) to coerce the partner into having sexual contact when the partner did not want to was included as violence.

The same criteria for violence were used to code preindex domestic and nondomestic violence. I advise using the same criteria when assessing a woman who has assaulted a partner.

GATHERING NECESSARY INFORMATION

Sometimes little information is available about the most recent incident, and more information should be sought before the index assault is identified. The perpetrator's prior police record or criminal history is essential information, and anyone conducting an assessment for use in criminal justice or intervention purposes should postpone scoring the ODARA until this information is obtained. It is also advisable to interview the partner or obtain information from a documented victim interview, especially about either partner's children. The absence of information is not normally a reason to select a different incident as the index assault, and it is always a reason to consider the feasibility of obtaining more documentation about the case.

SCORING ITEMS

Some ODARA items are scored with reference to events occurring at the index assault. Others are scored on the basis of events occurring before the index assault. Information pertaining to events that occurred on a separate occasion after the index assault is never used to score the ODARA. Each ODARA item is scored 0 or 1, and the total score is the sum of the item scores. Thus, the range of possible scores on the ODARA is 0 to 13.

Item 1: Pre-Index Domestic Assault in a Police or Criminal Record

For the purposes of scoring the ODARA, a domestic incident is defined as one in which the person being assessed assaulted a current or previous domestic cohabiting partner, the partner's children, or both, and that is recorded in a police occurrence report or criminal record. A domestic partner is defined as a person that the perpetrator is or was married to, is or was in a common-law relationship with, or lives or did live with for any length of time.

All of the following must be present:

- an act of violence (as defined above) carried out by the person being assessed,
- an incident that occurred on a separate occasion before the index assault, and
- police involvement or a subsequent report made to the police.

If any one of these criteria is absent, then score 0 for the item, even if every other criterion is present. These criteria are all required.

At least one of the following must be present:

- a victim who is a current or previous domestic partner of the person being assessed, or
- a victim who is the child of the perpetrator's current or previous domestic partner.

Either of these two criteria must be present to score 1 for the item. They do not both have to be present. If neither of these criteria is met, then score 0 for the item.

Do not include

- the index assault;
- incidents involving only pets or property;
- incidents reported in a medical record, civil or family court, or restraining order that are not recorded in a police occurrence report or criminal record; or
- incidents involving only strangers, acquaintances, friends, parents, siblings, other family members, or police officers.

Frequently Asked Question

Question. The perpetrator came to the attention of police for the first time on the night that the index assault occurred. During the investigation, the victim reported two other domestic assaults, one occurring the same afternoon, and one occurring the week before. Do these other assaults count as preindex domestic incidents, or are they all part of the index assault?

Answer. The assault taking place the week before can be used to score Pre-Index Domestic Assault, provided that the assault is documented in the police record as a discrete incident occurring on a specific date. The cluster rule applies here (see the earlier section on Identifying the Index Assault).

Item 2: Pre-Index Nondomestic Assault in a Police or Criminal Record

For the purposes of scoring the ODARA, a *nondomestic incident* is defined as one in which the person being assessed assaulted any person other than their current or previous domestic partner or the partner's children, and which is recorded in a police occurrence report or criminal record.

All of the following must be present:

- an act of violence as defined above, carried out by the person being assessed;
- an incident that occurred on a separate occasion before the index assault;
- police involvement or subsequent report made to the police; and
- a victim who is any person other than a current or previous domestic partner of the person being assessed or the partner's children.

If any one of these criteria is absent, then score 0 for the item, even if every other criterion is present. These criteria are all required.

Do not include

- the index assault,
- incidents involving only pets or property, or
- incidents involving only a current or previous domestic partner of the person being assessed or the partner's child.

Frequently Asked Question

Question. The perpetrator assaulted his mother, who lives in a basement suite. Does this incident count as domestic or nondomestic?

Answer. An assault on the perpetrator's mother, or any other member of his family of origin, counts as nondomestic for the purposes of scoring the ODARA. In the ODARA construction research and in validation studies conducted by members of the original ODARA research team, violence against a dating partner was also counted as nondomestic.

Item 3: Pre-Index Custodial Sentence of 30 Days or More

A custodial sentence includes only the final disposition handed down by the court for a criminal offense. It is not necessary for the person to have served the entire sentence, in order to score 1 for this item.

All of the following must be present:

- a sentence handed down before the index assault;
- a sentence resulting in incarceration;
- a sentence of 30 days or more; and
- actual admission to training school, youth custody, jail, federal correctional facility, or provincial or state correctional facility.

If any one of these criteria is absent, then score 0 for the item, even if every other criterion is present. These criteria are all required.

The custodial sentence need not have been given for a domestic offense; sentences for a nondomestic offense or any other criminal conviction should be included. Sentences that are served for any continuous or intermittent period should be included, as well as sentences that were not entirely (but at least partially) served in custody, as long as the total number of days in the custodial disposition handed down by the court was at least 30.

Do not include

- the sentence handed down for the index assault,
- time spent in a police holding cell or detained in a psychiatric hospital if not part of a sentence following conviction, or
- time spent in custody awaiting trial unless the sentence is stated as including time served (which may be a statutory requirement in some jurisdictions).

Frequently Asked Questions

Question. The perpetrator's criminal record shows a conditional or suspended sentence of 12 months. Can I use this sentence to score Pre-Index Custodial Sentence?

Answer. No. The criterion of actual admission into custody must be met. Do not count sentences that are served entirely in the community.

Question. The perpetrator was held in custody for 6 months before sentencing and then received a sentence of "1 day plus time served." Can I use this sentence to score Pre-Index Custodial Sentence?

Answer. Yes. If this disposition were specified as 1 day and 6 months or documented as "1 day and 6 months (time served)," then the total sentence is more than 30 days. It is the sentence that counts, not the number of days spent in custody after the sentence was handed down. If, however, the remand time is not specified in the sentence (e.g., the disposition is documented as, "1 day"), then the criteria for Pre-Index Custodial Sentence are not met.

Question. In my jurisdiction, a sentence to probation has an explicit custodial sentence attached to it that is invoked for a breach of probation. If I see that a perpetrator has been on probation, should I score this information under Pre-Index Custodial Sentence?

Answer. If the underlying sentence was for at least 30 days and was not explicitly a suspended sentence and resulted in custody, then yes. If any of these three conditions is not met, then the criteria for Pre-Index Custodial Sentence are not met.

Item 4: Failure on Pre-Index Conditional Release

Conditional release includes administrative release, bail, conditional discharge, parole, probation, promise to appear, suspended sentence, or any other occasion on which the perpetrator was at liberty in the community under supervision or other requirement ordered by a criminal court. It also includes no-contact, protection, or restraining orders imposed by a criminal or civil court, police, or other public authority. Some examples of conditional release failures are committing a new criminal offense, failing to appear for court, failing to attend an appointment with a probation officer, drinking when prohibited, having firearms when prohibited, coming to a person's home or workplace when prohibited, or contacting a person when prohibited.

At least one of the following must be present:

- any known violation of the terms of conditional release, whether or not the person being assessed was arrested or charged for it;
- a violation occurring at the time of the index assault or on a separate occasion prior to the index assault; and
- a charge for a criminal offense committed while on a conditional release ordered by a criminal court.

Any one of these criteria must be present to score 1 for the item. Not all the criteria have to be present. If none of these criteria are met, then score 0 for the item.

Do not include

- conditional releases that were obeyed, or
- conditional release failures that occurred on a separate occasion after the index assault.

Frequently Asked Questions

Question. The perpetrator's criminal record shows a conditional or suspended sentence of 12 months and a subsequent revocation of that sentence, resulting in some of that time (less than 30 days) served in a correctional institution. Should I score this information under Failure on Pre-Index Conditional Release or Pre-Index Custodial Sentence?

Answer. Both. This meets the criteria for a known violation of the terms of conditional release and a sentence of 30 days or more that resulted in actual admission to custody.

Question. The perpetrator had a condition to abstain from alcohol while on probation but lapsed and drank while watching a game on TV at a friend's house. Because the perpetrator was remorseful, agreed not to go to that friend's house again, and continued attending a substance use treatment group, the probation officer documented the alcohol use but did not pursue charges for a breach of probation. Does this count as a Failure on Pre-Index Conditional Release?

Answer. Yes. The perpetrator met the criteria for a known violation of the terms of conditional release. Criminal charges or revocation of conditional release are not required.

Item 5: Threat to Physically Harm or Kill at the Index Assault

For the purposes of scoring this item, a *threat* must be a clear indication of physical harm to a person. Normally this indication will be in the form of a specific verbal threat to harm a person physically. In a criminal record, evidence of a threat meeting the criteria for this item would be found in a charge of threatening, criminal threatening, uttering a threat, or terrorizing. Evidence of a physical gesture that is commonly recognized as a threat to harm a person physically can also be used to score this item.

Both of the following must be present:

- a threat to harm any person physically; and
- a threat made during the index assault, whether or not carried out.

These criteria are both required.

At least one of the following must be present:

- a threat made against any person, including police officers; or
- a criminal charge of threatening, uttering threats, or terrorizing.

Either of these criteria must be present to score 1 for the item. They do not both have to be present. If neither of these criteria is met, then score 0 for the item.

Do not include

- threats of emotional harm, financial harm, legal action, or custody dispute;
- threats against pets or property;
- threats of self-harm or suicide; or
- threats made on a separate occasion from the index assault.

Frequently Asked Questions

Question. The male perpetrator saw the female victim talking to another man at a party. Without saying anything, he glared at her in a way that she knew meant he was going to assault her. On their way home, he pulled the car off the road and committed the index assault. Can I use this information to score Threat to Physically Harm or Kill at the Index Assault?

Answer. No. Covert acts, or acts of omission, that are not commonly recognized as a threat cannot be used to score this item, even though the victim may feel that harm is imminent. The same is true for other behavior intended to scare a person without an overt threat. Although a victim may feel threatened by some actions by the perpetrator that cannot be classified as overt threats, in the ODARA development research, only acts that were clearly described as threats to harm a person physically were coded as threats. Similarly, in practice, there needs to be clear and objective evidence of a threat; a verbal threat is the clearest example.

Question. The perpetrator held a knife while sexually assaulting the victim. The victim complied out of fear that the perpetrator would use the knife. Can I use this information to score Threat to Physically Harm or Kill at the Index Assault?

Answer. No. An assault with a weapon is not sufficient evidence that the criteria for a threat were met.

Item 6: Confinement of the Partner at the Index Assault

For the purposes of scoring this item, confinement is defined as any act carried out to physically prevent the victim from leaving the scene of the incident. In most cases, confinement would be scored on the basis of evidence that the perpetrator kept the victim in a room with the exit barred. In a criminal record, evidence to score this item would be found in a charge of unlawful or forcible confinement or kidnapping arising from the index assault, provided the victim is known to be the partner.

In some cases, other acts by the perpetrator that deprived the victim of the ability to leave the scene could result in a criminal charge of unlawful confinement and therefore can be used to score this item (e.g., holding on to the victim while the victim was trying to escape, purposefully standing in the way of an escape route while the victim was trying to escape, removing or destroying the victim's clothing when the victim was trying to escape by going outdoors, forcibly damaging a vehicle or removing the keys while the victim was trying to escape in it). A required element in such cases is that the victim was trying to escape.

All of the following must be present:

- confinement of the partner who is the victim of the index assault;
- an act by which the person being assessed physically attempted to prevent the victim from leaving the location; and
- confinement carried out during the index assault, whether or not the victim eventually left the scene.

If any one of these criteria is absent, then score 0 for the item, even if every other criterion is present. These criteria are all required.

Do not include

- the perpetrator threatening to harm to the victim if the victim leaves,
- ripping out the telephone or cutting the telephone lines, or
- acts of confinement committed on a separate occasion from the index assault.

Frequently Asked Questions

Question. The perpetrator pinned the victim to the wall and punched the victim. The victim was not able to move while this assault took place. Does that count as confinement?

Answer. No. Restraint is not sufficient to conclude that an unlawful act of confinement has taken place. The primary evidence should be physical confinement in a locked room or other place from which the victim cannot escape. If escape is physically possible, a required element for this item is the victim's attempt to escape.

Question. The perpetrator was charged with criminal restraint arising from the index assault. Can I use this information to score Confinement of the Partner at the Index Assault?

Answer. Because the definition of criminal restraint varies across jurisdictions, more information is required. If the restraint was committed against the partner and committed by use of force rather than by threat or deception and in an attempt to restrict the victim's liberty or physical ability to leave the location, then yes. If any of these three conditions is not met, then the criteria for Confinement of the Partner at the Index Assault are not met.

Item 7: Victim Concern About Future Assaults

This item captures the victim's prediction of future assaults against the victim or the victim's children. Any statement made by the victim that indicates concern, fear, worry, or certainty pertaining to a possible future assault is considered an example of victim concern.

All of the following must be present:

- a statement made by the partner who is the victim of the index assault;
- a statement made in the victim's first reports to the police, or victim services if this information was not available to police, even if the victim subsequently expressed no concern; and
- a statement that indicates concern, fear, worry, or certainty pertaining to a possible future assault by the person being assessed.

If any one of these criteria is absent, then score 0 for the item, even if every other criterion is present. These criteria are all required.

At least one of the following must be present:

- a statement pertaining to possible future assaults against the victim of the index assault, or
- a statement pertaining to possible future assaults against the victim's children.

Either of these criteria must be present to score 1 for the item. They do not both have to be present. If neither of these criteria is met, then score 0 for the item.

Do not include

- the victim's fear for safety during the index assault,
- statements made by the victim on a separate occasion before the index assault, or
- inferences about concern based on protective action taken by the victim.

Frequently Asked Questions

Question. The victim has gone to a women's shelter and went back to her home to gather her property only when accompanied by a shelter support worker for protection. To me, it is clear that she is afraid of the perpetrator. Can I use this information to score Victim Concern?

Answer. No. A verbal statement by the victim is required. In the research, this variable was coded on the basis of overt behavior, usually a statement made to police, and was not inferred from other behavior.

Question. The victim states that the perpetrator would certainly commit another domestic assault given the opportunity; however, the victim is moving to another city, so they will no longer be in contact with each other. How should this response be scored?

Answer. Victim Concern should be scored 1 because the victim's statement indicates certainty of another assault. This item is not scored on the basis of a conditional probability, and assessors should not ask questions such as "Would this person assault you again if you stayed in the city . . . or moved out of state . . . or left the country?"

Item 8: More Than One Child Altogether

Add up the number of children the perpetrator has, plus any additional children the victim has. There must be more than one child in total to score 1 for this item.

Include the following:

- biological or adopted children of the person being assessed,
- biological or adopted children of the partner who is the victim of the index assault,
- minor or adult children who meet the above criteria, or
- children living with the victim or living elsewhere who meet the above criteria.

Do not include

- children who were either unborn or deceased at the time of the index assault; or
- children of a former partner who are not biologically related to, or adopted by, the person being assessed or the victim.

Frequently Asked Questions

Question. The perpetrator's ex-partner had children from a previous relationship who lived with the perpetrator during that relationship. These children now visit the perpetrator and the index victim every other weekend. Can I use this information to score More than One Child Altogether?

Answer. No. Only count children born to or adopted by the perpetrator or the index victim (or both).

Question. The perpetrator has one son and the index victim has one daughter, but they have no joint children. How should I score More than One Child Altogether?

Answer. Score the item 1 as both these children count toward the total.

Item 9: Victim's Biological Child From a Previous Partner

To score 1 for this item, the victim of the index assault must have a biological child whose other biological parent is not the perpetrator. Only one child is needed to score 1 for this item.

Include the following:

- biological children of the partner who is the victim of the index assault,
- minor or adult children who meet the first criterion, and
- children living with the victim or living elsewhere who meet the first two criteria.

Do not include

- biological children of the perpetrator,
- children who were adopted by the victim,

- children who are not the victim's biological children, or
- children who were deceased at the time of the index assault.

Frequently Asked Questions

Question. The female victim adopted a child at birth before her relationship with the perpetrator began. She feels just as much love and devotion as if she had given birth to this child. Can I use this information to score Victim's Biological Child From a Previous Partner?

Answer. No. In the ODARA development research, children who were known to be adopted were coded separately from biological children. It was the victim's biological children that predicted recidivism.

Question. The victim had a child with a previous partner who now has sole custody of the child. The perpetrator has no contact with this child. Does this child count for Victim's Biological Child From a Previous Partner?

Answer. Yes. The criteria pertain to the living existence of the child, not the perpetrator's relationship with that child.

Question. The victim had a child with a previous partner, and the perpetrator adopted this child. Do I count this child for More Than One Child Altogether or Victim's Biological Child From a Previous Partner?

Answer. Both. This child meets the criteria for More Than One Child Altogether and is the Victim's Biological Child From a Previous Partner.

Item 10: Pre-Index Violence Against a Nondomestic Victim

All of the following must be present:

- an act of violence (as defined earlier) carried out by the person being assessed;
- an incident that occurred on a separate occasion before the index assault; and
- a victim who is any person other than a current or previous domestic partner of the person being assessed, or the partner's children.

If any one of these criteria is absent, then score 0 for the item. These criteria are all required.

Police involvement is not required, and information used to score this item can come from sources other than criminal justice documentation. The required criteria for this item are a subset of the criteria for Pre-Index Nondomestic Assault, so that if Pre-Index Nondomestic Assault is scored 1, then Pre-Index Violence Against a Nondomestic Victim is also scored 1.

Frequently Asked Questions

Question. The perpetrator had a reputation for being a tough person during adolescence and is described as fighting a lot at that time, although there is no information about a specific event. Can I use this information to score Pre-Index Violence Against a Nondomestic Victim?

Answer. No. Reputations are not sufficient to conclude that an assault has been committed. A specific incident is required.

Question. The perpetrator has a police record for a violent assault, and a presentence report indicates that the victim was a dating partner. They had never lived together. Can I use this information to score Pre-Index Violence against a Nondomestic Victim?

Answer. Yes. A domestic partner is a partner that the perpetrator lives or did live with for any length of time. In the ODARA construction research and in validation studies conducted by members of the original ODARA research team, dating violence was counted as nondomestic.

Item 11: Two or More Indicators of Substance Abuse

To score 1 for this item, there must be more than one element of substance abuse present; alcohol use at the index assault is not sufficient by itself. The elements are listed from most common to least common according to the ODARA development research. All items pertain to the perpetrator who is being assessed.

At least two of the following must be present:

- the person consumed alcohol immediately before or during the index assault,
- the person used drugs immediately before or during the index assault,
- the person abused drugs and/or alcohol in the days or weeks before the index assault (e.g., alcohol intoxication, frequent alcohol use, use of street drugs, misuse of medication),
- the person noticeably increased abuse of drugs and/or alcohol in the days or weeks before the index assault (without a return to normal consumption before the index assault),
- the person has been more angry or violent when using drugs and/or alcohol before the index assault,
- the person consumed alcohol before or during a criminal offense before the index assault,

- the person's alcohol use before the index but since age 18 resulted in some problems or interference in the person's life, and
- the person's drug use before the index but since age 18 resulted in some problems or interference in the person's life.

Any two of these criteria must be present to score 1 for the item. Not all the criteria have to be present. If only one of these criteria is met, then score 0 for the item. Evidence for an alcohol or drug use problem or interference in the perpetrator's life can come from alcohol or drug use related to law violations resulting in a charge or revocation of conditional release; withdrawal symptoms or inability to decrease use; financial, job, relationship, legal, or health problems or other problems attributable to alcohol or drug use. Drugs that count for this item are illicit or street drugs, recreational drugs, or misused prescription medication.

Do not include medications taken as prescribed.

Frequently Asked Question

Question. The perpetrator did not use alcohol or drugs for several years before the index incident and is not known for becoming more angry or violent when using alcohol. However, at age 18, the perpetrator was charged for driving under the influence of alcohol. How should I score Substance Abuse?

Answer. This item should be scored 1. If the perpetrator was aged at least 18 years when charged with an alcohol-related criminal offense before the index assault, then two elements are satisfied: consumed alcohol before or during a prior criminal offense and alcohol use since age 18 resulted in problems (i.e., charged for a law violation).

Item 12: Assault on Index Victim When Pregnant

Information for scoring this item can come from sources other than criminal justice documentation, and the incident does not need to be known to the police.

All of the following must be present:

- an act of violence, as defined previously, carried out by the person being assessed;
- an incident against the partner who is the victim of the index assault; and
- the victim's pregnancy at the time of the assault.

If any one of these criteria is absent, then score 0 for the item, even if every other criterion is present. These criteria are all required. The index assault can count for this item. Score this item 0 for a male victim.

Do not include

- incidents involving only pets or property, or
- incidents that occurred when the victim was not pregnant.

Frequently Asked Questions.
Question. The perpetrator was convicted of an assault against a previous domestic partner who is not the index victim. The ex-partner was 5 months pregnant. Can I use this information to score Assault on Index Victim When Pregnant?

Answer. No. In the ODARA development research, this item was scored with respect to the index victim only.

Question. The victim was 6 weeks pregnant at the time of the index assault, but the perpetrator did not know. Can I use this information to score Assault on Index Victim when Pregnant?

Answer. Yes. In the ODARA development research, pregnancy was treated as a dichotomous variable (i.e., pregnant vs. not pregnant). Data were collected from police reports, so pregnancies were generally known to all parties. Perpetrators were not asked whether they knew about the pregnancy, so their knowledge could not be used as part of this item.

Item 13: Barriers to Victim Support

This item covers the victim's circumstances at the time of the index assault. Score it using information documented as close to the time of the index assault as possible. The elements are listed from most to least common according to the ODARA development research.

At least one of the following must be present:

- the victim of the index assault has one or more children aged 18 or under who live with the victim and for whom the victim provides care,
- the victim has no telephone (i.e., no cell phone and no land-line telephone in the home),
- the victim has no transportation (i.e., no access to a vehicle, no public transportation in the vicinity of the victim's home, and no money for a taxi or other paid transport),
- the victim is geographically isolated (i.e., living in a rural area with nobody living close by), or
- the victim consumed alcohol or drugs just before or during the index incident or has a history of alcohol or drug abuse (e.g., alcohol intoxication,

frequent alcohol use, use of illicit or street drugs, recreational drugs, abuse of medication).

Any one of these criteria must be present to score 1 for the item. Not all the criteria have to be present. If none of these criteria are met, then score 0 for the item.

Frequently Asked Questions

Question. None of the suggested barriers to support apply to the female victim, but she is of an ethnic minority in which a woman traditionally is subservient to her husband; in addition, there are no community domestic violence services in her minority language. Can I use this information to score Barriers to Victim Support?

Answer. No. In the ODARA development research, immigration issues and language barriers were recorded as circumstances that might increase the partner's vulnerability; however, there were insufficient data on these variables to establish an association with recidivism. Immigration patterns have changed globally since this research was conducted; however, further research that tests the incremental predictive validity of additional information is needed before items can be added to or modified on the ODARA.

ADJUSTING ODARA SCORES FOR ASSESSMENTS WITH AMBIGUOUS INFORMATION

If the available documentation indicates that an item might be present but the information is unclear or incomplete, the item may be considered ambiguous. It is better to seek more information before treating an item as missing, and this caveat is especially true for the perpetrator's criminal history (including prior domestic and nondomestic incidents, and correctional and conditional dispositions). In some circumstances, however, some items might be truly undefined. For example, a female victim might recall being assaulted on many past occasions but not be able either to recall or rule out a specific occasion on which she was pregnant during an assault, despite having given birth at least once during this time. In this case, Assault on the Index Victim When Pregnant could be treated as ambiguous.

Prorating is a standard assessment procedure for dealing with missing information. Prorating replaces missing information with data estimated from all items that are not missing. Prorating is preferable to scoring 0 for ambiguous items, which could underestimate risk. It is also preferable to scoring 1 for missing items, which could overestimate risk. Prorating should not, however, be used as an alternative to seeking as much information can be obtained.

The ODARA score can be prorated for up to five ambiguous items using the adjusted scores shown in Table 6.1. Analysis of ODARA construction data showed that missing more than five items reduced the accuracy of the ODARA to a point at which it was not statistically different from zero. To use Table 6.1, first add up the scores for the items that are present and find this score in the Raw Score column. Then identify the column for the number of items that are ambiguous. The number in the square where the row and column meet is the adjusted score. Interpret this number using Table 6.2.

For example, the perpetrator scores 2 on the ODARA, but there is a charge of assault on the criminal record without supplementary information as to whether the assault met the criteria for a Pre-Index Domestic Assault, or a Pre-Index Nondomestic Assault and thus Pre-Index Violence Against a Non-domestic Victim. With a raw score of 2, start from "2" in the Raw Score column and follow along the row until it meets the Number of Ambiguous Items column "3." The adjusted score is 3.

SAMPLE RISK ASSESSMENT REPORT SUMMARY AND NORMS FOR THE ODARA

The ODARA is an actuarial risk assessment tool for estimating the risk of domestic violence recidivism posed by an individual who has assaulted a partner. The higher the ODARA score, the more likely the perpetrator is to assault a partner again and the sooner, more frequent and severe future

TABLE 6.1. Prorating Table for Assessments With Ambiguous Items

	No. of ambiguous items				
Raw score	**1**	**2**	**3**	**4**	**5**
0	0	0	0	0	0
1	1	1	1	1	2
2	2	2	3	3	3
3	3	4	4	4	5
4	4	5	5	6	7+
5	5	6	7+	7+	7+
6	7+	7+	7+	7+	7+

Note. Do not use prorating as a substitute for seeking more information. Adapted from *Risk Assessment for Domestically Violent Men: Tools for Criminal Justice, Offender Intervention, and Victim Services* (p. 168), by N. Z. Hilton, G. T. Harris, & M. E. Rice, 2010, American Psychological Association (https://doi.org/10.1037/12066-000). Copyright 2010 by the American Psychological Association.

TABLE 6.2. Normative Data for ODARA Scores in a Population of Men With a Police Occurrence Report of Assault Against a Female Domestic Partner

ODARA score	% Recidivism	% In this range of scores	% Scoring lower	% Scoring higher
0	7	9	0	91
1	17	17	9	74
2	22	21	26	53
3	34	20	47	33
4	39	13	67	20
5-6	53	14	80	6
7-13	74	6	94	0

Note. ODARA = Distribution of Ontario Domestic Assault Risk Assessment. Recidivism is defined as a new assault against a female domestic partner identified by an occurrence report in police records or a charge in the criminal record, during an average follow-up of 4.9 years after the index assault. Data from Hilton et al. (2004); Hilton and Harris (2009b); and Hilton, Harris, Rice, et al. (2008); $N = 1{,}421$. Reprinted from *Risk Assessment for Domestically Violent Men: Tools for Criminal Justice, Offender Intervention, and Victim Services* (p. 170), by N. Z. Hilton, G. T. Harris, & M. E. Rice, 2010, American Psychological Association (https://doi.org/10.1037/12066-000). Copyright 2010 by the American Psychological Association.

assaults will be. The ODARA was developed in a study of 589 men known to police in the Province of Ontario, Canada, for physically assaulting their female partners and cross-validated in three further studies with similar samples. In an average follow-up of approximately 5 years after an index incident of domestic violence, 30% of men recidivated. The ODARA has since been validated in varied samples of male perpetrators. Studies with women who assaulted their partner have also been conducted; however, the current normative data table applies only to male perpetrators. The ODARA consists of 13 unique predictors of domestic violence recidivism, including domestic and nondomestic criminal history, threat and confinement during the index assault, substance abuse, children, and barriers to victim support. In the ODARA development research, only acts of physical violence met the definition of domestic violence recidivism. Of the men who recidivated, most assaulted the same partner as before.

The ODARA score for Mr. A was based on information ascertained at or before the index assault, which occurred on August 8, 2019, using available information from the correctional file compiled at the Probation and Parole Office in First City, Ontario. According to the information contained in these records, Mr. A scores 6 on the ODARA. As indicated by the normative data table (Table 6.2), fewer than 10% of the men in the ODARA construction and cross-validation studies obtained higher scores than Mr. A. When followed up for approximately 5 years, more than 50% of men in Mr. A's risk category committed a new domestic assault.

7 SCORING MANUAL FOR THE DOMESTIC VIOLENCE RISK APPRAISAL GUIDE

With the exception of score on the Psychopathy Checklist–Revised (PCL-R; Hare, 2003), all Domestic Violence Risk Appraisal Guide (DVRAG) items follow the same inclusion and exclusion criteria as the Ontario Domestic Assault Risk Assessment (ODARA), detailed in Chapter 6 and summarized here; however, most DVRAG items have nonunitary weights, and several are scored as continuous rather than dichotomous items. The final scoring practice case in the Appendix (Case A.4, Table A.4) shows how the ODARA and DVRAG items can be scored sequentially or simultaneously. For clarity in the scoring criteria, I use *perpetrator* to refer to the man who has assaulted his partner and whose risk is being assessed, and either *partner* or *victim* to refer to the partner who has been assaulted. I use male pronouns for the perpetrator and female pronouns for the partner who is the victim of the index assault because the DVRAG is not yet validated for other circumstances.

https://doi.org/10.1037/0000223-008
Domestic Violence Risk Assessment: Tools for Effective Prediction and Management, Second Edition, by N. Z. Hilton

ITEM SCORING

Item 1: Number of Pre-Index Assaults in a Police or Criminal Record

Count the number of physical assaults by the perpetrator against a current or previous cohabiting partner or her children, on a separate occasion prior to the index assault, and recorded in a police occurrence report or criminal record. Include any current or previous cohabiting partner or her children, but exclude incidents involving only abused pets or damaged property.

No. of assaults	Score
0	–1
1	0
≥2	+5

Item 2: Number of Pre-Index Nondomestic Assaults in a Police or Criminal Record

Count the number of physical assaults by the perpetrator on any person other than a current or previous cohabiting partner or her children, on a separate occasion prior to the index assault, and recorded in a police occurrence report or criminal record. Exclude incidents involving only abused pets or damaged property.

No. of assaults	Score
0	–1
≥1	+5

Item 3: Pre-Index Custodial Sentence of 30 Days or More

Score *no* if the perpetrator did not spend any time incarcerated as a result of a sentence handed down by the court for a criminal offense before the index assault. Score *yes* for any continuous or intermittent admission to training school, jail, federal correctional facility, or a provincial or state correctional facility, if the sentence was for at least 30 days. Exclude time spent in custody awaiting trial unless time served is explicitly stated as part of the sentence.

Response	Score
No	–1
Yes	+2

Item 4: Failure on Pre-Index Conditional Release

Score *no* if the perpetrator was not on conditional release at or before the index assault, or if he was but completed the conditions of release without failure. Score *yes* for any failure to obey a conditional release order that commenced before the index assault, whether or not the failure led to arrest, criminal charge, or revocation of conditional release.

Response	Score
No	–1
Yes	+2

Item 5: Threat to Physically Harm or Kill at the Index Assault

Score *yes* if the perpetrator made a threat of physical harm toward any person other than himself or incurred a criminal charge of threatening, uttering threats, threatening with a weapon, or equivalent charge arising from events at the index assault.

Response	Score
No	0
Yes	+1

Item 6: Confinement of the Partner at the Index Assault

Score *yes* if the perpetrator detained the index victim in a locked or barricaded physical space, or physically intervened with her attempt to leave the location.

Response	Score
No	0
Yes	+1

Item 7: Victim Concern About Future Assaults

Score *yes* if, at the time of the index victim's first report to police or documented interview with a victim service agency regarding the index assault, she made a verbal statement that specifies her concern, fear, worry, or certainty that perpetrator would assault her or her children in the future.

Response	Score
No	0
Yes	+2

Item 8: Number of Children

Add up the number of living, minor or adult, biological, or adopted children of the perpetrator, plus those additional children of the partner who is the index victim.

No. of children	Score
0-1	–1
≥2	+1

Item 9: Victim's Biological Children From a Previous Partner

Count all the living, minor or adult, biological children of the partner who is the index victim, whose other biological parent is not the perpetrator. Exclude adopted children.

No. of children	Score
0	–1
1	0
≥2	+2

Item 10: Pre-Index Violence Against a Nondomestic Victim

Score *yes* for any physical assault by the perpetrator on any person other than a current or previous cohabiting partner or her children, on a separate occasion before the index assault, whether or not recorded in a police occurrence report or criminal record.

Response	Score
No	0
Yes	+8

Item 11: Substance Abuse Score

Allot 1 point for each of the following: alcohol involved in the index assault, drugs involved in the index assault, alcohol or drug abuse in days or weeks before index assault, increased drug or alcohol use in days or weeks before index assault, more angry or violent when using drugs or alcohol, alcohol involved in a prior criminal offense, adult alcohol problem, adult drug problem. Exclude use of medications taken as prescribed. A *problem* includes law violations resulting in a charge or revocation of conditional release; financial, job, relationship, legal, or health problems; withdrawal symptoms; or inability to decrease use; any other problem resulting from substance use (alcohol, street drugs, or abuse of prescription medication).

No. of points	Score
0-1	–2
≥2	+2

Item 12: Assault on Index Victim When Pregnant

Score *yes* for any physical assault by the perpetrator on the partner (who is the victim of the index assault) when she was pregnant, on any occasion before or at the index assault, whether or not recorded in a police occurrence report or criminal record.

Response	Score
No	0
Yes	+5

Item 13: Barriers to Victim Support

Allot 1 point for each of the following: index victim has a child aged 18 who lives with her and for whom she provides care, index victim has neither telephone nor access to transportation, index victim is isolated geographically, index victim used alcohol in the index assault or has a history of alcohol or drug abuse. Note that the presence of both elements in a "nor/or" statement count as one barrier.

No. of points	Score
0	–1
1	0
≥2	+4

Item 14: Psychopathy Checklist-Revised Score

Full scoring criteria are available in Hare (2003).

PCL-R score	Score
≤ 9	−1
10–16	+1
≥ 17	+6

Alternative item scoring for DVRAG-4 method (see Scoring the DVRAG With PCL-R Facet 4 in Chapter 5, this volume).

PCL-R Facet 4 score	Score
0	−4
1	−2
2	0
3	+1
≥ 4	+4

ADJUSTING DOMESTIC VIOLENCE RISK APPRAISAL SCORES FOR ASSESSMENTS WITH AMBIGUOUS INFORMATION

On the ODARA, if there were no prorating system, leaving an item out would have the same effect on the total score as scoring the item 0. Any item that is left blank reduces the total score and possibly over- or underestimates the perpetrator's risk. That is why a prorating system was developed for the ODARA, which can be used for up to five items if the available information indicates that the item might be present but the details are unclear or incomplete for scoring purposes. Prorating is a standard assessment procedure for dealing with missing information that gives credit for an item based on the score obtained for the items that were scoreable. The prorating table in Chapter 6 makes this procedure easy for ODARA users.

In contrast, the DVRAG's use of both positive and negative weights means that an item value of 0 indicates that individuals having this characteristic reoffended at a rate that was close (within 5%) to the base rate. Therefore, on the DVRAG, assessors can give a score of 0 to a missing item, which gives credit for the item based on the normative average.

Prorating, however, can retain more predictive power than scoring items 0 and so is a desirable procedure if it can be done accurately. Prorating is more laborious for the DVRAG than the ODARA because of the item weights, but assessors can use the detailed steps provided here.

Calculations of the DVRAG's predictive accuracy in the combined sample of 649 cases revealed that it is robust in the face of up to five missing items, still predicting recidivism significantly better than the most accurate non-actuarial risk assessment. Results were best when the four criminal history items and the PCL-R were retained; consequently, I advise seeking more information if you have no criminal history information, just as with the ODARA. Any omission makes the estimated risk closer to the base rate than it might otherwise be, which could tend to underestimate risk (where the true score is positive) or to overestimate it (where the true score is negative). I suggest the following cautionary statements when communicating the assessment results with unscoreable items:

- When prorating is used: "It should be noted that there were [*insert number up to five*] items missing for Mr. B, and his DVRAG score was prorated for these items."
- When missing items are scored zero: "It should be noted that there were [*insert number up to five*] items missing for Mr. B, so his score is closer to the middle risk category than might be expected if complete information had been available."

If the available documentation indicates that an item might be present, but the information is unclear or incomplete, the item may be considered ambiguous. It is better to seek more information before treating an item as missing, and this caveat is especially true for the perpetrator's criminal history (including prior domestic and nondomestic incidents, and custodial and noncustodial dispositions). In some circumstances, however, some items are truly unknown.

If the Raw Sum of the Items That Are Scored Is Positive

1. Note the maximum possible positive score on each of the missing items and sum them.

   ___ + ___ + ___ + ___ + ___ = Total _____ (a)

2. Note the maximum possible positive scores on each of the scored items and sum them.

   ___ + ___ + ___ + ___ + ___ + ___ + ___ + ___ + ___ + ___ + ___ + ___ + ___ = Total _____ (b)

3. Note the actual obtained values on each of the items that are scored and sum them.

   ___ + ___ + ___ + ___ + ___ + ___ + ___ + ___ + ___ + ___ + ___ + ___ + ___ = Total _____ (c)

4. Divide the obtained sum (c) by the maximum possible (b). c ÷ b = _____ (d)

5. Multiply the obtained proportion (d) by the maximum possible on missing items (a). d × a = _____ (e)

6. Add the prorated score for missing items (e) to the obtained sum (c). e + c = _____ (f)

7. Round this result (f) to the nearest positive whole number for the final DVRAG score: ____

If the Raw Sum of the Items That Are Scored Is Negative

1. Note the most negative possible score on each of the missing items, and sum them.

   ___ + ___ + ___ + ___ + ___ = Total – ____ (a)

2. Note the most negative possible score on each of the scored items, and sum them.

   ___ + ___ + ___ + ___ + ___ + ___ + ___ + ___ + ___ + ___ + ___ + ___ + ___ = Total – _____ (b)

3. Note the actual obtained values on each of the items that are scored, and sum them.

   ___ + ___ + ___ + ___ + ___ + ___ + ___ + ___ + ___ + ___ + ___ + ___ + ___ = Total – _____ (c)

4. Divide the obtained sum (c) by the most negative possible (b). c ÷ b = ____ (d)

5. Multiply the obtained proportion (d) by the most negative possible on missing items (a). d × a = – ____ (e)

6. Subtract the absolute value of the prorated score for missing items (e) from the obtained sum. (c). c – |e| = – ____ (f)

7. Note that f should be a more extreme negative number than c.

8. Round this result (f) to the nearest negative whole number for the final DVRAG score: ____

SAMPLE RISK ASSESSMENT REPORT SUMMARY AND NORMS FOR THE DVRAG

The DVRAG is an actuarial risk assessment tool that ranks men with respect to risk for domestic violence recidivism and its frequency and severity. The higher the DVRAG score, the more likely the man is to assault a female cohabiting partner again, the more frequent and severe future assaults will be, and the sooner he will assault again. The DVRAG was developed in a study of 649 men in the Province of Ontario, Canada, who had a police record for physically assaulting their female partners, and had a corrections file permitting in-depth assessment. In an average follow-up of nearly 5 years after an index incident of domestic violence, 45% of men recidivated, most against the same partner as at the index. The DVRAG consists of 14 unique predictors of domestic violence recidivism, including score on the PCL-R (Hare, 2003), domestic and nondomestic criminal history, threat and confinement during the index assault, children in the relationship, substance abuse, and barriers to victim support. In the DVRAG development research, only acts of physical violence met the definition of domestic violence recidivism.

The DVRAG score for Mr. B was based on information ascertained at or before the index assault, which occurred on August 27, 2019, using information available in the file compiled at the Rainy Correctional Center. According to the information in these records, Mr. B scores +26 on the DVRAG. As indicated by the normative data table (see Table 7.1), 97% of men in the study described earlier obtained lower scores than Mr. B. When followed up for nearly 5 years, all (100%) men in Mr. B's risk category committed a new domestic assault that was recorded by police (see Table 7.2).

TABLE 7.1. Normative Data for the Distribution of Domestic Violence Risk Appraisal Guide (DVRAG) Scores

DVRAG score	% Scoring lower	DVRAG score	% Scoring lower
–10	0	8	74
–9	<2	9	77
–8	2	10	78
–7	4	11	81
–6	9	12	84
–5	15	13	86
–4	22	14	87
–3	27	15	89
–2	32	16	91
–1	38	17	92
0	43	18	93
1	48	19	94
2	54	20	95
3	58	21	96
4	63	24	97
5	65	26	98
6	68	≥31	≥99
7	71		

Note. Data from Hilton, Harris, Rice, et al. (2008).

TABLE 7.2. Normative Data and Probability of Recidivism for the Domestic Violence Risk Appraisal Guide (DVRAG) Risk Categories in a Population of Men With a Police Occurrence Report of Assault Against a Female Domestic Partner and an In-Depth Correctional File

Category: DVRAG score	% Recidivism	% In this category	% Scoring lower	% Scoring higher
1: –10 to –9	14	2	0	98
2: –8 to –5	24	20	2	78
3: –4 to –1	34	20	22	58
4: 0 to +3	44	20	43	37
5: +4 to +10	51	19	63	19
6: +11 to +23	71	16	81	3
7: +24 to +41	100	3	97	0

Note. Recidivism is defined as a new assault against a female domestic partner identified by an occurrence report in police records or a charge in the criminal record during an average follow-up of 4.8 years. Data from Hilton, Harris, Rice, et al. (2008).

PART III ADDITIONAL CONSIDERATIONS FOR RISK ASSESSMENT AND MANAGEMENT

8 CHOOSING A RISK ASSESSMENT APPROACH

Hypothesis Versus Evidence

Early in the 1990s, my late colleagues received an invitation to attend a meeting at which a select group of experts would confer on the identification of risk factors for violent recidivism. Inspired by the possibility of a checklist to predict violent behavior in forensic populations, they began a statistical analysis to examine which individual characteristics of men with a history of criminal charges for violence could adequately distinguish those who recidivate from those who do not recidivate. The resulting Violence Risk Appraisal Guide (VRAG) and Sex Offender Risk Appraisal Guide (Harris, Rice, et al., 2015) predicted violent recidivism with a large effect size. These tools have since seen dozens of replications, by Harris and colleagues and by other researchers, in various populations; in several countries, including the United States (Campbell, French, & Gendreau, 2009; Hanson & Morton-Bourgon, 2009; Harris et al., 2010; Harris, Rice, et al., 2015); and across diverse outcomes, including general violence by domestically violent men (Hilton et al., 2001). The revised VRAG (VRAG-R) had a large predictive effect among 1,261 men followed for up to 49 years (Rice et al., 2013), and studies have replicated its discriminant validity for violent recidivism

https://doi.org/10.1037/0000223-009
Domestic Violence Risk Assessment: Tools for Effective Prediction and Management, Second Edition, by N. Z. Hilton

(e.g., Glover et al., 2017; Hertz et al., 2019; Hogan & Olver, 2019; Olver & Sewall, 2018; see updates at https://www.vrag-r.org). The VRAG is the most frequently used actuarial violence risk assessment tool (Neal & Grisso, 2014).

The success of the VRAG family of tools, I believe, results from reliance on empirical research and an actuarial approach to its creation and interpretation. My colleagues and I used the same approach for our domestic violence risk assessment tools, the Ontario Domestic Assault Risk Assessment (ODARA; Hilton et al., 2004) and the Domestic Violence Risk Appraisal Guide (DVRAG; Hilton, Harris, Rice, et al., 2008). Nonempirical and intuitive approaches to risk assessment remain popular, however. Although this popularity often arises from anxiety about statistics and the scientific method, there is also optimism that clinical judgment can achieve benefits in violence prevention that empirical methods cannot. In this chapter, I discuss hypotheses about risk assessment that underlie this optimism and critically examine the evidence for them. I examine whether clinical judgment is essential to risk assessment, whether dynamic risk factors are superior to static risk factors, whether prediction models are incompatible with risk management, and whether individual risk can be inferred from actuarial data. I give examples from the VRAG and from an alternative approach, structured professional judgment (SPJ), which seeks a middle ground between clinical and empirical risk assessment. I draw on the empirical literature on domestic violence where possible.

HYPOTHESIS 1: CLINICAL JUDGMENT IS ESSENTIAL TO RISK ASSESSMENT

> The recommendation to apply guidelines rather than explicit instructions to the task of understanding risk potential in the individual case is because the evidence base is incomplete and flawed, which means that practitioners are required to use their judgement or discretion to bridge the gaps in their knowledge. (Logan & Lloyd, 2019, p. 3)

One sense of risk assessment is that of an informal, impressionistic evaluation based on personal considerations, experience, knowledge of the field, and ineffable qualities of the situation. This approach is often portrayed in movies by a wise and experienced clinician who says, "Given his history of abuse and rage, I think he's extremely dangerous; you'd better catch him before he kills again." In real life, this case review approach is ubiquitous, and many clinical decisions are based almost entirely on informal appraisals. Personnel decisions, too, are often based on an informal impression gleaned from unstructured interviews (e.g., Zhang et al., 2018). People make similar, intuitive decisions all the time about whom to choose as a domestic partner, what kind of car to buy, how to vote, and so on.

The Clinical-Actuarial Distinction

Human decision making has been studied for decades and spans many domains, including selecting people for employment or educational programs, diagnosing and prognosing medical conditions, forecasting weather, anticipating stock market performance, assessing insurance risks, and predicting criminal and violent recidivism (e.g., Swets et al., 2000). Decision making has been classified into two types: intuitive and mechanical. In the violence risk assessment field, the intuitive type is known as clinical or professional judgment, which includes using informal or intuitive processes to identify relevant information and combine such information to render a decision. When assessors use their professional experience, personal acumen, intuition, clinical observations, theoretical perspective, and memory for research findings and authoritative advice to determine which client characteristics and circumstances to synthesize into a decision, they are using professional judgment. When no decision-making method is specified in an assessment, it is usually the case that a professional judgment approach is being taken.

In contrast, actuarial risk assessment is a form of mechanical decision making that minimizes intuitive inferences by basing decisions on empirical relationships between predictor characteristics and outcomes (Dawes et al., 1989). In the actuarial assessment of the risk of violent recidivism, predictor items are chosen through well-designed follow-up studies that identify which items are related to the outcome. This research permits an optimal selection of items based on incremental validity—that is, selecting the most powerful predictors first and then adding items only when they improve prediction. In the actuarial method, data are entered into formulas or experience tables that provide information about the prevalence (or base rate) of an outcome that serve as an estimate of the outcome's probability. That is, actuarial assessment yields a numerical value for each case.

It probably comes as no surprise to learn that people are usually better off using some kind of formal assessment. For example, decisions about which car to buy could be based on systematically organized data about repair records, fuel mileage, resale value, and insurance rates. Personnel selection can be based on formal measures of aptitude and skills. The advantage of formal or mechanical decision making has been well established (if not well followed) for well more than 60 years. Decisions overall are better (more reliable, accurate, valid, profitable) when a mechanical or actuarial method is used instead of informal, impressionistic, or intuitive methods (e.g., Ægisdóttir et al., 2006; Grove, 2005; Swets et al., 2000). The same is true for domestic violence risk assessment (Seewald et al., 2017).

A simple rule for detecting whether a method is actuarial or clinical is that the actuarial method is well specified and, therefore, also amenable to replication, whereas the clinical method is neither clearly articulated nor easily reproduced (Grove & Meehl, 1996). Empirical research has shown that the actuarial method is more accurate, particularly for the risk of criminal and violent recidivism (Hilton et al., 2006; Harris, Rice, et al., 2015). Where actuarial systems are available, unstructured clinical judgment is indefensible on both ethical and scientific grounds (Dawes, 2005; Grove & Meehl, 1996). There have been many scientific tests in which "experts" are given information to aid their decisions (e.g., about diagnosis and prognosis, academic success, vocational performance, the risk of suicide or criminal activity) while the same set of facts is presented to a formula or mechanical process. Their accuracies are then compared, usually in terms of the proportion of correct statements. These studies have been gathered together in what is called "meta-analysis," using common metrics to derive a numerical statement as to whether either method shows an overall advantage. The actuarial approach has a consistent advantage, producing more accurate prediction of outcomes, especially for violent and criminal behavior (Ægisdóttir et al., 2006; M. A. Campbell et al., 2009; Grove, 2005; Hanson & Morton-Bourgon, 2009).

Clinical Judgment in Contemporary Violence Risk Assessment

At first glance, it would seem that actuarial risk assessments allow no room for any clinical judgment. Actuarial instruments by definition have a fixed list of (empirically selected) predictors that are scored according to exact, replicable criteria and combined in a specified manner to achieve a total score. Actuarial experience tables indicate the proportion of previously observed cases that met the criteria for subsequent violent conduct within specified periods of opportunity. In addition, the numerical score permits a rank ordering of all cases with respect to their assessed risk. This rank ordering is what permits assignment to correctional intervention (e.g., custody, community supervision, treatment) according to risk. Actuarial methods also have accompanying evidence of predictive validity and, typically, the potential for reliable scoring.

Some assessors, however, consider the rigidity of rules to be a weakness of actuarial risk assessment, along with its exclusion of variables that might predict recidivism in an individual case but are not empirically selected items (e.g., Douglas et al., 2014). The SPJ approach is a significant move toward incorporating clinical judgment into violence risk assessment (e.g., Douglas et al., 2014; Kropp & Hart, 2015). SPJ guides are not actuarial tools. They guide professionals to evaluate risk after consideration of a list of variables selected from the empirical and clinical literature, without explicit rules. Mechanical total scores on SPJ tools predict violent recidivism (e.g., K. M. Williams et al., 2017), including domestic violence (e.g., Helmus & Bourgon, 2011). The final professional judgment, however, uses an intuitive weighting of the item list plus an unlimited pool of characteristics that assessors deem relevant to an individual case.

The most widely used SPJ guide is the Historical–Clinical–Risk Management 20 (HCR-20; Webster et al., 1997; see also Neal & Grisso, 2014). The HCR-20 was recently restyled into the HCR-20 Version 3 (HCR-20-V3; Douglas et al., 2014), which eliminated item scores and increased the role of case formulation and summary clinical judgments. The equivalent guide for domestic violence is the SARA-V3 (Kropp & Hart, 2015). I introduced the SARA family of tools in Chapter 1 (in the section Domestic Violence Recidivism Assessment Tools and Guides).

Closely related to the hypothesis that clinical judgment is essential to risk assessment is the notion that the process is too complex for actuarial risk assessment. Hart et al. (2016) argued that "the complexity of violence risk assessment is best dealt with by developing decision making aids to assist an expert evaluator" (p. 16). I agree that assessing risk, identifying criminogenic needs, and providing evidence-based interventions tailored to individuals' treatment responsivity characteristics is challenging, and the field is a long way from ensuring that risk assessment leads to effective violence prevention (e.g., Viljoen et al., 2018). However, I have shown that, in an apparently complex case of a man with serial domestic offenses, the ODARA and DVRAG (actuarial tools) drew the same conclusion as assessors did using SPJ guidelines, without need for elaborate and time-consuming case formulation (Hilton, 2014). In other areas of human decision making, such as controlling the flow of air traffic and passengers, the complexity of the problem motivates experts not to abandon mechanical processes but to break down processes into subproblems governed by more detailed algorithms (e.g., Gawande, 2011; Ng et al., 2018). Furthermore, actuarial tools provide precise risk estimates, compared with clinical judgment that requires communication in vague labels such as *moderate risk*, which have no agreed meaning even among forensic clinicians (Hilton, Carter, Harris, & Sharpe, 2008; see Does Communicating Actuarial Plus Categorical Risk Improve Forensic Decisions? in Chapter 9, this volume).

Clinical Adjustment of Assessed Risk

Is there any room for clinical judgment in empirically supported risk assessment? I believe there is. I concur with Bornstein (2017), who explained, "even actuarial interpretation depends in part on the skill and judgment of the clinician" (p. 438). This is illustrated by the VRAG and DVRAG: Both need assessors to score the Psychopathy Checklist–Revised (PCL-R; Hare, 2003), a psychological assessment that requires clinical training and judgment to score. Judgment is also needed to determine the presence or severity of items based on the available information or whether the tool is suited to the individual, outcome, time frame, or question of interest on the basis of existing validation studies. Assessors also need clinical judgment to assign individuals to risk-informed management strategies—a task that research shows is still sadly deficient (Viljoen et al., 2018). Further, circumstances may require a case to be deemed an urgent priority for intervention, such as a threat of death made against a specific person. These instances of clinical judgment are compatible with assessment based primarily on actuarial risk.

However, it would be incorrect to modify risk estimates based on anomalous factors. There is evidence that deviating from actuarial results or structured guidelines produces worse prediction and poorer risk management decisions (Ansbro, 2010; Duwe & Rocque, 2018; Guay & Parent, 2018; McCafferty, 2017; Wormith et al., 2012). Clinicians' confidence in their judgments, moreover, bears little relation to their accuracy (e.g., Miller et al., 2015). Without the gathering, synthesizing, and weighing of extensive information that is beyond the information-processing capacity of most humans, nobody could claim to be an expert in the case of a new individual undergoing assessment. In contrast, consistent scoring and interpretation, and using only those items shown to have incremental validity, makes actuarial instruments a strong, defensible basis for decision making and effective resource allocation.

In contrast to forensic clinicians, antiviolence advocates such as women's shelter and transition house workers seem to attend to valid correlates of domestic violence recidivism, including substance abuse, children in the relationship, and domestic violence history (Cattaneo, 2007; as do women who have been victims of domestic violence, Connor-Smith et al., 2011). I think these professionals would be well positioned to assess violence risk because they are exposed to women returning to the shelter after a repeated episode of violence (a form of follow-up) and to clients who can provide detailed histories of their partners' violent behavior. However, there is no study yet of these professionals' ability to make reliable and accurate predictions of their clients' outcomes.

Conclusion

Although incorporating professional judgment might increase assessors' acceptance of empirically based risk assessment tools (e.g., Williams & Grant, 2006), I believe that the solution is not to encourage unspecified, idiosyncratic deviations from validated scales. Instead, I advise adhering to clear and simple actuarial scoring procedures and applying actuarial scores appropriately (Hilton et al., in press), using methods for incorporating risk scales into structured decision-making systems where available (e.g., McKee et al., 2007).

HYPOTHESIS 2: DYNAMIC RISK FACTORS ARE SUPERIOR TO STATIC RISK FACTORS

> Instruments that consist solely of static factors, or that treat risk factors as static, are valuable principally as classification tools: they identify something that has already happened or is happening now (such as a blip on a radar screen). . . . In contrast, instruments that include modifiable factors are designed to forecast, or estimate the likelihood of, a prospect that has yet to occur and may never. (Falzer, 2013, p. 45)

There is no question that correctional intervention needs to be concerned with risk factors that are changeable and amenable to modification through intervention, often called *dynamic* risk factors (e.g., Bonta & Andrews, 2017). Whether dynamic factors need to be included in risk assessments used to identify which individuals should have the highest priority for intervention is a different matter, however. Most clinicians think that tools that include dynamic variables are more useful for treatment planning, yet they do not use these tools to meet individuals' treatment needs (Viljoen et al., 2018). Furthermore, scholars disagree on what factors are dynamic and how to define and assess such factors. Thus, assessors cannot realize their hope of preventing violence simply by adding potentially changeable risk factors to a risk assessment tool.

Despite this unsure foundation, researchers and practitioners have hailed the incorporation of dynamic risk factors as an important advance in offending risk assessment (e.g., Bonta, 2007). Some called for supplementing risk assessment with "dynamic tools" to assess change during treatment (Olver & Wong, 2011, p. 124), which others argued was desirable yet premature based on the evidence available at the time (Harris & Rice, 2015). There is no research evidence yet that supports dynamic risk assessment in domestic violence, so in this section I draw upon the generally violent and sexually violent offending literatures.

Static Versus Dynamic Measurement

It is critical to think of the static–dynamic distinction in terms of measurement. Researchers generally agree that static risk factors do not change after measurement. Monahan and Skeem (2014) defined four categories of risk factors and called static factors *fixed markers*. Examples are age at first arrest, having ever been married, or having ever had a diagnosis of schizophrenia. Gender is another variable considered essentially static for the purposes of risk assessment; at least, no studies yet have examined transgender as a dynamic risk factor. Static risk factors, being unchanging, need only be measured once.

Some variables are risk factors (that is, they are related to recidivism), and they do change but are not changeable by treatment. Monahan and Skeem (2014) called these *variable markers*. An example is a person's age. Younger age is associated with increased risk of violent recidivism, including domestic violence (e.g., Richards et al., 2013). However, age cannot be changed by intervention. The predictive effect of age is surpassed by a static measure, age at first offense (Rice & Harris, 2014), and may be subsumed by other relatively fixed factors, such as psychopathic personality (Harris & Rice, 2015). Which age measure to use, and how it should impact treatment and release decision, remains highly debated in sex offense risk assessment (Seto, 2013), illustrating that even an apparently straightforward "dynamic" variable raises conceptual and methodological challenges.

Risk factors that are changeable through treatment but lack evidence for posttreatment change that reduces recidivism, are called *variable risk factors* (Monahan & Skeem, 2014) or *potentially variable risk factors* (Harris & Rice, 2015). An example is deviant sexual preferences. Men's sexual arousal can be measured using penile circumference or volume (see Seto, 2013, pp. 45–51, for a description of phallometry). Men who sexually assault adult women respond phallometrically to scenes of violent nonconsensual sex, and men who assault children respond to scenes of sexual activity with pubescent or younger children more than to consensual sex with adults

(Harris et al., 1992). But no research has yet shown that posttreatment change in sexual preferences alters the likelihood of recidivism.

Monahan and Skeem (2014) called *causal risk factors* those that when changed through treatment, measurably reduce the risk of recidivism. Studies reveal that scores on a set of putatively dynamic risk factors do improve prediction of sexual recidivism (e.g., Brankley et al., 2019; Olver, Mundt, et al., 2018; van den Berg et al., 2018) and violent recidivism among individuals in forensic settings (Penney et al., 2016). Testing causal risk factors is methodologically challenging and requires at least three time points (for baseline scores, change scores, and recidivism), variables that are sensitive to change and measured with good reliability, analyses that control for baseline scores as well as any other pertinent differences, samples large enough for statistical power, and so on. Controlling for initial static and dynamic scores substantially attenuates the predictive value of putatively dynamic factors or changes in risk scores (e.g., Brankley et al., 2019; Mastromanno et al., 2018; van den Berg et al., 2018).

Nevertheless, changes in actuarial risk measures significantly reduced (or increased) the rate of arrests for general offending in a sample of nearly 65,000 men and women on probation (Cohen et al., 2016) and contributed significantly to prediction models of violent reoffending among nearly 200,000 men and women released from custody (Howard & Dixon, 2013), controlling for initial risk scores. Other studies have shown similar results for different instruments and adult populations (e.g., De Vries Robbé et al., 2015; Labrecque et al., 2014; Vose et al., 2013). A review of studies linking change scores to general and violent recidivism indicated that the variables with the best evidence were antisocial personality, antisocial attitudes, antisocial beliefs, antisocial associates, substance use and social support (Serin et al., 2013), several of which are among the "central eight" risk factors for criminal recidivism (for a description of the central eight factors, see Bonta & Andrews, 2017, and Limits of Domestic Violence Theory in Chapter 1, this volume). This is crucial research and leagues ahead of current work on domestic violence risk assessment.

A final word on dynamic risk factor measurement: Two time points are necessary to detect change. With at least three waves of measurement, the association of change with subsequent recidivism can be detected (Bonta & Andrews, 2017, p. 18). And because measures vary in how reliable they are over time, change must exceed the error expected from test–retest unreliability (Helmus & Quinsey, 2020). Studies that measure potentially changeable factors only once are not testing their dynamic nature and cannot show whether dynamic factors improve risk assessment. "Dynamic" factors measured on a single occasion are de facto static measures. Harris and Rice (2015) argued, furthermore, that truly dynamic risk factors should be demonstrably changeable through intervention, and posttreatment change should add to the predictive accuracy of the best available static risk assessment, resulting in a more accurate prediction of recidivism among both treated and untreated individuals. This standard requires substantial extra time and effort to assess dynamic risk over and above the (often more predictive) static factors. But these criteria reflect assessors' expectations for dynamic risk assessment. Thus, there is not the obvious and overwhelming evidence for changeable risk factors that might be expected from the rhetoric on dynamic risk assessment.

Does Domestic Violence Risk Change Over Time?

Research using the SARA to reassesses domestic violence risk after intervention has shown that assessed risk can change. Lila et al. (2014) assessed 212 men before and after a court-mandated domestic violence treatment program in Spain. Most of the men (63%) were initially judged to be low risk using the SARA professional judgments. Men were followed for up to 25 months, and 38% were reconvicted for any assault or conditional release violation in this time. Changes in risk levels judged by treatment program staff before and after treatment were associated with lower recidivism, with an odds ratio of 16. This finding suggests that men who completed treatment and changed risk levels were 16 times less likely to be reconvicted than men who remained at high or moderate risk. However, the study did not control for initial SARA judgments or indicate whether initial judgments were associated with recidivism. Also, it is unclear how many men had different risk levels after treatment (some were judged to be higher risk), and how treatment dropouts were handled in the study design.

SARA scores and ratings have also changed across repeated contacts with police (Belfrage et al., 2012). Police scored and rated the SARA for 429 men arrested in Sweden for assault, threat, harassment, or breaches involving a female intimate partner. Among the 93 men who came to the attention of police for a second time, the average SARA score was higher on reassessment. Risk ratings also increased on average. Initial SARA scores predicted recidivism (and judgments approached significance). However, Belfrage and colleagues did not report whether change in risk scores improved prediction. Moreover, it was not clear that change in risk scores exceeded the fluctuations one might expect from imperfect interrater reliability. The stability of scores and ratings between the first and second assessments produced correlation coefficients of .71 and .45, respectively, which were similar to reported interrater reliabilities. Furthermore, officers were not masked to the previous SARA assessment, although this would be difficult to achieve because of the nature of the police investigation.

I explored ODARA change scores in a small convenience sample of 38 cases drawn from the ODARA validation research. The ODARA was scored at the first recidivistic offense, then again (unmasked) for the 14 men with further recidivism. From the first to second new offense, there was a small increase in ODARA scores, from an average of 5.3 to 5.9. The items most likely to change were conditional release failure, barriers to support, threat, and victim concern. The initial score predicted repeated recidivism better than the second (AUCs = .66 and .62, respectively), but neither was statistically significant in this small sample.

Studies of change scores take an important first step toward measuring changes in domestic violence risk and its relation to recidivism. Research that measures change in domestic violence risk, and how change relates to domestic violence recidivism, is still needed. I hope this critique of the hypotheses and evidence for dynamic risk will encourage others to replicate and refine the research conducted so far. Remember that to be usefully dynamic, risk change scores must provide information about recidivism risk over and above the information obtained from a single assessment. It is also important to establish good interrater reliability because poor rater agreement limits the conclusions that can be drawn about change in risk. Furthermore, little is known about test–retest reliability of domestic violence risk assessment tools, a statistic that shows the extent to which risk scores or judgments are stable over time, regardless of intervention. Clearly, the enterprise of dynamic risk assessment assumes natural fluctuations in risk, but the field lacks studies showing what the baseline expected variation is.

Possible Targets for Dynamic Assessment of Domestic Violence Risk

In the quest for dynamic risk assessment, the most promising variables are those which are consistently associated with domestic violence and amenable to intervention. Some potentially dynamic risk factors may be relatively stable, changing over a period of months or years (e.g., Hanson, Harris, et al., 2007). For example, as I described in Chapter 1, indicators of personality such as borderline personality disorder are consistently associated with domestic violence, and antisociality personality with its recidivism. Although personality tends to be stable in adulthood, Helmus and Quinsey

(2020) pointed out that even psychopathy has aspects that can and do vary over time, such as manipulative behavior.

Relatedly, substance use history is a robust risk factor for domestic violence recidivism, appearing on all major domestic violence risk assessment tools (see Chapter 1, this volume). Substance use treatment can reduce both alcohol use and the occurrence and frequency of domestic violence (e.g., O'Farrell & Murphy, 1995) and has been associated with changes in risk (Lila et al., 2014). Daily changes in alcohol use are related to patterns of domestic violence by men and women (e.g., Katerndahl et al., 2014). Other criminogenic needs are also priorities in the search for stable dynamic risk factors: procriminal attitudes, criminal associates, poor marital and family relationships, and employment or school problems. All are prevalent among men with a history of domestic violence in correctional (Stewart & Power, 2014) and forensic settings (Hilton & Radatz, 2018).

Capturing when a domestic offense is most likely might require consideration of additional variables. Helmus and Quinsey (2020) suggested that conditions that fluctuate more or less continuously might be most informative for dynamic risk assessment. Changes in coping and criminal attitudes measured at 3-month intervals, for example, predicted criminal recidivism among men on parole (Jones et al., 2010). Among individuals in forensic settings, measures of mood and compliance predicted antisocial behavior in the following month (Quinsey, Jones, Book, & Barr, 2006). The search for acute factors for domestic violence risk might begin with changes in substance use, anger or other aversive emotions, and relationship status. Stalking is a relatively understudied area of domestic violence that might have the potential for acute assessment (e.g., Eke, Hilton, Meloy, et al., 2011).

Hanson, Harris, and colleagues (2007) coined the term *acute dynamic variables* for highly transient conditions that last hours or days. There is no research indicating the most cost-effective schedule for reassessment, but there is converging evidence that the first few weeks or months after a domestic incident are the most likely to see a repeat offense. We found that the average time to reoffend—from the date of the index assault that made a case eligible for our study, to the date of the next domestic assault, regardless of time in custody—was 15 months (Hilton et al., 2004). In a study of men followed for up to 8 years after release to the community following correctional custody (Hilton et al., 2010), new charges of domestic violence occurred an average of 27 months later. In their study of nearly 30,000 men and women arrested for family violence, Stansfield and Williams (2014) broadened the outcome to new arrests for any family violence or violations of protective or restraining orders and found that most occurred within 200 days of the original arrest.

Dynamic Assessment and Protective Risk Factors

A related matter is the preference for protective factors over risk factors—that is, items that assess individuals' strengths and characteristics related to desistance from offending. The impetus for protective factor assessment comes largely from forensic psychiatry, where mental health recovery is a guiding value, and clinicians' efforts are directed toward improving patients' well-being at least as much as preventing their recidivism. Some researchers have welcomed protective factor assessment in the expectation that it will "aid in risk-management decision making and help inform strengths-based treatment efforts" (de Vries Robbé & Willis, 2017, p. 55). Others caution that protective factors should be more than risk factors scored in reverse (Harris & Rice, 2015).

One meta-analysis of studies using scales based on protective and risk factors found that outcomes related to postdischarge offending were better predicted than aggression and other problems within the hospital (O'Shea & Dickens, 2016). Furthermore, protective scales performed no better than risk scales. I share O'Shea and Dickens's (2016) conclusion that there is no empirical evidence yet supporting protective assessment for criminal justice populations.

Conclusion

Domestic violence has been considered a dynamic phenomenon, characterized by a cycle of tension, violence, and contrition (e.g., Walker, 2017) or a more complex labile pattern (e.g., Katerndahl et al., 2014). This work does not readily map onto current efforts to conduct dynamic risk assessment by measuring potentially changeable factors and their association with recidivism. Research to find treatable factors that are associated with changes in risk is desirable, but using potentially treatable characteristics to assess risk, in the absence of evidence that they improve prediction, confuses the two processes.

Atheoretical risk assessment that does not purport to measure change currently rests on a firmer empirical foundation than schemes that explicitly or implicitly assert causal relations or effectively promise reductions in offending if hypothesized causal factors are addressed. To date, no research has been conducted into truly dynamic assessment of domestic violence risk. Having set a standard for dynamic risk factors and established that there is insufficient evidence yet for causal, variable risk factors for domestic violence, it can be seen that assessors' embrace of dynamic risk assessment is an example of how hypothesis has preceded evidence, or even theory, about the causal mechanisms of criminal behavior.

HYPOTHESIS 3: PREDICTION MODELS ARE INCOMPATIBLE WITH RISK MANAGEMENT

> Risk is a state of potential that need not materialize. That is, a person can be high risk and yet not act violently. This may reflect successful management. This is contrasted with the concept of prediction, which is a definitive statement about that future that is incorrect if it does not materialize. Given the conceptual and pragmatic complexities of risk, use of a comprehensive, structured decision model is necessary. (Douglas et al., 2014, p. 101)

I hope it is already clear to readers that I study risk assessment in the hope of contributing to the management of domestic violence risk and, ultimately, to the prevention of domestic violence. Assessment and management are related but distinct tasks. Some scholars prefer to include risk management and risk communication under a broader definition of risk assessment; even so, assessment is the first step and informs efforts to contain or mitigate risk. Heilbrun (1997) first distinguished between prediction and management as two models of violence risk assessment. Heilbrun's argument was that the approach taken to risk assessment needs to be responsive to the legal context. For example, civil commitment or "dangerous offender" determination requires a model that maximizes predictive accuracy, whereas decisions related to competence to stand trial, community correctional sentences, and graduated release from institutional custody would need an assessment model that incorporates treatment plans and repeated evaluation and monitoring. Notably, Heilbrun pointed out that without postassessment monitoring of risk and modification of plans, the management approach is better conceptualized as a prediction model (Heilbrun, 1997, p. 352). That is, implementation, not instrumentation, distinguishes the prediction and management models.

Management-Model Risk Instruments?

Evaluating predictive accuracy is a generally accepted approach for measuring risk assessment validity. It does not mean that a tool is useful only to "predict" an individual outcome without concern for risk management. Testing the association between risk scores (or judgments) and outcomes like violent recidivism is necessary, regardless of whether the risk assessment produces an actuarial interpretation, a mechanical sum of risk factors present in a case, or a summary judgment of whether risk is high or low, or imminent, or specific to an individual person who may be victimized.

A misunderstanding stems from the notion that different risk assessment methods and variables are needed for prediction versus management.

Specifically, because SPJ tools guide assessors to consider how risk factors might affect risk, and to specify interventions to reduce the risk, it is argued that "SPJ tools offer distinct advantages over actuarial tests when one's goals include . . . to intervene to manage or reduce that risk" (Guy et al., 2012, p. 273). The argument that one type of tool is better than another for risk management implies that the tool not only predicts recidivism but also that variation in its items portends variation in risk and that intervening with these items reliably reduces risk: all prediction-based assumptions. (The reader may recognize these stipulations as criteria for the causal dynamic risk factor.)

Unfortunately, the variables that clinicians think are associated with violence risk are not necessarily empirically valid predictors. For example, variables that clinicians often consider important in correctional treatment—such as insight, treatment motivation, and attitudes minimizing offenses—were unrelated to violent recidivism in large samples of men discharged from forensic hospital (Harris & Rice, 2015). Furthermore, a systematic review of treatment evaluations showed that treatment for mental illness may improve individuals' mental health but have relatively little impact on recidivism risk (e.g., Morgan et al., 2012). It seems there is no getting around the need for a solid basis in predictive accuracy.

Theoretically Motivated Prediction

An alternative solution is to try to include risk factors that are informed by theory, whether in a risk assessment instrument or in the broader assessment process that includes suggestions for intervention (e.g., Mills, 2017). Theoretically important variables imply a (hypothesized) causal association. Causal theory can motivate items for consideration that should then be put to the test in follow-up studies and validation research. For example, the General Personality and Cognitive Social Learning theory of criminal conduct underlies the Risk–Need–Responsivity (RNR) model (Bonta & Andrews, 2017; see Limits of Domestic Violence Theory in Chapter 1, this volume). In a meta-analysis of 126 studies of men and women with mental illness in forensic or correctional settings, the central eight criminogenic risk factors motivated by the theory predicted recidivism substantially better than clinically motivated factors, such as psychiatric history (Bonta et al., 2014). Of course, empirical evidence can help inform and refine the theory, as it has certainly done in the RNR model.

In domestic violence, there is a large literature on theoretically motivated risk factors, as I reviewed in Chapter 1 (Theories of Risk for Domestic

Violence section), but little empirical evidence to suggest that one theory is more informative than another. The call to improve theoretically informed domestic violence intervention grows (e.g., Radatz & Hilton, 2019; Radatz & Wright, 2016; see also Chapter 4, Exhibit 4.1, this volume), but theoretically motivated domestic violence risk assessment is not yet a viable option.

Conclusion

Both policy and daily decisions about offending risk management must be sensitive to the likelihood of violent recidivism. To allocate resources such as custody, treatment, and victim assistance without regard to violence risk would be costly, ineffective, and unfair. Risk assessment tools can be used to evaluate risk-reduction policies (as I show in Chapter 10). But management-oriented risk assessment that rests on empirically unsupported assumptions that interventions aimed at the variables considered in the assessment will lower risk is inadvisable.

I believe the best articulated and supported framework currently available for accomplishing risk management is RNR. As well as defining how risk assessment begins the risk management process, evidence accumulated within the RNR model guides practitioners in the best supported treatment strategies—that is, social learning techniques such as cognitive behavior therapy with attention to individual characteristics that may affect response to treatment (e.g., age, education, language, culture, mental illness). Even so, to combine these risks, needs, responsivity factors, and potential scenarios of recidivism into a risk assessment and asserting that addressing them will reduce risk, reaches beyond the existing evidence.

HYPOTHESIS 4: INDIVIDUAL RISK CANNOT BE INFERRED FROM ACTUARIAL DATA

> Where the practitioner requires only a very quick, "ballpark" comparison, between his or her client and a group of people with a known rate of reoffending, and where the practitioner can be confident that his or her client is comparable to that group, an actuarial tool might be helpful if the practitioner ensures that they do not assume risk is being predicted in the individual case. (Logan, 2016, p. 585)

There is a sense in which one cannot draw firm conclusions about individuals using "group data." For example, data on the level of crime and poverty in various neighborhoods can indicate a relationship between poverty and crime at the neighborhood level (e.g., Pratt & Cullen, 2005) but do not allow researchers to conclude that there is necessarily a relationship between poverty and criminality at the individual level. It is an ecological fallacy to make inferences about individuals using data collected about groups and not individuals. As it turns out, research using individual measures of socioeconomic status and criminal behavior indicates that poverty is a relatively weak and indirect predictor of criminality among individuals (e.g., Bonta & Andrews, 2017, pp. 149–151; Sampson & Laub, 1994).

To create the ODARA and DVRAG, however, we coded information to score the tools and collected recidivism data on individual perpetrators, not "group" data in the sense of the neighborhood poverty and crime data in the previous paragraph. It is reasonable to infer one individual's risk from knowledge of how many similar people (in the group defined by their particular range of scores) were known to have recidivated. Actuarial instruments are designed to make an individual appraisal based on the known outcome of a group of individuals obtaining the same score. Because follow-up data are also measured at the individual level, they can be applied to a new individual without committing the ecological fallacy.

The Precision of Individual Risk Estimates

Indeed, actuarial risk assessment is the only current approach that yields individual estimates of the absolute probability of recidivism. This has been an area of controversy between proponents of clinical as opposed to empirical approaches to risk assessment. It has been argued that individual estimates are statistically unreliable, based on the size of individual confidence intervals. Confidence intervals indicate the level of precision of an average measure (as I described in Chapter 2, Exhibit 2.1). The misapplication of confidence interval formulae to individual cases earned resounding criticism (e.g., Hanson & Howard, 2010; Mossman & Sellke, 2007), including from scholars of statistics outside the field of violence risk assessment (Imrey & Dawid, 2015).

Despite the counterevidence, others concluded that actuarial data "cannot be used to estimate the specific probability or absolute likelihood that an individual person will commit violence in the future with any reasonable degree of precision or certainty" (Hart & Cooke, 2013, p. 95). Working with Christopher Lowenkamp, Grant Harris and I presented data to refute the reasoning and analysis behind the rejection of individual risk estimates. We demonstrated, in samples as large as 26,642 to as small as 90 (the sample size used by Hart and Cooke), that risk estimate precision depends on sample size (Harris, Lowenkamp, & Hilton, 2015). Actuarial estimates are typically derived from samples of at least several hundred cases. In short, the empirical procedures for developing actuarial risk assessment tools ensure that they are suited to inferring individual risk. As Helmus and Quinsey (2020) stated, "applying information from previous groups to individuals with similar characteristics (e.g., the same risk score) is not only defensible practice, but it is the strongest empirical evidence we currently have" (p. 135).

Individual Risk and Bias

A related concern is that an actuarial instrument cannot be used to infer an individual's risk until validated on a group bearing the individual's particular attributes. The feature of interest could be held by a subgroup of cases used in validation studies, such as being under 18 years or over 40 years, living in a city center or a rural community, or having a particular mental disorder. The VRAG tools have been shown to predict outcomes in a range of subgroups to whom actuarial assessment was once thought to be inapplicable, including individuals with schizophrenia, those with extreme psychopathy scores, older persons with a history of sex offenses, and those who have offenses against young people (Harris, Rice, et al., 2015). On the other hand, the feature of interest might be a distinctive set of traits not accounted for in data collection. This gap is of increasing concern as assessors, researchers, and policy makers become more aware of the potential for bias against individuals of Indigenous descent and other ethnic groups in how risk assessment procedures are developed and applied.

In the case of *Ewert v. Canada* (2018), a federal inmate identifying as Métis argued that certain assessment tools should not have been used to aid decisions about his custody and security because they had not been demonstrated to be accurate for people of Indigenous heritage. This case highlighted possible cultural bias in violence risk assessment and psychological assessment. Meta-analytic research and large-scale studies have shown that several structured risk assessment tools predict recidivism among both Indigenous and non-Indigenous groups, although effect sizes have been lower for Indigenous offenders (Gutierrez et al., 2016). The case sparked further research into possible cultural bias in risk assessment (e.g., Lee et al., 2020). Olver, Neumann, and colleagues (2018) found large predictive effects among both Indigenous and non-Indigenous men for scores on the PCL-R and its component factors, and few group differences in how PCL-R components uniquely contributed to recidivism; however, men of Indigenous heritage recidivated more than non-Indigenous men with the same PCL-R score, across follow-up times and outcomes. Olver, Neumann, and colleagues (2018) concluded that the PCL-R was appropriate for individuals of Indigenous ancestry and reminded assessors to be sensitive to cultural and individual differences. Cultural bias remains an important matter for future research in the field of risk assessment, and in domestic violence risk assessment specifically.

Bias can also be tied to socioeconomic status. Concern has arisen that risk factors such as lower education and unemployment could be indirect measures of lower socioeconomic status and that risk assessment tools including such factors could exacerbate inequities in the criminal justice system. In an attempt to study this bias experimentally, Skeem et al. (2020) presented judges with hypothetical case descriptions of either a casual laborer with no high school diploma or a computer retail store worker with a computer science degree. When given only a case summary, judges were more likely to sentence the store-worker than the laborer to jail. However, the opposite was true when judges were given information from a risk assessment tool (which included education and employment problems as a risk factor). Risk assessment tools may not be able to overcome systemic biases, including disproportionate criminal justice processing of ethnic minorities (e.g., Mears et al., 2016), or the possible risk-increasing effects of contact with the criminal justice system (e.g., Prins, 2019). Empirically supported methods are one of the best ways available to protect against bias in decision making (Gutierrez et al., 2016); even so, careful implementation, ongoing evaluation, and correction for disparities in policing, judicial, and correctional practice is required.

Although research designed to examine this issue is emerging (e.g., Stansfield & Williams, 2014), it remains understudied in domestic violence risk assessment and an important area for future research. The past body of violence risk assessment research shows that the strongest risk factors are consistent across methods and populations (e.g., Skeem & Monahan, 2011), and actuarial data can be interpreted as a valid estimate of risk notwithstanding individual differences in other characteristics. However, it can be argued that evidence should be presented for a tool's validity in ethnic subgroups specifically before it can be used—a call that, of course, applies equally to actuarial and SPJ assessments. In my career, I have preferred to speak only on matters for which I have a competent knowledge of the relevant empirical evidence. However, I am increasingly aware that silence on the issue of bias, and the White privilege that I and many of my professional colleagues in this field have, may contribute to systemic racism in the study and application of domestic violence risk assessment.

Research on the validity of the ODARA and other risk assessment tools in minority populations is essential, as are studies on not only the benefits but also the potential harms of domestic violence risk assessment to individuals who identify with racialized and marginalized groups.

Controversies in Inferring Individual Risk of Domestic Violence

A related criticism is that actuarial instruments rely on construction research using a single sample that renders them not generalizable to other populations (e.g., Douglas et al., 2014). In fact, both construction and cross-validation samples were included in the first published accounts of both the ODARA and the DVRAG (Hilton et al., 2004; Hilton, Harris, Rice, et al., 2008) and the ODARA has now been validated in other populations by me and other researchers (see Chapter 4, this volume). Note, however, that the absolute probabilities of recidivism reported for any sample may vary as a function of follow-up time, definition of recidivism, and other variables, so I encourage assessors not to rely solely on absolute recidivism estimates when making inferences about individual risk. Instead, interpretation should include the individual's rank order with respect to risk, which is more stable and generalizable.

Some authors have criticized actuarial tools for their focus on the likelihood of recidivism, a concern taken up by domestic violence researchers who argue that assessors should take into account not only the likelihood but also the nature, severity, frequency, and imminence of any future violence (e.g., Kropp & Hart, 2000). ODARA and DVRAG scores are associated with all of these characteristics; indeed, the DVRAG was constructed in part for its association with the severity and frequency of domestic violence recidivism (see the Selection of Predictors and Outcomes section in Chapter 5, this volume). Thus, the personal attributes that permit the actuarial identification of at least one domestic assault are the same as those that predict the total number of assaults, their total severity, and how soon they occur (e.g., Harris, Rice, et al., 2015; Hilton, Harris, Rice, et al., 2008).

However, the ability to forecast domestic homicide, specifically, especially against a particular, identifiable partner, remains a challenge. Homicide is a statistically rare event, and although that is no comfort at all to those who are victimized or their devastated survivors, it does mean that it is difficult to identify individuals at risk (e.g., Thornton, 2017). Out of hundreds of men that my colleagues and I identified in police records for assaulting their partner, only one later killed his partner in our study time frame averaging nearly 5 years (Hilton et al., 2004). This statistical challenge has not prevented efforts to create assessments that are sensitive to the risk of domestic homicide. Many domestic homicides are preceded by violence and other antisocial behavior that appears to go unheeded (e.g., Eriksson et al., 2019; Vatnar, Friestad, & Bjørkly, 2017), raising the call for homicide assessment protocols such as the Lethality Assessment Protocol (e.g., Grant & Cross-Denny, 2017). Case-control studies by researchers Jacquelyn Campbell (see Researcher Profile 1.1) and Myrna Dawson (see Researcher Profile 8.1) have been important to identifying risk markers of intimate partner homicides (e.g., J. C. Campbell et al., 2003; Dawson & Piscitelli, 2017). However, when individuals are matched on criminal history and personal characteristics, there are few risk factors that clearly distinguish domestic homicide from nonfatal cases, and these factors relate to antisociality rather than commonly perceived fatality risks such as suicidality (Jung & Stewart, 2019).

In a study of men who committed a lethal domestic homicide, those who had a police record of assault on an intimate partner before the homicide would have scored in the highest category of risk for domestic violence recidivism had they been assessed at the prior assault (Eke, Hilton, Harris, et al., 2011). Similar research found relatively high Danger Assessment scores in domestic homicide cases (e.g., Messing, Campbell, & Snider, 2017; see also Chapter 1, this volume). This certainly does not mean, however, that all or even most men who pose this level of risk for domestic violence recidivism will probably kill their partners. So far, there is no tool that can identify individuals who will commit domestic homicide in the future.

Conclusion

A substantial body of research supports the use of actuarial data to infer individual risk. An individual's risk of recidivism, and more importantly their rank order according to risk within a given population, is informative for both individual risk management and policy-level decisions about the intensity of treatment or security for persons in the criminal justice system. Actuarial data allow newly processed individuals to be matched to aggregate data, permitting the inference of individual risk and the effective application of policy across a system. Although there is the distinct concern for the risk of domestic homicide, it is not clear how risk assessment research will inform the prevention of domestic homicide specifically. Groups of researchers, practitioners, and advocates such as the Canadian Domestic Homicide Prevention Initiative (CDHPI.ca) are coming together to grapple with this vital question.

The link from risk assessment to prevention of violence requires that the assessed risk can be communicated effectively. In the next chapter, I look at this key component of any risk assessment and management process and examine the current research for improving the effectiveness of risk communication.

POINTS TO REMEMBER

- Clinical judgment may be needed for some risk assessment items but should not be relied on to determine the final risk summary or used to adjust an actuarial risk score.
- There is little evidence to date for causal risk factors for violence—factors that when changed through treatment, measurably reduce the risk of recidivism—and no research yet on usefully dynamic risk factors for domestic violence.
- Prediction-based risk assessment includes any method that assesses risk independent of postassessment monitoring of risk and plans that respond to changing individual needs.
- Statistical methods permit, and a substantial body of research supports, the use of actuarial data to infer individual risk. Actuarial tools measure individuals' risk using characteristics shown to increase predictive power in previous groups of individuals.
- Actuarial risk assessment tools for domestic violence are related to the occurrence, severity, and timing of recidivism, but no tool can yet predict domestic homicide.

QUESTIONS TO CONSIDER

1. Name the four types of risk factor. Give an example of each.
2. Describe one controversy in violence risk assessment that has yet to be addressed by domestic violence researchers.
3. Why would it be difficult to design an agreed-on, theoretically informed approach to domestic violence risk assessment?
4. What are some of the methodological challenges in conducting research to test causal risk factors? Imagine you are designing a study of dynamic

risk assessment for domestic violence. Choose one challenge and describe how you would overcome it.

5. What value might training as a clinician bring to violence risk assessment? What are the limitations of clinical judgment in risk assessment, and why might unstructured clinical judgment of violence risk remain popular despite contrary empirical support?

RESEARCHER PROFILE 8.1 MYRNA DAWSON, PhD

I began my undergraduate studies in journalism and gained work experience as a junior reporter on a community newspaper. The small Canadian town experienced a series of murders, and I was assigned to take photos of the accused for one of the trials and to cover a second trial. The convicted murderer whose case I reported on later wrote me a letter about what it meant to be imprisoned either physically or psychologically. These cases led me to think there was much more to understanding people who commit homicide than simply what is said in the courtroom.

During my time at this paper, I got to know a woman who, it turned out, was physically abused by her husband. Everyone seemed to know but just accepted it. When I was in graduate school, and working in a coffee shop, one of our regular customers who came in daily was killed by her husband. At the time, I was taking a class on women in the criminal justice system, and I read a report by Rosemary Gartner on domestic homicide. I realized this was what I wanted to work on, and Dr. Gartner eventually became my thesis supervisor for my PhD in sociology at the University of Toronto. Volunteering as a research assistant for the Intimate Femicide in Ontario study, led by the Women We Honour Action Committee and Dr. Gartner, had an important influence on my career. I traveled around the province to code data from prosecution files and police reports. I had an amazing experience and met many people working in the courts and law enforcement who later became contacts for my own research. As a condition of volunteering, I was able to use these data. This database now has about 8,500 cases, both female and male homicide victims, and I have used it to examine how the concept of intimacy is constructed in the courtroom, which typically leads to more lenient sentences. In the late 1990s, I was a research assistant for an evaluation study of Ontario's pilot specialized domestic violence courts. Again, I pored over the detailed information in hardcopy court files, and I continue this kind of research in my work as director of the Canadian

Femicide Observatory for Justice and Accountability and co-director of the Canadian Domestic Homicide Prevention Initiative.

Quantitative research is far more than simply crunching data, and it can be very time-consuming. Secondary data analysis can be valuable too; using the primary data means I can delve into the details, constructing a comprehensive understanding of what happened from various perspectives. One of the challenges is building trust with those from whom you want data, getting through all the legal and ethical requirements to obtain access to data, but it is worth it when access is granted. Since my work on the Intimate Femicide study, I have built a relationship with the Ontario Office of the Chief Coroner and continue to access these data. I also currently serve on the Ontario Domestic Violence Death Review Committee that reviews closed cases and makes recommendations for improving the system's response to domestic violence. Another challenge to working with large data sets is the risk of forgetting that there are real people behind these data. It's important for me to remember that these are the people I got into the research for, and they need to remain at the forefront of my mind.

My role as a Canada Research Chair has enhanced my time to travel and conduct research. I am comparing how Canada and Australia conduct domestic violence death reviews and how their courts construct and use the concept of intimacy. I have not forgotten my roots in journalism. It trained me to write simply and clearly, which is an important skill because good writing can really help researchers make an impact. Writing is still what I love to do the most.

About the Researcher

Dr. Dawson is a professor, Canada Research Chair in Public Policy in Criminal Justice, and director of the Centre for the Study of Social and Legal Responses to Violence at the University of Guelph.

9 RISK COMMUNICATION

The murder of Arlene May by Randy Iles, while he was on conditional release, was a tragic lesson in failed risk communication (see Introduction, this volume). In the aftermath of the May–Iles murder-suicide, there was much public discussion about the criminal justice system's apparent inability to assess and communicate the danger Randy Iles posed throughout the period leading up to the fatalities, especially during his court appearances. No actuarial risk assessment for domestic violence was available at that time, but Iles did have an extensive criminal history, including threats of violence. The courts, police services, and even a shelter Arlene May visited did have risk-relevant information, but their efforts to share and act on that information were insufficient, ineffectual, and—perhaps most important—uncoordinated.

A different, dramatic example of risk communication was seen in the case of Ralph Hadley. Ralph and Gillian Hadley married in 1997. Her two children lived with them, and they had a child together. Ralph was charged with criminal negligence causing bodily harm in an incident involving Gillian's son; this charge was withdrawn when he agreed to a peace bond.

https://doi.org/10.1037/0000223-010
Domestic Violence Risk Assessment: Tools for Effective Prediction and Management, Second Edition, by N. Z. Hilton

The next month, during an argument between the estranged couple, Ralph assaulted Gillian and was consequently charged with assault and breach of the peace bond. Ralph was released again on bail but continued to contact Gillian despite a no-contact order. When Gillian complained to the police about Ralph's repeated attempts to contact her, he was charged with this breach and with criminal harassment, and again released on bail with a new no-contact order. A police officer filed a brief stating that Ralph will "absolutely reoffend." A pretrial hearing on all outstanding charges eventually took place after 10 costly adjournments in the provincial court. Out on bail, Ralph broke into the matrimonial home, where Gillian was living. After a dramatic chase in front of the house, during which neighbors managed to rescue the baby, Ralph fatally shot first her and then himself (Brown, 2001; FACT Ontario, 2000).

Communication of risk, as this example makes clear, is not as straightforward as providing an assessment report. Effective risk communication is essential to the usefulness of a risk assessment tool, coherent functioning of the "system" responding to domestic violence, and adherence to the Risk–Needs–Responsivity (RNR) principles of effective correctional service (e.g., Bonta & Andrews, 2017). An actuarial risk score placed on court and criminal records and shared with community victim services, could serve as a fulcrum for a coordinated community response. In this chapter, I present evidence that actuarial risk assessment results can be communicated effectively, leading to good forensic decisions. Most of this work has been conducted with respect to general or sexual violence, but I will identify implications for domestic violence risk communication, and guide readers through a model for reporting results on the Ontario Domestic Assault Risk Assessment (ODARA; Hilton et al., 2004) and the Domestic Violence Risk Appraisal Guide (DVRAG; Hilton, Harris, Rice, et al., 2008). It is my fervent hope that the ODARA and DVRAG assessments are not merely scored and filed but tools for communication within and across criminal justice, intervention, and victim services.

"ASK THE EXPERT": WHAT DO FORENSIC PROFESSIONALS PREFER TO HEAR?

A popular way to determine the best approach to a task is to ask the people who are already doing it. When my colleagues and I began to study forensic risk communication, the few existing studies had surveyed clinicians about what they did. A major contributor to that work (as well as to current risk communication research) was Kirk Heilbrun (see Researcher Profile 9.1). Heilbrun et al. (1999) reported that only one of 55 clinicians used numerical ways to communicate violence risk. Half the respondents explained that they did not use probabilities because they did not believe the research literature justified them. Others said there was no suitable assessment or that numbers could be more misleading and open to misinterpretation than nonnumerical statements. Heilbrun and colleagues compared eight forms of risk communication (only five of which contained a conclusion about violence risk). The least popular option was "Express risk relative to norm or base rate for that population," and the most favored was "Describe recent and present behavior, give clinical impressions based on history, current behavior, mental status, and dynamics, and make a prediction." In subsequent surveys, simply identifying risk factors and specifying risk-reducing interventions were most popular among clinicians (Heilbrun et al., 2000, 2004). On average, the next most popular forms of risk communication were characterizing violence risk as high, moderate, or low or simply describing clinical features presumed to be relevant to risk. Thus, clinical description was preferred over any statement of the probability of violence.

Grann and Pallvik (2002) confirmed this preference when they found 56 nonnumerical expressions of degrees of risk among 122 actual forensic evaluations. It seemed that forensic clinicians endorsed clinical and intuitive approaches to both the evaluation of and their communication about violence risk. This preference for categorical risk communication remains into the mid-2010s. A survey of more than 2,000 risk assessors from 44 countries, known as IRiS (e.g., Singh et al., 2014), revealed that 85% of assessors worldwide communicate risk categorically, compared with 26% who use a dichotomy (e.g., "is likely to engage in violence") and only 14% who use probabilistic terms (e.g., percent likelihood of violence; Heilbrun et al., 2016). The most common reasons for rejecting numerical statements, in Heilbrun's earlier research, were negative and subjective: "I don't feel that precise" and "I don't know how to go from base rates to single cases" (Heilbrun et al., 1999, p. 403). These concerns appear to persist, despite a strong research foundation for the accuracy and precision of numerical approaches (Heilbrun et al., 2016; Neal & Grisso, 2014).

Studies show that "risk illiteracy" (Garcia-Retamero & Cokely, 2013) limits clinicians' ability to understand data that are important to decisions that depend on the magnitude of risk. More numerate people appear to make better decisions using numeric risk information because they deliberate and evaluate decisions more (Ghazal et al., 2014). They make better use of base rates, relative risks, and percentage information (e.g., Bodemer et al., 2014) and are less influenced by framing (e.g., being told that outcomes are 75% positive or 25% negative; e.g., Peters, 2012). In forensic decisions, more numerate people are less influenced by anecdotal information (e.g., Scurich, 2015) or by the listing of individual items from a risk assessment (e.g., Scurich, Monahan, & John, 2012), a practice that my colleagues and I found increases perceived risk (Hilton, Carter, et al., 2008). Yet even highly educated adults do poorly on statistical numeracy tests (e.g., Hilton et al., 2017; Taylor & Byrne-Davis, 2017). Risk-illiterate forensic decisions foster nonadherence to the RNR principles and could cause both unfair detention of individuals and avoidable harm to victims.

Another reason that assessors might prefer categorical risk communication is to make a presumptive judgment tied to a recommended action. For example, mock jurors were more likely to commit a man with a sex offense history to institutional treatment (having beyond a reasonable doubt that he was likely to reoffend) when risk was communicated categorically rather than probabilistically (Krauss et al., 2018). When clinicians use categorical labels to communicate risk in court, they are implicitly prescribing a course of action rather than simply providing the facts of assessed risk (Scurich, 2018; Varela et al., 2014). Jurors consider risk assessment reports more acceptable and important when cases score relatively high rather than low (e.g., Scurich & Krauss, 2013), and the effect is stronger when risk is communicated categorically rather than statistically (e.g., Varela et al., 2014).

I also think it possible that clinicians favor nonnumerical categories (e.g., low, moderate, or high risk) because they wish to communicate comparative risk. Comparative risk (as in rank order or percentile) is more useful than absolute probability because it permits more discrimination among individuals and does not fluctuate according to the particular definition of the outcome or the follow-up time of interest. Percentiles can be used to describe how risk scores are distributed in the population of persons known to offend and to indicate the proportion of cases that have the same or higher measured risk as the individual being assessed. Ironically, jurors and clinicians alike appear challenged to understand comparative risk (e.g., Varela et al., 2014) and may confuse it with absolute probability (e.g., Hilton et al., 2005).

WHAT DOES EFFECTIVE RISK COMMUNICATION LOOK LIKE?

Another way to decide the best way to communicate risk is to measure the effect of various methods. An inherent assumption is that there is an optimal outcome, or a performance standard, by which the proficiency of decision making can be evaluated: Objectively high-risk cases should receive greater supervision (or generally more intensive intervention) than lower risk cases. By this definition, all else being equal, the greater the difference between the use of secure custody for individuals of highest versus lowest risk, the greater is the forensic decision-making proficiency. Risk communication that results in the most proficient decisions is, I argue, the most effective communication. The difference between risk-related decisions for cases of objectively different risk provides a standard against which to measure the effect of risk communication (and other aspects of a system's performance).

Does Communicating Actuarial Risk Affect Forensic Decisions?

My study with Janet Simmons of decisions by an autonomous tribunal that determined the security placement of individuals held in forensic hospitals (Hilton & Simmons, 2001) has become an interesting story of the time taken for evidence-based risk assessment to influence decision making. The relevant legislation required the tribunal to base decisions primarily on the need to protect the public. Tribunals have a range of available options from detention in maximum security, to transfer to a less secure hospital, to discharge to the community with or without conditions.

Our study's principal concern was the extent to which actuarial risk scores influenced clinicians' recommendations to, and subsequent decisions by, the tribunal. Previous studies had concluded that such forensic tribunals were essentially "rubber-stamping" recommendations made by psychiatrists, although there was little relationship between clinical judgments and recidivism (e.g., Konečni & Ebbesen, 1984, p. 12; Quinsey et al., 1998). Therefore, we expected recommendations by clinicians, and psychiatrists in particular, to influence the tribunal strongly, but we also expected that scores on the Violence Risk Appraisal Guide (VRAG; Harris, Rice, et al., 2015) would influence them both. At the time, actuarial violence risk assessment was fairly new, and there was no evidence that tribunals would routinely use such information. Our expectations, however, were based on the fact that the VRAG had been developed in the study institution, hospital administrators and government officials had supported the VRAG's creation and implementation, and VRAG scores had been placed on individual patient records.

We collected data on decisions made since 1992, when the VRAG was first admitted in tribunal hearings. That same year, trained staff began completing the VRAG so that, by 1997, 90% of patients' files had a VRAG report soon after admission. The report provided the information considered for each patient's score on each item and a statement of the percentile rank, risk category (1–9), and probability of violent recidivism within a stated time frame (7 or 10 years) similar to that for the DVRAG (Chapter 7, Table 7.2). Tribunal decisions tended to be conservative, most resulting in no disposition change; therefore, we oversampled transfer and discharge decisions to bring the proportion of these cases to about a third.

It is important to note that in this study of risk-related decision proficiency, we were not evaluating the validity of actuarial or clinical assessment. VRAG scores were already established as an objective index of risk; the empirical question was whether clinical opinion and tribunal decision would be related to VRAG scores. If there was no VRAG score available to the tribunal hearing, it was obtained or scored later. The VRAG reports that were available entailed one form of risk communication, and we expected that their availability would improve decision-making proficiency by increasing the association between VRAG score and the tribunal decisions.

We found a large association between tribunal decisions and opinions given by psychiatrists and clinical teams. We were wrong, however, in our expectation that decisions would be related to the VRAG score. A very small association between VRAG score and tribunal decisions was detectable when the score was available and, in these cases, was the only thing related to tribunal decisions in addition to clinical opinion. The association between VRAG score and clinical opinion was essentially zero overall, and even a little worse when the score was known. Consequently, there was no difference in objective risk of violence between individuals who were detained in maximum security and those given a less secure placement. Clearly, neither the tribunal's decisions nor the advice received from clinicians showed evidence of forensic decision-making proficiency (Hilton & Simmons, 2001).

Courtroom judges' decision making can be similarly influenced by clinical opinion testimony over more accurate actuarial assessment (e.g., Blais, 2015). The Hilton and Simmons (2001) results showed that the tribunal, far from juggling multiple and sometimes conflicting sources of information, simply shifted most decision-making responsibility to the psychiatrists who testified about the best placement for the patients. In more than 90% of cases, this testimony exactly corresponded with the tribunal decision. A statistical model of clinical opinion revealed that men with more serious criminal histories, more institutional management problems over the previous year, less compliance with or response to psychiatric drugs, and men who were less physically attractive were least likely to garner a favorable recommendation from clinicians. Most of these characteristics are, in fact, irrelevant to the tribunal's primary mandate. On the basis of our experience on multidisciplinary clinical teams and our conversations with clinicians who testified at the tribunals, we concluded that the clinicians unsuccessfully attempted to balance the actuarial risk information with unaided clinical intuition or simply perceived actuarial risk to be irrelevant.

Consequently, recidivism among those released was significantly related to VRAG scores but not to clinical opinion. On the basis of observed rates of violent recidivism (Harris, Rice, et al., 2015), the expected rate of violent recidivism over the ensuing decade for individuals transferred or discharged from forensic hospital was nearly twice that which could have been achieved by release decisions governed by actuarial scores (Hilton & Simmons, 2001). Thus, effective risk communication could have cut the risk to society in half without an increase in the number or proportion of individuals detained.

A later study found some improvement in tribunal decisions made between 2000 and 2003—a modest statistical association between the VRAG and clinicians' advice to the tribunal—but no significant improvement in the proficiency of tribunal decisions (McKee et al., 2007). Then Crocker et al. (2014) read thousands of mental health tribunal decisions across Canada between 2000 and 2005 and found that decisions to discharge individuals were associated with scores on a structured risk assessment tool. Wilson et al. (2015) confirmed that decision-makers attended to the same risk factors that clinicians cited in their reports, although items pertaining to mental disorder symptoms and diagnoses were cited most often. Most recently, two colleagues and I examined decisions made at our institution in 2009 to 2012, up to 20 years after cases in the Hilton and Simmons study (Hilton, Simpson, & Ham, 2016). We now found that both clinical recommendations and dispositions to transfer patients were associated with VRAG scores. In multivariate analysis, the actuarial risk made no independent contribution to tribunal decisions after clinical opinions. This finding suggests that effective risk communication by assessors is key to risk-informed decisions and adherence to the first of the RNR principles. In the next sections, I examine what methods of communication can increase the influence of actuarial risk on forensic decisions.

Does Communicating Actuarial Risk Plus Risk Factors Improve Forensic Decisions?

In a first attempt to improve risk communication, my colleagues and I tested whether clinicians would use the VRAG more in security decisions when the actuarial risk score was clearly communicated, compared with only risk-relevant case information or risk-irrelevant case information (Hilton et al., 2005). As in previous studies of forensic decision-making, we limited the case information to a single paragraph plus a summary communication about the availability and results of "an actuarial risk assessment." Clinicians typically have much more information available but appear not to make use of it all in their decision making (Quinsey & Ambtman, 1979). In our study, each forensic clinician read two short case summaries of men described as patients in a maximum-security forensic hospital with either a 24% or 64% probability of violent recidivism within 10 years of opportunity, based on the VRAG. VRAG score was either explicitly stated or only implicitly available from the risk-relevant case information. The design was a 2 (24% vs. 64% probability) × 2 (risk-relevant vs. risk-irrelevant case information) × 2 (actuarial summary statement present vs. not). Clinicians estimated the likelihood of violent recidivism and compared it with that of other men detained in maximum security.

One might imagine that communicating the risk information twice—once in the risk-relevant case material and again in the actuarial summary—would improve its effectiveness. In fact, the effect was to increase the estimated risk, such that decisions were more conservative than accurate. Thus, contrary to the clinical lore that more information means more proficient decisions, providing case information reduced clinicians' accuracy, perhaps because they did not recognize that the risk-relevant information was subsumed by the actuarial summary statement.

Does Communicating Actuarial Plus Categorical Risk Improve Forensic Decisions?

In our next study, my colleagues and I wondered whether we could communicate actuarial risk more effectively if we provided nonnumerical categories to add emphasis to probabilistic information (Hilton, Carter, et al., 2008). We found no such evidence. Instead, there was substantial disagreement among forensic clinicians as to the numeric meaning associated with low, moderate, and high risk. On average, clinicians indicated that low risk was 0% to 27% likelihood of violent recidivism, moderate risk was 28% to 68%, and high risk was 69% to 100%. Averages, however, hid a great deal of disagreement: More than a third of the range that was moderate on average (38%–54%) was considered low by some participants and high by others.

We also found that forensic clinicians disagreed in the percentiles they thought should correspond to the three risk categories. The actual numbers they assigned to each comparative risk category were so similar to those for absolute likelihood of violent recidivism that clinicians evidently did not treat them as different metrics. Whereas probability of recidivism depends on the definition of recidivism and the time frame of interest, comparative risk depends on the population to which the individual is being compared (e.g., other men with a history of violent offenses, the general population). Our research has found that forensic clinicians do not distinguish between these fundamentally distinct concepts in practice.

This study was neither the first nor the last to report the lack of consensus on the meaning of nonnumerical risk categories among forensic and nonforensic assessors. Violence risk communication studies repeatedly show that nonnumerical risk terms are interpreted inconsistently, and yield overestimations of risk (e.g., Krauss et al., 2018) even when base rate data are provided (e.g., Varela et al., 2014; Walters et al., 2014). Probabilistic category estimates for violence risk have been obtained in more recent studies, including the IRiS survey, in which assessors estimated the maximum absolute probability for low risk and the minimum for high risk, without a stated time frame (average responses were 24% and 54%, respectively; Heilbrun et al., 2016, p. 158). However, category boundaries show some variability across studies and appear to be influenced by contextual factors such as the nature of the violent crime stated (e.g., Evans & Salekin, 2016; Knighton et al., 2014).

My colleagues and I demonstrated a context effect known as anchoring, whereby the risk level of one case influenced the perceived risk of a second case (Hilton, Carter, et al., 2008). We gave forensic clinicians a brief description of a group of men with a history of violent offenses who were described as having either a 10% probability of violent recidivism (10th percentile), a 48% probability (65th percentile), or an 82% probability (93rd percentile). Then we presented a brief description of a second group—the target group—that was always stated as having a 48% probability. Participants then rated the target group as low, moderate, or high risk. Although the target group did not vary in objective risk, participants judged them as high risk more often when the previous group had a 10% probability (see Figure 9.1). There was also a tendency to judge the target group as low risk more often when the previous group was at the 93rd percentile (Hilton, Carter, et al., 2008).

Readers familiar with the psychology of thinking (communicated so effectively by Kahneman, 2011) will not be surprised by the effects that individual or contextual characteristics can have on how information is perceived and used. Psychological research generally indicates that nonnumerical judgments show poor agreement and are invalidly influenced by context (e.g., Karelitz & Budescu, 2004). Research into medical risk communication has revealed aspects of the message that can influence people's understanding, including using frequencies versus percentages,

FIGURE 9.1. Percentage of Forensic Clinicians Rating the Same Target Group of Individuals as High Risk, as a Function of the Stated Risk of a Previous Group

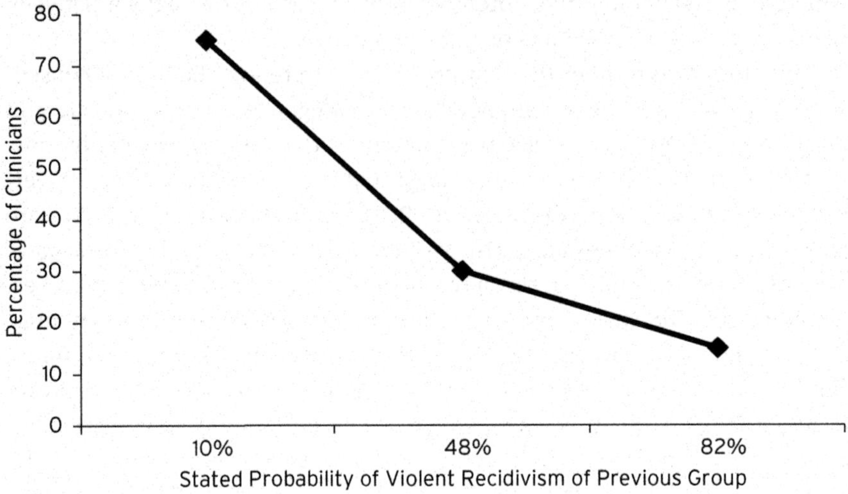

Note. The target risk group was identified as having a 48% probability of violent recidivism. Data from Hilton, Carter, Harris, and Sharpe (2008).

and presenting the benefits of action versus the adverse effects of inaction (for review, see Hilton, Scurich, & Helmus, 2015). For example, when students read a case summary in which there was "a 26% probability of violence occurring" they were more likely to commit the hypothetical individual to psychiatric hospital, compared with students who were told there was "a 74% probability of violence not occurring" (Scurich & John, 2011), evidencing poor reliability of decision making.

Reliability and Interpretation of Risk

In the ODARA and DVRAG construction and cross-validation studies, that were conducted on the basis of file coding, interrater reliability correlation coefficients of at least .80 on continuous measures were considered acceptable for inclusion in the research; in a field simulation, agreement was .95 between police officers (Hilton et al., 2004; and see Characteristics of the ODARA in Chapter 3, this volume). One problem for both research and practice is that if an instrument cannot be scored reliably, then it cannot reliably yield an accurate assessment of the risk of violence when used in practice. The less obvious concern is that assessors and decision-makers cannot effectively communicate and manage risk because they do not agree on the risk posed by an individual. This problem is exacerbated by lack of awareness of the amount of disagreement.

PROMISING PRACTICES IN VIOLENCE RISK COMMUNICATION

As the challenges to reliably and effectively communicating risk have been elucidated, scholars have updated recommendations for practice and policy (e.g., Hilton, Scurich, & Helmus, 2015; Scurich & John, 2012; Scurich, 2018; Stoff & Swerlick, 2013). I will describe two emerging suggestions for improvement that seem to show promise—visual aids and standardized categories—and nascent work on communicating change.

Using Graphs to Illustrate Risk Information

Researchers have experimented with graphs to aid comprehension of risk statistics. Statistics can be confusing, especially when combined with additional case information and for less numerate decision-makers, as I described earlier in this chapter. In experiments I conducted with Elke Ham, Kevin Nunes, Nicole Rodrigues, Cairina Frank, and Michael Seto, students made improved forensic decisions when they read statistical information supplemented with a visual aid, compared with statistics alone (Hilton et al., 2017). We defined effective decision making as assigning actuarially higher risk individuals to greater security (e.g., commit to maximum security vs. release to the community) than lower risk individuals. College students read case summaries and risk statistics based on the VRAG, with or without figures illustrating the VRAG results. We tested bar graphs illustrating either absolute probability of violent recidivism or percentile rank, a series of pie charts, and a risk thermometer (similar to a fundraising thermometer but in horizontal orientation). Without the graph, some participants assigned higher risk individuals to lower security than lower risk individuals. Graphs improved decision making overall, and the probability bar graph had the most beneficial effect. When we tested this bar graph with forensic clinicians, we found no overall effect on decision making; however, staff with more work experience on average only made proficient decisions when they viewed the graph (Hilton et al., 2017).

Batastini and colleagues (2019) tested a similar bar graph that displayed both 7- and 10-year probability of violent recidivism according to the VRAG; however, they included a statement cautioning against interpreting the actuarial probability as the individual's estimated risk. The graph had no effect overall on ratings of risk or danger.

In my recent research with Maaike Helmus (see Researcher Profile 9.2), we tested a bar graph, a risk thermometer, and an icon array in a study of sexual violence risk communication (Hilton & Helmus, 2020). Scores on an objective numeracy test were the biggest contributor to understanding the actuarial assessment results, but having any kind of graph made a significant improvement. Participants overestimated the risk of sexual recidivism; however, those who saw a graph perceived risk to be lower overall, and closer to the stated risk. Percentile information illustrated by an icon array graph produced the largest perceived difference between the actuarially higher and lower risk case. Icon arrays have shown much promise in medical risk communication because they can portray the sensitivity and specificity of screening tests by highlighting the proportion of cases with and without a positive test result and those with and without actual disease (e.g., Zikmund-Fisher et al., 2014). Assessors can use simple icon arrays to help communicate the risk of domestic violence recidivism associated with each ODARA risk category (Chapter 6, Figure 6.1).

Standardized Risk Levels

A group of criminal justice researchers, practitioners, and policy makers have proposed a common language for communicating general recidivism risk aimed at improving risk communication and the application of the RNR principles (Justice Center, 2017). They suggested a five-level system determined by absolute recidivism rates in a 2-year time frame. Absolute rates are the most often reported statistic when actuarial tools are used (e.g., Blais & Forth, 2014). They can be readily compared across studies and types of recidivism (e.g., violent, sexual, domestic) for the many violence risk assessment tools in use, unlike verbal categories or percentiles.

The proposed standardized risk levels incorporate both criminogenic needs and recidivism risk, defined as charges or convictions, in accordance with the normative data for leading actuarial tools (e.g., Hanson et al., 2017). Level I reflects a 2-year recidivism rate comparable to the base rate of offending behavior in the general population (less than 5%). Individuals at this level have no, few, mild, or transitory criminogenic needs requiring little or no correctional supervision and little expected risk reduction through treatment. Level V covers individuals with a 2-year recidivism rate at least 85% (average 90%); multiple chronic, severe, entrenched, and diverse criminogenic needs requiring intensive supervision; and extensive treatment with an initial emphasis on treatment readiness and behavioral management (Justice Center, 2017). Among individuals with a history of sex offenses, those in higher standardized categories had increasing rates of treatment needs and responsivity concerns, such as deviant sexual preference, child victims, impulsivity, and, to less extent, major mental illness (Hanson et al., 2017; Olver, Mundt, et al., 2018).

Standardized risk levels have not yet been created for domestic violence risk assessment. To do so will require some important practical decisions (as it has for risk categories for sexual offense recidivism; Hanson et al., 2017). For example, should the referent population be men who have assaulted their female partner, or defined more broadly? If the latter, then how will the different recidivism rates between men and women be handled? Given the lower rate of domestic violence recidivism compared with general recidivism (of which domestic recidivism is a subset), how many categories are needed; is there a meaningful Level V category for domestic violence recidivism; and, if so, then how should it be configured? Other decisions require estimates of the average rate of domestic offending in the general population, and rates (or other recidivism metric) of domestic violence recidivism. Although creating standardized risk levels for domestic violence recidivism would be challenging, it would yield worthwhile benefits for risk communication and allocation of resources. Currently, the ODARA does not share a common interpretation scheme with other widely used domestic violence risk assessment tools (described in Domestic Violence Recidivism Assessment Tools and Guides in Chapter 1). If standardized categories were developed on the basis of not only ODARA scores but also scores from other scales, assessors would be able to communicate the risk of domestic violence recidivism consistently, and to identify individuals in greatest need of intervention, regardless of the tool they choose to use.

Assessing and Communicating Change

As I described in Chapter 8 (Hypothesis 2), advances in the analysis of risk assessment scores over time have shown that scores can change and that change scores are associated with recidivism (e.g., Olver, Mundt, et al., 2018). Olver and colleagues provided a workbook application for assessors to compute recidivism estimates, and recommended tracking change scores cumulatively, capturing risk reduction over time. They observed, however, that the interpretation of change in risk is not intuitive. The meaning of a risk assessment score obtained after treatment, for example, depends on the magnitude of initial risk and the amount and degree of change following treatment. Individuals who reduce their risk may be better candidates for reduced security and supervision than those with the same initial risk who register no clinically significant change but may still fare worse than those with initially lower risk (e.g., Olver et al., 2015).

The ability to measure change in risk is an important direction for violence risk communication, especially as assessors wish to base their reports on dynamic factors. Studies with actuarial tools such as the ODARA and DVRAG are needed before domestic violence risk can be communicated in terms of change.

COMMUNICATING THE RISK OF DOMESTIC VIOLENCE: WHO, WHAT, WHERE, WHEN, WHY, AND HOW

The "Five Ws" of reporting remind the communicator to pack the most important information (in decreasing order of importance) into the opening paragraph of a story. When reporting on violence risk assessment, it is first necessary to state *who* is the subject of the assessment; in the case of the ODARA or DVRAG, the person identified as committing domestic violence. Although the ODARA can be conducted as part of a clinical interview with a client who has been assaulted by their partner (as I described in Victim Services in Chapter 4), the calculated risk is that posed by the individual who has committed the assault, not that necessarily faced by the client. In the ODARA construction sample, most men who recidivated did in fact assault the same woman as in the index assault, but some victimized a new partner or a previous partner. *Who* also includes the population to which the individual is being compared and their characteristics, with reference to the validation research on which actuarial norms are based. This reference provides the context (i.e., base rate) for interpreting the individual risk score.

What is defined as the risk of recidivism—that is, the probability of physical violence against an intimate partner. The rank of the individual score within the stated population must also be reported. On the basis of research described in this chapter, I believe a statement of the probability of recidivism will improve risk communication. Also, a statement of comparative risk such as percentile rank is essential to help decision-makers understand where a perpetrator stands in relation to others with respect to risk. For brief oral communication (e.g., in case conferences, interagency referrals), these two facts could suffice or may be conveyed through the standardized risk level. Actuarial risk assessment permits us to make conclusive statements about the probability of reoffending based on the individual's similarity to a group of individuals for whom the violent outcome was known. By the same token, the statement must always be connected to the known group. Thus, "men in this range of scores had approximately a 70% likelihood of recidivism," is preferred to "this man is 70% likely to recidivate" even though these statements are formally equivalent. A qualifying statement that the group data do not apply to the individual would be misleading, and I advise against such a statement.

Both the ODARA and DVRAG research defined recidivism according to police reports and criminal records, and when consulting the actuarial tables in the scoring manuals (Chapters 6 and 7), assessors should state the nature of the recidivism predicted. Reliance on official recidivism increases the utility of these tools throughout the criminal justice system. For cases without police involvement, however, official recidivism could substantially underestimate the actual rates of assault. In turn, our actuarial tables that include assaults not leading to charges or convictions may inflate perceived risk of adjudicated persons returning to court. Elsewhere, I have suggested using treatment intensity categories using data from men who were charged for their index assault (Radatz & Hilton, 2019; see Case Prioritization in Chapter 4, this volume). Where the ODARA or DVRAG are frequently used, I encourage assessors to devise actuarial tables for their own populations according to their needs (see Challenges to Effective Implementation in Chapter 10).

Where reminds assessors to state that the violence is expected to occur in a particular kind of relationship; specifically, against an adult intimate partner. Assessors might also state the region from which actuarial data were derived (Tables 6.2 and 7.2 pertain to data from Ontario, Canada) and the locations of validation studies (reviewed in Chapter 4).

When must also be stated in terms of the known follow-up period. Base rates of recidivism depend on the duration of the follow-up. If a decision concerned the lifetime likelihood of recidivism, actuarial tables that show rates from an average follow-up of under 5 years would underestimate the outcome of interest. Recidivism rates for actuarial categories cannot be directly extrapolated; for example, individuals in the highest risk categories are likely to show proportionately greater increases in risk as follow-up duration is increased. For decisions concerning shorter terms, the observed probabilities overestimate the outcome. It is difficult to imagine, however, circumstances in which a decision-maker is truly only concerned with a short time span and what happens later is legitimately of no concern. Assessors should also state when the index assault occurred. Risk scores are not invalidated when a new incident occurs, but a new domestic assault may prompt a review of current risks. Any new ODARA or DVRAG score should be communicated to all professionals involved with an individual's risk management.

Why could refer to the grounds on which the assessment is based. For example, the ODARA might be scored because a police investigation report indicates a domestic assault occurred, on the basis of statements made by the victim, accused, and witnesses. The information sources used to identify the index assault and score the items should be specified. The results of an ODARA scored on the basis of an interview with victim services client (I recommend a police record check whenever possible) should be communicated to the client as "according to your responses" or "based on the information you have provided." As well as using the documented police and criminal history to score the DVRAG, it is necessary to compile a psychosocial history (e.g., Harris, Rice, et al., 2015), possibly supplemented by an interview with the person being assessed, to score the PCL-R. All sources of information (including the referral) should be stated.

Written reports may also list the ODARA or DVRAG items and whether each contributed positively or negatively to the score. On one hand, reporting details about items in a risk assessment tool could lead to more conservative decisions (e.g., Hilton, Carter, et al., 2008), perhaps because decision-makers feel that there is more specific information to support a decision or to evaluate the relevance of the risk information to the individual (Scurich et al., 2012). On the other hand, listing the items promotes transparency and accountability of the assessment and assessor (e.g., Mills et al., 2011). A remedy for this dilemma is to link actuarial scores more strictly to actual decisions via a formal system that instantiates the decision policy (e.g., McKee et al., 2007). Some assessors wish to incorporate conceptually similar issues into the scoring. For example, one clinician reasoned that having young children makes it harder to access services, which explains why it is an ODARA item, and thus a partner's physical disability requiring wheelchair use should also garner a point on the ODARA. Although women with physical and other disabilities are vulnerable to abuse (e.g., Plummer & Findley, 2012), there were too few such cases in the ODARA construction research to indicate that it increased risk, so adding a point for disability is not valid. Similarly, reasoning that gambling problems are equivalent to substance abuse (because they both indicate impulse control problems) and adding a point for gambling is invalid. Empirically derived actuarial approaches add items only if they increase the predictive validity of the instrument over and above items already included. Even lengthy descriptions of the material used to score the items is of questionable value because that seems to result in more conservative decisions, as though more information means higher risk.

A similar concern arises with the question of whether to communicate risks in a positive or negative frame (e.g., Scurich & John, 2012), as strengths or weaknesses. Han and colleagues (2016) advised reporting risk in both positive and negative frames, and as both percentages and frequencies, as well as verbal explanations. Reporting choices must be made with not only a view to the intended audience's needs and preferences but also an understanding of the limits of human information processing and often unintended effects of communication (e.g., Kahneman, 2011). Many of the problems of invalid interpretation might best be resolved by incorporating actuarial scores explicitly into policy (McKee et al., 2007; see also Chapter 8, this volume).

My ideal for the ODARA/DVRAG risk assessment system is that it is accessible to everyone involved in the integrated community response to domestic violence. In particular, Norah Holder, the former director of the Sexual/Domestic Assault Program at the Orillia Soldiers Memorial Hospital, helped with transforming a research-based list of criteria into a series of questions that could be used as an interview with their clients (Hilton, Harris, & Holder, 2008). The program nurses were the first to use the ODARA with recently assaulted women, and provided valuable feedback, including the suggestion of using pie charts rather than statistical tables for interpreting scores. Partner assault clinic staff have told us that they appreciate being able to show clients the graphic interpretation materials (see Figures 6.1 and 6.2, Chapter 6, this volume) rather than just expressing their own professional opinion to their clients. The risk assessment results allow the information provided by the clients to be reframed and shared back with them in a way that helps them understand their situation and can be a motivation for clients to engage in safety planning and other steps to enhance their safety and well-being. As with risk management in the criminal justice system, safety planning is an important next step after risk assessment. In addition to sharing information and assisting with safety plans, there is emerging evidence that support services for individuals affected by domestic violence improve clients' outcomes by helping them build skills, offering encouragement, providing supportive counselling, increasing access to further community resources, and increasing social support and community engagement (e.g., Sullivan, 2018).

CONCLUSION

Regardless of the advice in this chapter about what should and should not be included in a risk assessment report, merely producing the report is not effective risk communication, even within a policy that directs decisions to be based on actuarial risk. The crucial test is whether the use, reporting, and implementation of a validated domestic violence risk assessment produces a measurable improvement in the allocation of resources—custody, conditional release, other intervention, or victim protection services—and ultimately reduces harm. I recommend that the probability of a specified outcome within a given time frame, and the percentile rank comparing the individual within a known population of domestic offenders, be the minimum information in a risk assessment summary. For optimal communication, this summary should be accompanied by a statement of the appropriate actions according to that risk, and these actions should be determined by empirically informed policy, as I describe in Chapter 10.

POINTS TO REMEMBER

- Medical and forensic professionals prefer risk to be communicated in terms of clinical impressions and nonnumerical categories such as "low risk" or "high risk," but studies show no reliable meaning of these nonnumerical terms.
- Forensic professionals can understand actuarial risk assessment results and are increasingly basing decisions on them.
- Verbal descriptions of risk, positive or negative framing, and the level of detail in a risk assessment report are among the factors that can inadvertently influence risk perceptions and decisions.
- Violence risk communication should include the probability of recidivism for the risk category in which the individual falls, the definition of recidivism (including behavior, time frame, and victim definition), and a report of the comparative risk.
- Graphs and standardized risk levels are emerging practices with the potential to improve violence risk communication.

QUESTIONS TO CONSIDER

1. Identify four variables shown to affect forensic risk communication.
2. "When followed up for approximately 5 years, more than 50% of men in Mr. X's risk category committed a new domestic assault." Rephrase this sentence using positive framing. What effect might this change have how Mr. X's risk is perceived?
3. Design graphs to illustrate and compare 17% and 39% probabilities of violence recidivism.
4. Research a case of domestic violence that made the news. How was risk described in court and talked about in the media? In what ways might the risk communication need to be improved to make it more effective?
5. Suppose an individual with a previous ODARA score of 5 is charged for assault on a new intimate partner. You conduct a new risk assessment and the ODARA score is now 4. How will you report the individual's risk of domestic violence recidivism? What factors might cause you to be cautious in reporting a change in risk?

RESEARCHER PROFILE 9.1
KIRK HEILBRUN, PhD

From my earliest days in graduate school (clinical psychology doctoral program, University of Texas at Austin), I was interested in crime and delinquency. This led me to seek a policy-relevant practicum position with the Texas Youth Council, the state agency responsible for operating the secure residential placements in Texas. My interest in this area was sharpened during a postdoctoral fellowship under Edwin Megargee at Florida State University (1981–1982). Megargee was one of the most prominent psychologists of his era to focus on crime, violence, and delinquency. This interest has persisted through jobs in forensic hospitals, a medical school and in my current position at Drexel University.

A major turning point for me was when I realized that violent behavior was largely influenced by factors beyond the scope of traditional symptoms of psychopathology, viewed through a psychodynamic lens (which was my training at the time). It was illuminating to consider violence as a form of aberrant behavior that nevertheless was strongly reinforced in certain contexts (e.g., instrumental aggression) and strongly subject to situational as well as personal influences. The movement toward considering violence as a public health problem rather than a clinical problem also considerably influenced me. Another eye-opener was realizing that the predominant research paradigm of the 1980s and 1990s (predicting violent behavior) yielded less valuable information than an approach that also provided guidance on reducing risk.

The work of forensic psychology researchers and correctional psychology researchers was not shared well in the 1990s—but when I began to follow the RNR work of Andrews, Bonta, and colleagues (e.g., Bonta & Andrews, 2017), it helped me a great deal in refining my thinking about useful ways of approaching human violence. My most influential contribution in this area would probably be Heilbrun (1997). I argued that there are some legal questions (e.g., civil commitment) for which a prediction of violent behavior provides the best answer. In most cases, however, the law asks questions that are best informed by accurate appraisal of how the risk can be managed or reduced as well as how high the risk is. This came at a time when prediction was the predominant, if not exclusive, goal of violence research. RNR was a distinct exception, but I wasn't familiar with it when I wrote this article.

I have an interest in violence and violent offending generally, although at times in my career, I have conducted research identifying a particular form of violence (e.g., homicide, serial homicide, sexual offending), and my work is relevant to how all forms of violence risk is communicated. I am now working on a project that incorporates risk communication into the appraisal of individuals who received mandatory life incarceration sentences as juveniles and are being considered for resentencing pursuant to recent U.S. Supreme Court decisions. These decisions do not clearly identify reoffending risk as a component of the resentencing decision, instead focusing on rehabilitation. But I think that rehabilitation is clearly linked to risk in this context. I have also found that the general public views risk as so important that it drowns out other influences (Heilbrun et al., 2018). The next step will examine ways to put risk in perspective so it remains one consideration—but not the only one. I see next steps as involving more intervention research and a growing collaboration within psychology across domestic violence and other outcomes that can benefit from more consistently applied methods.

About the Researcher

Dr. Heilbrun is a professor of psychology at Drexel University and a licensed psychologist.

RESEARCHER PROFILE 9.2
L. MAAIKE HELMUS, PhD

I'm often asked what attracted me to the work I do, and I think part of it is that I was a child in the height of the 1980s "Stranger Danger" craze. My parents had a book filled with horrifying images and stories of all the ways that strangers want to hurt you. My well-intentioned parents regularly read it to me before bedtime, spawning a childhood full of recurring nightmares about strangers. I often wonder whether my being drawn to this field can be explained by wanting to understand something I was so afraid of growing up. Plus, who wouldn't want to devote their career to studying criminal behavior after watching *Silence of the Lambs*?

While I was a criminology student at Carleton University (concentrating in psychology and minoring in law), I had an opportunity to work in the Corrections Research Unit at Public Safety Canada with R. Karl Hanson. Karl became a wonderful mentor and friend, and I stayed at Public Safety for 10 years. Their research focused on sex offender risk assessment. I was fascinated with the idea of using empirical research to address practical problems facing criminal justice agencies: How do we prioritize resources? How intensively should we supervise offenders? How do we know who needs treatment most and what should be treated?

I also loved statistics (a surprise to me and everyone who knew me, but a lesson in how applying the material to something you care about can be motivating) and understanding how the statistical approaches we use may influence the answers we get. Like many things, doing research well is hard work. It requires a flexible understanding of statistical approaches and their strengths and weaknesses and also recognizing that no single study is a determinant of truth; rather, replication and meta-analyses are required to understand what works best for whom and under what conditions.

My main research concerns how to improve forensic decision making. Daily decisions in criminal justice have a huge impact on offenders' lives and implications for public safety. I'm interested in how to make decisions more empirically defensible: transparent, accurate, fair, reliable, and cost-effective. I'm also becoming more interested in risk communication—how to communicate the results of risk assessments in clear and unbiased ways. A good risk assessment will only go so far if decision-makers don't understand the information well enough to guide their decisions, or if the way we communicate the results contributes to systematic biases in interpretation.

My research focuses on risk assessment tools for sex offenders and violent offenders. I am part of the development team for the Static-99R,

Static-2002-R, STABLE/ACUTE-2007, CPORT, and the VRAG-R. Sex offenders as a group have some unique risk factors (e.g., sexual preoccupation, emotional identification with children, sex as coping, deviant sexual interests) and specialized sex offender risk assessment scales work best. I wonder whether domestic offenders also have unique risk factors, or whether tools designed for violent offenders are appropriate for this group. As an undergraduate, I conducted a meta-analysis of domestic violence risk assessment and found that domestic-specific scales performed no better than general offending scales (Hanson, Helmus, & Bourgon, 2007). Maybe the domestic scales existing in 2007 weren't optimally combining the general and domestic-specific risk factors. I think the field needs a more comprehensive meta-analysis on psychologically meaningful risk factors for domestic violence recidivism. I hope to continue this work and examine whether intimate partner rapists more closely resemble sex offenders or domestic violence offenders.

About the Researcher

Dr. Helmus is an assistant professor of criminology at Simon Fraser University, Burnaby, BC, Canada.

10 IMPLEMENTING ACTUARIAL RISK ASSESSMENT

In Part II, I showed how the Ontario Domestic Assault Risk Assessment (ODARA) predicted recidivism in the original construction sample of men with a police record for domestic violence and also in other samples studied by the original research team and by independent researchers. In this chapter, I consider how that knowledge can be used to increase both the safety of partners and fairness to individuals who have assaulted them. When Harris, Rice, and Quinsey (1993) developed the Violence Risk Appraisal Guide (VRAG) in the early 1990s, knowledge translation for most researchers still consisted of publishing an article in the peer-reviewed literature. These researchers went further, providing information to decision makers such as clinical administrators and policy makers, and conducting VRAG training sessions for clinicians. They hoped that circulating the first actuarial tool to predict violent recidivism among men with a history of serious violent offenses would ensure that it would soon be adopted in the forensic and criminal justice systems. They hoped, moreover, that a measurable improvement in public safety would result. It soon turned out that doing that research was only the first and easiest part. Getting a new instrument

https://doi.org/10.1037/0000223-011
Domestic Violence Risk Assessment: Tools for Effective Prediction and Management, Second Edition, by N. Z. Hilton

into use even in the hospital and province where it was developed would prove to be much more daunting.

In this chapter, I summarize the VRAG implementation experience and review research on other policy changes in the criminal justice system's response to domestic violence that inspired my colleagues and me to continue our efforts in this field. I then recount events that facilitated the ODARA's adoption in Ontario, and the hurdles faced, before discussing practical issues of scoring and training. I offer guidelines for embedding actuarial risk assessment in domestic violence policy, providing examples from others who have adopted the ODARA for use in criminal justice, domestic violence intervention, and victim services.

HOW POLICY DECISIONS CAN AFFECT CRIMINAL JUSTICE OUTCOMES

In the 1990s, Provincial government officials mandated use of the VRAG, and provided resources to ensure risk assessments were conducted on patients in all of Ontario's forensic hospitals. However, these policies lapsed once the particular individuals who implemented them moved to other positions. Without sustained policy, some of the greatest opposition to the VRAG came from clinicians at the hospital where it had been developed, perhaps because of the tendency for people to be less open to new ideas that differ from dominant ways of thinking, especially people who consider themselves experts in a given area (e.g., Kahneman, 2011; Ottati et al., 2015). Forensic hospitals are predominantly guided by a medical model, and many clinicians reject any form of checklist that they fear might undervalue their knowledge, add extra work, limit their professional judgment, or diminish their authority (e.g., Gawande, 2011; Russ et al., 2015). Twenty years passed before it could be confidently said that forensic decisions were influenced by actuarial risk (Hilton, Simpson, & Ham, 2016; see Does the Communication of Actuarial Risk Affect Forensic Decisions? in Chapter 9, this volume). Thus, where policy may have been necessary at first, in its absence, the strong empirical support for violence risk assessment, and a general uptake of evidence-based practice in clinical settings, may have led clinicians to eventually consider this new practice.

In Canada, correctional systems are not so overtly medical, and policies have long been in place to ensure that assessment and programming are evidence-based. Standardized risk and criminogenic need assessments are a routine part of correctional intake procedures (e.g., Bourgon et al., 2018). In fact, in my experience of working with people implementing actuarial risk assessment in Canada and the United States, actuarial risk assessments are more likely to be adopted in correctional systems than forensic hospitals, perhaps due in part to the correctional system's higher proportion of psychologists over medical or nursing staff (e.g., Singh et al., 2014), as psychologists are often trained in a variety of standardized testing and assessment tools.

Mandatory Arrest

In the 1980s in Canada and the United States, mounting pressure from groups advocating on behalf of "battered women" and a changing political climate with regard to domestic violence resulted in proarrest legislation (Hilton & Harris, 2009a). Mandatory arrest policies increased arrests (Jaffe et al., 1986) and domestic violence led to criminal justice responses comparable to those for other violent crimes, even though arrest was far from universally applied in the 1990s and early 2000s, as illustrated by researchers such as Myrna Dawson (e.g., Dawson & Hotton, 2014; see also Researcher Profile 8.1). Domestic violence now represents more than one quarter of all police-reported victims of violent offenses in Canada (e.g., Burczycka & Conroy, 2017) and is the single largest category of calls to police in the United States (e.g., Klein, 2009).

Evaluations of the effect of arrest on domestic assault recidivism include an influential study by Sherman and Berk (1984) of 314 individuals (98% male) in Minneapolis, Minnesota, and subsequent replications in other U.S. cities. The effects of arrest varied according to follow-up time, source of outcome data (partner report vs. official record), employment, postarrest counseling, and other factors (Berk et al., 1992; Miller, 2003; Pate & Hamilton, 1992; Sherman et al., 1992). Other studies found no support for effects of arrest; when data were combined across studies and reanalyzed, arrest was found to produce a slight reduction in domestic violence overall (Maxwell et al., 2002), but an increase in recidivism among antisocial individuals (Johnson & Goodlin-Fahncke, 2015) who may be at higher risk of domestic violence recidivism (as I discussed in the section Typologies in Chapter 1 of this volume).

When my colleagues and I evaluated the effect of arrest in the ODARA construction sample (Hilton, Harris, & Rice, 2007), we controlled for prearrest actuarial risk for domestic assault recidivism, as measured by the ODARA. We found that police officers were more likely to arrest men who were higher in prearrest risk, even though the officers were unaware of actual ODARA scores (the ODARA was scored later by research assistants). Police were also more likely to arrest men who had committed more serious assaults. Similar findings have been reported in Australia and Europe: Physical assault, partner's fear, no-contact order violations, substance abuse, and previous domestic incidents were among the variables that increased the likelihood of police judging individuals to be at risk and pressing criminal charges (Perez Trujillo & Ross, 2008), and more postarrest interventions were used in cases judged to be higher risk (Belfrage et al., 2012), confirming our impression that arrest is associated with prearrest risk of recidivism.

In our study, arrested men were more likely to commit a new assault in the 5-year follow-up (Hilton, Harris, & Rice, 2007). But this effect was entirely attributable to the fact that police arrested men already at relatively high risk for recidivism. When ODARA score was entered first into a regression analysis, arrest added nothing to the prediction of recidivism. We also found no effect of arrest on time elapsed before reoffending and no effect among men with higher ODARA scores. However, among men with average or lower ODARA scores, those who were arrested spent more time without assaulting a partner again than did men not arrested. For lower risk men at least, then, arrest might have had the benefit of delaying recidivism.

Another benefit of proarrest policies is that they may help reduce biases inherent in human decision making, such as the influence of race on arrest (Eitle, 2005). There remains controversy regarding possible unintended effects of mandatory arrest, such as the impact on dual arrest of both parties in the domestic incident (e.g., Fraehlich & Ursel, 2014). Gerstenberger and Williams (2013), though, found that single arrests were more likely than dual arrests when measured risk was higher, in a large sample of men and women arrested for intimate partner violence in Connecticut. Their study supports the conclusion that arrest decisions are sensitive to domestic violence risk. Other research suggests that notifying police and getting help from victim support services, rather than arrest per se, reduces subsequent domestic violence (e.g., Xie & Lynch, 2017). Whether any benefit can be attributed to current policies of arrest and prosecution or whether apparent effects depend on some subsequent criminal justice or extra-legal intervention has yet to be determined.

No-Drop Prosecution

The well-known Duluth model project ensured that each criminal justice juncture had formal guidelines to limit discretion, including no-drop prosecution. The model emerged in the 1980s. It was developed by women's advocates in Duluth, Minnesota, working with criminal justice and nongovernmental agencies to develop and monitor a coordinated system, with the aim of increasing accountability among men who assault their partners (e.g., Gondolf, 2010; Pence & Shepard, 1999). Probation officers placed individuals into risk categories based on their abuse histories, and courts could order individuals into domestic violence treatment that targeted attitudes, power, and control in the intimate relationship. The model spread across the United States and beyond (e.g., Pence & Shepard, 1999). Evaluation of the Duluth model first centered on the treatment component, yielding a small effect, although the studies suffered from judicial overrides of randomization to intervention, high treatment dropout rates, and low follow-up response rates (e.g., Babcock et al., 2004; Herman et al., 2014). One study evaluated the outcome of the coordinated community response as a whole. Community members in 10 U.S. cities implementing such models did not report different rates of domestic violence than those in 10 non-implementing cities (Post et al., 2010).

Garner and Maxwell (2009) reviewed no-drop prosecution policies in the context of the U.S. Violence Against Women Act of 1994. They reported increases in arrested cases leading to prosecution, and prosecution leading to conviction of domestic violence cases. After the legislation, two thirds of arrests led to prosecution, and half of prosecutions led to conviction, similar to rates in jurisdictions outside the United States. A systematic review of the effects of criminal justice sanctions, however, found that most showed no effect on domestic violence recidivism (Maxwell & Garner, 2012). Where effects were observed, the most promising results were for prosecution, for which there were 6 times as many results supporting beneficial effects as adverse effects. Undermining this promising result, however, was the revelation that the research methods of existing studies were too weak to detect effects, either beneficial or adverse.

A notable discovery from studies of criminal justice responses to domestic violence is that criminal sanctions are often applied in the United States, Canada, Europe, and Australia (e.g., Garner & Maxwell, 2009) and that communities support arrest, prosecution, treatment, and even incarceration for individuals who commit domestic offenses (e.g., Post et al., 2010). This culture of support for criminal processing of domestic violence not only inspires efforts to implement risk assessment across sectors responding to domestic violence but also creates the need for risk-informed policies and procedures to handle the burden of domestic violence within the system.

ONTARIO'S DOMESTIC ASSAULT RISK ASSESSMENT

Support for the implementation of the ODARA came from the Ontario Provincial Police (OPP), who collaborated on the research leading to its development. In particular, Kate Lines, who was Detective Chief Inspector at the time the research collaboration began, had been involved with an interministerial committee responding to the inquest into the May–Iles domestic homicide described in the Introduction to this volume. She was committed to the aims of this research and gained the full support of the OPP Behavioural Sciences and Analysis Section. She also succeeded in hiring three new threat analysis officers with primary responsibility for developing officer training and implementation of the ODARA.

Together with OPP threat analysts, the ODARA research team created instructional materials for police officers and provided information sessions to government ministers, officials, and judicial decision makers. The result was a risk assessment tool developed in collaboration with the very personnel and organization that would lead its use and implementation, founded on a cocreation process considered best practice in knowledge translation (e.g., Greenhalgh et al., 2016). The OPP took responsibility for training police officers and participated extensively in a pilot project that aimed to have the ODARA become required evidence at bail hearings of men charged with domestic assault. Although this project encountered hurdles (described later in this chapter), it worked very well at the policing level. The ODARA is now embedded in the domestic violence risk management report used by police services across Ontario.

Getting the ODARA Scored

Getting the ODARA scored as soon as possible on eligible cases is an essential first step in the successful use of the ODARA/DVRAG system. To simplify scoring, ODARA item scores are simple dichotomies that can be tallied easily on a single-sheet scoring form to be used along with detailed scoring and interpretation materials that were developed with feedback from users. Information was considered for inclusion in the ODARA only if it could be readily obtained during frontline police investigations (see Using Available Data in Chapter 3 this volume). Training materials were designed to ensure that potential ODARA users were informed as to why each item was on the assessment (and why others were not).

Training Users to Score the ODARA Reliably

A survey of Canadian police officers revealed that most were familiar with domestic violence risk assessment, rated it as helpful, and would use a risk assessment tool if they had sufficient training (M. A. Campbell et al., 2018). However, more than half reported that they had received no formal training in domestic violence. Training and testing on use of the risk assessment tool is essential because an actuarial tool that could not be reliably scored by its intended users would be of little practical value.

The first tests of interrater agreement showed that the ODARA was reliably scored by a variety of professionals. Specifically, interrater reliability coefficients were at least .90 for trained research coders, and for police officers who were given the scoring sheet but had no specific training on how to score the ODARA (Hilton et al., 2004). To promote assessors' adherence to the scoring criteria, my colleagues and I then created and evaluated a detailed instruction booklet and training sessions, applying the educational principles of repetition of material, association of material with existing knowledge, and repeated testing (Hilton, Harris, Rice, et al., 2007). We used trainees' feedback at each session to improve future content.

By the time of the transition to online training (described in the next section), we had conducted nearly 50 training sessions for potential users of the ODARA, with attendees from community victim services such as shelters, transition homes, and hospital-based partner assault clinics, as well as child protection workers, counselors and clinicians, correctional and law enforcement officers. All sessions were led by at least two trainers from our team. We used case videos for scoring practice rather than live role plays because videos were standard stimuli, providing exactly the same information each time they were presented. We created the scripts for these videos on the basis of randomly selected cases from the ODARA research, but we elaborated on the information in the police reports and changed names, locations, and several other details to create a simulated clinical interview with the woman who has been assaulted. The scripts were performed by members of our research department or the local community and were digitally recorded and edited at our hospital.

The interviews proceeded quickly, questions were omitted if they could be answered using responses to previous questions, and some responses were deliberately ambiguous. These features made the videos a good scoring challenge and permitted us to evaluate the improvement in scoring accuracy before and after training. When trainees viewed and scored the first video, they had not yet learned the full scoring criteria. When they scored the second video, they had been exposed to a detailed presentation of all the scoring criteria and scored a practice case video together. A total of 201 trainees completed the evaluation and showed a statistical improvement in their scoring after the training. Before training, trainees' average scores were incorrect by more than 1 point; after training, the mean error was reduced to just over half a point (Hilton, Harris, Rice, et al., 2007). One case appeared easier to score than the other one, a problem addressed by *counterbalancing*—alternating the order of videos at each training session. By the end of training, trainees scored both test cases equally well.

Next, we tested how much the apparent training effect was simply due to practice; that is, whether the experience of scoring one case makes it easier to score another. We asked 61 new trainees to score the two cases one right after the other; this test demonstrated no significant improvement (Hilton, Harris, Rice, et al., 2007).

Not all domestic violence risk assessors can attend classroom training, and those who do attend still need to refer to the scoring criteria each time they use the ODARA. In this book, I have included all the elements of ODARA training that are possible to provide in written form: literature reviews to help the reader integrate the new knowledge with existing knowledge, the research background and performance statistics of the ODARA, detailed scoring instructions, responses to frequently asked questions, and practice cases with feedback. In addition, ODARA training was transformed into an online, restricted-access e-learning program.

Online Training: "ODARA 101"

ODARA 101 is currently hosted by the Waypoint Centre for Mental Health Care at https://odara.waypointcentre.ca. As in classroom training, trainees can receive an ODARA certificate when they score 10 standard cases with an interrater reliability of .75, using a single measures intraclass correlation (ICC) requiring absolute agreement on ODARA risk category. ODARA 101 was launched in 2012, following an evaluation that compared success on the scoring test among 42 people who had recently participated in classroom training with 45 trainees who evaluated a prerelease version of the e-training (Hilton & Ham, 2015). Trainees included counselors, police officers, shelter staff, and mental health workers, among others. They all scored 10 written cases, formatted as police occurrence reports and simulated victim interviews. The average ICC for classroom trainees was identical to that for e-learning users: .92. All classroom trainees completed the test, and all but one passed on their first attempt, whereas the completion and pass rate was only 86% for e-learning. However, this success rate is substantially better than the 42% of trainees who completed and passed the test during a mail-in distance training approach that was tried before developing the e-learning program. In addition, e-learning was more cost-effective than classroom training. Trainees felt the program was professional and user-friendly, and they appreciated the convenience of taking training at their own pace.

A few years later, I worked with a team to update the program technology and make the content more representative of trainees' diverse experiences (Ham et al., 2019). We created case scenarios from stories gathered through collaborations with domestic violence transition house and counseling agency staff across the Province of Saskatchewan. We turned these stories into simulated interview transcripts designed to respectfully reflect women's experiences of domestic violence in rural, remote, Indigenous, and multicultural urban communities. We edited the interviews to ensure anonymity as well as a range of ODARA scores, and set them in shelters, domestic assault clinics, victim crisis services, and police investigations. We video-recorded 13 scenarios for use in practice and testing components of ODARA 101. Training content was also translated from English into French, and the new system allowed organization administrators to assign and monitor their staff's training. Of 223 trainees who participated during beta-testing, 78% passed first time, with an average ICC of .82. Some trainees reported that the newly automated, randomized test was more challenging than the previous format, and our evaluation included participants who took the test using videoed rather than written cases, who tended to perform less well. Still, 68 participants who completed an evaluation survey rated the program as being user-friendly, of good quality and utility, and an improvement over the older program.

Domestic Violence Risk Appraisal Guide Training

Scoring and training for the DVRAG entail a different set of challenges. The DVRAG requires considerably more clinical information about the individual and more time to score than does the ODARA, especially because it includes the Psychopathy Checklist–Revised (PCL-R, Hare, 2003). Thus, the DVRAG allows an important role for clinical expertise. In particular, a total score on the PCL-R is required to score this DVRAG item.

The PCL-R is a psychological test that is used to measure psychopathy and is robustly associated with violence risk (e.g., K. M. Williams et al., 2017). It can be scored from information available in individuals' correctional records along with a structured interview with the individual, or from correctional or forensic file information alone. Training must be obtained from authorized trainers through http://hare.org or online at https://www.gifrinc.com/pcl-r-and-pcl-sv-training. ODARA 101 provides training on the scoring criteria for the remaining DVRAG items, and assessors with access to a reliable PCL-R score documented by a qualified assessor can score the remaining items according to the manual in Chapter 7, this volume.

Using the Ontario Domestic Assault Risk Assessment in Court

The DVRAG has not been used in court to my knowledge at the time of writing. The ODARA, in contrast, has received much uptake with domestic violence assessors and has been admitted in several jurisdictions. To the best of my knowledge, there have been few problems in using the ODARA in higher courts, but my colleagues and I initially experienced some difficulties when working with prosecutors to support its use in bail court.

Bail courts in Ontario, Canada, are presided over by lay justices of the peace, and government officials stipulated that the justices could not be offered training on risk assessment for fear of infringing on judicial independence. Denial of bail was so common that, at the time, more than 60% of prisoners in Ontario's correctional system were on remand, not sentenced (Webster et al., 2009). The government had endorsed a tool previously created by the OPP as recommended practice across the province (Ontario Ministry of the Solicitor General, 2000) and were cautious of creating a new policy about the ODARA. We were not involved in the government's strategic planning for adoption of the ODARA in bail courts, although it depended on expert testimony from us. Lawyers disagreed with ODARA scoring criteria that included criminal behavior not resulting in conviction (and we had concerns about the effects of changing scoring criteria on predictive accuracy). They hoped for an eventual appeal to a higher court that would produce a binding ruling mandating the ODARA in bail court. After 2 years, this approach was abandoned.

During this attempt, meanwhile, police officers scored the ODARA in hundreds of cases, and decisions about whether to detain accused persons for a bail hearing were made more strongly in accord with actuarial risk than before the ODARA was available (Hilton, Harris, & Rice, 2007). ODARA scores were also associated with denial of bail, suggesting that the bail court pilot led to improved risk-related decisions. Furthermore, the ODARA was used with good results in Ottawa, Canada's capital city, and it continues to be used and presented in bail courts today, as well as in probation and parole decisions across the province.

LESSONS LEARNED FROM ODARA IMPLEMENTATION EXPERIENCES

As the Ontario experience shows, merely developing and sharing a risk assessment tool is not sufficient for successful implementation. I have been privileged to consult on and assist with implementation efforts in other jurisdictions and fortunate to hear both the success stories and challenges of these experiences, some of which I describe in this section, with the permission of those who shared them with me. Lessons learned include the importance of (a) objectively stated policy, (b) training users in the actuarial system and its application, (c) cooperation and coordination among agencies implementing and enforcing the policy, and (d) methods for evaluating outcomes and revising implementation policies.

Specifying Policy

Some scholars have attempted to elucidate the principles associated with the successful adoption of innovations in society in general and public policy in particular (e.g., Dopson et al., 2003; Handley et al., 2016; Sarkies et al., 2017). Briefly, evidence-based policy innovations are more likely to succeed when they have opinion leaders and peer champions who can muster passion and emotional commitment by communicating the importance of change, building a shared vision, and providing sustained support, all low-cost strategies. Policies are also more successful when they are adaptable to the context, when they solve a problem or offer an advantage important to the organization, when benefits outweigh costs, and when adoption of the policy does not carry risks (e.g., Greenhalgh et al., 2004; Purtle, Dodson, & Brownson, 2018).

There are many examples of embedding formulaic systems in policies and procedures that improve the health and safety of citizens. Air travel safety, air traffic control, medical surgery, and epidemic monitoring are notable examples (e.g., Gawande, 2011; Ng et al., 2018; Spreco & Timpka, 2016). Precedents also exist for embedding formulaic systems in criminal justice legislation. For example, "sexually violent predator" commitment statutes require individuals over a given score on a specified sexual offense risk assessment tool to be identified (e.g., DeMatteo et al., 2015). Widespread adoption of specific tools to aid bail decisions has led to lower risk individuals being substantially more likely to be released on nonmonetary bail, higher risk individuals being relatively more likely to be detained, and less pretrial custody overall without substantial changes in rearrests, at least in the short term (e.g., Stevenson, 2018). Reductions in pretrial custody have also been reported (e.g., Walton, 2019). Advisory risk-informed guidelines, rather than mandatory formalistic models, maintain judicial discretion; however, they also leave room for human biases to persist, including racial discrimination (e.g., Stevenson, 2018). Implementing actuarial risk assessment as part of bail reform, in particular, has raised questions about the balance of judicial and legislative authority, access to criminal records needed to score several items, and the potential for police officers to over-score items and for judges to override assessed risk (e.g., Walton, 2019). Jurisdictions adopting the ODARA as part of their community response to domestic violence have had to address these tensions.

I believe that a policy to use actuarial tools to make forensic decisions and allocate criminal justice resources can increase fairness to individuals charged with criminal offenses. A lesson learned from the bail court pilot project (as well as experience with the VRAG) is that official policies stating when and how actuarial tools are to be used are a needed first step to increase the likelihood that the tools will be used (Harris & Rice, 2007; McKee et al., 2007). Some busy professionals are inclined to perform a clinical judgment first, and then use actuarial tools in cases they deem high risk; if the tool contradicts the intuition, they might ignore the actuarial data. In court this could mean that, although all assessments are disclosed, the prosecutor continues to present a case as high risk even though it falls in one of the lower actuarial categories. As a result, individuals might receive a more restrictive intervention than they would under a system that routinely based allocation of resources on actuarial risk.

I have worked with jurisdictions that specified policies for use of the ODARA by law enforcement officers. For example, the Northwest Territories, Canada, introduced the ODARA as the result of several years of planning between the Department of Health and Social Services and the Department of Justice. Upon implementation, the Royal Canadian Mounted Police (RCMP) "G" Division established a policy for the use of the ODARA, which helps ensure police officers use the tool in each domestic violence case they attend, and train new recruits through ODARA 101 (Northwest Territories Department of Justice, 2012).

Alternatively, legislation could specify that a valid risk assessment tool that is determined by an arm's length committee be used at these junctures. This was the approach taken in Maine. In recognition that risk assessment tools may change, the statutes reference law enforcement officers' "good faith effort to administer a validated, evidence-based domestic violence risk assessment recommended by the Maine Commission on Domestic and Sexual Abuse and approved by the Maine Department of Public Safety" (An Act to Adopt the Use of Standardized Risk Assessment in the Management of Domestic Violence Crimes, 2012). The Commission, a multidisciplinary stakeholders group, recommended the ODARA, following a working group review of validated domestic violence risk assessment tools. The ODARA is intended to influence decisions from bail through probation. Additional statutory language requires law enforcement officers to provide the results of the assessment to the bail commissioner (who sets and executes bail), bail commissioners to make a good faith effort to obtain the risk assessment results before setting bail, and judicial officers setting bail to take into account any evidence that the defendant poses a danger to the safety of others in the community, including the risk assessment results. The Maine Criminal Justice Academy developed minimum standards and, together with the Maine Chiefs of Police Association, developed model policy language for implementation by all law enforcement agencies regarding use of the ODARA. The same approach was taken by the State of New Mexico (State of New Mexico, 2008), which amended its Criminal Procedure Act (§31-12-12 D), mandating that all funded domestic violence treatment providers conduct an initial assessment with each participant. The ODARA was chosen by the State's Domestic Violence Offender Treatment Intervention program, a group that has 33 member agencies. This approach facilitates oversight of implementation as well as responsiveness to advances in research, training, and practice of domestic violence risk assessment that may make a new or modified tool preferable.

Legislation could mandate use of the ODARA (or other validated tool) at a number of junctures in the criminal justice system. Police officers can be required to submit an ODARA score to prosecutors in all eligible cases with clear evidence of domestic assault. Legislation could specify that the ODARA score be disclosed to both sides at bail hearings and state a cutoff score for presumption of bail, save for specified exceptional circumstances. For example, if a decision were made to deny bail to the 10% highest scoring people assessed on the ODARA, then bail statistics and actuarial data could be used to determine the appropriate cutoff score and the number of places in jail required to implement such a policy. A similar approach could be used to determine treatment intensity (Radatz & Hilton, 2019; see Case Prioritization in Chapter 4, this volume). A suitable cutoff can be selected using the statistical properties of the receiver operating characteristic area under the curve (see AUC and Related Accuracy Statistics in Chapter 2), the distribution of scores in a jurisdiction (to estimate how many cases would be affected), and the resources available to implement the policy, balanced with decision-making costs and benefits (e.g., Harris & Rice, 2007; Mossman, 2013). The minimum and maximum weight to be placed on the ODARA score, compared with other relevant considerations under the law (e.g., offense severity, impact on individuals who were assaulted), could be specified in regulations. Specification makes the decision explicit and transparent and, accordingly, helps guard against bias.

The DVRAG could play a role in postconviction decisions. To the extent that reduced recidivism is a goal of sentencing and conditional release decisions, the more weight given for factors empirically related to risk, the more successful the policy will be. The weighting of actuarial scores and other necessary considerations (e.g., offense severity, impact on individuals who were assaulted) can be made explicit and formulaic in forensic security and other conditional release decisions (e.g., McKee et al., 2007). Correctional policy could mandate that individuals with higher DVRAG scores receive more intensive interventions aimed at reducing recidivism, in accordance with the principles of effective correctional service (e.g., Bonta & Andrews, 2017; see Limits of Domestic Violence Theory in Chapter 1, this volume). Policies for parole and probation could ensure greater supervision and monitoring of individuals with higher DVRAG scores, specifying how each score translates into eligibility for probation or parole, and the intensity of services. If, for example, it were decided that 100 hours of court-mandated treatment would be the presumptive condition imposed on all individuals convicted of domestic assault who had at least a 50% likelihood of reoffending within 2 years, actuarial norms could be used to anticipate the number who would qualify and the resources required to implement the policy.

Training Users

To implement an actuarial tool effectively, education about the tools and their application would be required for all professionals who provide domestic violence services. Training to a certifiable standard could be specified for all assessors who administer the ODARA or DVRAG, as well as education about their indicated uses and limitations. Each criminal justice partner would require knowledge of policy guidelines about correctional and community interventions for individuals at each level of assessed risk.

For example, when the Maine Judicial Branch began a project to provide judicial monitoring of individuals who have perpetrated domestic violence, they brought me and a colleague to Maine to provide three trainings. First, a session was provided for decision makers from the domestic violence resource centers of the Maine Coalition to End Domestic Violence (MCEDV), child protection services, law enforcement, pretrial services, probation, and treatment programs, about the development and administration of ODARA. Next, a smaller multidisciplinary group who would sustain the project as trainers going forward participated in a train-the-trainer course. One of us also gave a keynote presentation at a multidisciplinary conference on domestic violence courts and judicial monitoring. Later, the Maine

Criminal Justice Academy delivered initial mandatory training for all law enforcement officers statewide regarding the ODARA, and the Judicial Branch coordinated training for all judges and all bail commissioners statewide about the development and use of ODARA. Only after these trainings did law enforcement officers, pretrial services, specialized probation officers, and advocates from the domestic violence resource centers begin using the ODARA. Statewide implementation by law enforcement was coordinated by the MCEDV in partnership with the Cumberland County Violence Intervention Partnership (VIP). These experts have since provided consultation and training to other jurisdictions exploring ODARA implementation, including California, Delaware, Illinois, Iowa, Kentucky, Maryland, Massachusetts, Missouri, New Jersey, New Orleans, New York, North Dakota, Oregon, Pennsylvania, Texas, Virginia, and Washington State (e.g., Luppi & Colpitts, 2014).

This cascading approach to training has been repeated in many other jurisdictions implementing the ODARA. For example, five trainers and policy advisors from the New Brunswick Department of Public Safety attended the first train-the-trainer course offered in Penetanguishene in 2006. As Canada's only officially bilingual province, the Government of New Brunswick translated the scoring instructions and case videos we provided them (similar to those now in ODARA 101) into French. With these materials, Department of Public Safety trainers trained, tested, and certified all their community corrections probation officers, and also provided training to the Department of Justice in Newfoundland and Labrador.

A team from the Saskatchewan Department of Public Safety and Policing also attended a train-the-trainer course and then rolled out training across the province (Province of Saskatchewan, 2009). In-person training has been found helpful for explaining how and why the ODARA is to be reported and used, as well as for giving individual learners feedback on their test results and showing them how to improve for retesting. When one trainer moved to a position in court-based victim services, he also trained those staff. When other trainers were lost to promotion and other changes, the province contracted with a psychologist in private practice to complete trainer-training and provide ongoing training. Managing their own training also allows Saskatchewan to set their own certification standard, requiring 90% correct item scores as well as reliability on total scores.

Most ODARA training is now provided online through ODARA 101 (Hilton & Ham, 2015; Ham et al., 2019; described earlier in this chapter). The training and practice sections can be completed in a group setting, creating a venue for networking and discussion. This option was chosen at first by the Provincial Association for Transition Houses and Services of

Saskatchewan (PATHS). Not satisfied with the relevance and accessibility of ODARA 101 to service providers across the diverse province, however, PATHS began face-to-face training (https://pathssk.org/training), then partnered with us to improve ODARA 101 content and format (Ham et al., 2019). Online training makes it possible for just about every agency to keep its staff trained, despite turnover. At the same time, cross-sector ODARA training sessions can provide an opportunity for professionals to interact on neutral territory and to discuss shared concerns. PATHS's leadership in providing training in domestic violence risk to not only its own member agencies but also to professionals in other sectors, for example, has increased recognition and respect for shelter workers' role in the community response to domestic violence.

Cooperation and Coordination Among Agencies

Readers will note that one theme of this book is that the interests of all those involved in domestic violence are best served when everyone works together to address important problems. Specifically, I believe that, after emergency responses where needed, the next step to ensuring a safe and cost-effective course of action involves law enforcement officers, court officials, correctional services staff, forensic clinicians, court-based victim support workers, health care providers, and the staff of shelters, transition houses, and other domestic violence resources all evaluating the risk represented by each of their cases using a common and accurate metric. I opened this book with an example of a real case in which failure to arrive at a common understanding of one individual's risk resulted in tragedy. I have also described research showing that informal or intuitive practices are inadequate for the task of arriving at this common understanding. To be sure, truly effective strategies to mitigate the risk are still required. Nevertheless, a shared approach to risk assessment is an essential first step.

I highly value my partnership with my colleagues in the OPP, which began when we collaborated to create a risk assessment tool suitable for not only law enforcement but also other agencies that are part of the community response to domestic violence. This collaboration, despite real and fundamental differences in organizational culture and tradition, between one government agency responsible for a large police service and another agency responsible for health care, stands as a tangible example of the sort of cooperation and collaboration that I speak to.

Similarly, Maine's ODARA implementation experience points to the value of MCEDV's collaborative partnerships: with the Commission for their report to legislature, the VIP and law enforcement agencies to begin using the ODARA, and the police training academy responsible for training all officers. An existing interest in risk assessment, and champions for domestic violence risk assessment especially, were also keys to their success. Likewise, in Canada's Northwest Territories, the introduction of the ODARA was a result of several years of planning between the Department of Health and Social Services and the Department of Justice. After the RCMP established its policy for the use of the ODARA, the tool was also made part of the Territorial Government funded Community Counselling Program Standards.

Other jurisdictions have combined training with implementation planning, to enhance interagency cooperation and coordination. I facilitated 2 days of such planning for the Iowa State Court, Judicial Branch with participants who represented the attorney general's office, the Iowa Law Enforcement Academy, special crimes prosecutors, victim advocates, and the Department of Health's Violence Prevention Coordinator. Johnson County, Iowa, already had a well-coordinated response to domestic and sexual violence and were familiar with risk assessment tools based on scientific research when it was awarded a grant for a pilot program using the ODARA (Hermiston, 2017). Also contributing to their successful implementation was the team of three champions working collaboratively, including an Iowa City Police domestic violence investigator, an Assistant County Attorney, and an executive director from the Domestic Violence Intervention Program. All had extensive experience and held respected positions in their fields. They understood the ODARA well and how it supports alignment of resources to cases according to risk. They worked together to train hundreds of officers within 2 years, as well as probation officers, domestic violence treatment supervisors, victim advocates, prosecutors, judges, and child protection workers who may use the ODARA or need to interpret the score. In-person training meant content could be tailored to the needs of professionals from each sector and provided the venue for frank and respectful communication.

Case-coordination teams or high-risk response protocol teams are widely used and provide another opportunity for consolidating multiple stakeholder partnerships. New Brunswick's coordinated community response teams, for example, are led by community victim services, and there is no requirement for assaults to have been reported to police (New Brunswick Office of the Chief Coroner, 2018).

Evaluating Outcomes and Revising Policy

Evaluating whether intended outcomes are achieved is an important part of effective policy. In Canada, the Corrections and Conditional Release Act (1992) stands as an example of criminal justice policy that included a statutory requirement for evaluation. The act had a clause requiring a parliamentary review of its provisions and operation a few years after implementation. As part of this review, several research evaluations were conducted, and several modifications to the policy were made. For a similar policy that mandated the use of the ODARA, the evaluation component could require that records be kept of the numbers of domestic violence incidents attended by police, the proportion for whom ODARA scores were produced, and statistics about the ODARA scores of individuals detained by police, denied bail, sentenced, mandated to and actually attending treatment, denied parole, and so on.

In New Brunswick, a strong spirit of collaboration helped initiate implementation efforts, and continual monitoring helps sustain it. Public safety agents well versed in the ODARA conduct on-site policy audits and review whether the ODARA is scored in eligible cases. A lack of specialized domestic violence officers, however, hampers consistent use of the ODARA. Researchers have found that officers scored the tool in 60% of eligible cases and were less likely to use it when not recommending charges (Ballucci et al., in press). Using the ODARA selectively in cases that are perceived as higher risk could lead to actuarially risky cases going unnoticed because they appear to be nonrisky, and potential disparities in the criminal justice response. A restricted range of values can also result in underestimates of predictive accuracy. New Brunswick researchers are currently conducting ODARA validation studies.

In Maine, the MCEDV conducted online surveys of law enforcement officers and domestic violence resource center advocates statewide, to assess their use of the ODARA. Results indicated that officers across the state are using the ODARA, and the ODARA is informing bail-setting. In addition, the ODARA is considered helpful to risk communication, risk management, and safety planning with people who are victims of domestic abuse and violence. The surveys revealed some shared concerns, largely around ongoing training needs to ensure the ODARA is used only in cases involving eligible crimes and eligible relationships.

These kinds of evaluation can help identify weaknesses in the implementation and where policy may need to be modified, processes clarified, and training and other resources enhanced. The policy's effectiveness can also be evaluated by examining how closely ODARA or DVRAG scores are related to criminal justice, domestic violence treatment, and safety planning decisions, using the same logic as in studies of forensic and tribunal decisions (Hilton, Simpson, & Ham, 2016; Hilton & Simmons, 2001; McKee et al., 2007; see Does the Communication of Actuarial Risk Affect Forensic Decisions? in Chapter 9, this volume). In the case of a policy regarding use of the ODARA, the correlation between a forensic decision and the ODARA score would be used to evaluate how well the decisions match that which would be made based on the risk principle of effective correctional service.

Ideally, efficacy would be determined experimentally by randomly implementing the policy in some jurisdictions and not in others, or even randomly applying the policy to some individuals and not others. An experimental evaluation method would also increase the likelihood of detecting unintended consequences. For example, mandating use of the ODARA in bail decisions might produce the desirable difference between individuals who are released and those who are detained. But if this result occurred at the cost of a great increase in custody spaces devoted to domestic violence cases, such that individuals with a higher risk of committing other, nondomestic violence had to be released (because there was no place to detain them), an apparently effective domestic violence policy might be achieved at unacceptable cost both to individuals who perpetrate domestic violence and to individuals victimized by nondomestic offenses. Rigorous quantitative evaluation can be designed to detect such adverse outcomes.

Challenges to Effective Implementation

I have witnessed many inspirational examples of partnerships and collaborations. I recognize, however, that gaining cooperation among government agencies is easier said than done. An apparently desirable goal can be readily derailed by agencies having conflicting interests. Real interagency cooperation requires leadership in arranging contingencies so that all involved share the same interests. Actuarial tools can support cooperation by offering a common language for talking about risk.

Dedicated champions of evidence-based practice in criminal justice, domestic violence treatment, and community victim services are often key to sustaining successful implementation. I have also seen promising initiatives fizzle out despite best intentions because a key player leaves the organization, receives a different portfolio, or is promoted to a position that does not allow the time for continuing the role of champion. Natural leaders may emerge during the implementation process, and multiple stakeholder planning meetings can also be an opportunity to identify potential champions. Recognizing these individuals, and supporting them with both encouragement and resources, are crucial steps in sustaining an effective implementation. Providing champions with growth opportunities, such as developing their leadership skills and having some oversight of the implementation even if they move into new organizational roles, can also be considered part of an implementation strategy.

Not having access to the information necessary to scoring the ODARA can be an obstacle to its adoption. In New Mexico, all male and female adults referred for domestic violence treatment are assessed using the ODARA, since early 2019. Publicly available criminal records facilitate scoring of multiple items. The ODARA score can be submitted during bail and protection order hearings and criminal trials and may influence detention and custody decisions, where the default pretrial decision is community release. This is the strategy adopted by El Puente, an approved intervention provider agency in Socorro County, who have observed that magistrates and judges appear more likely to use the information if police and criminal records that back up the item scores are submitted as exhibits. Treatment providers can usually access criminal information needed to score the ODARA, but not all are familiar with how to access and interpret the data, leading to some scoring discrepancies between agencies. This challenge raises the need to train all ODARA users in not only how to score the ODARA but also jurisdiction- and agency-level procedures for obtaining and interpreting the required information.

I recognize that the current lack of actuarial norms for women who commit domestic violence, and validation research with individuals who assault same-sex partners, remains a challenge for agencies seeking to adopt the ODARA for all their domestic violence cases. Some agencies have opted to use the tool and conduct their own operational and validation research. I work with these organizations whenever I can, advising on follow-up studies to validate the ODARA in their populations. I encourage implementers to conduct such research even if using the ODARA only for men who assault female partners, as locally derived norms can optimize the application of actuarial risk assessment in their jurisdictions.

CONCLUSION

I have seen some of these strategies working among the agencies I have supported in adopting the ODARA. Incorporating a validated actuarial risk assessment system into an empirically informed systemic response to domestic violence can increase fairness to all parties, can be used to evaluate the appropriateness, effectiveness, and efficiency of the system's response, and provides a defensible basis for action that defends against accusations of dereliction of duty should a tragedy occur. And, I hope, against the occurrence of such tragedies, preventing suffering among individuals who become victims of domestic violence and their children.

POINTS TO REMEMBER

- The ODARA can be completed easily and accurately by police officers and other frontline users with minimal training; the DVRAG requires expertise to score the PCL-R.
- The examples of ODARA implementation in criminal justice, domestic violence treatment, and victim service sectors across jurisdictions in the United States and Canada illustrate the benefits of collaborative planning and the need for careful training and evaluation.
- Fairness to individuals accused of domestic assault, and safety planning for those affected by the violence, can be enhanced by the use of a shared risk metric among victim services, the criminal justice system, and domestic violence treatment programs.
- Policy should be evaluated in terms of reduction of violent recidivism and monitored with respect to the correlation of decisions with actuarial risk score.
- Involving key players and enlisting opinion leaders and peer champions from the outset, as well as ensuring shared goals, are essential for successful teamwork.

QUESTIONS TO CONSIDER

1. Name six jurisdictions where the ODARA has been adopted into policy or practice.
2. Describe two hurdles that implementers have faced and strategies to overcome them.
3. Why is online training for domestic violence risk assessment useful for many assessors? Why do some prefer in-person training?
4. Imagine you work for a community domestic violence treatment program that receives referrals from a probation service and works closely with community victim services. How would you choose and implement a tool for risk assessment and communication?
5. What are some of the practical, scientific, legal, and ethical issues in implementing legislation requiring the use of a specific risk assessment tool? How might they be resolved in a way that balances fairness to individuals charged with domestic violence, safety for their partners, and needs of the criminal justice system?

11 QUESTIONS AND ANSWERS ABOUT THE ONTARIO DOMESTIC ASSAULT RISK ASSESSMENT AND THE DOMESTIC VIOLENCE RISK APPRAISAL GUIDE SYSTEM

As principal author of the Ontario Domestic Assault Risk Assessment (ODARA; Hilton et al., 2004) and the Domestic Violence Risk Appraisal Guide (DVRAG; Hilton, Harris, Rice, et al., 2008), I have provided dozens of classroom training sessions for diverse groups of professionals and volunteers interested in using these actuarial assessment tools. I have evaluated the online ODARA training program and consulted with governments in Canada, the United States, and elsewhere to train criminal justice officials and community agency staff on actuarial violence risk assessment tools. I have been asked many questions about the ODARA and DVRAG. Responses to the most frequently asked questions are reproduced here to help readers grappling with the same issues. For full item scoring criteria and interpretation materials, see Chapters 6 and 7, this volume. For scoring practice, see the Appendix.

For most questions, a short, unqualified answer often suffices. So, for each question in this chapter, I provide a brief response to satisfy readers who want such confirmation. A brief supporting explanation then follows, usually pointing readers to key aspects of how the original research was done.

https://doi.org/10.1037/0000223-012
Domestic Violence Risk Assessment: Tools for Effective Prediction and Management, Second Edition, by N. Z. Hilton

TABLE 11.1. Quick Guide to Eligibility Criteria and Use of the Ontario Domestic Assault Risk Assessment (ODARA) and Domestic Violence Risk Appraisal Guide (DVRAG)

	ODARA	DVRAG
Person to be assessed	Male adult who has assaulted a female intimate partner May also be used to assess a female adult who has assaulted a male partner	
Index assault criteria	Physical assault including physical contact with the partner or a credible threat of death with a weapon in hand in the presence of the partner Index assault reported to police (exception may be made when using the ODARA only to support a partner who has been assaulted)	
Timing of index assault	The most recent occurrence that meets the index assault criteria (regardless of criminal charges)	
Information sources	Police record and criminal history; for partner-only use, supplementing partner interview with official reports is advised where possible	Police record, criminal history, and forensic, clinical, or correctional assessment information sufficient for scoring the Psychopathy Checklist-Revised (PCL-R; Hare, 2003) or PCL-R Facet 4
Population to which norms apply	Men who committed an index assault that appeared in police records	Men who committed an index assault that appeared in police records and for whom in-depth case information is obtained during probation, parole, or corrections or forensic detention for any offense
Conditions of use	Whenever sufficient information is available	Whenever a reliable PCL-R score or PCL-R Facet 4 score is available and an ODARA score is either unavailable or at least 2

Last, I provide more detailed or qualified information on some topics. For those who just want to know whether they have a case that meets the eligibility criteria, I provide an at-a-glance guide (see Table 11.1).

APPLICATION TO ELIGIBLE CASES AND RELEVANT POPULATIONS

Question

Can the ODARA and DVRAG be used only for men who are violent toward female partners? Should I use another assessment that is for all kinds of relationship violence?

Answer

The ODARA was developed and tested originally for male-to-female domestic assaults; it has since been validated with women who assault their partners and in samples including dating relationships.

When my colleagues and I pulled a new sample of 200 cases from police reports similar to those used for the ODARA construction research, there were insufficient cases in which a woman was identified as the sole or primary aggressor to test the ODARA's predictive accuracy, and fewer than five cases of assault in same-sex relationships. The ODARA's predictive accuracy has since been tested in small studies involving women who assaulted their partners (see Women Who Assault Their Partners in Chapter 4, this volume), with mixed results, and more validation research is needed. Much larger samples (at least several hundred cases) are needed to create an actuarial table, like the ones in Chapters 6 and 7, for the interpretation of women's risk of recidivism. For now, the ODARA can be used to compare a woman's risk with that of other women who have assaulted their partners, to identify the highest priority for supervision, custodial treatment, and other services for women with domestic offenses.

Several tests of the ODARA's predictive accuracy have included dating relationships and found no evidence that they are different in terms of the distribution of the ODARA or its predictive accuracy (see Dating and Same-Sex Relationships in Chapter 4, this volume). There are no separate actuarial tables to use for dating violence cases. Violence risk assessment research does not indicate that the predictors of violent recidivism differ for individuals who are not currently in a marital or cohabiting relationship (although having never been so is a risk factor for general violence).

More Information

The same limitation applies to nonactuarial domestic risk assessments; that is, no norms have been delineated for cases of violence in dating relationships, and little or no empirical evidence yet supports their use for female-to-male violence or violence in the relationships of sexual and gender minorities. Some jurisdictions use the ODARA in these cases, provided the remaining eligibility criteria are met. Assessors and policy makers may face a difficult choice between using the ODARA, a locally developed but unvalidated tool, or unaided professional judgement. I advise adding a cautionary statement about the limited validation research in such cases. I also encourage organizations using the ODARA to evaluate its use, including predictive validity, especially when applying it to understudied populations.

Question

The data that were used to create the ODARA and DVRAG came from police records in one province of Canada. How can I be sure that the ODARA and DVRAG generalize to all the racial, ethnic, religious, socioeconomic, and geographic communities of my own jurisdiction?

Answer

Several steps can be taken to assess whether there are reasonable grounds to believe an assessment tool is appropriate for a given individual or population.

Confidence in the appropriate application of any risk assessment tool to a new individual or population is increased by such factors as diversity in the construction samples, similarities between construction and new samples, an accumulation of research supporting generalizability, and studies of discriminative validity, calibration, and bias involving specific communities.

The sampling strategy in the ODARA and DVRAG construction research excluded no individuals on the basis of race, ethnicity, socioeconomic status, or similar variables. In fact, race, ethnicity, and religion were not available in the police record systems we used. The data represented all areas policed by the Ontario Provincial Police across the province, plus approximately 50 municipalities with their own police services, and Indigenous communities. This sampling procedure increases confidence that the predictive value of the ODARA and DVRAG is generally applicable to men who commit domestic violence in the Province of Ontario, although different groups might exhibit different rates of violence overall. Assessors can evaluate whether their populations are sufficiently similar to use these tools. This is an important step in selecting any risk assessment tool or guide.

Studies conducted to date show evidence of the ODARA's predictive validity in different regions, in samples drawn from different criminal justice contexts, and for different outcomes (I reviewed this research in Chapter 4, this volume). Limited calibration work indicates that new ODARA norms should be determined for certain populations (e.g., for women who assault their partners). Although similar evidence has yet to accumulate for the DVRAG, a well-established field of violence prediction research has shown that the strongest predictors of violent behavior are consistent across demographic characteristics. Researchers have begun to focus on ethnic bias in violence risk assessment (see Individual Risk and Bias in Chapter 8), and this topic remains worthy of research in domestic violence risk assessment.

More Information

Research into criminal offending generally indicates that the best predictors of violence are valid across demographic characteristics (see Finding Representative Cases, Chapter 3). Cross-validations of the ODARA and DVRAG are consistent with this body of research. That is, the ODARA was not developed using samples from predominantly large urban areas, but its predictive value was confirmed in samples from the Greater Toronto Area, Canada's largest and most ethnically diverse metropolis. The ODARA has generalized well outside of Ontario and Canada, providing further grounds for using the ODARA and DVRAG with confidence in other jurisdictions.

Another aspect of this question is the potential for ethnic bias as a result of using an assessment that does not pay attention to demographic characteristics or biases in the criminal justice system. For example, persons of Indigenous descent are represented more among arrested, convicted, and incarcerated individuals than in the general population, which has sparked controversy and legal challenge over the use of assessment tools for this group (see Individual Risk and Bias, Chapter 8). Although little is yet known about how systemic bias affects domestic violence risk assessment, I believe actuarial risk assessment can be part of the solution by offering a first and transparent step in the process of apportioning effective and appropriate services.

In summary, there are reasonable grounds to believe that the ODARA and DVRAG will be valid predictors of domestic violence recidivism in diverse groups. Continued research is required, and I encourage local validations in jurisdictions where these tools are being adopted.

Question

The partner obtained a civil court restraining order on the basis of an act of violence that was not reported to police. Police became involved later when the individual violated the restraining order. Can the ODARA be scored in this case, with the index assault being the assault history described in the restraining order application?

Answer

Previously unreported domestic assaults can be used as the index assault when they have become the subject of a police investigation.

The index assault is the most recent incident known to the police in which the individual engaged in violence against an intimate partner. If it can be established that an assault occurred in the past (meeting the criteria of physical contact with the partner or a credible threat of death with a weapon in hand in the presence of the partner), and this evidence is contained in the police report filed subsequently for a nonviolent offense, then it is an eligible index assault.

More Information

An exception is made when the ODARA is scored entirely from an interview with a partner who is familiar with the individual's criminal history. This might happen at a community victim service when the ODARA is being used only to support victim safety planning and not for use in court. In this case, the assessor should communicate to the client that the ODARA's predictive validity has not been established using partner interviews alone, and that the individual's risk could be different were a police record check to show a different history.

Question

I work with individuals who are convicted of domestic offenses and serving a probation sentence. The majority of my cases fall into the highest categories on the ODARA, so should I use some other assessment method?

Answer

The DVRAG is suitable for individuals with more in-depth clinical information and can discriminate among those with relatively high scores better than the ODARA.

The distribution of ODARA scores in the correctional population is skewed toward the higher end because the justice system tends to filter out lower risk individuals from the point of police contact through to court decisions. In the correctional sample used in the DVRAG construction research, a quarter of the individuals who scored in the highest ODARA category fell into the highest DVRAG category. The DVRAG requires a full criminal history and in-depth information to score the Psychopathy Checklist–Revised (PCL-R; Hare, 2003); the DVRAG-4 can be scored with PCL-R Facet 4 items. I describe the DVRAG research in Chapter 5, and the full scoring manual appears in Chapter 7.

RISK ASSESSMENT ITEMS

Question

Why does the ODARA give 2 points against individuals for violent behavior towards people other than their partner and children (i.e., Pre-Index Nondomestic Assault and Pre-Index Assault Against a Nondomestic Victim)? What if I am evaluating a man who was arrested for assault years ago after he got drunk at a football game and got into a fight?

Answer

Violence in general is such a strong predictor that having an identified incident of violence against others and having a police report for such violence both independently predicted domestic violence recidivism.

Each item on the ODARA was incorporated into the tool when the analyses indicated that it contributed to the prediction of domestic violence recidivism even after all other items were taken into account. The statistical procedure that led to the creation of the ODARA identified two items measuring the use of nondomestic violence. The two items are not the same—both require an identifiable incident of violence, but only one requires a police report—but can pertain to the same incident, if the individual was violent and has a police record for this violence. In essence, the statistical selection procedure resulted in a system that weights general violence according to its ability to predict domestic violence recidivism.

More Information

Actuarial risk assessment tools often employ weighted items. Some behaviors contribute more to the score than others because they are stronger predictors of violent recidivism than others are. Criminal behavior, especially violence, was measured in a variety of ways in the ODARA construction research. The predictive strength of general violence resulted in two items reflecting this behavior being selected by statistical analysis because they independently predicted recidivism. That is, having a police record for nondomestic violence predicted domestic violence recidivism even when the occurrence of violence against others was already taken into account. The predictive strength of nondomestic violence is also reflected in the substantial weights given to these two items in the DVRAG. It was not the only characteristic that we measured and coded in more than one way. For example, from a range of variables pertaining to children of the individuals being assessed or their partner, both the total number of children and the children from the partner's previous relationship independently predicted recidivism.

Question

The ODARA is based on static variables. Shouldn't violence risk assessment include both static and dynamic risk? For example, should abstention from alcohol lower the risk score?

Answer

The information captured by the ODARA can be ascertained at the time of the index assault and used to help make immediate and longer-term decisions. There is no available evidence to support altering the score on the basis of changes occurring after the index assault.

In the violence risk assessment literature, there are currently a number of definitions for a *dynamic* variable (see Chapter 8, Hypothesis 2, this volume). To the extent that dynamic means potentially changeable, several ODARA items are dynamic. To the extent that dynamic means a causal risk factor that is changeable through intervention with a consequent reduction in recidivism, the most promising candidate for domestic violence risk assessment is substance use. There is some evidence that treatment is related to risk, and day-to-day changes in alcohol intake are related to patterns of domestic violence (see Possible Targets for Dynamic Assessment of Domestic Violence Risk, Chapter 8). The ODARA and DVRAG capture index and preindex indicators of substance use and related problems that are strong predictors of domestic violence recidivism, rather than postindex changes. Further research is required to identify how changes in causal risk factors can be incorporated into otherwise static measures (i.e., any assessment that is conducted at one point in time).

More Information

While recognizing the need for research into dynamic risk assessment, I do not view *dynamic* as something that an assessor believes might change in the future, something that an individual promises to do (e.g., stop drinking), or a condition of release. The ODARA score should not be altered because of such things. A useful kind of dynamic risk factor would capture fluctuations that occurred during community supervision and that indicated changes in the risk of imminent violence. Some preliminary work has shown promising results with the prediction of violent and sexual recidivism using posttreatment change scores (e.g., Olver, Mundt, et al., 2018). There is no evidence yet that similar patterns hold for predicting imminent domestic violence. Without this evidence, adjusting the ODARA or DVRAG score for events that occur during supervision introduces unacceptable intuitive judgment. A related matter is whether risk should be reassessed after a new domestic assault. ODARA and DVRAG scores can move either up (e.g., increased criminal history) or down (e.g., different index behaviors or partner circumstances). There is no evidence yet of an advantage to reassessment, but some assessors prefer to do so to keep their records current. I recommend that agencies choose whether or not to reassess risk in all cases and embed this decision in their policies and procedures.

Question

The ODARA and DVRAG give too limited a picture of an individual's risk. Adding more items and areas to explore would help me feel that I am covering all the important aspects of the case. Wouldn't a more comprehensive assessment be more accurate?

Answer

The items on the ODARA and DVRAG were selected from among many that were coded from police reports and correctional files. The surviving items include all those that had unique predictive validity in a series of statistical analyses.

To maximize predictive accuracy, an assessment does not need to include every predictor, only the ones that afford incremental validity. Adding variables that are not as strongly related to recidivism to the assessment can reduce overall predictive accuracy and increase measurement error. In Chapter 5, I describe the search for items to add to the ODARA, which resulted in the selection of one additional item (PCL-R score). Tests of many other potential items, including variables specific to domestic relationships and family violence, did not find any that improved on the predictive accuracy of the DVRAG.

More Information

In Chapter 1, I showed that not all the characteristics typical of individuals who assault their partners predict recidivism. Some can actually be unhelpful as predictors. For example, men who assault their partners are more likely than other men to self-report being abused as a child or witnessing domestic violence as a child. In the follow-up research I describe in Chapter 5, as well as studies conducted by other researchers, however, violence in the family of origin did not predict recidivism. Future research could identify new possibilities for improving domestic violence risk assessment. However, adding items to the ODARA or DVRAG without empirical validation would create a risk assessment of unknown validity and could reduce predictive accuracy. In the meantime, the best protection against missing important risk information is to read all available documentation carefully, to adhere to the scoring criteria for each item, and to prorate scores only when the available documentation indicates that an item might be present but the information is unclear or incomplete.

INTERPRETATION OF SCORES

Question

The average length of the follow-up study in the ODARA research was almost 5 years. What if I need to know a man's risk of recidivism in the next year?

Answer

The percentile (rank order) indicates how an individual compares with other men with a record of domestic assault with respect to risk, regardless of the time frame of interest.

The ODARA has successfully predicted domestic violence recidivism in follow-up periods as short as 6 months and as long as 9 years (I review these validations in Chapter 4). Meanwhile, it is important to note that rank order is perhaps the most useful piece of information about risk when it comes to making decisions about priority for custody, supervision, treatment, and partner safety. For assessors concerned about interpreting absolute risk of recidivism across different time periods, it is important to be aware that the actual likelihood of new police reports for domestic violence would be expected to be lower (especially for the lowest risk categories) than the norms indicate over a time period less than 5 years, and higher (especially for the highest risk categories) during a longer time period. In contrast, percentiles rank individuals according to their risk of recidivism notwithstanding the duration of follow-up. Furthermore, individuals with the highest ODARA scores tended to meet the criteria for recidivism the soonest.

More Information

Although there is growing evidence that ODARA scores predict how soon recidivism will occur, in the ODARA construction research, it was often not known whether or how long individuals were remanded in custody before trial, for the index assault or any other offenses, which limits any point estimate of the net elapsed time until recidivism. A reasonable estimate of the upper limit of the average timing of recidivism across the construction sample is approximately 15 months. The ODARA is correlated with the number of recidivistic offenses in a given time, and by inference also correlated with how soon the first offense will occur. Thus, whether an assessor is concerned about any act of domestic assault, the anticipated number of assaults, the likely injury resulting, or how soon recidivism might occur, the ODARA and DVRAG provide relevant information.

Question

You say that an individual's risk summary statement must always refer to the group data. Does this mean that the risk only actually applies to the group, not an individual?

Answer

The actuarial risk of the group that an individual belongs to does apply to the individual.

The study of violent outcomes among a group of individuals in follow-up research permits statements about the probability that violent recidivism will be committed by members of that group; that is, by individuals who are similar on characteristics that afforded incremental validity to the prediction of outcomes in the studied group. In a way, this research formalizes the process that is used in nonactuarial decisions routinely made by clinicians and other assessors that require the assessor to make connections between individuals and a reference group. For example, clinical diagnosis is made with reference to clinical data about individuals with similar symptoms, or to the results of a clinical assessment that has been standardized on groups with similar symptoms. Clinicians take into account what they recall about their past experience with other cases and what they understand about the structured assessments they use to diagnose each new individual. It is, indeed, appropriate to operate as though each member of a group with the same computed level of risk shares the same likelihood of recidivism implied by the risk categories; failure to do so has been called the "aggregate/individual" or "nomothetic/ideographic" error (Grove & Meehl, 1996) and has been roundly criticized by the risk assessment research community (e.g., Hanson & Howard, 2010; Imrey & Dawid, 2015; Mossman & Sellke, 2007; see The Precision of Individual Risk Estimates, Chapter 8, this volume).

More Information

The presence of recidivism is a categorical outcome; that is, its presence is something different from its absence. In contrast, frequency and severity of recidivism are continuous measures: one occurrence is more than zero, two is more than one, and so on. A risk assessment score is a continuous variable also; that is, a higher number represents a greater risk. However, to provide stable probabilities of recidivism, a range of scores is often broken into a category, and the probability of recidivism is given as the proportion of individuals with scores in that category who recidivated in follow-up research. In the DVRAG, for example, there is a wide range of scores, and all are collapsed into seven categories with a corresponding risk level. In the ODARA, because of the dichotomous scoring, there is a smaller range of scores, and a higher proportion of cases with a given score, permitting stable estimates of recidivism for some particular scores; therefore, the five lowest categories comprise only one score each.

Question

I am concerned primarily about domestic murder. The ODARA/DVRAG system is not designed to predict lethality, so should I use another assessment that is?

Answer

The ODARA and DVRAG were not designed to assess the risk of lethal domestic violence specifically, but higher scores do indicate risk of more severe future assaults.

Statistically rare outcomes such as domestic homicide are much more difficult to predict than is overall domestic violence, and no actuarial risk assessment has been developed on a follow-up study focused on lethal outcomes. Moreover, sometimes it is only a matter of timely and expert medical intervention that makes the difference between murder and an assault with a nonlethal outcome. I believe that there is great value in engaging in risk management and safety planning in all such cases regardless of whether the outcome is expected to be lethal. The ODARA and DVRAG construction studies included all postindex incidents in which an act of violence met the definition of domestic assault recidivism.

More Information

Predicting specific kinds of violence is more difficult than predicting violence overall. Although there are published assessments intended to assess the risk of lethality, none has yet been demonstrated to predict domestic murder in a follow-up study. Future research addressing this question would require an extraordinarily large sample from a high-risk population. Meanwhile, in a retrospective study of domestic homicide cases, the ODARA yielded average scores just under seven for cases that did not have prior police reports of domestic violence and nine for cases with police histories, when scored from information documented before a lethal assault in a small number of cases (Eke, Hilton, Harris, et al., 2011).

Throughout this book, I have recommend using the ODARA/DVRAG system in all cases of domestic assault and devoting more risk management effort and resources to higher risk cases; this includes developing and adhering to a safety plan for the partner. Attention could be increased in the presence of the individual's use of firearms or strangulation, divorce or separation, the partner having a new sexual partner, and the partner being of childbearing age or having a child from a sexual relationship other than with the individual being assessed, because these factors were the strongest correlates of domestic homicide in studies of women lethally assaulted by their male partners (e.g., J. C. Campbell, Messing, & Williams, 2017; J. C. Campbell, Webster, & Glass, 2009) and might indicate the timing of serious violence. That is, actuarial scores indicate who is at greatest risk for violence, and these other factors could indicate when such violence might occur.

RESOURCES REQUIRED FOR SCORING THE TOOLS

Question

The ODARA is just one more piece of paperwork in a domestic investigation and takes too long for a police officer to complete. The DVRAG demands evaluation of psychopathy, and we do not have time for that.

Answer

Officers can obtain information for scoring the ODARA during the routine incident investigation and interview with the partner who has been assaulted.

The ODARA items were all selected from information available to police, so scoring should take only a few minutes once a domestic investigation is underway. When scoring the ODARA, be sure to use the dichotomous (yes–no) scoring method, not the item weights used for the DVRAG. The DVRAG contains the PCL-R score, a measure of psychopathy and probably the single most important psychological assessment for forensic evaluation. If the ODARA indicates a score of 2 or more and a reliable PCL-R score can be obtained, we recommend scoring the DVRAG or DVRAG-4; if not, the ODARA gives a valid estimate of violence risk.

Question

Why can't I score the ODARA or DVRAG from an interview with the individual being assessed? They have no reason to lie about things like the number of children they have or things they know I can check in the criminal record.

Answer

Official records should be used whenever possible to maximize the accuracy of the score.

The ODARA and DVRAG were created from research that used criminal record information; wherever possible, that is the way these tools should be applied in practice. I strongly advise obtaining a police record check to score the ODARA and using a full correctional or forensic clinical file to score the DVRAG. If you have no reliable information about the individual's criminal history, or the index assault, or the partner's circumstances (including children in the relationship) then you should seek more information before scoring the ODARA. Without sufficient information to score the PCL-R (or its Facet 4 items), you should seek more information before scoring the DVRAG or use the ODARA instead.

More Information

Lying and conning are defining features of psychopathy. So too are glibness and superficial charm, so an interviewer might not recognize when an individual with these characteristics is not being honest about their criminal history. A full diagnostic assessment of psychopathy requires both an interview by a skilled and qualified interviewer and a criminal file review. Future research could create an interview or paper-and-pencil test for individuals that assesses their risk of domestic violence recidivism; however, the research on which the ODARA and DVRAG are based depended principally on other sources of information. Consequently, I cannot recommend the ODARA and DVRAG be completed on the basis of an interview with the individual being assessed.

Question

Actuarial risk assessment is not perfect and takes more time than just asking the partner's opinion. Don't women who have been assaulted by their partner know the individual's violence potential best?

Answer

Women's statements about their partner's potential for violence do predict recidivism well, but the other items on the ODARA and DVRAG improve on that prediction.

Women's ability to predict reassaults might come from their intimate knowledge of the individual's behavior and the proximal predictors of their violence. This knowledge is not always accessible to other people and is difficult to capture in empirical research studies. The ODARA construction research showed, however, that including partners' predictions on the ODARA improves on the predictive accuracy of both.

More Information

As I described in Chapter 1 (see Vulnerability Factors Among Women Who Are Assaulted), women's predictions are correlated with domestic violence in subsequent months and years. The partner's statement of concern was selected in the statistical process used to create the ODARA because of its predictive accuracy over and above many other variables that were tested. A woman's fear for her children especially might prompt her to leave an abusive relationship, which in turn may be a proximal risk factor for assault. There are limits, however, on the accuracy of partners' predictions. Sometimes women minimize the violence or are overly optimistic about their ability to end their relationship with the abusive partner.

COURT ISSUES

Question

The ODARA research used research assistants' judgments to ascertain whether violence occurred at the index assault and recidivism. Would it not be more applicable to the courts if the research had been based on criminal convictions?

Answer

Although it is possible that some courts would consider a tool that assesses risk on the basis of convictions to be more relevant, decisions about bail and conditional release sentencing are to some extent concerned with the risk of any detected offense. The ODARA was designed to predict police occurrence reports or charges of domestic violence rather than whether an individual is convicted.

The ODARA and DVRAG assess the risk of a domestic assault that comes to the attention of the criminal justice system. The extensive literature on unreported crime suggests that the published norms will underestimate the true likelihood of another domestic assault. In general, actuarial risk assessment tools that have been admitted into evidence use criminal conduct measured by police report, arrest, charge, or conviction, rather than conviction alone, because such broader measures capture more closely the true rate of recidivism. Basing ODARA eligibility, item scoring, and recidivism only on convictions could result in poorer predictive validity.

More Information

In court settings, it is important to separate the task of risk assessment and the process of determining guilt. Forensic decisions are often made based on a person's conduct regardless of criminal conviction (e.g., roadside suspensions of drivers' licenses based on breathalyzer readings or a police officer's opinion that a person is impaired, the granting of search warrants upon evidence of criminal activity that might be uncovered, limitations imposed on personal liberty pertaining to possible terrorist activity). The VRAG tools have been admitted as evidence many times at such preventive detention sentencing proceedings for persons with mental disorder, even though they consider past criminal charges that have not resulted in conviction. Bail courts, especially, can deny bail if the accused person might commit a new offense while awaiting trial or violate other conditions of release; the ODARA has been shown to be directly relevant to these questions.

Meanwhile, for those whose sole concern is whether an individual will be convicted of subsequent assault on a partner, a test of this outcome found that the ODARA predicts criminal conviction for domestic assault recidivism with a medium effect size, area under the curve (AUC) = .66, 95% confidence interval [.53, .78] (see AUC and Related Accuracy Statistics in Chapter 2), under conservative conditions whereby men who were not charged or whose charges were withdrawn or unresolved at the time of coding were counted as nonrecidivists. The argument against restricting ODARA scoring to offenses resulting in convictions is not intended to suggest that research criteria for recidivism replace legal standards for culpability; these issues are entirely separate. When it comes to domestic violence risk assessment, though, police reports appear to be at least as valid legal findings of guilt for identifying risk factors for future violence.

Question

You have suggested that the ODARA can be used to help make decisions about bail. Wouldn't that usurp the court's prerogative to make decisions?

Answer

The ODARA is a decision support tool that provides information about grounds that are important to the granting of bail, especially whether there is a substantial likelihood that the accused person would commit another offense if released.

Bail courts in Ontario can detain an accused person on three grounds: to ensure they attend court for trial, to protect the safety of the public, and to maintain confidence in the justice system (which essentially concerns the severity of the offense). The ODARA provides information on the first two grounds. The ODARA scoring manual (see Chapter 6, this volume) does not specify cutoff scores for denying bail. In any jurisdiction, a decision would have to be made about which scores are appropriate for requiring a bail hearing, and any other conditional release decision based on available resources, the acceptability of recidivism, and justice needs. In sum, I hope that the ODARA can be useful to bail decisions, but to assist with rather than to usurp the function of the bail court.

More Information

The particular matter of bail court is raised because the ODARA makes possible the use of actuarial risk assessment for domestic violence suitable for the time frame of bail court. Actuarial risk information has an extensive history of being admitted to higher courts and given weight in sentencing decisions, as well as in parole board decisions and mental health tribunals. In bail court, the primary evidence is usually provided by police, in the form of written reports submitted by the prosecution and viva voce testimony. Police services now routinely use some form of risk checklist, and the admission of domestic and other risk assessment tools as evidence into bail court is a growing practice.

Question

Several items are based on what the alleged victim reported at the time of the index assault. Should the ODARA score be revised when alleged victims recant their allegation?

Answer

The ODARA score predicts recidivism using information available at the time of the index assault. There is no available evidence that supports altering the score using information about events that occur later.

The investigation that occurred within the first few hours after the index assault was reported to police was the basis for the ODARA research. ODARA items were partly, but not exclusively, based on partner statements documented in the police report. Investigating officers typically interviewed other witnesses and gathered other evidence. Statements by the persons involved made in subsequent days and weeks were not used. Future research could test whether additional information, such as events occurring after the index assault but before a criminal justice or risk management decision, improves prediction of subsequent domestic violence recidivism. In the meantime, altering or setting aside the ODARA score based on later statements would not be justified.

APPORTIONING RESOURCES ACCORDING TO RISK

Question

Even the lowest risk categories on the ODARA and DVRAG have a nonzero likelihood of recidivism. This shows that all individuals are at some risk, so shouldn't they all be denied bail and all given the best treatment we have to offer?

Answer

There is variation among people who commit domestic violence, with some more likely to recidivate than others. Giving the same intervention to all individuals could leave those who need more intervention at risk and could increase risk among those of lowest risk.

To have a realistic prospect of altering the likelihood of recidivism, interventions must abide by the Risk–Need–Responsivity (RNR) principles of correctional intervention, as I described in earlier chapters (e.g., Limits of Domestic Violence Theory in Chapter 1). First, intervention must be delivered in accordance with risk; those cases of highest risk must receive proportionately more intensive service. Interventions aimed at the lowest risk groups have the potential to increase the likelihood of reoffending.

More Information

Interventions must target criminogenic needs—changeable characteristics associated with recidivism. Substance use and antisocial conduct are examples of empirically supported targets for intervention. Low self-esteem, anxiety, and personal distress are examples of unsupported targets, and interventions to increase self-esteem and reduce anxiety or distress could increase the likelihood of violence. As I described in Chapter 2 (see Risk Assessment for Domestic Violence Treatment), therapies aimed at changing attitudes and beliefs about gender roles, although popular domestic violence treatment targets, lack good research support, so it is not known whether they reduce risk (or potentially increase it). Effective interventions for criminogenic needs are highly structured, largely skills-based, and help participants learn new behaviors. Interventions also require a formal ongoing monitoring system to ensure that service providers follow the curriculum, where available, and adhere to the other principles of effective intervention. Such a system would include preintervention risk assessment to determine treatment intensity and follow-up with participants to evaluate success and inform program improvements.

Question

What if a man's ODARA or DVRAG score places him in a relatively low-risk category, but he has stated that he will kill his wife and children when he is released? Do I have to override the actuarial score and use my discretion in this case?

Answer

A policy incorporating the duty to protect can be implemented without use of a clinical override of the ODARA or DVRAG score.

The duty to protect a person who is the object of a specific and credible threat of violence imposes a legal and moral obligation to act, regardless of the probability of recidivism. It should not be a matter of clinical discretion but rather a matter of policy to intervene with individuals who make specific threats of violence regardless of their actuarial risk. A policy can be implemented that not only states the default level of intervention at certain ODARA or DVRAG scores but also provides for custody or close supervision in cases in which an individual makes a direct threat. This approach is quite different from using one's judgment to alter a risk score or deviate from an interpretation based on the experience table.

More Information

A valid risk assessment supports the first principle of effective correctional service, but it is not the only consideration. It is reasonable, as a matter of policy rather than an aspect of risk assessment, to take steps to protect someone who has been threatened with further violence. It is customary in many jurisdictions for the bail court to require a promise of good behavior before an accused person is released. Forensic clinicians can offer treatment for people with symptoms of mental illness as an appropriate and humane intervention, even though they are not criminogenic needs or ODARA/DVRAG items. In contrast, secure custody might be reserved for individuals with relatively high scores on a violence risk assessment tool.

BROADER CONCERNS

Question

The ODARA and DVRAG are entirely empirically based and atheoretical. Wouldn't risk assessment be more useful if it helped to explain domestic violence?

Answer

The process of domestic violence risk assessment can help generate explanations for the violence that may guide risk management decisions or help assessors frame their understanding of the individual. However, theories of domestic violence recidivism are not well developed, and the highest risk cases can be identified without a theoretical framework.

Often in classroom training sessions, participants ask why a particular item is on the ODARA. The correct answer is, of course, "because it predicted domestic violence recidivism." But *why* and *how* it predicts are often topics of much discussion. Theoretical explanations can be both fascinating and useful for designing interventions such as treatment; however, risk assessment can be done successfully without any reference to causal pathways. Some characteristics that distinguish individuals who assault their partners from those who do not might also predict their recidivism or help identify those most at risk of assaulting their partners again. Alcohol use is one variable that might aid both prediction and explanation (see Possible Targets for Dynamic Assessment of Domestic Violence Risk, Chapter 8). There is no necessary overlap, however, and blending the risk assessment task with attempts to explain an individual's behavior could lead assessors to make empirically unsupported adjustments to the risk score.

More Information

In considering this question, it is important to understand what "theory" is. In one sense, a theory is a hunch, guess, or hypothesis about relationships. Police have made much practical use of the hypothesis that fingerprints are unique without having to know the genetic and prenatal environmental reasons for their uniqueness. Indeed, knowing why fingerprints are unique has not led to more accurate identifications than were achieved before. In the same way, useful risk assessment instruments have been developed primarily by including variables that have been found to be empirically related to recidivism, without necessarily knowing why. Current actuarial systems, although not themselves explanations of crime and violence, must be consistent with causal explanations because they predict relevant outcomes. In contrast, because unaided clinical judgment is weakly or not related to recidivism, one may legitimately conclude that it is not generally based on a valid explanation of violence. The empirical superiority of actuarial data over clinical intuition implies that clinicians should set aside clinical intuition and theories of violence to optimize risk-related decisions.

Question

Violence against women is a product of sexist society, and risk assessment just individualizes the problem. Don't we need a more fundamental change?

Answer

Sexism and other systemic prejudice could be at the root of much violence and compound the problem of violence against women, specifically. Nevertheless, individual differences do exist in proclivity for violent behavior.

The primary function of domestic violence risk assessment is to identify those individuals who are most likely to assault their partner again or to do so more severely. This information can then be used to reduce the occurrence of violence through increased supervision, more intensive treatment, or more secure custody, where appropriate. The same information can also be used to advise people who have been assaulted of the potential for repeated violence by their partner or ex-partner and to advocate for increased protection and support for them and their families. I believe that actuarial risk assessment is one tool in a multifaceted approach to reducing violence against women and can be used at the same time as making efforts to change societal factors.

CONCLUSION

In my experience, most of the questions and concerns exemplified in these 20 examples are motivated by a genuine desire to do as good a job as possible. Most assessors want a thorough understanding simply to prevent potential victimization while avoiding unnecessary restriction of persons accused or convicted of domestic violence. On the other hand, human nature entails a strong and irresistible expectation that the behavior of other humans is understandable and predictable from our observations and interactions with them. People readily accept that scientific methods could result in better medicines, aircraft, and refrigerators than they could create themselves. But it is much harder to accept that science has anything special to offer interpersonal domains such as personnel selection, education, mental health, or violence risk assessment.

My responses to these questions are influenced to a large extent by my psychological perspective on criminal behavior. Readers who favor a more sociopolitical perspective, or who are primarily concerned with the effects of prejudice and disadvantage, may be more interested in social justice solutions to crime rather than the assessment of individual violence risk. Sociological and psychological theories of crime have their respective research methods and bodies of evidence, and both literatures have produced critiques of actuarial risk assessment. There are legal and ethical implications of domestic violence risk assessment that must be grappled with.

Sometimes, however, it may be difficult for readers to distinguish attempts to improve risk assessment and its application from poorly conducted research and commentaries that promote misunderstanding of statistical arguments.

When I have proffered advice in this book, my bias is in favor of the empirical evidence pertaining to the prediction of violent recidivism, and of domestic violence recidivism in particular. Scientific studies, although not perfect, repeatedly show that accurate (and professionally competent) decisions about the risk of subsequent violence require certain pieces of information, especially details of the individual's criminal record. It is because of the robust association between preindex assaults, conditional release failures, and custodial sentences and recidivism that these variables were selected through the statistical analyses used to construct the ODARA. In the case of in-depth forensic risk assessment, measuring psychopathic traits permits greater accuracy in risk assessment than is possible without measuring it. Not allocating the resources needed to obtain such information and incorporating it into decision-making risks accepting avoidable revictimization, unnecessary incarceration, or other undesirable outcomes. The ODARA and DVRAG are tools for ensuring that criminal justice, treatment, and victim support services gather and integrate this information into the allocation of risk management resources.

AFTERWORD

Future Directions in Domestic Violence Risk Assessment Research and Practice

Since the first edition of this book a decade ago, there has been substantial growth in domestic violence risk assessment research. New tools have appeared, validation studies have expanded beyond samples of men who assault their female partners, and many jurisdictions have adopted assessment tools into practice in criminal justice, treatment, and victim service contexts. Many of these developments have been in response to demands from assessors in the field. Risk assessment research has also been drawn along by progress in the broader field of violence prediction, which has seen advances in addressing statistical and ethical challenges to risk assessment and its applications. These developments point to promising directions for domestic violence risk assessment and many promising opportunities for related research.

NEXT STEPS IN DOMESTIC VIOLENCE RISK ASSESSMENT RESEARCH

The research described in this book constitutes the entire contribution of actuarial methods to domestic violence risk assessment that I am aware of and comprises a shorter history than that of violence prediction in general. So much has happened in the latter field since Monahan's (1981) germinal monograph stating that clinicians' predictions of violence are correct no more than one time out of three that, when I read those words as a student, I could

https://doi.org/10.1037/0000223-013
Domestic Violence Risk Assessment: Tools for Effective Prediction and Management, Second Edition, by N. Z. Hilton

not imagine I would publish the first actuarial risk assessment for domestic violence nearly 25 years later. The first decade of violence risk assessment research saw an increase in prediction accuracy for general violent recidivism. So far, research has not shown that domestic violence recidivism can consistently be predicted with the same accuracy as can general violence recidivism. There could be a limit set by the smaller target that researchers have to aim at: not just any criminal violence but just that directed at intimate partners. Finding ways to improve the detection of domestic violence from official records of assaults and testing the benefits of data collection from multiple sources, including all parties involved in domestic assaults, will challenge researchers to expand their methods and enhance their collaborative partnerships.

Just one decade ago, I did not anticipate that, despite a teeming literature on domestic violence risk assessment by now, little would look beyond men's violence against women. We have seen that most risk assessment research has yet to include women who commit domestic violence. No tool has been developed specifically for women or incorporated risk factors that may be unique to violence by women, let alone by transgendered persons or those in same-sex relationships. Although such specialized tools might turn out to be unnecessary, more research is needed to examine gender differences in domestic violence risk assessment. Indeed, research with more inclusive samples might discover how existing tools can be modified to optimize predictive accuracy (both discrimination and calibration) for domestic violence in intimate partner relationships involving any genders, and specifically in currently underserved communities.

The exploration of cultural bias has been identified as a key next step for research in risk assessment (see Individual Risk and Bias in Chapter 8). Researchers are creating and critiquing methods for testing bias and are grappling with related ethical and legal issues. Scientific and cross-discipline research on cultural bias in violence prediction is likely to increase over the next decade, and studies in domestic violence risk assessment will need to follow this direction.

Future research on the Ontario Domestic Assault Risk Assessment (ODARA) and Domestic Violence Risk Appraisal Guide (DVRAG) in particular could explore the effects of adjusting the item scoring criteria. Although field tests of scoring fidelity and interrater reliability remain important, it may be valuable for assessors and policy-makers to know the degree to which deviating from item scoring and prorating procedures affect predictive validity. Researchers could explore how the needs apparent in specific contexts affect risk assessment, such as services for newcomer communities who might be lacking criminal history, or courtrooms in which attorneys and judges may argue for using convictions rather than police reports. Studies could be designed to test the addition of potential predictors that are of interest to assessors, such as suicide threats or animal abuse, perhaps using different samples and information sources from those used in the ODARA and DVRAG research. Another potential addition is professional judgment: Could assessors make a post-ODARA judgment of risk that shows interrater reliability and incremental predictive validity over the ODARA score? Other adjustments made on the basis of observed behavior change could also be investigated. For example, can individuals' risk category be reduced if they remain offense-free in the community for a given time period, or if they exhibit certain measurable changes in evidence-based domestic violence treatment? Validation studies for the DVRAG and its risk categories, with or without such additions and adjustments, are still needed in a variety of contexts, using scores from either researchers or assessors.

Another direction that risk assessment research might take is to explore how interactions between two or more variables can improve predictive validity. For example, both alcohol use and antisociality are associated with domestic violence outcomes, but how does alcohol use affect the association between antisociality and domestic violence, and how might knowing about that interaction improve domestic violence risk assessment? In the related area of sexual offending, the combination of two key predictors—Psychopathy Checklist–Revised scores and results of sexual preference testing—increases risk of sexual recidivism; however, it is not yet clear how to combine these variables to improve risk assessment (e.g., Hawes et al., 2013). To do so may require delving into the field of nonarbitrary metrics, capturing the interaction using cut-off scores for each variable that reflect a real difference in the underlying characteristics (e.g., Blanton & Jaccard, 2006; R. K. Hanson, personal communication, June 2, 2019). Researchers have experimented with nonarbitrary metrics for categorizing and communicating risk assessment results. Perhaps this approach will one day improve domestic violence risk assessment.

Theory development and testing remains a substantial gap in domestic violence research. Although theory has generated ideas for potential predictors for testing, the creation and application of risk assessment tools have been empirically driven. Theoretically motivated risk factors for the occurrence of domestic violence have not necessarily translated into predictors of domestic violence recidivism in follow-up research (e.g., adverse childhood experiences, see Exhibit 1.1). Moreover, empirically supported predictors could be considered relevant to multiple theoretical perspectives;

for example, children in the relationship, especially minor children, could be related to domestic violence recidivism for reasons to do with the age–crime curve, parental stress, evolved sexual jealousy, antisocial personality, or some combination of these or other possible explanations (see the section Child Abuse in Chapter 4). A more robust theoretical literature to inform domestic violence risk assessment would include tests of competing theories that make different hypotheses about the effects of variables or that are instantiated by different variables.

NEW DEVELOPMENTS IN DOMESTIC VIOLENCE RISK ASSESSMENT

The tools set out in this book are only the beginning of the risk assessment and management processes. Communicating the assessed risk to people who need it for their decision making, such as judges, parole officers, psychiatric review boards, or partners planning for their own safety, is also part of the process. For many practitioners, specifying risk management strategies is a formal part of this communication. Emerging research shows that agencies are most likely to enact recommendations that involve strict enforcement of criminal justice sanctions and least likely to engage with the mental health, family, and social needs of individuals charged with criminal offenses (Dyck et al., 2018; Ennis, Hargreaves, & Gulayets, 2015). This finding suggests that more attention is needed to understand how risk assessment services can reach their full potential. Efforts to strengthen the process from risk assessment to the enactment of risk management strategies could focus on improving access to rehabilitative interventions for individuals assessed to be at relatively high risk of domestic violence recidivism, and especially to effective interventions that target criminogenic needs.

Other unfolding developments include incorporating situational factors that may affect imminent risk of domestic violence. Even tools that measure purportedly dynamic risk factors do so in a static manner (i.e., measured at a single point in time) rather than capturing changing contextual information. Situational factors such as use of firearms or other weapons might be especially relevant to the risk of domestic homicide (e.g., J. C. Campbell et al., 2007; Folkes et al., 2013). Until truly dynamic methods of domestic violence risk assessment are developed, it will be important to examine how practitioners can incorporate changeable, situational risk factors into their risk management strategies without losing the benefit of information provided by existing risk assessment tools.

CONCLUSION

Some of these matters are controversial, in that people do not agree on how to balance the desire to implement change with the need for adequate research to support that change. Often, urgent issues precede the evidence base for responding to them, as I illustrated in Chapter 8. Domestic violence risk assessment is a rapidly developing practice, but one for which the empirical base is also growing. Collaborations between researchers, assessors, and policy makers enhance the practical utility of research and its application in criminal justice, domestic violence treatment, and community victim services. This book has been written with all these audiences in mind. I hope that its overview of domestic violence risk assessment, the ODARA and DVRAG tools, and considerations in risk assessment and risk management will inform and inspire all those working to end domestic violence.

Appendix

CASE MATERIALS FOR SCORING PRACTICE

These case materials are provided for scoring practice. All are fictional cases, informed by my research experience with police reports and stories from domestic violence victims. The transcripts are not intended to illustrate exemplary interviewing techniques; in fact, some items are deliberately left to learners to piece together to challenge learners to examine the scoring criteria carefully and consider the handling of ambiguous information. Correct scores for each case are listed at the end of this appendix, with a brief explanation. Cases A.1 and A.2 present details about a police report regarding a single occurrence of domestic violence. Case A.3 presents a transcript of an interview conducted by a community victim service provider with a person who has been assaulted, rather than a police report. Case A.4 presents more in-depth information about an individual being assessed, including multiple police occurrence reports and a psychosocial assessment report prepared by a forensic clinician. Tables at the end of the appendix present Ontario Domestic Assault Risk Assessment (ODARA; Hilton et al., 2004) scores for all four cases, as well as Domestic Violence Risk Appraisal Guide (DVRAG; Hilton, Harris, Rice, et al., 2008) scores for Case A.4.

The psychosocial report for the DVRAG case in Case A.4 was created according to the example psychosocial history provided by Harris, Rice, et al. (2015) and is a realistic example of how the DVRAG may be scored from forensic material. The information considered for scoring the Psychopathy Checklist–Revised (PCL-R; Hare, 2003) in this case is indicated in the psychosocial report by PCL-R items in parentheses at the end of the relevant paragraphs.

CASE A.1: POLICE OCCURRENCE REPORT, ANDALUS MACDONALD

Occurrence 01-021050 (Domestic Assault)

Involved Persons

- **Accused:** Macdonald, Andalus, 10 Mackenzie Street, Abbott, ON. Date of birth 1981-04-09. Employer: First Time Leasing. Relationship to victim: Spouse.
- **Charged:** Assault (spousal), 2019-06-21. Released on recognizance, next hearing 1000 hr, 07-14
- **Victim:** Macdonald, Arial, 10 Mackenzie Street, Abbott, ON. Date of birth 1987-03-15. Employer: First Public School.
- **Witness, complainant:** Thompson, Calisto (age 14), 10 Mackenzie Street, Abbott, ON. Date of birth 2005-05-21. Employer: Student

History

Dispatched following call received from a child stating their stepdad had hit their mom. There are no current alerts for persons at this address. Officers were admitted to the residence by person identifying himself as Andalus Macdonald (accused). Also present in the home was Arial Macdonald (victim) and her son from her first marriage, who lives with them and was present during the assault.

Incident

At approximately 1700 hr Andalus and Arial Macdonald were in their kitchen discussing the overuse of data on their family phone plan. Mr. Macdonald was very upset at the expense saying that someone would have to pay for it, and it wouldn't be him. He felt the son, who streamed podcasts when the Wi-Fi was down, should be responsible for the cost. Ms. Macdonald did not agree. The argument became heated and loud. When Ms. Macdonald tried to leave the kitchen, Mr. Macdonald punched her in the back and then stormed out of the house. The son called 911 at this time.

Ms. Macdonald texted her sister to see if she and the son could go there for the night, but Mr. Macdonald returned to the kitchen and grabbed the phone out of her hand saying, "I'm going to cut you both out of the plan from now on." Ms. Macdonald decided to remain at home and wait for the accused to calm down. The police arrived at 1735 hr. Mr. Macdonald expressed regret for the incident and said it was probably best if Ms. Macdonald did go to stay with her sister for a while.

Victim Statement

Ms. Macdonald states that she and the accused have been married for 6 years. She denies any previous assaults or threats by the accused. She states that the accused had been consuming a large amount of alcohol before the incident (three to four bottles of beer), which was unusual for him as neither of them typically consume much alcohol except when having friends over.

Criminal Record

Date	Location	Charge	Sentence
2017-07-27	Bowell, ON	Operating a vehicle while impaired	6 months' probation (license suspension; refrain from consuming alcohol; keep the peace)

CASE A.2: POLICE OCCURRENCE REPORT, CORBEL TUPPER

Occurrence 01-040314 (Domestic Assault)

Involved Persons

- **Accused:** Tupper, Corbel, 317 King Street South, Meighen, ON. Date of birth 1992-05-10. Employer: First Regional Hospital. Relationship to victim: Dating partner.
- **Charged:** Assault, 2019-06-22. Held for bail hearing, next appearance 1000 hr, 07-14
- **Victim, complainant:** Laurier, Edessa, 1703–2019 Borden Avenue, Meighen, ON. Date of birth 1995-03-17. Employer: First Home Realty.

History

Dispatched following call received from a woman reporting that she was being held captive by her boyfriend Corbel Tupper (accused). Current alerts indicate Tupper is on probation. On attending the premises, officers could not get a response at the door, but communications center reported the caller could hear us from the bedroom closet where she was trapped. Officers were admitted to the residence by the apartment supervisor and located the woman in the bedroom closet, which was barricaded with a heavy piece of furniture. There was an odor of urine and the woman moved with some difficulty stating she had been crouched in the closet for at least a day and a half.

Incident

On the night of 21 June, Mr. Tupper had visited the apartment of Edessa Laurier (victim) for a date. He had asked her to meet him at the bus stop outside the building, but she declined because of the weather. He was unusually critical of her appearance and behavior, including her choice to drink a flavored spritzer. He had brought wine and he insisted that they both drink it.

At approximately 2200 hr Mr. Tupper began to smoke marijuana, and Ms. Laurier requested that he smoke on the balcony and then leave as she wished to go to sleep. Mr. Tupper began accusing her of having other men in her apartment. She said "Goodnight" and walked away from him into her bedroom. He followed and pushed her to the floor then sat on her legs and punched her in the back and sides, saying, "This is what I'll do to you if I find out you've been seeing anyone else." He then searched her room for "evidence," emptying her underwear from her drawers and pulling everything out of her closet. She shouted at him to stop, then started to call a friend for help, but he kicked the phone out of her hand. She then went to run out of the bedroom, but the accused caught her and pulled her back into the room, dragging her to the closet. He then pushed the drawers in front of the door. He spent the night sleeping in the bedroom ignoring her pleas to let her out or to allow her some water or food. She states that she slept intermittently and upon waking today realized that Mr. Tupper had gone or was sleeping. She could see that her phone had fallen close to the closet door and made attempts to push the closet door open until she could reach far enough to get hold of it.

Victim Statement

Ms. Laurier states that she and Mr. Tupper have been dating for 5 months, and this is the first time he has been violent toward her, although he has been increasingly controlling and at times "creepy." She states that when they were first seeing each other, a previous girlfriend of the accused contacted her to warn her of his jealous and violent behavior, which apparently started when she was pregnant with their now 2-year-old child. As a result, Ms. Laurier states she is now scared of future violence by Mr. Tupper. Neither party has other children, and Ms. Laurier denies any possibility of pregnancy.

An ambulance was called and Ms. Laurier was transported to hospital as a precaution due to her distressed and dehydrated state. Victim services to follow up. Officers remained at the scene while the building supervisor changed the apartment door lock. Mr. Tupper was located at his place of employment and taken into custody without incident.

Criminal Record

Date	Location	Charge	Sentence
2017-01-19	Bennett, ON	Assault	18 months' probation (refrain from consuming alcohol; keep the peace)
2015-04-18	St. Laurent, ON	Assault	6 months' probation (refrain from consuming alcohol; keep the peace)

CASE A.3: VICTIM SERVICES INTERVIEW TRANSCRIPT, FRANKLIN DIEFENBAKER

INTERVIEWER: Mr. Diefenbaker, I appreciate you coming into the office for this follow-up today. I thought that the injury to your head might make it difficult for you to get here.

CLIENT: Well, I'm not comfortable enough yet to drive here, but a friend drove me to the subway, and it was just a few stops.

INTERVIEWER: How are things at home since the police were there on the weekend?

CLIENT: Quiet, I guess. I guess it'll be that way until my wife is back home, or we decide what we're going to do. I called our son, he's pretty good about it all, he says I can come stay with him and the kids if I want to.

INTERVIEWER: That's good. Do you or your wife have any other children?

CLIENT: We have a daughter. We haven't seen her in a while. She left home when she was 22 and doesn't visit. She won't talk to her mother at all, but it's mutual.

INTERVIEWER: I'd like to talk more about your situation and what you can expect to happen over the next few days and weeks regarding the charges against your wife. We can also talk about safety planning for you during this time. One of the things that can help us with that is a brief risk assessment. We use the ODARA. It was created to assess the risk that a man who has assaulted a female partner will do so again in the future, and most of the interpretation is based on men as the person being assessed; however, there's also evidence that higher ODARA scores are related to increased risk among women who assault their male partners. It can give us an idea of your wife's risk. It only takes about 10 minutes to run through the questions with you, and we can pull some of the information from the police record. Are you interested in doing this?

CLIENT: OK, yes.

INTERVIEWER: All right then. Let's start with some details about the assault last week. Did your wife threaten to harm or kill you or anyone else?

CLIENT: Yes. While she was throwing everything around the kitchen, she was yelling, "I've had it now. I'm going to kill you this time!" I thought she might, too.

INTERVIEWER: That sounds like it would have been frightening for you. At that time, did she do anything to prevent you leaving the location?

CLIENT: Not really. I mean, there's stuff flying around and I had to dodge it to get to the door. That's how I got the cut on my head.

INTERVIEWER: How did you leave the situation?

CLIENT: I got out of the kitchen. I went for the phone, but she punched me in the arm and then she pulled the phone right out of the wall. So I turned around and left the apartment. My neighbor down the hall was standing listening at their door. I guess he heard the fuss. He just pulled me into his apartment, and it was him who called the police.

INTERVIEWER: Did she come after you at all?

CLIENT: No, once I got out the front door, she just slammed it shut and kept hollering.

INTERVIEWER: Had either of you had anything to drink just before or during the assault?

CLIENT: No, I had just come home from work, so I had just had a shower and nothing to eat or drink yet. She had though, she was already into a bottle of wine. That's when the trouble starts, you see?

INTERVIEWER: Is she more angry or violent when she uses drugs or alcohol?

CLIENT: She's way more violent when she drinks. It's a real problem. Just the alcohol, mind you. She's not a drug user.

INTERVIEWER: So she didn't use drugs just before or during this assault?

CLIENT: No. Not me either, never been into any of that. I'm not a teetotaler, mind you. I do like to have a gin and tonic some evenings. I've just never been one to drink that much, and I don't use drugs. I've never known my wife to use drugs either.

INTERVIEWER: Did she abuse alcohol in the past few days or weeks?

CLIENT: No, that's the sad thing. It's been going well for a few weeks.

INTERVIEWER: Before this time, have police ever come because she was hitting you?

CLIENT: No. My son almost called them once when he realized the violence was still going on. I hadn't let on for a few years, but she hit me in the face with a glass one time when he was over at our place, and it all came out. The drinking and the pushing me around has been going on a long time, you see. Ever since the kids started school, just about. He almost called the police that day, but I asked him not to.

INTERVIEWER: So, have police ever been involved because she was threatening you?

CLIENT: No.

INTERVIEWER: Or threatening your son? Or your daughter?

CLIENT: No, they never came before.

INTERVIEWER: Do you know if the police have dealt with her because she was hitting or threatening another partner?

CLIENT: Oh, gosh no. Anyway, it would have been so long ago that she was going out with someone else before she met me.

INTERVIEWER: Before this time, have the police ever had to deal with her for any other kind of violence?

CLIENT: No, she's never been involved with the police or courts at all in the past.

INTERVIEWER: So, is she violent to people other than you or your children?

CLIENT: Well, she's always shouting at the neighbors, especially when she has been drinking and she thinks they're making too much noise, or leaving their garbage out, that sort of thing. One day late last summer, a young woman in the building wouldn't take it and shouted right in her face, and my wife slapped her and pulled her hair. The woman kicked her and called her a few choice names, until her friends talked her down. Nobody called the police then either.

INTERVIEWER: We've already talked about your two children. Are you concerned that your wife will assault either you or your son or daughter again in the future?

CLIENT: Well, I don't think it will stop. I'd like it to. But I don't know how we can continue our marriage. She'll have to do something to change, stop drinking for good or something, and if she doesn't then she'll just keep on with these violent rages that she has. I don't think I can take any more of this.

INTERVIEWER: It sounds like you've been assaulted many times. We can talk about some of your options and the services at our agency that can support you in your next steps. Let me ask first about your situation where you're living right now. Do you have a phone in your home, or a cell phone?

CLIENT: We have a phone.

INTERVIEWER: Do you have access to transportation?

CLIENT: Yes, I have the car that I normally use. There's the subway, too, if I'm up to a bit of a walk first.

INTERVIEWER: OK, that's good. Do you have any questions for me about what we've been talking about so far?

The victim services worker refers to the police record, which confirms responses provided by the client. The worker and client now discuss the ODARA results and prepare a safety plan.

CASE A.4: DOMESTIC VIOLENCE RISK APPRAISAL GUIDE CASE MATERIAL, MALGUN PEARSON

Occurrence 01-010190329 (Domestic Assault)

Involved Persons

- **Accused:** Pearson, Malgun, 379 Trudeau Street, Clark, ON. Date of birth: 1963-06-17. Employer: First Marina. Relationship to victim: Spouse.

- **Charged:** Assault (spousal), impaired driving, dangerous driving, 2019-03-29. Held for bail hearing, next appearance 1000 hr, 04-17.
- **Victim:** Pearson, Lucida, 379 Trudeau Street, Clark, ON. Date of birth: 1968-02-21. Employer: First Street Pharmacy.
- **Witness, complainant:** Turner, Sonny (age 26), 24 Mulroney Street, Clark, ON. Date of birth 1992-05-12. Employer: FirstLife Insurance.
- **Witness:** Turner, Princess (age 23), 379 Trudeau Street, Clark, ON. Date of birth 1995-06-13. Employer: First Tech Recruitment.
- **Witness:** Pearson, Sweetie (age 17), 379 Trudeau Street, Clark, ON. Date of birth: 2002-02-14. Employer: Student, Premiere High School.

History

Dispatched to residence following a call stating an assault was in progress. On arrival, officers were met on the front porch by a young man identifying himself as the caller who reported that his mother (Lucida Pearson, victim) had been assaulted by his stepfather (Malgun Pearson, accused). Also present were Lucida's two daughters who live at this residence. The accused had left the premises in his vehicle, apparently under the influence of alcohol, and a police bulletin was issued with the vehicle description. The accused has two prior assaults on record (incidents 01-0204594 and 01-036475). No other charges or alerts on record.

Incident

On March 29, 2019, at approximately 1815 hr, the entire family was present at their residence. They had been having dinner, and the adults had consumed alcoholic beverages during the meal. The accused began complaining to the victim about the quality of the meal. Ms. Pearson stated that Mr. Pearson did not have any sympathy for her condition as she has been suffering a bad cold for 2 weeks. He called her "lazy and whiny" and threw the remains of his dinner plate in the sink. When Ms. Pearson told him to put the remains in the compost bin instead, he smashed the plate on the floor. He then picked up a broken piece of plate and held it to her throat, while gripping her by the hair. When the other family members protested, the accused slapped Ms. Pearson in the face with the back of his hand and left the kitchen. At that time, the victim's son contacted the police.

Ms. Pearson sustained a swollen right eye and a scratch on her neck. Medical attention was obtained, and victim services were notified. Mr. Pearson was apprehended at First Street Pub, charged, and taken into custody.

Victim Statement

Ms. Pearson states that she and Mr. Pearson have been married since May 23, 1998. She states that there has been recent escalation in frequency of his aggressive behavior. However, she denies being concerned about future assaults against her or the children because she feels that, this time, he will get help for his behavior. She admits to having two beers to drink this evening, which she states is "no more than usual" during family get-togethers, but it might have made her more tired than usual as she has been feeling unwell and struggling to keep up with family responsibilities, including ensuring her 17-year-old attends school and completes homework.

Occurrence 02-0204594 (Assault, Fail to Comply)

Involved Persons

- **Accused:** Pearson, Malgun, 379 Trudeau Street, Clark, ON. Date of birth: 1963-06-17. Employer: First Marina. Relationship to victim: none.
- **Charged:** Assault, fail to comply with probation order, 2015-10-19. Released on recognizance, next appearance 1000 hr, 11-01.
- **Victim, complainant:** Campbell, Sylfaen, 248 Chrétien Close, Martin, ON. Date of birth 1970-05-01. Employer: First Security.
- **Witness:** Pearson, Lucida, 379 Trudeau Street, Clark, ON. Date of birth: 1968-02-21. Employer: First Street Pharmacy.

History

Police received a call at 1437 hr Saturday October 19, 2015, from a person stating they had been assaulted while enforcing security at First Mall. Officers attended the mall security office and spoke with Sylfaen Campbell, who was observed to have bruising along the forearms and left cheekbone. The accused was identified as Malgun Pearson. Pearson is currently on probation for a spousal assault (01-036475).

Incident

The accused and victim were shopping in First Groceries when Pearson became argumentative and distressed, shouting that he was going to kill himself. Grocery store staff called mall security, and Campbell attended the scene. Initial attempts at de-escalation appeared to be effective and Pearson agreed to accompany Campbell to the mall security office. When Campbell turned to open the office door, Pearson attacked Campbell with repeated blows to the face and upper body. Additional security guards came to Campbell's aid and arrested Pearson under section 494 of the Criminal Code.

Occurrence 03-036475 (Domestic Assault)

Involved Persons

- **Accused:** Pearson, Malgun, 379 Trudeau Street, Clark, ON. Date of birth: 1963-06-17. Employer: First Marina. Relationship to victim: spouse.
- **Charged:** Assault (spousal), 2015-08-25. Released on recognizance, next appearance 1000 hr, 11-01.
- **Victim, complainant:** Pearson, Lucida, 379 Trudeau Street, Clark, ON. Date of birth: 1968-02-21. Employer: First Street Pharmacy.

History

Dispatched to the residence following a call from a woman requesting help with her angry husband. There are no alerts or prior reports for this location or either party. Upon arrival, officers could not get a response at the front door. Mr. Malgun Pearson (accused) was located on the patio at the rear of the house and admitted officers to the premises through the back gate. Ms. Lucida Pearson (spouse/victim) came down from an upstairs room when officers called out to any other occupants.

Incident

This incident occurred on August 25, 2015, at approximately 1700 hr. Mr. Pearson had been cooking on the barbeque while Ms. Pearson made other preparations for dinner. Mr. Pearson began insulting Ms. Pearson's housekeeping and cooking abilities. She angrily threw a kitchen towel at the accused and said, "Do it yourself then" and attempted to leave the patio into the house. He darted into the doorway to prevent her leaving. He then hit her with the barbeque spatula until she managed to escape into the house. Mr. Pearson agreed with Ms. Pearson's account of events, but he stated that he is under a lot of stress lately and was struggling with his mood. He was arrested and charged with assault without incident.

Victim Statement

Ms. Pearson states that she and Mr. Pearson have been married since May 23, 1998. They have a 13-year-old daughter, and Ms. Pearson has two children aged 21 and 18 from her previous marriage, who live with them. She denies previous physical assaults; however, there have been previous threats of physical harm, and she is now concerned about future assaults against her or the children. She denies any alcohol use by either party on this occasion.

Psychosocial Assessment Report

Interview Details

- **Name:** Malgun Pearson
- **Case Number:** 2019-329
- **Date of admission**: 6 July 2019
- **Date of report:** 24 July 2019
- **Legal documentation:** Found guilty of assault (spousal) and sentenced to 90 days plus 18 months' probation on 27 June 2019
- **Date of birth:** 17 June 1963 (Harper, ON, Canada)
- **Next of kin:** Lucida Pearson (spouse)
- **Occupation:** Coffeeshop manager
- **Case historian:** Vani Macdonald, MSW
- **Information sources:** Patient, spouse, stepmother, sister, Provincial Police Service reports, National Police Fingerprint Service reports, First Secondary School records, First Marina (Mr. Pearson's employer), Provincial Correctional Institution

Circumstances Leading to Admission

Mr. Malgun Pearson, a 56-year-old, married man was admitted to the First Institute Secure Assessment Unit on 6 July 2019. He had been charged and subsequently found guilty of assault against his wife of 21 years. He was also charged with impaired driving following the assault, for which he pleaded guilty. A charge of dangerous driving was withdrawn. He was sentenced by Provincial Court on 27 June 2019 to 90 days plus 18 months' probation for the assault and fined $1,000 for the impaired driving. He was detained in the Provincial Correctional Institution since that date and was brought to the Secure Assessment Unit for assessment following repeated disruptive behavior and self-harm (PCL-R 14, 20).

Current Offense Information

The police report indicates that on 29 March 2019, Mr. Pearson assaulted his wife, 51-year-old Lucida Pearson, during a family dinner at their home, after an argument about the quality of the meal and what to do with the remains on his plate. She sustained a swollen eye and a scratch on her neck, from a broken piece of plate that Mr. Pearson held to her neck. There was no property damage reported other than the plate which Mr. Pearson broke. According to the police report, the two parties concur on the events of the incident, and they both gave similar descriptions of the events during their interviews with me. In conversations with me, both parties agreed that they had been consuming alcohol with the meal. Ms. Pearson reports that Mr. Pearson had become aggressive more often than usual before the index assault (i.e., minor assaults occurring every few weeks instead of once or twice per year) but could not provide further details of any specific incidents and none were reported to police. She feels that on this occasion the violence occurred "out of the blue" and was especially surprising because, in the past, he would control his temper in front of the children. She feels that his driving off after the incident, without considering whether he was fit to drive after drinking, was reckless and bound to get him into trouble (PCL-R 8, 10, 14, 15).

Mr. Pearson was released on bail without incident until he was convicted of assault for the above offense. According to correspondence from the Provincial Correctional Institution, Mr. Pearson was remorseful upon arrival at the institution and within 48 hours began to appear despondent and spent most of his time curled up on his bunk, apparently crying. He complained of inability to sleep and lack of appetite. He was observed to be irritable with staff or others in custody who spoke to him and was the apparent victim of a violent altercation with another man in custody on the same unit who accused him of stealing a magazine. He was then placed in segregation on a suicide watch until transfer to this hospital could be arranged (PCL-R 10, 14).

Family History

Mr. Pearson's father, Hodes Pearson, was born in 1936 and worked at a coffeeshop chain most of his life until retiring at age 65. Hodes married Mr. Pearson's mother, Candara Pearson, in 1963. The marriage was strained by Candara's poor mental health. When Mr. Pearson was 14 years old, his parents divorced, and Hodes married again. Mr. Pearson's stepmother, Euphemia, was born in 1941 and worked as an accounts receivable clerk until retiring at age 67. She states that she has been in good health until recent problems with arthritis. Both Hodes and Euphemia are reported to be occasional drinkers with no major mental health problems. They continue to live independently in a retirement village in Harper, ON.

The mother, Candara Pearson, was born in 1938. She suffered from mental illness, which was variously diagnosed over the years as major depressive disorder, bipolar disorder, and schizoaffective disorder. Mr. Pearson describes remembering his mother as very loving and involved with his caretaking when she was well but with long bouts of inability to care for him when she was ill. He states that he spent much of the time playing alone and later with his sister who is 6 years his junior. Candara died of heart failure at age 49 (PCL-R 7).

Mr. Pearson's younger sister Georgia, age 50, is a clinical psychologist specializing in trauma-related disorders. She reports having struggled with anxiety during adolescence, which is now under control. She describes looking up to her brother when she was very young and concurs that their mother was gentle and loving when she was well. She states that they have stayed in touch throughout their adulthood and get along fine as long as they avoid discussing politics, but their relationship is mainly limited to holiday get-togethers at Georgia's initiative.

Lucida Pearson, aged 51, married Mr. Pearson in 1998 at age 30 years. She arrived in Canada as a refugee with her mother and two older siblings in the 1970s and states that she identifies as Canadian. Her first husband was her high school sweetheart; they married right after graduation and had two children together, but the marriage did not work out and ended amicably after 10 years. She worked in office administration and then as a cashier in a pharmacy before returning to college part time to qualify as a pharmacy technician. She met Mr. Pearson in the coffeeshop where he worked, as she frequently spent afternoons studying there. She states that Mr. Pearson accepted her two children, although he was "never a very involved father." They have one child together, who is now 17 and has some learning disabilities. Ms. Pearson states that it has always been up to her to make sure this child received the support she needed and that helping her with homework has been increasingly stressful due to the daughter's growing disinterest in completing school. Ms. Pearson states that she and Mr. Pearson have generally been happy with where they have ended up in life and that they have good friendships with a few neighbors and coworkers. She describes herself as an occasional drinker, usually joining others in "a drink or two" when her family gathers for holidays or family dinners. She states that Mr. Pearson has similar drinking habits, except that there have been times in his life when he chose to drink on his own while watching TV for long hours on weekends, which she associates with times when his mood was "low." She expresses strong feelings of affection and loyalty to Mr. Pearson. She states that she is not afraid of Mr. Pearson and that she is more concerned that he gets the help he needs to feel better about himself and control his "temper."

Childhood

Mr. Pearson lived with both parents until they divorced when he was 14 and then with his father and stepmother, who moved into the family home. He describes himself as a capable person who learned to take care of himself at an early age because of his mother's illnesses and his father's long hours at work. He was an only child until age 6 and then prided himself on being in charge of his sister. He denies any involvement with child protection services but states that neighbors sometimes made sure he and his sister were fed when his mother was ill.

Mr. Pearson admits to becoming depressed during his adolescence, which he attributes to the difficulties of his parents' divorce and adjusting to living with his stepmother. He states that he was managing "just fine" without a stepmother and resented what he saw as her overinvolvement, although they got along better when he left home at age 18. He states that he twice ran away from home, once telling a friend's family that he had permission to stay over for the weekend, and once staying almost a week with a girlfriend while her parents were away. Both were occasioned by arguments with his stepmother about his friends and school grades. He admits to entering his neighborhood variety store about seven or eight times through an unlocked back door store when he was 16, at first with two friends and later on his own. They stole candy and cigarettes from the rear storage room. They were not caught, and the store owner eventually began locking the rear door. Mr. Pearson states that his smoking habit was established at that time, and he has been unable to quit despite several attempts, one lasting for nearly 3 months; currently he smokes half a pack a day (PCL-R 18, 20).

Education

Mr. Pearson began school at age 5 and completed Grade 12 at age 18. His elementary education was uneventful, with no record of behavior problems, and he was an average student, preferring music and mathematics. He states that he was good friends with a boy in his elementary school who later moved away, and he had only "passing" friendships in high school. The stepmother reports that she and his father wanted him to go to college, but he refused, saying that he wanted to "get out in the world" and start working. Mr. Pearson states that he considered getting more education later, but the time never seemed right (PCL-R 12).

Occupational

Mr. Pearson had a few short-lived jobs stocking shelves and on factory lines before moving to the coffeeshop chain. There, he worked as a warehouse operator then baker and eventually worked his way up to store manager. He states that he finds that he gets on "well enough" with his coworkers and employees, who are mostly women, but that he relies on others to "deal with the young ones," whom he states don't have the same attitude to work (PCL-R 16).

Medical

Mr. Pearson reports that he may have been premature and underweight at birth, based on some family conversations that he recalls. There is no information available about specific pregnancy or perinatal difficulties. He reports no major childhood injuries or serious illnesses that he can recall, other than repeated ear infections. He was hospitalized for acute respiratory problems in 2004, 2008, and 2010, after which he was diagnosed with chronic obstructive pulmonary disease. This problem is managed with the use of inhaled steroids. However, he wheezed noticeably during our interview.

Psychiatric

This is Mr. Pearson's first admission to a psychiatric facility. He admits to experiencing depressed moods a number of times since adolescence, sometimes taking to his bed for "days at a time" but going back to work when he was out of sick time. He states it "never occurred" to him to see a doctor or therapist. He agrees that he feels "more depressed than normal" since the index incident and receiving his sentence. He denies feeling suicidal or intending any self-harm, either currently or while at the correctional institute. He states that he punched the walls and floor in anger at being in custody, not as intentional self-harm. He states he is not sure whether it is worse to be seen as "mad" rather than "bad." There are no reports of self-harm, altercations, or irritable behavior since his admission to the Secure Assessment Unit. However, during our interview he seemed apathetic, saying, "What difference will it make, anyway?" The psychiatric assessment by Dr. May, in her report dated 10 July 2019, indicated a provisional diagnosis of major depressive disorder with anxious distress, and alcohol use disorder. Dr. May has requested cognitive and neuropsychological testing (PCL-R 3, 5, 10).

Substance Use

Mr. Pearson reports going to "a few" parties as a teenager but was not often invited. He would drink beer or liquor if it was provided, and shared his parents' supply of alcohol "sometimes" when he had friends over at his home, between ages 14 and 17. However, he did have enough money to pay for alcohol. He reports using marijuana "two or three times" around age 14 but did not enjoy the effects. He denies any current substance use other than long-term cigarette smoking and occasional alcohol consumption. Police records indicate that Mr. Pearson's blood alcohol level was at just over the legal limit at the time of arrest for the index assault (PCL-R 15).

Criminal History

Consistent with Mr. Pearson's statements, records indicate only three preindex criminal charges. One is for an earlier assault on his wife in August 2015, for which he was charged with assault. He pleaded guilty and received probation. He expressed remorse to me for this assault, saying that he had been struggling with a depressed mood and that work had been stressful at the time because of building renovations. The other charges are for an assault on a security guard and breach of conditions in October 2015, a few months after the first domestic assault. Mr. Pearson told me that "maybe I was mistaken," but he thought that the security guards were about to assault him. He again attributed the incident, and an argument with his wife that preceded it, to stress, this time caused by the demands of being on probation for the earlier domestic assault. No juvenile record is available, and Mr. Pearson denies any other criminal charges (PCL-R 16, 19, 20).

Adult Relationships and Sexual History

Mr. Pearson states that he suffered a lot of anxiety during adolescence and was bullied by some of his peers until he attended a large high school that afforded him a relative amount of anonymity; he was relieved to be "lost in the crowd." He states that he had "a few" girlfriends between the ages of 14 and 16, and these relationships mostly consisted of sitting together during class or lunch, long phone conversations after school, and the occasional movie. His earliest sexual intercourse was at age 17, at the home of a girl he dated for a few months. His next relationship that he considers "serious" began when he was 19, with a woman he met at work who was a year older than he. This relationship lasted about 4 years, ending 2 months after they moved in together and the woman told him she now realized she did not want to spend the rest of her life with him. Mr. Pearson describes being "really shaken up" by this breakup. He missed her and became withdrawn from social activity for a couple of years, switching jobs from the warehouse to the baker position to "make a clean break." He met his wife, the victim of the index assault, while working in the coffeeshop.

He states that they exchanged phone numbers and talked occasionally for about a year before he had the courage to ask her on a date. Both parties state that it was Lucida who asked him to marry her (PCL-R 11, 17).

Mr. Pearson describes his marriage as "fine" but states that he has been under a lot of stress lately and finds it difficult not to be angry with what he describes as his wife's "petty annoyances" over "every stupid little thing." He described the index offense as an instance of her difficult behavior but was unable to provide any other examples. Ms. Pearson also states that their marriage has been "mostly good" but describes Mr. Pearson as more "grouchy and irritable" and "difficult to handle" in the past few years, especially when he forgets things and needs to be reminded or told what to do. She gave three examples of occasions when he pushed, grabbed, or slapped her or tried to prevent her walking away from an argument, in between the two incidents for which he was charged with domestic assault (PCL-R 7, 8, 10, 11, 16).

Interviewer's Impressions

I spoke with Mr. Pearson briefly the day he was brought to the Secure Assessment Unit and then for 3 hours 1 week later. During our first interaction, he was withdrawn and tearful. During the full interview, he was mostly calm but occasionally agitated and tearful, especially when discussing his wife and events at and since the index offense. He appeared eager to comply with the interview and was generally forthcoming with information, which largely concurred with other informants and official documents. He answered all my questions and elaborated when probed for more detail, occasionally asking whether his answers would be included in my report. He stated that he was not interested in attending treatment groups or social activities in the unit because he is nervous around the other patients. He requested meeting with me or the unit psychology staff for individual therapy. He expressed the hope that he would soon be able to return home (PCL-R 1, 5, 7, 13, 16).

ODARA AND DVRAG SCORES FOR PRACTICE CASES

This section provides the ODARA scores for cases A.1 through A.4, and the DVRAG and DVRAG-4 score for Case A.4. In Tables A.1 to A.4, brief explanations are provided for item scores, followed by total and prorated scores as appropriate.

TABLE A.1. Ontario Domestic Assault Risk Assessment Scoring for Andalus Macdonald

0, 1, or ?	Item	Explanation
0	1. Pre-index domestic assault in a police or criminal record	None on criminal record; victim denies any previous assaults by accused
0	2. Pre-index nondomestic assault in a police or criminal record	None on criminal record
0	3. Pre-index custodial sentence of 30 days or more	Only probation on record
0	4. Failure on pre-index conditional release	No evidence of violations
0	5. Threat to physically harm or kill at the index assault	No threat of physical harm
0	6. Confinement of the partner at the index assault	Victim tried to leave, he did not prevent her, and he left the house
0	7. Victim concern about future assaults	No statement of concern
1	8. More than one child altogether	Son who called police, and victim's daughter from her first marriage
1	9. Victim's biological child from a previous partner	Victim's daughter from her first marriage
0	10. Pre-index assault against a non-domestic victim	No evidence of previous assaults
1	11. Two or more indicators of substance abuse	Pre-index operating vehicle while impaired; three to four bottles of beer at index
0	12. Assault on index victim while she was pregnant	No mention of pregnancy
1	13. Barriers to victim support	Minor child to care for
4	Raw total	Sum of items scored 1
4	Final score (risk category)	0 ambiguous items

TABLE A.2. Ontario Domestic Assault Risk Assessment Scoring for Corbel Tupper

0, 1, or ?	Item	Explanation
?	1. Pre-index domestic assault in a police or criminal record	Two prior assaults; in absence of more details, this item is ambiguous
?	2. Pre-index nondomestic assault in a police or criminal record	Two prior assaults; in absence of more details, this item is ambiguous
0	3. Pre-index custodial sentence of 30 days or more	Only probation on record
1	4. Failure on pre-index conditional release	Current alerts indicate Tupper is on probation
1	5. Threat to physically harm or kill at the index assault	Punched her in the back and sides saying, "This is what I'll do to you if I find out you've been seeing anyone else."
1	6. Confinement of the partner at the index assault	She ran out of the bedroom; the accused pulled her back into the room and pushed the drawers to block the door.
1	7. Victim concern about future assaults	Victim states she is now scared of future violence by the accused
0	8. More than one child altogether	Accused has one child with previous girlfriend
0	9. Victim's biological child from a previous partner	No indication of other children
	10. Pre-index assault against a non-domestic victim	Previous assaults ambiguous
1	11. Two or more indicators of substance abuse	He insisted that they both drink wine at index, and he smoked marijuana at index
0	12. Assault on index victim while she was pregnant	Index victim denies any possibility of pregnancy
1	13. Barriers to victim support	No evidence of her being responsible for children, has phone, bus stop nearby, not geographically isolated; she chose spritzer and he insisted she drink wine
6	Raw total	Sum of items scored 1
7–13	Final score (risk category)	Prorated for three ambiguous items

TABLE A.3. Ontario Domestic Assault Risk Assessment Scoring for Information Provided by Franklin Diefenbaker

0, 1, or ?	Item	Explanation
0	1. Pre-index domestic assault in a police or criminal record	Never involved with police or courts
0	2. Pre-index nondomestic assault in a police or criminal record	Never involved with police or courts
0	3. Pre-index custodial sentence of 30 days or more	Never involved with police or courts
0	4. Failure on pre-index conditional release	Never involved with police or courts
1	5. Threat to physically harm or kill at the index assault	"I'm going to kill you this time!"
0	6. Confinement of the partner at the index assault	Ran out of apartment; she slammed door after him
1	7. Victim concern about future assaults	"I don't think it will stop"
1	8. More than one child altogether	Son and daughter
0	9. Victim's biological child from a previous partner	"Our son . . . We have a daughter"
1	10. Pre-index assault against a non-domestic victim	Slapped neighbor during specified incident
1	11. Two or more indicators of substance abuse	Drank wine at index; more violent when she drinks
0	12. Assault on index victim while she was pregnant	This item is treated as 0 automatically because the victim identifies as male
0	13. Barriers to victim support	Not responsible to care for minor children, phone in home, has car, not geographically isolated, no substance use at index or history
5	Raw total	Sum of items scored 1
5	Final score (risk category)	0 ambiguous items

TABLE A.4. Ontario Domestic Assault Risk Assessment and Domestic Violence Risk Appraisal Guide Scoring for Malgun Pearson

Item 0, 1, or ?	Item	Explanation	DVRAG Score
1	1. Pre-index domestic assault in a police or criminal record	Pre-index occurrence 01-036475 domestic assault	0
1	2. Pre-index nondomestic assault in a police or criminal record	Pre-index occurrence 01-0204594 assault on mall security	5
0	3. Pre-index custodial sentence of 30 days or more	Only probation on record	-1
1	4. Failure on pre-index conditional release	Pre-index occurrence 01-0204594 includes fail to comply	2
0	5. Threat to physically harm or kill at the index assault	No indication of threat to physically harm	0
0	6. Confinement of the partner at the index assault	Pre-index confinement not counted	0
0	7. Victim concern about future assaults	Denies being concerned about future assaults at index; pre-index concern not counted	0
1	8. More than one child altogether	Three children, two live at the same residence	1
1	9. Victim's biological child from a previous partner	Two children from her previous marriage	2
1	10. Pre-index assault against a non-domestic victim	Assault on mall security during specified incident	8
0	11. Two or more indicators of substance abuse	Drinking with dinner at index, impaired driving at index not counted, no other evidence	-2
0	12. Assault on index victim while she was pregnant	No assaults previous to occurrence 01-036475	0
1	13. Barriers to victim support	17-year-old child requires care; consumed alcohol at index	4
	14. Psychopathy Checklist-Revised score	PCL-R score range = 10-16 (or PCL-R Facet 4 score = 3)	1
7	Raw ODARA total	Sum of items	20
7-13	Final ODARA score	DVRAG Category	6
		Percentile	95

References

Ægisdóttir, S., White, M. J., Spengler, P. M., Maugherman, A. S., Anderson, L. A., Cook, R. S., Nichols, C. N., Lampropoulos, G. K., Walker, B. S., Cohen, G., & Rush, J. D. (2006). The Meta-Analysis of Clinical Judgment Project: Fifty-six years of accumulated research on clinical versus statistical prediction. *The Counseling Psychologist, 34*(3), 341–382. https://doi.org/10.1177/0011000005285875

Ali, P. A., & Naylor, P. B. (2013). Intimate partner violence: A narrative review of the feminist, social and ecological explanations for its causation. *Aggression and Violent Behavior, 18*(6), 611–619. https://doi.org/10.1016/j.avb.2013.07.009

Allen, C. T., Swan, S. C., Maas, C. D., & Barber, S. (2015). A comparison of the structural factors of the Propensity for Abusiveness Scale for women and men in a domestic violence treatment program. *Journal of Interpersonal Violence, 30*(13), 2326–2343. https://doi.org/10.1177/0886260514552450

American Psychiatric Association. (2013). *Diagnostic and statistical manual of mental disorders* (5th ed.). https://doi.org/10.1176/appi.books.9780890425596

An Act to Adopt the Use of Standardized Risk Assessment in the Management of Domestic Violence Crimes, 2019-A M.R.S. §4012(6) (2012).

Andrews, D., & Bonta, J. (2001). *LSI-R user's manual*. Multi-Health Systems.

Ansbro, M. (2010). The nuts and bolts of risk assessment: When the clinical and actuarial conflict. *Howard Journal of Criminal Justice, 49*(3), 252–268. https://doi.org/10.1111/j.1468-2311.2010.00614.x

Archer, J. (2013). Can evolutionary principles explain patterns of family violence? *Psychological Bulletin, 139*(2), 403–440. https://doi.org/10.1037/a0029114

Arias, E., Arce, R., & Vilariño, M. (2013). Batterer intervention programmes: A meta-analytic review of effectiveness. *Intervención Psicosocial, 22*(2), 153–160. https://doi.org/10.5093/in2013a18

Askeland, I. R., & Heir, T. (2014). Psychiatric disorders among men voluntarily in treatment for violent behaviour: A cross-sectional study. *BMJ Open, 4*(4), e004485. https://doi.org/10.1136/bmjopen-2013-004485

Au, A., Cheung, G., Kropp, R., Yuk-chung, C., Lam, G. L. T., & Sung, P. (2008). A preliminary validation of the Brief Spousal Assault Form for the Evaluation of Risk (B-SAFER) in Hong Kong. *Journal of Family Violence, 23*(8). 727–735. https://doi.org/10.1007/s10896-008-9198-z

Averdijk, M., & Elffers, H. (2012). The discrepancy between survey-based victim accounts and police reports revisited. *International Review of Victimology, 18*(2), 91–107. https://doi.org/10.1177/0269758011432955

Babcock, J., Armenti, N., Cannon, C., Lauve-Moon, K., Buttell, F., Ferreira, R., Cantos, A., Hamel, J., Kelly, D., Jordan, C., Lehmann, P., Leisring, P. A., Murphy, C., O'Leary, K. D., Bannon, S., Salis, K. L., & Solano, I. (2016). Domestic violence perpetrator programs: A proposal for evidence-based standards in the United States. *Partner Abuse, 7*(4), 355–460. https://doi.org/10.1891/1946-6560.7.4.355

Babcock, J. C., Green, C. E., & Robie, C. (2004). Does batterers' treatment work? A meta-analytic review of domestic violence treatment. *Clinical Psychology Review, 23*(8), 1023–1053. https://doi.org/10.1016/j.cpr.2002.07.001

Baldwin, L. (Chair). (1999). *Working toward a seamless community and justice response to domestic violence: A five year plan for Ontario* [Unpublished Report to the Attorney General of Ontario by the Joint Committee on Domestic Violence]. Toronto, Ontario, Canada. https://archive.org/details/mag_00007588

Ballucci, D., Campbell, M. A., & Gill, C. (in press). Use of the ODARA by police officer for intimate partner violence: Implications for practice in the field. *Community Safety and Well-Being.*

Barnes, J. C., TenEyck, M., Boutwell, B. B., & Beaver, K. M. (2013). Indicators of domestic/intimate partner violence are structured by genetic and nonshared environmental influences. *Journal of Psychiatric Research, 47*(3), 371–376. https://doi.org/10.1016/j.jpsychires.2012.10.016

Batastini, A. B., Hoeffner, C. E., Vitacco, M. J., Morgan, R. D., Coaker, L. C., & Lester, M. E. (2019). Does the format of the message affect what is heard? A two-part study on the communication of violence risk assessment data. *Journal of Forensic Psychology Research and Practice, 19*(1), 44–71. https://doi.org/10.1080/24732850.2018.1538474

Beattie, S., David, J. D., & Roy, J. (2018). *Homicide in Canada, 2017.* Statistics Canada. https://www150.statcan.gc.ca/n1/en/pub/85-002-x/2018001/article/54980-eng.pdf?st=iIxGMhYO

Becerra-García, J. A. (2015). Neuropsychology of domestic violence: A comparative preliminary study of executive functioning. *Medicine, Science, and the Law, 55*(1), 35–39. https://doi.org/10.1177/0025802414525148

Belfrage, H., & Strand, S. (2012). Measuring the outcome of structured spousal violence risk assessments using the B-SAFER: Risk in relation to recidivism and intervention. *Behavioral Sciences & the Law, 30*(4), 420–430. https://doi.org/10.1002/bsl.2019

Belfrage, H., Strand, S., Storey, J. E., Gibas, A. L., Kropp, P. R., & Hart, S. D. (2012). Assessment and management of risk for intimate partner violence by police officers using the Spousal Assault Risk Assessment Guide. *Law and Human Behavior, 36*(1), 60–67. https://doi.org/10.1037/h0093948

Bell, K. M., & Naugle, A. E. (2008). Intimate partner violence theoretical considerations: Moving towards a contextual framework. *Clinical Psychology Review, 28*(7), 1096–1107. https://doi.org/10.1016/j.cpr.2008.03.003

Berk, R. A., Campbell, A., Klap, R., & Western, B. (1992). A Bayesian analysis of the Colorado Springs Spouse Abuse Experiment. *The Journal of Criminal Law & Criminology, 83*(1), 170–200. https://doi.org/10.2307/1143828

Berk, R., & Hyatt, J. (2015). Machine learning forecasts of risk to inform sentencing decisions. *Federal Sentencing Reporter, 27*(4), 222–228. https://doi.org/10.1525/fsr.2015.27.4.222

Berk, R. A., Sorenson, S. B., & Barnes, G. (2016). Forecasting domestic violence: A machine learning approach to help inform arraignment decisions. *Journal of Empirical Legal Studies, 13*(1), 94–115. https://doi.org/10.1111/jels.12098

Beyer, K., Wallis, A. B., & Hamberger, L. K. (2015). Neighborhood environment and intimate partner violence: A systematic review. *Trauma, Violence & Abuse, 16*(1), 16–47. https://doi.org/10.1177/1524838013515758

Birkley, E. L., & Eckhardt, C. I. (2015). Anger, hostility, internalizing negative emotions, and intimate partner violence perpetration: A meta-analytic review. *Clinical Psychology Review, 37*, 40–56. https://doi.org/10.1016/j.cpr.2015.01.002

Blais, J. (2015). Preventative detention decisions: Reliance on expert assessments and evidence of partisan allegiance within the Canadian context. *Behavioral Sciences & the Law, 33*(1), 74–91. https://doi.org/10.1002/bsl.2155

Blais, J., & Forth, A. E. (2014). Prosecution-retained versus court-appointed experts: Comparing and contrasting risk assessment reports in preventative detention hearings. *Law and Human Behavior, 38*(6), 531–543. https://doi.org/10.1037/lhb0000082

Bland, M., & Ariel, B. (2015). Targeting escalation in reported domestic abuse. *International Criminal Justice Review, 25*(1), 30–53. https://doi.org/10.1177/1057567715574382

Blanton, H., & Jaccard, J. (2006). Arbitrary metrics in psychology. *American Psychologist, 61*(1), 27–41. https://doi.org/10.1037/0003-066X.61.1.27

Bodemer, N., Meder, B., & Gigerenzer, G. (2014). Communicating relative risk changes with baseline risk. *Medical Decision Making, 34*(5), 615–626. https://doi.org/10.1177/0272989X14526305

Bokhari, E., & Hubert, L. (2018). The lack of cross-validation can lead to inflated results and spurious conclusions: A re-analysis of the MacArthur Violence Risk Assessment Study. *Journal of Classification, 35*(1), 147–171. https://doi.org/10.1007/s00357-018-9252-3

Bonta, J. (2007). Offender risk assessment and sentencing. *Canadian Journal of Criminology and Criminal Justice, 49*(4), 519–529. https://doi.org/10.3138/cjccj.49.4.519

Bonta, J., & Andrews, D. A. (2017). *The psychology of criminal conduct*. Routledge.

Bonta, J., Blais, J., & Wilson, H. A. (2014). A theoretically informed meta-analysis of the risk for general and violent recidivism for mentally disordered offenders. *Aggression and Violent Behavior, 19*(3), 278–287. https://doi.org/10.1016/j.avb.2014.04.014

Bornstein, R. F. (2017). Evidence-based psychological assessment. *Journal of Personality Assessment, 99*(4), 435–445. https://doi.org/10.1080/00223891.2016.1236343

Bourgon, G., Mugford, R., Hanson, R. K., & Coligado, M. (2018). Offender risk assessment practices vary across Canada. *Canadian Journal of Criminology and Criminal Justice, 60*(2), 167–205. https://doi.org/10.3138/cjccj.2016-0024

Brankley, A. E., Babchishin, K. M., & Hanson, R. K. (2019, September). STABLE–2007 demonstrates predictive and incremental validity in assessing risk-relevant propensities for sexual offending: A meta-analysis. *Sexual Abuse, 13*, 1079063219871572. Advance online publication. https://doi.org/10.1177/1079063219871572

Brazil, K. J., & Forth, A. E. (2020). Psychopathy and the induction of desire: Formulating and testing an evolutionary hypothesis. *Evolutionary Psychological Science, 6*(1), 64–81. https://doi.org/10.1007/s40806-019-00213-0

Breiman, L. (2001). Statistical modeling: The two cultures. *Statistical Science, 16*(3), 199–231. https://doi.org/10.1214/ss/1009213726

Brown, D. (2001, December 7). Turning domestic violence into a religion: Inquest on epic social debate. *The Ottawa Citizen*.

Buchanan, K. (2009). *Risk assessment and spousal violence predictive validity and cultural applicability* [Unpublished doctoral dissertation]. University of Regina.

Burczycka, M., & Conroy, M. (2017). *Family violence in Canada: A statistical profile, 2015*. Statistics Canada. https://www150.statcan.gc.ca/n1/en/pub/85-002-x/2017001/article/14698-eng.pdf?st=tU_bB4-4

Burge, S. K., Katerndahl, D. A., Wood, R. C., Becho, J., Ferrer, R. L., & Talamantes, M. (2016). Using complexity science to examine three dynamic patterns of intimate partner violence. *Families, Systems & Health, 34*(1), 4–14. https://doi.org/10.1037/fsh0000170

Buzawa, E. S., Buzawa, C. G., & Stark, E. D. (2017). *Responding to domestic violence: The integration of criminal justice and human services* (5th ed.). Sage. https://doi.org/10.1007/978-3-319-56721-1

Cafferky, B. M., Mendez, M., Anderson, J. R., & Stith, S. M. (2018). Substance use and intimate partner violence: A meta-analytic review. *Psychology of Violence, 8*(1), 110–131. https://doi.org/10.1037/vio0000074

Cala, M. J., Trigo, M. E., & Saavedra, F. J. (2016). Women's disengagement from legal proceedings for intimate partner violence: Sociodemographic and psychological variables. *The European Journal of Psychology Applied to Legal Context, 8*(1), 35–42. https://doi.org/10.1016/j.ejpal.2015.10.002

Campbell, J. (1981). Misogyny and homicide of women. *Advances in Nursing Science, 3*(2), 67–86. https://doi.org/10.1097/00012272-198101000-00007

Campbell, J. C. (1986). Nursing assessment for risk of homicide with battered women. *Advances in Nursing Science, 8*(4), 36–51. https://doi.org/10.1097/00012272-198607000-00006

Campbell, J. C. (2004). Helping women understand their risk in situations of intimate partner violence. *Journal of Interpersonal Violence, 19*(12), 1464–1477. https://doi.org/10.1177/0886260504269698

Campbell, J. C., Glass, N., Sharps, P. W., Laughon, K., & Bloom, T. (2007). Intimate partner homicide: Review and implications of research and policy. *Trauma, Violence & Abuse, 8*(3), 246–269. https://doi.org/10.1177/1524838007303505

Campbell, J. C., Messing, J. T., & Williams, K. R. (2017). Prediction of homicide of and by battered women. In J. C. Campbell & J. T. Messing (Eds.), *Assessing dangerousness: Domestic violence offenders and child abusers* (3rd ed., pp. 107–138). Springer. https://doi.org/10.1891/9780826133274.0005

Campbell, J. C., Webster, D., Koziol-McLain, J., Block, C., Campbell, D., Curry, M. A., Gary, F., Glass, N., McFarlane, J., Sachs, C., Sharps, P., Ulrich, Y., Wilt, S. A., Manganello, J., Xu, X., Schollenberger, J., Frye, V., & Laughon, K. (2003). Risk factors for femicide in abusive relationships: Results from a multisite case control study. *American Journal of Public Health, 93*(7), 1089–1097. https://doi.org/10.2105/AJPH.93.7.1089

Campbell, J. C., Webster, D. W., & Glass, N. (2009). The Danger Assessment: Validation of a lethality risk assessment instrument for intimate partner femicide. *Journal of Interpersonal Violence, 24*(4), 653–674. https://doi.org/10.1177/0886260508317180

Campbell, M. A., French, S., & Gendreau, P. (2009). The prediction of violence in adult offenders. *Criminal Justice and Behavior, 36*(6), 567–590. https://doi.org/10.1177/0093854809333610

Campbell, M. A., Gill, C., & Ballucci, D. (2017). Informing police response to intimate partner violence: Predictors of perceived usefulness of risk assessment screening. *Journal of Police and Criminal Psychology, 33*(2), 175–187. https://doi.org/10.1007/s11896-017-9244-y

Cannon, C., Hamel, J., Buttell, F. P., & Ferreira, R. (2016). A survey of domestic violence perpetrator programs in the United States and Canada: Findings and implications for policy and intervention. *Partner Abuse, 7*(3), 226–276. https://doi.org/10.1891/1946-6560.7.3.226

Cantos, A. L., Goldstein, D. A., Brenner, L., O'Leary, K. D., & Verborg, R. (2015). Correlates and program completion of family only and generally violent perpetrators of intimate partner violence. *Behavioral Psychology, 23*(3), 549–569.

Cantos, A. L., Kosson, D. S., Goldstein, D. A., & O'Leary, K. D. (2019). Treatment impact on recidivism of family only vs. generally violent partner violence perpetrators. *International Journal of Clinical and Health Psychology, 19*(3), 171–180. https://doi.org/10.1016/j.ijchp.2019.05.002

Capaldi, D. M., Kim, H. K., & Shortt, J. W. (2007). Observed initiation and reciprocity of physical aggression in young, at-risk couples. *Journal of Family Violence, 22*(2), 101–111. https://doi.org/10.1007/s10896-007-9067-1

Capaldi, D. M., Knoble, N. B., Shortt, J. W., & Kim, H. K. (2012). A systematic review of risk factors for intimate partner violence. *Partner Abuse, 3*(2), 231–280. https://doi.org/10.1891/1946-6560.3.2.231

Capaldi, D. M., Shortt, J. W., Kim, H. K., Wilson, J., Crosby, L., & Tucci, S. (2009). Official incidents of domestic violence: Types, injury, and associations with nonofficial couple aggression. *Violence and Victims, 24*(4), 502–519. https://doi.org/10.1891/0886-6708.24.4.502

Cattaneo, L. B. (2007). Contributors to assessments of risk in intimate partner violence: How victims and professionals differ. *Journal of Community Psychology, 35*(1), 57–75. https://doi.org/10.1002/jcop.20134

Cattaneo, L. B., Bell, M. E., Goodman, L. A., & Dutton, M. A. (2007). Intimate partner violence victims' accuracy in assessing their risk of re-abuse. *Journal of Family Violence, 22*(6), 429–440. https://doi.org/10.1007/s10896-007-9097-8

Cattaneo, L. B., & Goodman, L. A. (2003). Victim-reported risk factors for continued abusive behavior: Assessing the dangerousness of arrested batterers. *Journal of Community Psychology, 31*(4), 349–369. https://doi.org/10.1002/jcop.10056

Chan, K. L. (2014). Assessing the risk of intimate partner violence in the Chinese population. *Violence Against Women, 20*(5), 500–516. https://doi.org/10.1177/1077801214535107

Chavis, A. Z., & Hill, M. S. (2008). Integrating multiple intersecting identities: A multicultural conceptualization of the power and control wheel. *Women & Therapy, 32*(1), 121–149. https://doi.org/10.1080/02703140802384552

Cheng, S.-Y., Davis, M., Jonson-Reid, M., & Yaeger, L. (2019). Compared to what? A meta-analysis of batterer intervention studies using nontreated controls or comparisons. *Trauma, Violence & Abuse*, 1524838019865927. Advance online publication. https://doi.org/10.1177/1524838019865927

Chiffriller, S. H., & Hennessy, J. J. (2009). An empirically generated typology of men who batter. *Victims & Offenders, 5*(1), 1–24. https://doi.org/10.1080/15564880903048552

Clift, R. J. W., Thomas, L. A., & Dutton, D. G. (2005). Two-year reliability of the Propensity for Abusiveness Scale. *Journal of Family Violence, 20*(4), 231–234. https://doi.org/10.1007/s10896-005-5986-x

Cohen, J. (1992). A power primer. *Psychological Bulletin, 112*(1), 155–159. https://doi.org/10.1037/0033-2909.112.1.155

Cohen, T. H., Lowenkamp, C. T., & VanBenschoten, S. W. (2016). Does change in risk matter? *Criminology & Public Policy, 15*(2), 263–296. https://doi.org/10.1111/1745-9133.12190

Collins, A. M., Bouffard, L. A., & Wilkes, N. (2019). Predicting recidivism among defendants in an expedited domestic violence court. *Journal of Interpersonal Violence*, 886260518822343. Advance online publication. https://doi.org/10.1177/0886260518822343

Connor-Smith, J. K., Henning, K., Moore, S., & Holdford, R. (2011). Risk assessments by female victims of intimate partner violence: Predictors of risk perceptions and comparison to an actuarial measure. *Journal of Interpersonal Violence, 26*(12), 2517–2550. https://doi.org/10.1177/0886260510383024

Connors, A. D., Mills, J. F., & Gray, A. L. (2012). An evaluation of intimate partner violence intervention with incarcerated offenders. *Journal of Interpersonal Violence, 27*(6), 1176–1196. https://doi.org/10.1177/0886260511424499

Connors, A. D., Mills, J. F., & Gray, A. L. (2013). Intimate partner violence intervention for high-risk offenders. *Psychological Services, 10*(1), 12–23. https://doi.org/10.1037/a0028979

Cook, A. N., Murray, A. A., Amat, G., & Hart, S. D. (2014). Using structured professional judgment guidelines in threat assessment and management: Presentation, analysis, and formulation of a case of serial intimate partner violence. *Journal of Threat Assessment and Management, 1*(2), 67–86. https://doi.org/10.1037/tam0000011

Corrections and Conditional Release Act 1992, Section 233, SC 1992, c 20. https://laws-lois.justice.gc.ca/eng/acts/C-44.6/

Corvo, K., & Johnson, P. (2013). Sharpening Ockham's Razor: The role of psychopathology and neuropsychopathology in the perpetration of domestic violence. *Aggression and Violent Behavior, 18*(1), 175 to 182. https://doi.org/10.1016/j.avb.2012.11.017

Costa, B. M., Kaestle, C. E., Walker, A., Curtis, A., Day, A., Toumbourou, J. W., & Miller, P. (2015). Longitudinal predictors of domestic violence perpetration and victimization: A systematic review. *Aggression and Violent Behavior, 24*, 261–272. https://doi.org/10.1016/j.avb.2015.06.001

Crane, C. A., & Easton, C. J. (2017). Integrated treatment options for male perpetrators of intimate partner violence. *Drug and Alcohol Review, 36*(1), 24–33. https://doi.org/10.1111/dar.12496

Crane, C. A., Oberleitner, L. M. S., & Easton, C. J. (2013). Sub-clinical trauma in the treatment of partner violent offenders with substance dependence. *Advances in Dual Diagnosis, 6*(1), 5–13. https://doi.org/10.1108/17570971311308980

Crocker, A. G., Nicholls, T. L., Charette, Y., & Seto, M. C. (2014). Dynamic and static factors associated with discharge dispositions: The national trajectory project of individuals found not criminally responsible on account of mental disorder (NCRMD) in Canada. *Behavioral Sciences & the Law, 32*(5), 577–595. https://doi.org/10.1002/bsl.2133

Cubellis, M. A., Peterson, B. E., Henninger, A. M., & Lee, D. (2018). Childhood sexual abuse and antisocial traits and behaviors: A gendered examination of the factors associated with perpetration of intimate partner violence. *Journal of Interpersonal Violence, 33*(20), 3125–3161. https://doi.org/10.1177/0886260516633692

Cubells, J., & Calsamiglia, A. (2018). Do we see victims' agency? Criminal justice and gender violence in Spain. *Critical Criminology, 26*(1), 107–127. https://doi.org/10.1007/s10612-017-9379-2

Cumming, G., & Finch, S. (2005). Inference by eye: Confidence intervals and how to read pictures of data. *American Psychologist, 60*(2), 170–180. https://doi.org/10.1037/0003-066X.60.2.170

Cunha, O., Braga, T., & Gonçalves, R. A. (2018). Psychopathy and intimate partner violence. *Journal of Interpersonal Violence*. Advance online publication. https://doi.org/10.1177/0886260518754870

Cunha, O., & Gonçalves, R. A. (2013). Intimate partner violence offenders: Generating a data-based typology of batterers and implications for treatment. *The European Journal of Psychology Applied to Legal Context, 5*(2), 131–139. https://doi.org/10.5093/ejpalc2013a2

Dawes, R. M. (2005). The ethical implications of Paul Meehl's work on comparing clinical versus actuarial prediction methods. *Journal of Clinical Psychology, 61*(10), 1245–1255. https://doi.org/10.1002/jclp.20180

Dawes, R. M., Faust, D., & Meehl, P. E. (1989). Clinical versus actuarial judgment. *Science, 243*(4899), 1668–1674. https://doi.org/10.1126/science.2648573

Dawson, M., & Hotton, T. (2014). Police charging practices for incidents of intimate partner violence in Canada. *Journal of Research in Crime and Delinquency, 51*(5), 655–683. https://doi.org/10.1177/0022427814523787

Dawson, M., & Piscitelli, A. (2017). Risk factors in domestic homicides: Identifying common clusters in the Canadian context. *Journal of Interpersonal Violence*, 886260517729404. Advance online publication. https://doi.org/10.1177/0886260517729404

DeMatteo, D., Murphy, M., Galloway, M., & Krauss, D. A. (2015). A national survey of state sexually violent person (SVP) legislation: Procedures, policy and practice. *International Journal of Forensic Mental Health, 14*, 245–266. https://doi.org/10.1080/14999013.2015.1110847

De Vries Robbé, M., de Vogel, V., Douglas, K. S., & Nijman, H. L. I. (2015). Changes in dynamic risk and protective factors for violence during inpatient forensic psychiatric treatment: Predicting reductions in postdischarge community recidivism. *Law and Human Behavior, 39*(1), 53–61. https://doi.org/10.1037/lhb0000089

de Vries Robbé, M., & Willis, G. M. (2017). Assessment of protective factors in clinical practice. *Aggression and Violent Behavior, 32*, 55–63. https://doi.org/10.1016/j.avb.2016.12.006

Dichter, M. E., & Gelles, R. J. (2012). Women's perceptions of safety and risk following police intervention for intimate partner violence. *Violence Against Women, 18*(1), 44–63. https://doi.org/10.1177/1077801212437016

Díez, C., Kurland, R. P., Rothman, E. F., Bair-Merritt, M., Fleegler, E., Xuan, Z., Galea, S., Ross, C. S., Kalesan, B., Goss, K. A., & Siegel, M. (2017). State intimate partner violence–related firearm laws and intimate partner homicide rates in the United States, 1991 to 2015. *Annals of Internal Medicine, 167*(8), 536–543. https://doi.org/10.7326/M16-2849

Dobash, R. E., & Dobash, R. (1979). *Violence against wives*. The Free Press.

Dopson, S., Locock, L., Gabbay, J., Ferlie, E., & Fitzgerald, L. (2003). Evidence-based medicine and the implementation gap. *Health: An Interdisciplinary Journal for the Social Study of Health, Illness and Medicine, 7*(3), 311–330. https://doi.org/10.1177/1363459303007003004

Douglas, K. S., Hart, S. D., Webster, C. D., Belfrage, H., Guy, L. S., & Wilson, C. M. (2014). Historical-Clinical-Risk Management–20, Version 3 (HCR-20V3): Development and overview. *International Journal of Forensic Mental Health, 13*(2), 93–108. https://doi.org/10.1080/14999013.2014.906519

Drawbridge, D. C., Todorovic, K., Winters, G. M., & Vincent, G. M. (2019). Implementation of risk-need-responsivity principles into probation case planning. *Law and Human Behavior, 43*(5), 455–467. https://doi.org/10.1037/lhb0000351

Dutton, D. G. (2007). *The abusive personality: Violence and control in intimate relationships* (2nd ed.). Guilford Press.

Dutton, D. G. (2012). The case against the role of gender in intimate partner violence. *Aggression and Violent Behavior, 17*(1), 99–104. https://doi.org/10.1016/j.avb.2011.09.002

Dutton, D. G., & Golant, S. K. (1995). *The batterer: A psychological profile*. Basic Books.

Dutton, D. G., Landolt, M. A., Starzomski, A., & Bodnarchuk, M. (2001). Validation of the Propensity for Abusiveness Scale in diverse male populations. *Journal of Family Violence, 16*(59), 59–73. https://doi.org/10.1023/A:1026528510057

Duwe, G., & Rocque, M. (2018). The home-field advantage and the perils of professional judgment: Evaluating the performance of the Static-99R and the MnSOST-3 in predicting sexual recidivism. *Law and Human Behavior, 42*(3), 269–279. https://doi.org/10.1037/lhb0000277

Dyck, H. L., Campbell, M. A., & Wershler, J. L. (2018). Real-world use of the risk-need-responsivity model and the level of service/case management inventory with community-supervised offenders. *Law and Human Behavior, 42*(3), 258–268. https://doi.org/10.1037/lhb0000279

Echeburúa, E., Amor, P. J., Loinaz, I., & de Corral, P. (2010). Escala de Predicción del Riesgo de Violencia Grave contra la pareja–Revisada (EPV-R). [Severe Intimate Partner Violence Risk Prediction Scale–Revised]. *Psicothema, 22*(4), 1054–1060.

Eckhardt, C. I., & Crane, C. A. (2014). Male perpetrators of intimate partner violence and implicit attitudes toward violence: Associations with treatment outcomes. *Cognitive Therapy and Research, 38*(3), 291–301. https://doi.org/10.1007/s10608-013-9593-5

Eitle, D. (2005). The influence of mandatory arrest policies, police organizational characteristics, and situational variables on the probability of arrest in domestic violence cases. *Crime and Delinquency, 51*(4), 573–597. https://doi.org/10.1177/0011128705277784

Eke, A. W., Hilton, N. Z., Harris, G. T., Rice, M. E., & Houghton, R. E. (2011). Intimate partner homicide: Risk assessment and prospects for prediction. *Journal of Family Violence, 26*(3), 211–216. https://doi.org/10.1007/s10896-010-9356-y

Eke, A. W., Hilton, N. Z., Meloy, J. R., Mohandie, K., & Williams, J. (2011). Predictors of recidivism by stalkers: A nine-year follow-up of police contacts. *Behavioral Sciences & the Law, 29*(2), 271–283. https://doi.org/10.1002/bsl.975

Eke, A. W., Meloy, J. R., Brooks, K., Jean, L., & Hilton, N. Z. (2014). Threats, approach behavior, and violent recidivism among offenders who harass Canadian justice officials. *Journal of Threat Assessment and Management, 1*(3), 188–202. https://doi.org/10.1037/tam0000016

Ennis, L., Hargreaves, T., & Gulayets, M. (2015). The Integrated Threat and Risk Assessment Centre: A program evaluation investigating the implementation of threat management recommendations. *Journal of Threat Assessment and Management, 2*(2), 114–126. https://doi.org/10.1037/tam0000040

Ennis, L., Toop, C., Jung, S., & Bois, S. (2017). Instrumental and reactive intimate partner violence: Offender characteristics, reoffense rates, and risk management. *Journal of Threat Assessment and Management, 4*(2), 61–76. https://doi.org/10.1037/tam0000080

Eriksson, L., Mazerolle, P., Wortley, R., Johnson, H., & McPhedran, S. (2019). The offending histories of homicide offenders: Are men who kill intimate partners distinct from men who kill other men? *Psychology of Violence, 9*(4), 471–480. https://doi.org/10.1037/vio0000214

Evans, S. A., & Salekin, K. L. (2016). Violence risk communication: What do judges and forensic clinicians prefer and understand? *Journal of Threat Assessment and Management, 3*(3–4), 143–164. https://doi.org/10.1037/tam0000062

Ewert v. Canada, 2018 SCC 30 [2018] 2 S.C.R. 165. https://scc-csc.lexum.com/scc-csc/scc-csc/en/item/17133/index.do

Falzer, P. R. (2013). Valuing structured professional judgment: Predictive validity, decision-making, and the clinical-actuarial conflict. *Behavioral Sciences & the Law, 31*(1), 40–54. https://doi.org/10.1002/bsl.2043

Farrington, D. P. (1985). Predicting self-reported and official delinquency. In D. P. Farrington & R. Tarling (Eds.), *Prediction in criminology* (pp. 150–173). State University of New York.

Farrington, D. P., & Ttofi, M. M. (2014). Criminal careers in self-reports compared with official records. *Criminal Behaviour and Mental Health, 24*(4), 225–228. https://doi.org/10.1002/cbm.1932

Farrington, D. P., Ttofi, M. M., Crago, R. V., & Coid, J. W. (2014). Prevalence, frequency, onset, desistance and criminal career duration in self-reports compared with official records. *Criminal Behaviour and Mental Health, 24*(4), 241–253. https://doi.org/10.1002/cbm.1930

Felitti, V. J., Anda, R. F., Nordenberg, D., Williamson, D. F., Spitz, A. M., Edwards, V., Koss, M. P., & Marks, J. S. (1998). Relationship of childhood abuse and household dysfunction to many of the leading causes of death in adults: The Adverse Childhood Experiences (ACE) Study. *American Journal of Preventive Medicine, 14*(4), 245–258. https://doi.org/10.1016/s0749-3797(98)00017-8

Fernández Suárez, A., Pérez, B., Herrero, J., Juarros-Basterretxea, J., & Rodríguez-Díaz, F. J. (2018). The role of psychopathic traits among intimate partner–violent men: A systematic review. *Revista Iberoamericana de Psicología y Salud, 9*(2), 84–114.

Flores, A. W., Holsinger, A. M., Lowenkamp, C. T., & Cohen, T. H. (2017). Time-free effects in predicting recidivism using both fixed and variable follow-up periods. *Criminal Justice and Behavior, 44*(1), 121–137. https://doi.org/10.1177/0093854816678649

Foa, E. B., Cascardi, M., Zoellner, L. A., & Feeny, N. C. (2000). Psychological and environmental factors associated with partner violence. *Trauma, Violence & Abuse, 1*(1), 67–91. https://doi.org/10.1177/1524838000001001005

Folkes, S. E. F., Hilton, N. Z., & Harris, G. T. (2013). Weapon use increases the severity of domestic violence but neither weapon use nor firearm access increases the risk or severity of recidivism. *Journal of Interpersonal Violence, 28*(6), 1143–1156. https://doi.org/10.1177/0886260512468232

Fowler, D. R., Cantos, A. L., & Miller, S. A. (2016). Exposure to violence, typology, and recidivism in a probation sample of domestic violence perpetrators. *Child Abuse & Neglect, 59*, 66–77. https://doi.org/10.1016/j.chiabu.2016.07.007

Fowler, K. A., & Westen, D. (2011). Subtyping male perpetrators of intimate partner violence. *Journal of Interpersonal Violence, 26*(4), 607–639. https://doi.org/10.1177/0886260510365853

Fox, G. L., & Benson, M. L. (2006). Household and neighborhood contexts of intimate partner violence. *Public Health Reports, 121*(4), 419–427. https://doi.org/10.1177/003335490612100410

Fox, J. A., & Fridel, E. E. (2017). Gender differences in patterns and trends in U.S. homicide, 1976–2015. *Violence and Gender, 4*(2), 37–43. https://doi.org/10.1089/vio.2017.0016

Fraehlich, C., & Ursel, J. (2014). Arresting women: Pro-arrest policies, debates, and developments. *Journal of Family Violence, 29*(5), 507–518. https://doi.org/10.1007/s10896-014-9605-6

Garcia-Retamero, R., & Cokely, E. T. (2013). Communicating health risks with visual aids. *Current Directions in Psychological Science, 22*(5), 392–399. https://doi.org/10.1177/0963721413491570

Garner, J. H., & Maxwell, C. D. (2009). Prosecution and conviction rates for intimate partner violence. *Criminal Justice Review, 34*(1), 44–79. https://doi.org/10.1177/0734016808324231

Gawande, A. (2011). *The checklist manifesto: How to get things right*. Metropolitan.

Gayford, J. J. (1975). Battered wives: (a) Research on battered wives. *Royal Society of Health Journal, 95*(6), 288–289. https://doi.org/10.1177/146642407509500609

Gerbrandij, J., Rosenfeld, B., Nijdam-Jones, A., & Galietta, M. (2018). Evaluating risk assessment instruments for intimate partner stalking and intimate partner violence. *Journal of Threat Assessment and Management, 5*(2), 103–118. https://doi.org/10.1037/tam0000101

Gerstenberger, C., Stansfield, R., & Williams, K. R. (2019). Intimate partner violence in same-sex relationships: An analysis of risk and rearrest. *Criminal Justice and Behavior, 46*(11), 1515–1527. https://doi.org/10.1177/0093854819871984

Gerstenberger, C. B., & Williams, K. R. (2013). Gender and intimate partner violence: Does dual arrest reveal gender symmetry or asymmetry? *Journal of Interpersonal Violence, 28*(8), 1561–1578. https://doi.org/10.1177/0886260512468325

Gerth, J., Rossegger, A., Bauch, E., & Endrass, J. (2017). Assessing the discrimination and calibration of the Ontario Domestic Assault Risk Assessment in Switzerland. *Partner Abuse, 8*(2), 168–189. https://doi.org/10.1891/1946-6560.8.2.168

Gerth, J., Rossegger, A., Singh, J. P., & Endrass, J. (2015). Assessing the risk of intimate partner violence: Validating the DyRiAS in Switzerland. *Archives of Forensic Psychology, 1*(2), 1–15.

Gerth, J., Rossegger, A., Urbaniok, F., & Endrass, J. (2014). The Ontario Domestic Assault Risk Assessment (ODARA)—Validity and authorized German translation of an intimate partner violence screening tool. *Fortschritte der Neurologie-Psychiatrie, 82*(11), 616–626. https://doi.org/10.1055/s-0034-1384915

Ghazal, S., Cokely, E. T., & Garcia-Retamero, R. (2014). Predicting biases in very highly educated samples: Numeracy and metacognition. *Judgment and Decision Making, 9*(1), 15–34.

Gladwell, M. (2005). *Blink: The power of thinking without thinking*. Little, Brown.

Glass, N., Perrin, N., Hanson, G., Bloom, T., Gardner, E., & Campbell, J. C. (2008). Risk for reassault in abusive female same-sex relationships. *American Journal of Public Health, 98*(6), 1021–1027. https://doi.org/10.2105/AJPH.2007.117770

Glover, A. J. J., Churcher, F. P., Gray, A. L., Mills, J. F., & Nicholson, D. E. (2017). A cross-validation of the Violence Risk Appraisal Guide–Revised (VRAG-R) within a correctional sample. *Law and Human Behavior, 41*(6), 507–518. https://doi.org/10.1037/lhb0000257

Godbout, N., Daspe, M.-È., Lussier, Y., Sabourin, S., Dutton, D., & Hébert, M. (2017). Early exposure to violence, relationship violence, and relationship satisfaction in adolescents and emerging adults: The role of romantic attachment. *Psychological Trauma: Theory, Research, Practice and Policy, 9*(2), 127–137. https://doi.org/10.1037/tra0000136

Godbout, N., Vaillancourt-Morel, M.-P., Bigras, N., Briere, J., Hébert, M., Runtz, M., & Sabourin, S. (2019). Intimate partner violence in male survivors of child maltreatment: A meta-analysis. *Trauma, Violence & Abuse, 20*(1), 99–113. https://doi.org/10.1177/1524838017692382

Goldfarb, D., Goodman, G. S., Larson, R. P., Eisen, M. L., & Qin, J. (2018). Long-term memory in adults exposed to childhood violence: Remembering genital contact nearly 20 years later. *Clinical Psychological Science, 7*(2), 381–396. https://doi.org/10.1177/2167702618805742

Goldstein, D. A., Cantos, A. L., Brenner, L. H., Verborg, R. J., & Kosson, D. S. (2016). Perpetrator type moderates the relationship between severity of intimate partner violence and recidivism. *Criminal Justice and Behavior, 43*(7), 879–898. https://doi.org/10.1177/0093854815616841

Gondolf, E. W. (2010). The contributions of Ellen Pence to batterer programming. *Violence Against Women, 16*(9), 992–1006. https://doi.org/10.1177/1077801210379330

Gondolf, E. W., & Wernik, H. (2009). Clinician ratings of batterer treatment behaviors in predicting reassault. *Journal of Interpersonal Violence, 24*(11), 1792–1815. https://doi.org/10.1177/0886260508325493

Goodman, L. A., Dutton, M. A., & Bennett, L. (2000). predicting repeat abuse among arrested batterers. *Journal of Interpersonal Violence, 15*(1), 63–74. https://doi.org/10.1177/088626000015001005

Government of Canada. (2018). *Canadian police information centre*. http://www.cpic-cipc.ca/index-eng.htm

Graham, L. M., Sahay, K. M., Rizo, C. F., Messing, J. T., & Macy, R. J. (2019). The validity and reliability of available intimate partner homicide and reassault risk assessment tools: A systematic review. *Trauma, Violence & Abuse*, 1524838018821952. Advance online publication. https://doi.org/10.1177/1524838018821952

Graham-Kevan, N., & Archer, J. (2003). Physical aggression and control in heterosexual relationships: The effect of sampling. *Violence and Victims, 18*(2), 181–196. https://doi.org/10.1891/vivi.2003.18.2.181

Grann, M., & Långström, N. (2007). Actuarial assessment of violence risk: To weigh or not to weigh? *Criminal Justice and Behavior, 34*(1), 22–36. https://doi.org/10.1177/0093854806290250

Grann, M., & Pallvik, A. (2002). An empirical investigation of written risk communication in forensic psychiatric evaluations. *Psychology, Crime & Law, 8*(1), 113–130. https://doi.org/10.1080/10683160208401812

Grann, M., & Wedin, I. (2002). Risk factors for recidivism among spousal assault and spousal homicide offenders. *Psychology, Crime & Law, 8*(1), 5–23. https://doi.org/10.1080/10683160208401806

Grant, T. M., & Cross-Denny, B. (2017). Lethality assessment protocol. *Criminal Justice Review, 42*(4), 384–399. https://doi.org/10.1177/0734016817699672

Gray, A. L. (2012). *Assessing risk for intimate partner violence: A cross-validation of the ODARA and DVRAG within a sample of incarcerated offenders* [Unpublished master's thesis]. Carleton University.

Greenhalgh, T., Jackson, C., Shaw, S., & Janamian, T. (2016). Achieving research impact through co-creation in community-based health services: Literature review and case study. *The Milbank Quarterly, 94*(2), 392–429. https://doi.org/10.1111/1468-0009.12197

Greenhalgh, T., Robert, G., Macfarlane, F., Bate, P., & Kyriakidou, O. (2004). Diffusion of innovations in service organizations: Systematic review and recommendations. *The Milbank Quarterly, 82*(4), 581–629. https://doi.org/10.1111/j.0887-378x.2004.00325.x

Grove, W. M. (2005). Clinical versus statistical prediction: The contribution of Paul E. Meehl. *Journal of Clinical Psychology, 61*(10), 1233–1243. https://doi.org/10.1002/jclp.20179

Grove, W. M., & Meehl, P. E. (1996). Comparative efficiency of informal (subjective, impressionistic) and formal (mechanical, algorithmic) prediction procedures: The clinical-statistical controversy. *Psychology, Public Policy, and Law, 2*(2), 293–323. https://doi.org/10.1037/1076-8971.2.2.293

Guay, J.-P., & Parent, G. (2018). Broken legs, clinical overrides, and recidivism risk: An analysis of decisions to adjust risk levels with the LS/CMI. *Criminal Justice and Behavior, 45*(1), 82–100. https://doi.org/10.1177/0093854817719482

Guldimann, A., Brunner, R., Schmid, H., & Habermeyer, E. (2016). Supporting threat management with forensic expert knowledge: Protecting public officials and private individuals. *Behavioral Sciences & the Law, 34*(5), 645–659. https://doi.org/10.1002/bsl.2254

Gutierrez, L., Helmus, L. M., & Hanson, R. K. (2016). What we know and don't know about risk assessment with offenders of Indigenous heritage. *Journal of Threat Assessment and Management, 3*(2), 97–106. https://doi.org/10.1037/tam0000064

Guy, L. S., Packer, I. K., & Warnken, W. (2012). Assessing risk of violence using structured professional judgment guidelines. *Journal of Forensic Psychology Practice, 12*(3), 270–283. https://doi.org/10.1080/15228932.2012.674471

Ham, E., Hilton, N. Z., Giesbrecht, C. J., & Macdonald, S. (2019). ODARA 101: Look what's new! *Crime Science, 26*(1), 6–8.

Hamberger, L. K., & Hastings, J. E. (1989). Counseling male spouse abusers: Characteristics of treatment completers and dropouts. *Violence and Victims, 4*(4), 275–286. https://doi.org/10.1891/0886-6708.4.4.275

Hamberger, L. K., Larsen, S., & Campbell, J. (2016). Methodological contributions to the gender symmetry debate and its resolution. *Journal of Family Violence, 31*(8), 989–993. https://doi.org/10.1007/s10896-016-9873-4

Hamby, S. (2016). Self-report measures that do not produce gender parity in intimate partner violence: A multi-study investigation. *Psychology of Violence, 6*(2), 323–335. https://doi.org/10.1037/a0038207

Han, P. K. J., Piccirillo, J., Gutheil, C., Williams, D., Wartak, M. M., Dufault, C., Hallen, S., Lucas, F. L., & Joekes, K. (2016). Development and evaluation of an online risk communication teaching program for medical students. *Medical Science Educator, 26*(4), 557–567. doi:10.1007/s40670-016-0290-3

Handley, M. A., Gorukanti, A., & Cattamanchi, A. (2016). Strategies for implementing implementation science: A methodological overview. *Emergency*

Medicine Journal, 33(9), 660–664. https://doi.org/10.1136/emermed-2015-205461

Hanson, R. K. (2017). Assessing the calibration of actuarial risk scales: A primer on the E/O index. *Criminal Justice and Behavior, 44*(1), 26–39. https://doi.org/10.1177/0093854816683956

Hanson, R. K., Babchishin, K. M., Helmus, L. M., Thornton, D., & Phenix, A. (2017). Communicating the results of criterion referenced prediction measures: Risk categories for the Static-99R and Static-2002R sexual offender risk assessment tools. *Psychological Assessment, 29*(5), 582–597. https://doi.org/10.1037/pas0000371

Hanson, R. K., Cadsky, O., Harris, A., & Lalonde, C. (1997). Correlates of battering among 997 men: Family history, adjustment, and attitudinal differences. *Violence and Victims, 12*(3), 191–208. https://doi.org/10.1891/0886-6708.12.3.191

Hanson, R. K., Harris, A. J. R., Scott, T. L., & Helmus, L. (2007). *Assessing the risk of sexual offenders on community supervision: The Dynamic Supervision Project* (User report, Corrections research). Public Safety Canada. https://www.publicsafety.gc.ca/cnt/rsrcs/pblctns/ssssng-rsk-sxl-ffndrs/index-en.aspx#a08

Hanson, R. K., Helmus, L., & Bourgon, G. (2007). *The validity of risk assessments for intimate partner violence: A meta-analysis* (Report No. 2007-07). Public Safety Canada.

Hanson, R. K., & Howard, P. D. (2010). Individual confidence intervals do not inform decision-makers about the accuracy of risk assessment evaluations. *Law and Human Behavior, 34*(4), 275–281. https://doi.org/10.1007/s10979-010-9227-3

Hanson, R. K., & Morton-Bourgon, K. E. (2009). The accuracy of recidivism risk assessments for sexual offenders: A meta-analysis of 118 prediction studies. *Psychological Assessment, 21*(1), 1–21. https://doi.org/10.1037/a0014421

Hardesty, J. L., Khaw, L., Ridgway, M. D., Weber, C., & Miles, T. (2013). Coercive control and abused women's decisions about their pets when seeking shelter. *Journal of Interpersonal Violence, 28*(13), 2617–2639. https://doi.org/10.1177/0886260513487994

Harding, H. G., & Helweg-Larsen, M. (2009). Perceived risk for future intimate partner violence among women in a domestic violence shelter. *Journal of Family Violence, 24*(2), 75–85. https://doi.org/10.1007/s10896-008-9211-6

Hare, R. D. (2003). *Hare Psychopathy Checklist–Revised (PCL-R)* (2nd ed.). Multi-Health Systems.

Hare, R. D. (2016). Psychopathy, the PCL-R, and criminal justice: Some new findings and current issues. *Canadian Psychology, 57*(1), 21–34. https://doi.org/10.1037/cap0000041

Harrell, F. E., Jr., Lee, K. L., & Mark, D. B. (1996). Multivariable prognostic models: Issues in developing models, evaluating assumptions and adequacy, and measuring and reducing errors. *Statistics in Medicine, 15*(4), 361–387.

https://doi.org/10.1002/(SICI)1097-0258(19960229)15:4<361::AID-SIM168>3.0.CO;2-4

Harris, G. T., & Hilton, N. Z. (2001). Theoretical note: Interpreting moderate effects in interpersonal violence. *Journal of Interpersonal Violence, 16*(10), 1094–1098. https://doi.org/10.1177/088626001016010008

Harris, G. T., Hilton, N. Z., & Rice, M. E. (2011). Explaining the frequency of intimate partner violence by male perpetrators. *Criminal Justice and Behavior, 38*(4), 309–331. https://doi.org/10.1177/0093854810397449

Harris, G. T., Hilton, N. Z., Rice, M. E., & Eke, A. W. (2007). Children killed by genetic parents versus stepparents. *Evolution and Human Behavior, 28*(2), 85–95. https://doi.org/10.1016/j.evolhumbehav.2006.08.001

Harris, G. T., Lowenkamp, C. T., & Hilton, N. Z. (2015). Evidence for risk estimate precision: Implications for individual risk communication. *Behavioral Sciences & the Law, 33*(1), 111–127. https://doi.org/10.1002/bsl.2158

Harris, G. T., & Rice, M. E. (2003). Actuarial assessment of risk among sex offenders. *Annals of the New York Academy of Sciences, 989*(1), 198–210. https://doi.org/10.1111/j.1749-6632.2003.tb07306.x

Harris, G. T., & Rice, M. E. (2007). Characterizing the value of actuarial violence risk assessments. *Criminal Justice and Behavior, 34*(12), 1638–1658. https://doi.org/10.1177/0093854807307029

Harris, G. T., & Rice, M. E. (2015). Progress in violence risk assessment and communication: Hypothesis versus evidence. *Behavioral Sciences & the Law, 33*(1), 128–145. https://doi.org/10.1002/bsl.2157

Harris, G. T., Rice, M. E., Hilton, N. Z., Lalumiére, M. L., & Quinsey, V. L. (2007). Coercive and precocious sexuality as a fundamental aspect of psychopathy. *Journal of Personality Disorders, 21*(1), 1–27. https://doi.org/10.1521/pedi.2007.21.1.1

Harris, G. T., Rice, M. E., & Quinsey, V. L. (1993). Violent recidivism of mentally disordered offenders: The development of a statistical prediction instrument. *Criminal Justice and Behavior, 20*(4), 315–335. https://doi.org/10.1177/0093854893020004001

Harris, G. T., Rice, M. E., & Quinsey, V. L. (2010). Allegiance or fidelity? A clarifying reply. *Clinical Psychology: Science and Practice, 17*(1), 82–89. https://doi.org/10.1111/j.1468-2850.2009.01197.x

Harris, G. T., Rice, M. E., Quinsey, V. L., Chaplin, T. C., & Earls, C. (1992). Maximizing the discriminant validity of phallometric assessment data. *Psychological Assessment, 4*(4), 502–511. https://doi.org/10.1037/1040-3590.4.4.502

Harris, G. T., Rice, M. E., Quinsey, V. L., & Cormier, C. A. (2015). *Violent offenders: Appraising and managing risk* (3rd ed.). American Psychological Association. https://doi.org/10.1037/14572-000

Harris, G. T., Skilling, T. A., & Rice, M. E. (2001). The construct of psychopathy. *Crime and Justice, 28*, 197–264. https://doi.org/10.1086/652211

Hart, S. D., & Cooke, D. J. (2013). Another look at the (im-)precision of individual risk estimates made using actuarial risk assessment instruments.

Behavioral Sciences & the Law, 31(1), 81–102. https://doi.org/10.1002/bsl.2049

Hart, S. D., Douglas, K. S., & Guy, L. S. (2016). The structured professional judgement approach to violence risk assessment: Origins, nature, and advances. In *The Wiley-Blackwell handbook on the assessment, treatment and theories of sexual offending*. https://onlinelibrary.wiley.com/doi/10.1002/9781118574003.wattso030

Hawes, S. W., Boccaccini, M. T., & Murrie, D. C. (2013). Psychopathy and the combination of psychopathy and sexual deviance as predictors of sexual recidivism: Meta-analytic findings using the Psychopathy Checklist–Revised. *Psychological Assessment, 25*(1), 233–243. https://doi.org/10.1037/a0030391

Heckert, D. A., & Gondolf, E. W. (2004). Battered women's perceptions of risk versus risk factors and instruments in predicting repeat reassault. *Journal of Interpersonal Violence, 19*(7), 778–800. https://doi.org/10.1177/0886260504265619

Heilbrun, K. (1997). Prediction versus management models relevant to risk assessment: The importance of legal decision-making context. *Law and Human Behavior, 21*, 347–359. https://doi.org/10.1023/A:1024851017947

Heilbrun, K., Durham, K., Thornewill, A., Schiedel, R., Pietruszka, V., Phillips, S., Locklair, B., & Thomas, J. (2018). Life-sentenced juveniles: Public perceptions of risk and need for incarceration. *Behavioral Sciences & the Law, 36*(5), 587–596. https://doi.org/10.1002/bsl.2377

Heilbrun, K., Newsham, R., & Pietruszka, V. (2016). Risk communication: An international update. In J. P. Singh, S. Bjørkly, & S. Fazel (Eds.), *International perspectives on violence risk assessment* (pp. 150–165). Oxford University Press. https://doi.org/10.1093/acprof:oso/9780199386291.003.0009

Heilbrun, K., O'Neill, M. L., Stevens, T. N., Strohman, L. K., Bowman, Q., & Lo, Y. W. (2004). Assessing normative approaches to communicating violence risk: A national survey of psychologists. *Behavioral Sciences & the Law, 22*(2), 187–196. https://doi.org/10.1002/bsl.570

Heilbrun, K., O'Neill, M. L., Strohman, L. K., Bowman, Q., & Philipson, J. (2000). Expert approaches to communicating violence risk. *Law and Human Behavior, 24*(1), 137–148. https://doi.org/10.1023/A:1005435005404

Heilbrun, K., Philipson, J., Berman, L., & Warren, J. (1999). Risk communication: Clinicians' reported approaches and perceived values. *The Journal of the American Academy of Psychiatry and the Law, 27*(3), 397–406.

Helmus, L., & Bourgon, G. (2011). Taking stock of 15 years of research on the Spousal Assault Risk Assessment Guide (SARA): A critical review. *International Journal of Forensic Mental Health, 10*(1), 64–75. https://doi.org/10.1080/14999013.2010.551709

Helmus, L. M., & Babchishin, K. M. (2017). Primer on risk assessment and the statistics used to evaluate its accuracy. *Criminal Justice and Behavior, 44*(1), 8–25. https://doi.org/10.1177/0093854816678898

Helmus, L. M., & Quinsey, V. L. (2020). Predicting violent reoffending with the VRAG-R: Overview, controversies, and future directions for actuarial risk scales. In S. Wormith, L. Craig, & T. Hogue (Eds.), *What works in violence risk management: Theory, research, and practice* (pp. 119–144). Wiley-Blackwell.

Helmus, L. M., & Thornton, D. (2015). Stability and predictive and incremental accuracy of the individual items of Static-99R and Static-2002R in predicting sexual recidivism. *Criminal Justice and Behavior, 42*(9), 917–937. https://doi.org/10.1177/0093854814568891

Hendricks, B., Werner, T., Shipway, L., & Turinetti, G. J. (2006). Recidivism among spousal abusers: Predictions and program evaluation. *Journal of Interpersonal Violence, 21*(6), 703–716. https://doi.org/10.1177/0886260506287310

Henrichs, J., Bogaerts, S., Sijtsema, J., & Klerx-van Mierlo, F. (2015). Intimate partner violence perpetrators in a forensic psychiatric outpatient setting: Criminal history, psychopathology, and victimization. *Journal of Interpersonal Violence, 30*(12), 2109–2128. https://doi.org/10.1177/0886260514552272

Henry, C. (2018). Exposure to domestic violence as abuse and neglect: Constructions of child maltreatment in daily practice. *Child Abuse & Neglect, 86*, 79–88. https://doi.org/10.1016/j.chiabu.2018.08.018

Herman, K., Rotunda, R., Williamson, G., & Vodanovich, S. (2014). Outcomes from a Duluth model batterer intervention program at completion and long term follow-up. *Journal of Offender Rehabilitation, 53*(1), 1–18. https://doi.org/10.1080/10509674.2013.861316

Hermiston, L. (2017, April 4). Johnson County using tool to assess domestic violence risk. *The Gazette*. https://www.thegazette.com/subject/news/public-safety/johnson-county-using-tool-to-assess-domestic-violence-risk-20170404/

Hertz, P. G., Eher, R., Etzler, S., & Rettenberger, M. (2019). Cross-validation of the revised version of the Violence Risk Appraisal Guide (VRAG-R) in a sample of individuals convicted of sexual offenses. *Sexual Abuse*. Advance online publication. https://doi.org/10.1177/1079063219841901

Hilton, N. Z. (1989). One in ten: The struggle and disempowerment of the battered women's movement. *Canadian Journal of Family Law, 7*, 313–335.

Hilton, N. Z. (1992). Battered women's concerns about their children witnessing wife assault. *Journal of Interpersonal Violence, 7*(1), 77–86. https://doi.org/10.1177/088626092007001007

Hilton, N. Z. (2014). Actuarial assessment in serial intimate partner violence: Comment on Cook, Murray, Amat, and Hart. *Journal of Threat Assessment and Management, 1*(2), 87–92. https://doi.org/10.1037/tam0000013

Hilton, N. Z., Carter, A. M., Harris, G. T., & Sharpe, A. J. B. (2008). Does using nonnumerical terms to describe risk aid violence risk communication? Clinician agreement and decision making. *Journal of Interpersonal Violence, 23*(2), 171–188. https://doi.org/10.1177/0886260507309337

Hilton, N. Z., & Eke, A. W. (2016). Non-specialization of criminal careers among intimate partner violence offenders. *Criminal Justice and Behavior, 43*(10), 1347–1363. https://doi.org/10.1177/0093854816637886

Hilton, N. Z., & Ennis, L. (2020). Intimate partner violence risk assessment and management: An RNR approach to threat assessment. In S. J. Wormith, L. A. Craig, & T. Hogue (Eds.), *What works in violence risk management: Theory, research and practice* (pp. 163–182). Wiley-Blackwell.

Hilton, N. Z., & Ham, E. (2015). Cost-effectiveness of electronic training in domestic violence risk assessment: ODARA 101. *Journal of Interpersonal Violence, 30*(6), 1065–1073. https://doi.org/10.1177/0886260514539762

Hilton, N. Z., Ham, E., & Green, M. M. (2019). Adverse childhood experiences and criminal propensity among intimate partner violence offenders. *Journal of Interpersonal Violence, 34*(19), 4137–4161. https://doi.org/10.1177/0886260516674943

Hilton, N. Z., Ham, E., Nunes, K. L., Rodrigues, N. C., Frank, C., & Seto, M. C. (2017). Using graphs to improve violence risk communication. *Criminal Justice and Behavior, 44*(5), 678–694. https://doi.org/10.1177/0093854816668916

Hilton, N. Z., & Harris, G. T. (2005). Predicting violence by serious wife assaulters: A critical review and implications for policy and practice. *Trauma, Violence & Abuse, 6*, 3–23. https://doi.org/10.1177/1524838004272463

Hilton, N. Z., & Harris, G. T. (2009a). Criminal justice responses to partner violence: History, evaluation, and lessons from interventions for criminal conduct. In D. Whitaker & J. Lutzker (Eds.), *Preventing partner violence: Research and evidence-based intervention strategies* (pp. 219–243). American Psychological Association. https://doi.org/10.1037/11873-010

Hilton, N. Z., & Harris, G. T. (2009b). How nonrecidivism affects predictive accuracy: Evidence from a cross-validation of the Ontario Domestic Assault Risk Assessment (ODARA). *Journal of Interpersonal Violence, 24*(2), 326–337. https://doi.org/10.1177/0886260508316478

Hilton, N. Z., Harris, G. T., & Holder, N. L. (2008). Actuarial violence risk assessment in hospital-based partner assault clinics. *Canadian Journal of Nursing Research, 40*, 56–70.

Hilton, N. Z., Harris, G. T., Popham, S., & Lang, C. (2010). Risk assessment among incarcerated male domestic violence offenders. *Criminal Justice and Behavior, 37*(8), 815–832. https://doi.org/10.1177/0093854810368937

Hilton, N. Z., Harris, G. T., Rawson, K., & Beach, C. A. (2005). Communicating violence risk information to forensic decision makers. *Criminal Justice and Behavior, 32*(1), 97–116. https://doi.org/10.1177/0093854804270630

Hilton, N. Z., Harris, G. T., & Rice, M. E. (2000). The functions of aggression by male teenagers. *Journal of Personality and Social Psychology, 79*(6), 988–994. https://doi.org/10.1037/0022-3514.79.6.988

Hilton, N. Z., Harris, G. T., & Rice, M. E. (2001). Predicting violence by serious wife assaulters. *Journal of Interpersonal Violence, 16*(5), 408–423. https://doi.org/10.1177/088626001016005002

Hilton, N. Z., Harris, G. T., & Rice, M. E. (2006). Sixty-six years of research on the clinical versus actuarial prediction of violence. *The Counseling Psychologist, 34*(3), 400–409. https://doi.org/10.1177/0011000005285877

Hilton, N. Z., Harris, G. T., & Rice, M. E. (2007). The effect of arrest on wife assault recidivism, controlling for pre-arrest risk. *Criminal Justice and Behavior, 34*(10), 1334–1344. https://doi.org/10.1177/0093854807300757

Hilton, N. Z., Harris, G. T., & Rice, M. E. (2010). *Risk assessment for domestically violent men: Tools for criminal justice, offender intervention, and victim services*. American Psychological Association. https://doi.org/10.1037/12066-000

Hilton, N. Z., Harris, G. T., & Rice, M. E. (2015). The step-father effect in child abuse: Comparing discriminative parental solicitude and antisociality. *Psychology of Violence, 5*(1), 8–15. https://doi.org/10.1037/a0035189

Hilton, N. Z., Harris, G. T., Rice, M. E., Eke, A. W., & Lowe-Wetmore, T. (2007). Training front-line users in the Ontario Domestic Assault Risk Assessment (ODARA): A tool for police domestic investigations. *The Canadian Journal of Police & Security Services, 5*(1), 92–96.

Hilton, N. Z., Harris, G. T., Rice, M. E., Houghton, R. E., & Eke, A. W. (2008). An in-depth actuarial assessment for wife assault recidivism: The Domestic Violence Risk Appraisal Guide. *Law and Human Behavior, 32*(2), 150–163. https://doi.org/10.1007/s10979-007-9088-6

Hilton, N. Z., Harris, G. T., Rice, M. E., Lang, C., Cormier, C. A., & Lines, K. J. (2004). A brief actuarial assessment for the prediction of wife assault recidivism: The Ontario domestic assault risk assessment. *Psychological Assessment, 16*(3), 267–275. https://doi.org/10.1037/1040-3590.16.3.267

Hilton, N. Z., Harris, G. T., Rice, M. E., Smith Krans, T., & Lavigne, S. E. (1998). Antiviolence education in high schools: Implementation and evaluation. *Journal of Interpersonal Violence, 13*, 726–742. https://doi.org/10.1177/088626098013006004

Hilton, N. Z., & Helmus, L. M. (2020). Using graphs in sexual violence risk communication: Benefits may depend on the risk metric. *Sexual Abuse*. Advance online publication. https://doi.org/10.1177/1079063220951191

Hilton, N. Z., Pham, A., Jung, S., Nunes, K., & Ennis, L. (2020). Risk scores and reliability of the SARA, SARAV3, B-SAFER, and ODARA among intimate partner violence (IPV) cases referred for threat assessment. *Police Practice and Research*. Advance online publication. https://doi.org/10.1080/15614263.2020.1798235

Hilton, N. Z., Popham, S., Lang, C., & Harris, G. T. (2014). Preliminary validation of the ODARA for female intimate partner violence offenders. *Partner Abuse, 5*(2), 189–203. https://doi.org/10.1891/1946-6560.5.2.189

Hilton, N. Z., & Quinsey, V. L. (2017). Domestic Violence Risk Appraisal Guide can be scored with PCL-R Facet 4. *Crime Science, 24*, 14–16.

Hilton, N. Z., & Radatz, D. L. (2018). The criminogenic and noncriminogenic treatment needs of intimate partner violence offenders. *International Journal of Offender Therapy and Comparative Criminology, 62*(11), 3247–3259. https://doi.org/10.1177/0306624X17740015

Hilton, N. Z., & Radatz, D. L. (in press). The association of criminogenic needs with ODARA treatment categories. *Psychological Services*.

Hilton, N. Z., Rice, M. E., Harris, G. T., Judd, B., & Quinsey, V. L. (in press). The Violence Risk Appraisal Guide, Sex Offender Risk Appraisal Guide and Violence Risk Appraisal Guide–Revised for Violence Risk Assessment and the Ontario Domestic Assault Risk Assessment and Domestic Violence Risk Appraisal Guide for Domestic Assault Risk. In R. K. Otto & K. S. Douglas (Eds.), *Handbook of violence risk assessment* (2nd ed.). Routledge.

Hilton, N. Z., Scurich, N., & Helmus, L.-M. (2015). Communicating the risk of violent and offending behavior: Review and introduction to this special issue. *Behavioral Sciences & the Law, 33*(1), 1–18. https://doi.org/10.1002/bsl.2160

Hilton, N. Z., & Simmons, J. L. (2001). The influence of actuarial risk assessment in clinical judgments and tribunal decisions about mentally disordered offenders in maximum security. *Law and Human Behavior, 25*(4), 393–408. https://doi.org/10.1023/A:1010607719239

Hilton, N. Z., Simpson, A. I., & Ham, E. (2016). The increasing influence of risk assessment on forensic patient review board decisions. *Psychological Services, 13*(3), 223–231. https://doi.org/10.1037/ser0000068

Hines, D. A., & Saudino, K. J. (2004). Genetic and environmental influences on intimate partner aggression: A preliminary study. *Violence and Victims, 19*(6), 701–718. https://doi.org/10.1891/vivi.19.6.701.66341

Hirschel, D., & Buzawa, E. S. (2013). The impact of offenders leaving the scene on the police decision to arrest in cases of intimate partner violence. *Violence Against Women, 19*(9), 1079–1103. https://doi.org/10.1177/1077801213501843

Hirschel, D., Hutchison, I. W., & Shaw, M. (2010). The interrelationship between substance abuse and the likelihood of arrest, conviction, and re-offending in cases of intimate partner violence. *Journal of Family Violence, 25*(1), 81–90. https://doi.org/10.1007/s10896-009-9272-1

Hogan, N. R., & Olver, M. E. (2019). Static and dynamic assessment of violence risk among discharged forensic patients. *Criminal Justice and Behavior, 46*(7), 923–938. https://doi.org/10.1177/0093854819846526

Hoge, R. D., & Andrews, D. A. (2002). *Youth Level of Service/Case Management Inventory (YLS/CMI)*. Multi-Health Systems.

Holder, R. L., & Daly, K. (2018). Sequencing justice: A longitudinal study of justice goals of domestic violence victims. *British Journal of Criminology, 58*(4), 787–804. https://doi.org/10.1093/bjc/azx046

Holt, S., Buckley, H., & Whelan, S. (2008). The impact of exposure to domestic violence on children and young people: A review of the literature. *Child Abuse & Neglect, 32*(8), 797–810. https://doi.org/10.1016/j.chiabu.2008.02.004

Holtzworth-Munroe, A., Bates, L., Smutzler, N., & Sandin, E. (1997). A brief review of the research on husband violence: I. Maritally violent versus nonviolent men. *Aggression and Violent Behavior, 2*(1), 65–99. https://doi.org/10.1016/S1359-1789(96)00015-8

Holtzworth-Munroe, A., Meehan, J. C., Herron, K., Rehman, U., & Stuart, G. L. (2003). Do subtypes of maritally violent men continue to differ over time?

Journal of Consulting and Clinical Psychology, 71(4), 728–740. https://doi.org/10.1037/0022-006X.71.4.728

Holtzworth-Munroe, A., & Stuart, G. L. (1994). Typologies of male batterers: Three subtypes and the differences among them. *Psychological Bulletin, 116*(3), 476–497. https://doi.org/10.1037/0033-2909.116.3.476

Howard, P. D. (2017). The effect of sample heterogeneity and risk categorization on area under the curve predictive validity metrics. *Criminal Justice and Behavior, 44*(1), 103–120. https://doi.org/10.1177/0093854816678899

Howard, P. D., & Dixon, L. (2013). Identifying change in the likelihood of violent recidivism: Causal dynamic risk factors in the OASys violence predictor. *Law and Human Behavior, 37*(3), 163–174. https://doi.org/10.1037/lhb0000012

Huss, M. T., & Langhinrichsen-Rohling, J. (2006). Assessing the generalization of psychopathy in a clinical sample of domestic violence perpetrators. *Law and Human Behavior, 30*(5), 571–586. https://doi.org/10.1007/s10979-006-9052-x

Huss, M. T., & Ralston, A. (2008). Do batterer subtypes actually matter? Treatment completion, treatment response, and recidivism across a batterer typology. *Criminal Justice and Behavior, 35*(6), 710–724. https://doi.org/10.1177/0093854808316218

Imrey, P., & Dawid, A. (2015). A commentary on statistical assessment of violence recidivism risk. *Statistics and Public Policy, 2*(1), e1029338. https://doi.org/10.1080/2330443X.2015.1029338

Jackson, M. A., Sippel, L. M., Mota, N., Whalen, D., & Schumacher, J. A. (2015). Borderline personality disorder and related constructs as risk factors for intimate partner violence perpetration. *Aggression and Violent Behavior, 24*, 95–106. https://doi.org/10.1016/j.avb.2015.04.015

Jaffe, P. G., Campbell, M., Olszowy, L., & Hamilton, L. H. A. (2014). Paternal filicide in the context of domestic violence: Challenges in risk assessment and risk management for community and justice professionals. *Child Abuse Review, 23*(2), 142–153. https://doi.org/10.1002/car.2315

Jaffe, P., Wolfe, D. A., Telford, A., & Austin, G. (1986). The impact of police charges in incidents of wife abuse. *Journal of Family Violence, 1*(1), 37–49. https://doi.org/10.1007/BF00977031

Johnson, D. (2005). *Signposts of success: Interpreting Ontario's elementary school test scores*. C.D. Howe Institute. https://www.cdhowe.org/public-policy-research/signposts-success-interpreting-ontarios-elementary-school-test-scores

Johnson, M. P. (2011). Gender and types of intimate partner violence: A response to an anti-feminist literature review. *Aggression and Violent Behavior, 16*(4), 289–296. https://doi.org/10.1016/j.avb.2011.04.006

Johnson, M. P., Leone, J. M., & Xu, Y. (2014). Intimate terrorism and situational couple violence in general surveys: Ex-spouses required. *Violence Against Women, 20*(2), 186–207. https://doi.org/10.1177/1077801214521324

Johnson, R. R., & Goodlin-Fahncke, W. (2015). Exploring the effect of arrest across a domestic batterer typology. *Juvenile & Family Court Journal, 66*(1), 15–30. https://doi.org/10.1111/jfcj.12024

Jones, N. J., Brown, S. L., & Zamble, E. (2010). Predicting criminal recidivism in adult male offenders. *Criminal Justice and Behavior, 37*(8), 860–882. https://doi.org/10.1177/0093854810368924

Juarros-Basterretxea, J., Herrero, J., Fernández-Suárez, A., Pérez, B., & Rodríguez-Díaz, F. J. (2018). Are generalist batterers different from generally extra-family violent men? A study among imprisoned male violent offenders. *The European Journal of Psychology Applied to Legal Context, 10*(1), 8–14. https://doi.org/10.5093/ejpalc2018v10n1a1

Jung, S., & Buro, K. (2017). Appraising risk for intimate partner violence in a police context. *Criminal Justice and Behavior, 44*(2), 240–260. https://doi.org/10.1177/0093854816667974

Jung, S., & Stewart, J. (2019). Exploratory comparison between fatal and non-fatal cases of intimate partner violence. *Journal of Aggression, Conflict and Peace Research, 11*(3), 158–168. https://doi.org/10.1108/JACPR-11-2018-0394

Justice Center. (2017). *A five-level risk and needs system: Maximizing assessment results through the development of a common language.*

Kahneman, D. (2011). *Thinking, fast and slow*. Anchor.

Karelitz, T. M., & Budescu, D. V. (2004). You say "probable" and I say "likely": Improving interpersonal communication with verbal probability phrases. *Journal of Experimental Psychology: Applied, 10*(1), 25–41. https://doi.org/10.1037/1076-898X.10.1.25

Katerndahl, D., Burge, S., Ferrer, R., Becho, J., & Wood, R. (2014). Multi-day recurrences of intimate partner violence and alcohol intake across dynamic patterns of violence. *Journal of Evaluation in Clinical Practice, 20*(5), 711–718. https://doi.org/10.1111/jep.12218

Kelley, M. L., & Braitman, A. L. (2016). Antisocial personality disorder and physical partner violence among single and dual substance-abusing couples *Journal of Family Violence, 31*(4), 423–431. https://doi.org/10.1007/s10896-016-9802-6

Kimber, M., Adham, S., Gill, S., McTavish, J., & MacMillan, H. L. (2018). The association between child exposure to intimate partner violence (IPV) and perpetration of IPV in adulthood-A systematic review. *Child Abuse & Neglect, 76*, 273–286. https://doi.org/10.1016/j.chiabu.2017.11.007

Kimmes, J. G., Mallory, A. B., Spencer, C., Beck, A. R., Cafferky, B., & Stith, S. M. (2019). A meta-analysis of risk markers for intimate partner violence in same-sex relationships. *Trauma, Violence & Abuse, 20*(3), 374–384. https://doi.org/10.1177/1524838017708784

Klein, A. R. (2009). *Practical implications of current domestic violence research: For law enforcement, prosecutors and judges*. U.S. Department of Justice,

National Institute of Justice Special Report. https://www.ncjrs.gov/pdffiles1/nij/225722.pdf

Knighton, J. C., Murrie, D. C., Boccaccini, M. T., & Turner, D. B. (2014). How likely is "likely to reoffend" in sex offender civil commitment trials? *Law and Human Behavior, 38*(3), 293–304. https://doi.org/10.1037/lhb0000079

Konečni, V. J., & Ebbesen, E. B. (1984). The mythology of legal decision making. *International Journal of Law and Psychiatry, 7*(1), 5–18. https://doi.org/10.1016/0160-2527(84)90003-7

Krauss, D. A., Cook, G. I., & Klapatch, L. (2018). Risk assessment communication difficulties: An empirical examination of the effects of categorical versus probabilistic risk communication in sexually violent predator decisions. *Behavioral Sciences & the Law, 36*(5), 532–553. https://doi.org/10.1002/bsl.2379

Kropp, P. R., & Hart, S. D. (2000). The Spousal Assault Risk Assessment (SARA) Guide: Reliability and validity in adult male offenders. *Law and Human Behavior, 24*(1), 101–118. https://doi.org/10.1023/A:1005430904495

Kropp, P. R., & Hart, S. D. (2004). *The development of the Brief Spousal Assault Form for the Evaluation of Risk (B-SAFER): A tool for criminal justice professionals*. Department of Justice Canada. https://www.justice.gc.ca/eng/rp-pr/fl-lf/famil/rr05_fv1-rr05_vf1/index.html

Kropp, P. R., & Hart, S. D. (2015). *SARA-V3: User guide for the third edition of the Spousal Assault Risk Assessment Guide*. ProActive ReSolutions.

Kropp, P. R., Hart, S. D., & Belfrage, H. (2010). *Brief Spousal Assault form for the Evaluation of Risk (B-SAFER)*. ProActive ReSolutions.

Kropp, P. R., Hart, S. D., & Lyon, D. R. (2002). Risk assessment of stalkers. *Criminal Justice and Behavior, 29*(5), 590–616. https://doi.org/10.1177/009385402236734

Kropp, P. R., Hart, S. D., Webster, C. D., & Eaves, D. (1999). *Spousal assault risk assessment guide*. Multi-Health Systems.

Kuijpers, K. F., Van der Knaap, L. M., & Winkel, F. W. (2012). Victims' influence on intimate partner violence revictimization: An empirical test of dynamic victim-related risk factors. *Journal of Interpersonal Violence, 27*(9), 1716–1742. https://doi.org/10.1177/0886260511430389

Labrecque, R. M., Smith, P., Lovins, B. K., & Latessa, E. J. (2014). The importance of reassessment: How changes in the LSI-R Risk Score can improve the prediction of recidivism. *Journal of Offender Rehabilitation, 53*(2), 116–128. https://doi.org/10.1080/10509674.2013.868389

Larsen, S. E., & Hamberger, L. K. (2015). Men's and women's experience of IPV Part II: A review of new developments in comparative studies in clinical populations. *Journal of Family Violence, 30*(8), 1007–1030. https://doi.org/10.1007/s10896-015-9730-x

Lauch, K. M., Hart, K. J., & Bresler, S. (2017). Predictors of treatment completion and recidivism among intimate partner violence offenders. *Journal of*

Aggression, Maltreatment & Trauma, 26(5), 543–557. https://doi.org/10.1080/10926771.2017.1299824

Lauria, I., McEwan, T. E., Luebbers, S., Simmons, M., & Ogloff, J. R. P. (2017). Evaluating the Ontario Domestic Assault Risk Assessment in an Australian frontline police setting. *Criminal Justice and Behavior, 44*(12), 1545–1558. https://doi.org/10.1177/0093854817738280

Lawson, J. (2019). Domestic violence as child maltreatment: Differential risks and outcomes among cases referred to child welfare agencies for domestic violence exposure. *Children and Youth Services Review, 98*, 32–41. https://doi.org/10.1016/j.childyouth.2018.12.017

Lee, S. C., Hanson, R. K., & Blais, J. (2020). Predictive accuracy of the Static-99R and Static-2002R risk tools for identifying Indigenous and White individuals at high risk for sexual recidivism in Canada. *Canadian Psychology, 61*(1), 42–57. https://doi.org/10.1037/cap0000182

Levin, S. K., Nilsen, P., Bendtsen, P., & Bülow, P. (2019). Adherence to planned risk management interventions in Swedish forensic care: What is said and done according to patient records. *International Journal of Law and Psychiatry, 64*, 71–82. https://doi.org/10.1016/j.ijlp.2019.02.003

Liem, M., Levin, J., Holland, C., & Fox, J. A. (2013). The nature and prevalence of familicide in the United States, 2000–2009. *Journal of Family Violence, 28*(4), 351–358. https://doi.org/10.1007/s10896-013-9504-2

Lila, M., Oliver, A., Catalá-Miñana, A., & Conchell, R. (2014). Recidivism risk reduction assessment in batterer intervention programs: A key indicator for program efficacy evaluation. *Psychosocial Intervention, 23*(3), 217–223. https://doi.org/10.1016/j.psi.2014.11.001

Logan, C. (2016). Structured professional judgment: Applications to sexual offender risk assessment and management. In A. Phenix & H. M. Hoberman (Eds.), *Sexual offending: Predisposing antecedents, assessment and management* (pp. 571–588). Springer. https://doi.org/10.1007/978-1-4939-2416-5_26

Logan, C., & Lloyd, M. (2019). Violent extremism: A comparison of approaches to assessing and managing risk. *Legal and Criminological Psychology, 24*(1), 141–161. https://doi.org/10.1111/lcrp.12140

Loinaz, I. (2014). Typologies, risk and recidivism in partner-violent men with the B-SAFER: A pilot study. *Psychology, Crime & Law, 20*(2), 183–198. https://doi.org/10.1080/1068316X.2013.770854

López-Ossorio, J. J., González Álvarez, J. L., Buquerín Pascual, S., García, L. F., & Buela-Casal, G. (2017). Risk factors related to intimate partner violence police recidivism in Spain. *International Journal of Clinical and Health Psychology, 17*(2), 107–119. https://doi.org/10.1016/j.ijchp.2016.12.001

Luppi, F., & Colpitts, J. (2014). *A roadmap to risk assessment: ODARA and Maine's CCR* [Webinar]. Battered Women's Justice Project. https://www.bwjp.org/resource-center/resource-results/a-roadmap-to-risk-assessment-odara-and-maine-s-ccr.html

Macy, R. J., & Goodbourn, M. (2012). Promoting successful collaborations between domestic violence and substance abuse treatment service sectors: A review of the literature. *Trauma, Violence & Abuse, 13*(4), 234–251. https://doi.org/10.1177/1524838012455874

Mager, K. L., Bresin, K., & Verona, E. (2014). Gender, psychopathy factors, and intimate partner violence. *Personality Disorders, 5*(3), 257–267. https://doi.org/10.1037/per0000072

Mason, R., Wolf, M., O'Rinn, S., & Ene, G. (2017). Making connections across silos: Intimate partner violence, mental health, and substance use. *BMC Women's Health, 17*(1), 29. Advance online publication. https://doi.org/10.1186/s12905-017-0372-4

Mastromanno, B., Brookstein, D. M., Ogloff, J. R. P., Campbell, R., Chu, C. M., & Daffern, M. (2018). Assessing change in dynamic risk factors in forensic psychiatric inpatients: Relationship with psychopathy and recidivism. *The Journal of Forensic Psychiatry & Psychology, 29*(2), 323–336. https://doi.org/10.1080/14789949.2017.1377277

Maxwell, C. D., & Garner, J. H. (2012). The crime control effects of criminal sanctions for intimate partner violence: 1989–2014. *Partner Abuse, 3*(4), 469–500. https://doi.org/10.1891/1946-6560.3.4.469

Maxwell, C. D., Garner, J. H., & Fagan, J. A. (2002). The preventive effects of arrest on intimate partner violence: Research, policy and theory. *Criminology & Public Policy, 2*(1), 51–80. https://doi.org/10.1111/j.1745-9133.2002.tb00107.x

McCafferty, J. T. (2017). Professional discretion and the predictive validity of a juvenile risk assessment instrument: Exploring the overlooked principle of effective correctional classification. *Youth Violence and Juvenile Justice, 15*(2), 103–118. https://doi.org/10.1177/1541204015622255

McEwan, T. E., Shea, D. E., & Ogloff, J. R. P. (2019). The development of the VP-SAFvR: An actuarial instrument for police triage of Australian family violence reports. *Criminal Justice and Behavior, 46*(4), 590–607. https://doi.org/10.1177/0093854818806031

McKee, S. A., Harris, G. T., & Rice, M. E. (2007). Improving forensic tribunal decisions: The role of the clinician. *Behavioral Sciences & the Law, 25*(4), 485–506. https://doi.org/10.1002/bsl.768

McKee, S. A., & Hilton, N. Z. (2019). Co-occurring substance use, PTSD, and IPV victimization: Implications for female offender services. *Trauma, Violence, & Abuse, 20*(3), 303–314. https://doi.org/10.1177/1524838017708782

McTague, J. (2018). *Validation of the Ontario Domestic Assault Risk Assessment (ODARA) instrument with men and women* [Unpublished master's thesis]. University of New Brunswick.

Mears, D. P., Cochran, J. C., & Lindsey, A. M. (2016). Offending and racial and ethnic disparities in criminal justice. *Journal of Contemporary Criminal Justice, 32*(1), 78–103. https://doi.org/10.1177/1043986215607252

Mehta, S., Bastero-Caballero, R. F., Sun, Y., Zhu, R., Murphy, D. K., Hardas, B., & Koch, G. (2018). Performance of intraclass correlation coefficient (ICC) as a reliability index under various distributions in scale reliability studies. *Statistics in Medicine, 37*(18), 2734–2752. https://doi.org/10.1002/sim.7679

Ménard, K. S., Anderson, A. L., & Godboldt, S. M. (2009). Gender differences in intimate partner recidivism. *Criminal Justice and Behavior, 36*(1), 61–76. https://doi.org/10.1177/0093854808325905

Mental Health Centre Penetanguishene Research Department. (2005). *Ontario Domestic Assault Risk Assessment General Scoring Criteria* [Booklet].

Messing, J. T., Amanor-Boadu, Y., Cavanaugh, C. E., Glass, N. E., & Campbell, J. C. (2013). Culturally competent intimate partner violence risk assessment: Adapting the Danger Assessment for immigrant women. *Social Work Research, 37*(3), 263–275. https://doi.org/10.1093/swr/svt019

Messing, J. T., Campbell, J. C., & Snider, C. (2017). Validation and adaptation of the danger assessment-5: A brief intimate partner violence risk assessment. *Journal of Advanced Nursing, 73*(12), 3220–3230. https://doi.org/10.1111/jan.13459

Messing, J. T., Campbell, J., Sullivan Wilson, J., Brown, S., & Patchell, B. (2017). The Lethality Screen: The predictive validity of an intimate partner violence risk assessment for use by first responders. *Journal of Interpersonal Violence, 32*(2), 205–226. https://doi.org/10.1177/0886260515585540

Messing, J. T., Campbell, J., Webster, D. W., Brown, S., Patchell, B., & Wilson, J. S. (2015). The Oklahoma Lethality Assessment Study: A quasi-experimental evaluation of the Lethality Assessment Program. *The Social Service Review, 89*(3), 499–530.

Messing, J. T., O'Sullivan, C. S., Cavanaugh, C. E., Webster, D. W., & Campbell, J. (2017). Are abused women's protective actions associated with reduced threats, stalking, and violence perpetrated by their male intimate partners? *Violence Against Women, 23*(3), 263–286. https://doi.org/10.1177/1077801216640381

Messing, J. T., & Thaller, J. (2013). The average predictive validity of intimate partner violence risk assessment instruments. *Journal of Interpersonal Violence, 28*(7), 1537–1558. https://doi.org/10.1177/0886260512468250

Milaniak, I., & Widom, C. S. (2015). Does child abuse and neglect increase risk for perpetration of violence inside and outside the home? *Psychology of Violence, 5*(3), 246–255. https://doi.org/10.1037/a0037956

Miller, D. J., Spengler, E. S., & Spengler, P. M. (2015). A meta-analysis of confidence and judgment accuracy in clinical decision making. *Journal of Counseling Psychology, 62*(4), 553–567. https://doi.org/10.1037/cou0000105

Miller, J. (2003). An arresting experiment: Domestic violence victim experiences and perceptions. *Journal of Interpersonal Violence, 18*(7), 695–716. https://doi.org/10.1177/0886260503251130

Mills, J. F. (2017). Violence risk assessment: A brief review, current issues, and future directions. *Canadian Psychology/Psychologie Canadienne, 58*(1), 40–49. https://doi.org/10.1037/cap0000100

Mills, J. F., Kroner, D. F., & Morgan, R. D. (2011). *Clinician's guide to violence risk assessment*. Guilford Press.

Monahan, J. (1981). *Predicting violent behavior: An assessment of clinical techniques*. Sage.

Monahan, J., Metz, A. L., Garrett, B. L., & Jakubow, A. (2020). Risk assessment in sentencing and plea bargaining: The roles of prosecutors and defense attorneys. *Behavioral Sciences & the Law, 38*(1), 1–11. https://doi.org/10.1002/bsl.2435

Monahan, J., & Skeem, J. L. (2014). Risk redux: The resurgence of risk assessment in criminal sanctioning. *Federal Sentencing Reporter, 26*(3), 158–166. https://doi.org/10.1525/fsr.2014.26.3.158

Monahan, J., & Skeem, J. L. (2014). Risk redux: The resurgence of risk assessment in criminal sanctioning. *Federal Sentencing Reporter, 26*(3), 158–166. https://doi.org/10.1525/fsr.2014.26.3.158

Monahan, J., Steadman, H. J., Robbins, P. C., Appelbaum, P., Banks, S., Grisso, T., Heilbrun, K., Mulvey, E. P., Roth, L., & Silver, E. (2005). An actuarial model of violence risk assessment for persons with mental disorders. *Psychiatric Services, 56*(7), 810–815. https://doi.org/10.1176/appi.ps.56.7.810

Monahan, J., Steadman, H. J., Silver, E., Appelbaum, P. S., Robbins, P., & Mulvey, E. P. (2001). *Rethinking risk assessment: The MacArthur study of mental disorder and violence*. Oxford University Press.

Monsalve, S., Ferreira, F., & Garcia, R. (2017). The connection between animal abuse and interpersonal violence: A review from the veterinary perspective. *Research in Veterinary Science, 114*, 18–26. https://doi.org/10.1016/j.rvsc. 2017.02.025

Morgan, R. D., Flora, D. B., Kroner, D. G., Mills, J. F., Varghese, F., & Steffan, J. S. (2012). Treating offenders with mental illness: A research synthesis. *Law and Human Behavior, 36*(1), 37–50.

Moser, A. E. (2012). *Validation and expansion of the Ontario Domestic Assault Risk Assessment (ODARA) instrument: An early warning system* [Unpublished master's thesis]. University of New Brunswick.

Moser, A. E., & Campbell, M. A. (2012). *Validation and expansion of the Ontario Domestic Assault Risk Assessment (ODARA) instrument: An early warning system*. Centre for Criminal Justice Studies & Psychology Department, University of New Brunswick. https://www.unb.ca/saintjohn/ccjs/_resources/pdf/odarapoliceresponse2012.pdf

Mossman, D. (2013). Evaluating risk assessments using receiver operating characteristic analysis: Rationale, advantages, insights, and limitations. *Behavioral Sciences & the Law, 31*(1), 23–39. https://doi.org/10.1002/bsl.2050

Mossman, D., & Sellke, T. (2007). Avoiding errors about "margins of error." *The British Journal of Psychiatry, 191*(6), 561–561. https://doi.org/10.1192/bjp.191.6.561

Murphy, C. M., Morrel, T. M., Elliott, J. D., & Neavins, T. M. (2003). A prognostic indicator scale for the treatment of partner abuse perpetrators. *Journal of Interpersonal Violence, 18*(9), 1087–1105. https://doi.org/10.1177/0886260503254515

Nazarewicz, J. (2020). *"You fight like a girl": Intimate partner abuse perpetration and recidivism amongst Australian women* [Unpublished doctoral dissertation]. Swinburne University of Technology, Melbourne, Australia.

Neal, T. M. S., & Grisso, T. (2014). Assessment practices and expert judgment methods in forensic psychology and psychiatry. *Criminal Justice and Behavior, 41*(12), 1406–1421. https://doi.org/10.1177/0093854814548449

Nesset, M. B., Lara-Cabrera, M. L., Dalsbø, T. K., Pedersen, S. A., Bjørngaard, J. H., & Palmstierna, T. (2019). Cognitive behavioural group therapy for male perpetrators of intimate partner violence: A systematic review. *BMC Psychiatry, 19*(1), 11. Advance online publication. https://doi.org/10.1186/s12888-019-2010-1

New Brunswick Office of the Chief Coroner. (2018). *Recommendations from the Domestic Violence Death Review Committee 2017.* https://voixfemmesnb-voiceswomennb.ca/content/dam/gnb/Departments/ps-sp/pdf/Publications/DomesticViolence2017.pdf

Ng, K. K. H., Lee, C. K. M., Chan, F. T. S., & Lv, Y. (2018). Review on meta-heuristics approaches for airside operation research. *Applied Soft Computing, 66,* 104–133. https://doi.org/10.1016/j.asoc.2018.02.013

Nguyen, T. P., Karney, B. R., & Bradbury, T. N. (2017). Childhood abuse and later marital outcomes: Do partner characteristics moderate the association? *Journal of Family Psychology, 31*(1), 82–92. https://doi.org/10.1037/fam0000208

Nicolaidis, C., Curry, M. A., Ulrich, Y., Sharps, P., McFarlane, J., Campbell, D., Gary, F., Laughon, K., Glass, N., & Campbell, J. (2003). Could we have known? A qualitative analysis of data from women who survived an attempted homicide by an intimate partner. *Journal of General Internal Medicine, 18*(10), 788–794. https://doi.org/10.1046/j.1525-1497.2003.21202.x

Northwest Territories Department of Justice. (2012). *Department of Justice strategic plan: 5 year implementation strategy 2012–2017.* https://www.assembly.gov.nt.ca/sites/default/files/12-11-05td93-173.pdf

O'Farrell, T. J., & Murphy, C. M. (1995). Marital violence before and after alcoholism treatment. *Journal of Consulting and Clinical Psychology, 63*(2), 256–262. https://doi.org/10.1037/0022-006x.63.2.2

O'Leary, K. D., Tintle, N., & Bromet, E. (2014). Risk factors for physical violence against partners in the U.S. *Psychology of Violence, 4*(1), 65–77. https://doi.org/10.1037/a0034537

Okano, M., Langille, J., & Walsh, Z. (2016). Psychopathy, alcohol use, and intimate partner violence: Evidence from two samples. *Law and Human Behavior, 40*(5), 517–523. https://doi.org/10.1037/lhb0000192

Olver, M. E., Beggs Christofferson, S. M., & Wong, S. C. P. (2015). Evaluation and applications of the clinically significant change method with the Violence Risk Scale-Sexual Offender version: Implications for risk-change communication. *Behavioral Sciences & the Law, 33*(1), 92–110. https://doi.org/10.1002/bsl.2159

Olver, M. E., & Jung, S. (2017). Incremental prediction of intimate partner violence: An examination of three risk measures. *Law and Human Behavior, 41*(5), 440–453. https://doi.org/10.1037/lhb0000251

Olver, M. E., Mundt, J. C., Thornton, D., Beggs Christofferson, S. M., Kingston, D. A., Sowden, J. N., Nicholaichuk, T. P., Gordon, A., & Wong, S. C. P. (2018). Using the Violence Risk Scale-Sexual Offense version in sexual violence risk assessments: Updated risk categories and recidivism estimates from a multi-site sample of treated sexual offenders. *Psychological Assessment, 30*(7), 941–955. https://doi.org/10.1037/pas0000538

Olver, M. E., Neumann, C. S., Sewall, L. A., Lewis, K., Hare, R. D., & Wong, S. C. P. (2018). A comprehensive examination of the psychometric properties of the Hare Psychopathy Checklist–Revised in a Canadian multisite sample of Indigenous and non-Indigenous offenders. *Psychological Assessment, 30*(6), 779–792. https://doi.org/10.1037/pas0000533

Olver, M. E., & Sewall, L. A. (2018). Cross-validation of the discrimination and calibration properties of the VRAG-R in a treated sexual offender sample. *Criminal Justice and Behavior, 45*(6), 741–761. https://doi.org/10.1177/0093854818762483

Olver, M. E., & Wong, S. C. P. (2011). A comparison of static and dynamic assessment of sexual offender risk and need in a treatment context. *Criminal Justice and Behavior, 38*(2), 113–126. https://doi.org/10.1177/0093854810389534

Ontario, F. A. C. T. (2000). *Timeline of events around the murder-suicide of Gillian and Ralph Hadley*. http://fact.on.ca/hadley/timeline.htm

Ontario Ministry of the Solicitor General. (2000). *A guide to the domestic violence supplementary report form.*

Ontario Office of the Chief Coroner. (1998). *Inquest into the deaths of Arlene May and Randy Iles, February 16–July 2, 1998.* http://www.oaith.ca/assets/files/Publications/May-Iles-inquest-recommendations.pdf

Ontario Office of the Chief Coroner. (2017). *Domestic violence death review committee 2016 annual report.* http://cdhpi.ca/sites/cdhpi.ca/files/2016%20DVDRC%20Annual%20Report%20Accessible%20%28ENGLISH%29.pdf

Ørke, E. C., Vatnar, S. K. B., & Bjørkly, S. (2018). Risk for revictimization of intimate partner violence by multiple partners: A systematic review. *Journal of Family Violence, 33*(5), 325–339. https://doi.org/10.1007/s10896-018-9952-9

O'Shea, L. E., & Dickens, G. L. (2016). Performance of protective factors assessment in risk prediction for adults: Systematic review and meta-analysis. *Clinical Psychology: Science and Practice, 23*(2), 126–138. https://doi.org/10.1111/cpsp.12146

Ottati, V., Price, E. D., Wilson, C., & Sumaktoyo, N. (2015). When self-perceptions of expertise increase closed-minded cognition: The earned dogmatism effect. *Journal of Experimental Social Psychology, 61*, 131–138. https://doi.org/10.1016/j.jesp.2015.08.003

Pate, A. M., & Hamilton, E. E. (1992). Formal and Informal deterrents to domestic violence: The Dade County Spouse Assault Experiment. *American Sociological Review, 57*(5), 691–697. https://doi.org/10.2307/2095922

Payne, J. L., & Piquero, A. R. (2016). The concordance of self-reported and officially recorded lifetime offending histories: Results from a sample of Australian prisoners. *Journal of Criminal Justice, 46*, 184–195. https://doi.org/10.1016/j.jcrimjus.2016.05.004

Payton, M. E., Greenstone, M. H., & Schenker, N. (2003). Overlapping confidence intervals or standard error intervals: What do they mean in terms of statistical significance? *Journal of Insect Science, 3*(1), 34. https://doi.org/10.1093/jis/3.1.34

Pence, E. L., & Shepard, M. F. (1999). Developing a coordinated community response. In M F. Shepard & E. L. Pence (Eds.), *Coordinating community responses to domestic violence* (pp. 3–24). Thousand Oaks, CA: Sage.

Penney, S. R., Marshall, L. A., & Simpson, A. I. F. (2016). The assessment of dynamic risk among forensic psychiatric patients transitioning to the community. *Law and Human Behavior, 40*(4), 374–386. https://doi.org/10.1037/lhb0000183

Perez Trujillo, M., & Ross, S. (2008). Police response to domestic violence: Making decisions about risk and risk management. *Journal of Interpersonal Violence, 23*(4), 454–473. https://doi.org/10.1177/0886260507312943

Peters, E. (2012). Beyond comprehension: The role of numeracy in judgments and decisions. *Current Directions in Psychological Science, 21*(1), 31–35. https://doi.org/10.1177/0963721411429960

Peterson, C., Kearns, M. C., McIntosh, W. L., Estefan, L. F., Nicolaidis, C., McCollister, K. E., Gordon, A., & Florence, C. (2018). Lifetime economic burden of intimate partner violence among U.S. adults. *American Journal of Preventive Medicine, 55*(4), 433–444. https://doi.org/10.1016/j.amepre.2018.04.049

Peterson-Badali, M., Skilling, T., & Haqanee, Z. (2015). Examining implementation of risk assessment in case management for youth in the justice system. *Criminal Justice and Behavior, 42*(3), 304–320. https://doi.org/10.1177/0093854814549595

Petersson, J., Strand, S., & Selenius, H. (2019). Risk factors for intimate partner violence: A comparison of antisocial and family-only perpetrators. *Journal of Interpersonal Violence, 34*(2), 219–239. https://doi.org/10.1177/0886260516640547

Pinto, L. A., Sullivan, E. L., Rosenbaum, A., Wyngarden, N., Umhau, J. C., Miller, M. W., & Taft, C. T. (2010). Biological correlates of intimate partner violence perpetration. *Aggression and Violent Behavior, 15*(5), 387–398. https://doi.org/10.1016/j.avb.2010.07.001

Piquero, A. R., Theobald, D., & Farrington, D. P. (2014). The overlap between offending trajectories, criminal violence, and intimate partner violence. *International Journal of Offender Therapy and Comparative Criminology, 58*(3), 286–302. https://doi.org/10.1177/0306624X12472655

Plummer, S. B., & Findley, P. A. (2012). Women with disabilities' experience with physical and sexual abuse: Review of the literature and implications for the field. *Trauma, Violence & Abuse, 13*(1), 15–29. https://doi.org/10.1177/1524838011426014

Pollock, W., Menard, S., Elliott, D. S., & Huizinga, D. H. (2015). It's official: Predictors of self-reported vs. officially recorded arrests. *Journal of Criminal Justice, 43*(1), 69–79. https://doi.org/10.1016/j.jcrimjus.2014.12.004

Post, L. A., Klevens, J., Maxwell, C. D., Shelley, G. A., & Ingram, E. (2010). An examination of whether coordinated community responses affect intimate partner violence. *Journal of Interpersonal Violence, 25*(1), 75–93. https://doi.org/10.1177/0886260508329125

Pratt, T. C., & Cullen, F. T. (2005). Assessing macro-level predictors and theories of crime: A meta-analysis. *Crime and Justice, 32*, 373–450. https://doi.org/10.1086/655357

Prins, S. J. (2019). Criminogenic or criminalized? Testing an assumption for expanding criminogenic risk assessment. *Law and Human Behavior, 43*(5), 477–490. https://doi.org/10.1037/lhb0000347

Pritchard, D. A. (1977). Linear versus configural statistical prediction. *Journal of Consulting and Clinical Psychology, 45*(4), 559–563. https://doi.org/10.1037/0022-006X.45.4.559

Province of Saskatchewan. (2009). *08–09 annual report*. Ministry of Justice and Attorney General. https://publications.saskatchewan.ca/#/products/28607

Purtle, J., Dodson, E. A., & Brownson, R. C. (2018). Policy dissemination research. In R. B. Brownson, G. A. Colditz, & E. K. Proctor (Eds.), *Dissemination and implementation research in health: Translating science into practice* (2nd ed., pp. 433–447). Oxford University Press.

Quinsey, V. L., & Ambtman, R. (1979). Variables affecting psychiatrists' and teachers' assessments of the dangerousness of mentally ill offenders. *Journal of Consulting and Clinical Psychology, 47*(2), 353–362. https://doi.org/10.1037/0022-006X.47.2.353

Quinsey, V. L., Jones, G. B., Book, A. S., & Barr, K. N. (2006). The dynamic prediction of antisocial behavior among forensic psychiatric patients: A prospective field study. *Journal of Interpersonal Violence, 21*(12), 1539–1565. https://doi.org/10.1177/0886260506294238

Quinsey, V. L., Khanna, A., & Malcolm, P. B. (1998). A retrospective evaluation of the Regional Treatment Centre Sex Offender Treatment Program. *Journal of Interpersonal Violence, 13*(5), 621–644. https://doi.org/10.1177/088626098013005005

Radatz, D. L. (2015). *Domestic violence, batterer intervention, and effective correctional programming* [Unpublished doctoral dissertation]. University of Nebraska, Lincoln.

Radatz, D. L., & Hilton, N. Z. (2019). Determining batterer intervention program treatment intensities: An illustration using the Ontario Domestic Assault Risk Assessment. *Partner Abuse, 10*(3), 269–282. https://doi.org/10.1891/1946-6560.10.3.269

Radatz, D. L., & Wright, E. M. (2016). Integrating the principles of effective intervention into batterer intervention programming. *Trauma, Violence & Abuse, 17*(1), 72–87. https://doi.org/10.1177/1524838014566695

Rettenberger, M., & Eher, R. (2013). Actuarial risk assessment in sexually motivated intimate-partner violence. *Law and Human Behavior, 37*(2), 75–86. https://doi.org/10.1037/b0000001

Rice, M. E., & Harris, G. T. (1995). Violent recidivism: Assessing predictive validity. *Journal of Consulting and Clinical Psychology, 63*(5), 737–748. https://doi.org/10.1037/0022-006x.63.5.737

Rice, M. E., & Harris, G. T. (2005). Comparing effect sizes in follow-up studies: ROC Area, Cohen's *d*, and *r*. *Law and Human Behavior, 29*(5), 615–620. https://doi.org/10.1007/s10979-005-6832-7

Rice, M. E., & Harris, G. T. (2014). What does it mean when age is related to recidivism among sex offenders? *Law and Human Behavior, 38*(2), 151–161. https://doi.org/10.1037/lhb0000052

Rice, M. E., Harris, G. T., & Lang, C. (2013). Validation of and revision to the VRAG and SORAG: The Violence Risk Appraisal Guide–Revised (VRAG-R). *Psychological Assessment, 25*(3), 951–965. https://doi.org/10.1037/a0032878

Richards, T. N., Jennings, W. G., Tomsich, E. A., & Gover, A. R. (2013). A longitudinal examination of offending and specialization among a sample of Massachusetts domestic violence offenders. *Journal of Interpersonal Violence, 28*(3), 643–663. https://doi.org/10.1177/0886260512455519

Richards, T. N., Tillyer, M. S., & Wright, E. M. (2017). Intimate partner violence and the overlap of perpetration and victimization: Considering the influence of physical, sexual, and emotional abuse in childhood. *Child Abuse & Neglect, 67*, 240–248. https://doi.org/10.1016/j.chiabu.2017.02.037

Robinson, A. L., Pinchevsky, G. M., & Guthrie, J. A. (2018). A small constellation: Risk factors informing police perceptions of domestic abuse. *Policing and Society, 28*(2), 189–204. https://doi.org/10.1080/10439463.2016.1151881

Rock, R. C., Sellbom, M., Ben-Porath, Y. S., & Salekin, R. T. (2013). Concurrent and predictive validity of psychopathy in a batterers' intervention sample. *Law and Human Behavior, 37*(3), 145–154. https://doi.org/10.1037/lhb0000006

Romero-Martínez, Á., Lila, M., & Moya-Albiol, L. (2016). Empathy impairments in intimate partner violence perpetrators with antisocial and borderline traits: A key factor in the risk of recidivism. *Violence and Victims, 31*(2), 347–360. https://doi.org/10.1891/0886-6708.vv-d-14-00149

Russ, S. J., Sevdalis, N., Moorthy, K., Mayer, E. K., Rout, S., Caris, J., Mansell, J., Davies, R., Vincent, C., & Darzi, A. (2015). A Qualitative evaluation of the barriers and facilitators toward implementation of the WHO Surgical Safety Checklist across hospitals in England. *Annals of Surgery, 261*(1), 81–91. https://doi.org/10.1097/sla.0000000000000793

Ryan, T. J. (2016). *An examination of the interrater reliability and concurrent validity of the Spousal Assault Risk Assessment Guide–Version 3 (SARA-V3)* [Unpublished doctoral dissertation]. Simon Fraser University.

Sampson, R. J., & Laub, J. H. (1994). Urban poverty and the family context of delinquency: A new look at structure and process in a classic study. *Child Development, 65*(Spec. No. 2), 523–540. https://doi.org/10.2307/1131400

Sarkies, M. N., Bowles, K.-A., Skinner, E. H., Haas, R., Lane, H., & Haines, T. P. (2017). The effectiveness of research implementation strategies for promoting evidence-informed policy and management decisions in healthcare: A systematic review. *Implementation Science, 12*, Article 132. https://doi.org/10.1186/s13012-017-0662-0

Schafers, C. L. (2019). *Risk, responsivity and the treatment process in an intimate partner violence group program* [Unpublished doctoral dissertation]. University of Saskatchewan.

Schwartz, I. M., York, P., Nowakowski-Sims, E., & Ramos-Hernandez, A. (2017). Predictive and prescriptive analytics, machine learning and child welfare risk assessment: The Broward County experience. *Children and Youth Services Review, 81*, 309–320. https://doi.org/10.1016/j.childyouth.2017.08.020

Scurich, N. (2015). The differential effect of numeracy and anecdotes on the perceived fallibility of forensic science. *Psychiatry, Psychology and Law, 22*(4), 616–623. https://doi.org/10.1080/13218719.2014.965293

Scurich, N. (2018). The case against categorical risk estimates. *Behavioral Sciences & the Law, 36*(5), 554–564. https://doi.org/10.1002/bsl.2382

Scurich, N., & John, R. S. (2011). The effect of framing actuarial risk probabilities on involuntary civil commitment decisions. *Law and Human Behavior, 35*(2), 83–91. https://doi.org/10.1007/s10979-010-9218-4

Scurich, N., & John, R. S. (2012). Prescriptive approaches to communicating the risk of violence in actuarial risk assessment. *Psychology, Public Policy, and Law, 18*(1), 50–78. https://doi.org/10.1037/a0024592

Scurich, N., & Krauss, D. A. (2013). The effect of adjusted actuarial risk assessment on mock-jurors' decisions in a sexual predator commitment proceeding. *Jurimetrics, 53*(4), 395–413. https://www.jstor.org/stable/24395656

Scurich, N., Monahan, J., & John, R. S. (2012). Innumeracy and unpacking: Bridging the nomothetic/idiographic divide in violence risk assessment. *Law and Human Behavior, 36*(6), 548–554. https://doi.org/10.1037/h0093994

Seewald, K., Rossegger, A., Urbaniok, F., & Endrass, J. (2017). Assessing the risk of intimate partner violence: Expert evaluations versus the Ontario Domestic Assault Risk Assessment. *Journal of Forensic Psychology Research and Practice, 17*(4), 217–231. https://doi.org/10.1080/24732850.2017.1326268

Sentürk, A. B., Wesemüller, M., & Rettenberger, M. (2016). Kriminalprognose bei häuslicher gewalt validierung der Deutschsprachigen version des Ontario Domestic Assault Risk Assessment (ODARA) an weiblichen und männlichen häuslichen Gewalttätern [Risk assessment in cases of domestic violence—A validation of the German version of the Ontario Domestic Assault Risk Assessment (ODARA) with female and male domestic violence offenders]. *Rpsych Rechtspsychologie, 2*(3), 330–344. https://doi.org/10.5771/2365-1083-2016-3-330

Serie, C. M. B., van Tilburg, C. A., van Dam, A., & de Ruiter, C. (2017). Spousal assaulters in outpatient mental health care: The relevance of structured risk assessment. *Journal of Interpersonal Violence, 32*(11), 1658–1677. https://doi.org/10.1177/0886260515589932

Serin, R. C., Lloyd, C. D., Helmus, L., Derkzen, D. M., & Luong, D. (2013). Does intra-individual change predict offender recidivism? Searching for the Holy Grail in assessing offender change. *Aggression and Violent Behavior, 18*(1), 32–53. https://doi.org/10.1016/j.avb.2012.09.002

Seto, M. C. (2013). *Internet sex offenders*. American Psychological Association. https://doi.org/10.1037/14191-000

Sherman, L. W., & Berk, R. A. (1984). The specific deterrent effects of arrest for domestic assault. *American Sociological Review, 49*(2), 261–272. https://doi.org/10.2307/2095575

Sherman, L. W., Schmidt, J. D., Rogan, D. P., Smith, D. A., Gartin, P. R., Cohn, E. G., Collins, J., & Bacich, A. R. (1992). The variable effects of arrest on criminal careers: The Milwaukee Domestic Violence Experiment. *The Journal of Criminal Law & Criminology*, *83*(1), 137–169. https://doi.org/10.2307/1143827

Shorey, R. C., Elmquist, J., Ninnemann, A., Brasfield, H., Febres, J., Rothman, E. F., Schonbrun, Y. C., Temple, J. R., & Stuart, G. L. (2012). The association between intimate partner violence perpetration, victimization, and mental health among women arrested for domestic violence. *Partner Abuse*, *3*(1), 3–21. https://doi.org/10.1891/1946-6560.3.1.3

Shorey, R. C., Febres, J., Brasfield, H., & Stuart, G. L. (2012). The prevalence of mental health problems in men arrested for domestic violence. *Journal of Family Violence*, *27*(8), 741–748. https://doi.org/10.1007/s10896-012-9463-z

Shrout, P. E., & Fleiss, J. L. (1979). Intraclass correlations: Uses in assessing rater reliability. *Psychological Bulletin*, *86*(2), 420–428. https://doi.org/10.1037/0033-2909.86.2.420

Singh, J. P., Desmarais, S. L., Hurducas, C., Arbach-Lucioni, K., Condemarin, C., Dean, K., Doyle, M., Folino, J. O., Godoy-Cervera, V., Grann, M., Ho, R. M. Y., Large, M. M., Nielsen, L. H., Pham, T. H., Rebocho, M. F., Reeves, K. A., Rettenberger, M., de Ruiter, C., Seewald, K., & Otto, R. K. (2014). International perspectives on the practical application of violence risk assessment: A global survey of 44 countries. *International Journal of Forensic Mental Health*, *13*(3), 193–206. https://doi.org/10.1080/14999013.2014.922141

Skeem, J. L., & Lowenkamp, C. T. (2016). Risk, race, and recidivism: Predictive bias and disparate impact. *Criminology*, *54*(4), 680–712. https://doi.org/10.1111/1745-9125.12123

Skeem, J. L., & Monahan, J. (2011). Current directions in violence risk assessment. *Current Directions in Psychological Science*, *20*(1), 38–42. https://doi.org/10.1177/0963721410397271

Skeem, J. L., Scurich, N., & Monahan, J. (2020). Impact of risk assessment on judges' fairness in sentencing relatively poor defendants. *Law and Human Behavior*, *44*(1), 51–59. https://doi.org/10.1037/lhb0000360

Snider, C., Webster, D., O'Sullivan, C. S., & Campbell, J. (2009). Intimate partner violence: Development of a brief risk assessment for the emergency department. *Academic Emergency Medicine*, *16*(11), 1208–1216. https://doi.org/10.1111/j.1553-2712.2009.00457.x

Sorenson, S. B., & Schut, R. A. (2018). Nonfatal gun use in intimate partner violence: A systematic review of the literature. *Trauma, Violence & Abuse*, *19*(4), 431–442. https://doi.org/10.1177/1524838016668589

Spreco, A., & Timpka, T. (2016). Algorithms for detecting and predicting influenza outbreaks: Metanarrative review of prospective evaluations. *BMJ Open*, *6*(5), e010683. https://doi.org/10.1136/bmjopen-2015-010683

Stansfield, R., & Williams, K. R. (2014). Predicting family violence recidivism using the DVSI–R: Integrating survival analysis and perpetrator characteristics. *Criminal Justice and Behavior*, *41*(2), 163–180. https://doi.org/10.1177/0093854813500776

Stare, B. G., & Fernando, D. M. (2014). Intimate partner violence typology and treatment. *The Family Journal, 22*(3), 298–303. https://doi.org/10.1177/1066480714529747

State of New Mexico. (2008). Criminal Procedure Act, Article 12, Section 31-12-12. https://laws.nmonesource.com/w/nmos/Chapter-31-NMSA-1978#!b/31-12-12

Stevenson, M. T. (2018). Assessing risk assessment in action. *Minnesota Law Review, 103*, 303–384. https://doi.org/10.2139/ssrn.3016088

Stevenson, R., Fitzgerald, A., & Barrett, B. J. (2018). Keeping pets safe in the context of intimate partner violence: Insights from domestic violence shelter staff in Canada. *Affilia, 33*(2), 236–252. https://doi.org/10.1177/0886109917747613

Stewart, L. A., Gabora, N., Kropp, P. R., & Lee, Z. (2014). Effectiveness of risk-needs-responsivity-based family violence programs with male offenders *Journal of Family Violence, 29*(2), 151–164. https://doi.org/10.1007/s10896-013-9575-0

Stewart, L. A., & Power, J. (2014). Profile and programming needs of federal offenders with histories of intimate partner violence. *Journal of Interpersonal Violence, 29*(15), 2723–2747. https://doi.org/10.1177/0886260514526059

Stith, S. M., Green, N. M., Smith, D. B., & Ward, D. B. (2008). Marital satisfaction and marital discord as risk markers for intimate partner violence: A meta-analytic review. *Journal of Family Violence, 23*(3), 149–160. https://doi.org/10.1007/s10896-007-9137-4

Stoff, B. K., & Swerlick, R. A. (2013). Reframing risk part II: Methods for improving medical risk communication. *Journal of the American Academy of Dermatology, 69*(4), 637–639. https://doi.org/10.1016/j.jaad.2013.02.026

Storey, J. E., Gibas, A. L., Reeves, K. A., & Hart, S. D. (2011). Evaluation of a violence risk (threat) assessment training program for police and other criminal justice professionals. *Criminal Justice and Behavior, 38*(6), 554–564. https://doi.org/10.1177/0093854811403123

Storey, J. E., Kropp, P. R., Hart, S. D., Belfrage, H., & Strand, S. (2014). Assessment and management of risk for intimate partner violence by police officers using the Brief Spousal Assault Form for the Evaluation of Risk. *Criminal Justice and Behavior, 41*(2), 256–271. https://doi.org/10.1177/0093854813503960

Storey, J. E., & Strand, S. (2017). The influence of victim vulnerability and gender on police officers' assessment of intimate partner violence risk. *Journal of Family Violence, 32*(1), 125–134. https://doi.org/10.1007/s10896-016-9905-0

Straus, M. A., Hamby, S. L., Boney-McCoy, S., & Sugarman, D. B. (1996). The Revised Conflict Tactics Scales (CTS2): Development and preliminary psychometric data. *Journal of Family Issues, 17*(3), 283–316. https://doi.org/10.1177/019251396017003001

Stuart, E. P., & Campbell, J. C. (1989). Assessment of patterns of dangerousness with battered women. *Issues in Mental Health Nursing, 10*(3–4), 245–260. https://doi.org/10.3109/01612848909140848

Stuart, G. L., McGeary, J., Shorey, R. C., & Knopik, V. S. (2016). Genetics moderate alcohol and intimate partner violence treatment outcomes in a randomized controlled trial of hazardous drinking men in batterer intervention programs: A preliminary investigation. *Journal of Consulting and Clinical Psychology, 84*(7), 592–598. https://doi.org/10.1037/a0040219

Sullivan, C. M. (2018). Understanding how domestic violence support services promote survivor well-being: A conceptual model. *Journal of Family Violence, 33*(2), 123–131. https://doi.org/10.1007/s10896-017-9931-6

Svalin, K., Mellgren, C., Levander, M. T., & Levander, S. (2018). Police employees' violence risk assessments: The predictive validity of the B-SAFER and the significance of protective actions. *International Journal of Law and Psychiatry, 56*, 71–79. https://doi.org/10.1016/j.ijlp.2017.09.001

Swets, J. A., Dawes, R. M., & Monahan, J. (2000). Psychological science can improve diagnostic decisions. *Psychological Science in the Public Interest, 1*(1), 1–26. https://doi.org/10.1111/1529-1006.001

Swogger, M. T., Walsh, Z., & Kosson, D. S. (2007). Domestic violence and psychopathic traits: Distinguishing the antisocial batterer from other antisocial offenders. *Aggressive Behavior, 33*(3), 253–260. https://doi.org/10.1002/ab.20185

Swogger, M. T., Walsh, Z., Kosson, D. S., Cashman-Brown, S., & Caine, E. D. (2012). Self-reported childhood physical abuse and perpetration of intimate partner violence. *Criminal Justice and Behavior, 39*(7), 910–922. https://doi.org/10.1177/0093854812438160

Taxman, F. S., Pattavina, A., & Caudy, M. (2014). Justice reinvestment in the United States: An empirical assessment of the potential impact of increased correctional programming on recidivism. *Victims & Offenders, 9*(1), 50–75. https://doi.org/10.1080/15564886.2013.860934

Taylor, A., & Byrne-Davis, L. (2017). Clinician numeracy: Use of the medical interpretation and numeracy test in foundation trainee doctors. *Numeracy, 10*(2), Article 5. Advance online publication. https://doi.org/10.5038/1936-4660.10.2.5

Teicher, M. H., & Samson, J. A. (2016). Annual Research Review: Enduring neurobiological effects of childhood abuse and neglect. *Journal of Child Psychology and Psychiatry, and Allied Disciplines, 57*(3), 241–266. https://doi.org/10.1111/jcpp.12507

Theobald, D., Farrington, D. P., Coid, J. W., & Piquero, A. R. (2016). Are male perpetrators of intimate partner violence different from convicted violent offenders? Examination of psychopathic traits and life success in males from a community survey. *Journal of Interpersonal Violence, 31*(9), 1687–1718. https://doi.org/10.1177/0886260515569061

Thijssen, J., & de Ruiter, C. (2011). Identifying subtypes of spousal assaulters using the B-SAFER. *Journal of Interpersonal Violence, 26*(7), 1307–1321. https://doi.org/10.1177/0886260510369129

Thornton, S. (2017). Police attempts to predict domestic murder and serious assaults: Is early warning possible yet? *Cambridge Journal of Evidence-Based Policing, 1*(2–3), 64–80. https://doi.org/10.1007/s41887-017-0011-1

Trinh, B. V. (2010). *A replication study of the Domestic Violence Risk Appraisal Guide (DVRAG)* [Unpublished doctoral dissertation]. Alliant International University.

Turner, E., Medina, J., & Brown, G. (2019). Dashing hopes? The predictive accuracy of domestic abuse risk assessment by police. *British Journal of Criminology, 59*(5), 1013–1034. https://doi.org/10.1093/bjc/azy074

Tutty, L. M., & Koshan, J. (2013). Calgary's specialized domestic violence court: An evaluation of a unique model. *Alberta Law Review, 50*(4), 731–755. https://doi.org/10.29173/alr74

Ulmer, J. C. (2015). *The Ontario Domestic Assault Risk Assessment (ODARA): A validation and comparison study for an Oregonian law enforcement agency* [Doctoral dissertation, George Fox University]. https://digitalcommons.georgefox.edu/psyd/177

van den Berg, J. W., Smid, W., Schepers, K., Wever, E., van Beek, D., Janssen, E., & Gijs, L. (2018). The predictive properties of dynamic sex offender risk assessment instruments: A meta-analysis. *Psychological Assessment, 30*(2), 179–191. https://doi.org/10.1037/pas0000454

van der Put, C. E., Gubbels, J., & Assink, M. (2019). Predicting domestic violence: A meta-analysis on the predictive validity of risk assessment tools. *Aggression and Violent Behavior, 47,* 100–116. https://doi.org/10.1016/j.avb.2019.03.008

Varela, J. G., Boccaccini, M. T., Cuervo, V. A., Murrie, D. C., & Clark, J. W. (2014). Same score, different message: Perceptions of offender risk depend on Static-99R risk communication format. *Law and Human Behavior, 38*(5), 418–427. https://doi.org/10.1037/lhb0000073

Vatnar, S. K. K., Friestad, C., & Bjørkly, S. (2017). Intimate partner homicide in Norway 1990–2012: Identifying risk factors through structured risk assessment, court documents, and interviews with bereaved. *Psychology of Violence, 7*(3), 395–405. https://doi.org/10.1037/vio0000100

Viljoen, J. L., Cochrane, D. M., & Jonnson, M. R. (2018). Do risk assessment tools help manage and reduce risk of violence and reoffending? A systematic review. *Law and Human Behavior, 42*(3), 181–214. https://doi.org/10.1037/lhb0000280

Vose, B., Smith, P., & Cullen, F. T. (2013). Predictive validity and the impact of change in total LSI–R score on recidivism. *Criminal Justice and Behavior, 40*(12), 1383–1396. https://doi.org/10.1177/0093854813508916

Walker, L. E. (2017). *The battered woman syndrome* (4th ed.). Springer.

Walsh, Z., Swogger, M. T., O'Connor, B. P., Chatav Schonbrun, Y., Shea, M. T., & Stuart, G. L. (2010). Subtypes of partner violence perpetrators among male and female psychiatric patients. *Journal of Abnormal Psychology, 119*(3), 563–574. https://doi.org/10.1037/a0019858

Walters, G. D., Kroner, D. G., DeMatteo, D., & Locklair, B. R. (2014). The impact of base rate utilization and clinical experience on the accuracy of judgments made with the HCR-20. *Journal of Forensic Psychology Practice, 14*(4), 288–301. https://doi.org/10.1080/15228932.2014.941726

Walton, M. (2019). Bail reform and intimate partner violence in Maine. *Maine Law Review, 71*(1). *Article, 6,* 1–43.

Ward-Lasher, A., Sheridan, D. J., Glass, N. E., & Messing, J. T. (2017). Prediction of interpersonal violence: An introduction. In J. C. Campbell & J. T. Messing (Eds.), *Assessing dangerousness: Domestic violence offenders and child abusers* (3rd ed., pp. 1–32). Springer.

Wareham, J., Boots, D. P., & Chavez, J. M. (2009). A test of social learning and intergenerational transmission among batterers. *Journal of Criminal Justice, 37*(2), 163–173. https://doi.org/10.1016/j.jcrimjus.2009.02.011

Watt, M. E., & Scrandis, D. A. (2013). Traumatic childhood exposures in the lives of male perpetrators of female intimate partner violence. *Journal of Interpersonal Violence, 28*(14), 2813–2830. https://doi.org/10.1177/0886260513488694

Webster, C. D., Douglas, K. S., Eaves, D., & Hart, S. D. (1997). *HCR–20. Assessing the risk of violence. Version 2*. Simon Fraser University and Forensic Psychiatric Services Commission of British Columbia.

Webster, C. M., Doob, A. N., & Myers, N. M. (2009). The parable of Ms Baker: Understanding pre-trial detention in Canada. *Current Issues in Criminal Justice, 21*(1), 79–102. https://doi.org/10.1080/10345329.2009.12035834

Weisz, A. N., Black, B. M., Lucero, J. L., Kaiser, A., Rose, I., & Muzzi, D. (2012). Batterers' intervention: How group leaders assess the risk levels of participants. *Journal of Offender Rehabilitation, 51*(6), 414–433. https://doi.org/10.1080/10509674.2012.693901

Weisz, A. N., Tolman, R. M., & Saunders, D. G. (2000). Assessing the risk of severe domestic violence. *Journal of Interpersonal Violence, 15*(1), 75–90. https://doi.org/10.1177/088626000015001006

Whittington, R., Hockenhull, J. C., McGuire, J., Leitner, M., Barr, W., Cherry, M. G., Flentje, R., Quinn, B., Dundar, Y., & Dickson, R. (2013). A systematic review of risk assessment strategies for populations at high risk of engaging in violent behaviour: Update 2002-8. *Health Technology Assessment, 17*(50), i–xiv, 1–128. Advance online publication. https://doi.org/10.3310/hta17500

Wijenayake, S., Graham, T., & Christen, P. (2018). A decision tree approach to predicting recidivism in domestic violence. In M. Ganji, L. Rashidi, B. Fung, & C. Wang (Eds.), *Trends and applications in knowledge discovery and data mining: PAKDD 2018* (Vol. 11154). Springer. https://doi.org/10.1007/978-3-030-04503-6_1

Williams, K. M., Wormith, J. S., Bonta, J., & Sitarenios, G. (2017). The use of meta-analysis to compare and select offender risk instruments: A commentary on Singh, Grann, and Fazel (2011). *International Journal of Forensic Mental Health, 16*(1), 1–15. https://doi.org/10.1080/14999013.2016.1255280

Williams, K. R. (2012). Family violence risk assessment: A predictive cross-validation study of the Domestic Violence Screening Instrument–Revised (DVSI-R). *Law and Human Behavior, 36*(2), 120–129. https://doi.org/10.1037/h0093977

Williams, K. R., & Grant, S. R. (2006). Empirically examining the risk of intimate partner violence: The revised Domestic Violence Screening Instrument (DVSI-R). *Public Health Reports, 121*(4), 400–408. https://doi.org/10.1177/003335490612100408

Williams, K. R., & Houghton, A. B. (2004). Assessing the risk of domestic violence reoffending: A validation study. *Law and Human Behavior, 28*(4), 437–455. https://doi.org/10.1023/B:LAHU.0000039334.59297.f0

Williams, K. R., & Stansfield, R. (2017). Disentangling the risk assessment and intimate partner violence relation: Estimating mediating and moderating effects. *Law and Human Behavior, 41*(4), 344–353. https://doi.org/10.1037/lhb0000249

Wilson, C. M., Crocker, A. G., Nicholls, T. L., Charette, Y., & Seto, M. C. (2015). The use of risk and need factors in forensic mental health decision-making and the role of gender and index offense severity. *Behavioral Sciences & the Law, 33*(1), 19–38. https://doi.org/10.1002/bsl.2162

Winstok, Z. (2017). Critical review of Hamby's (2014) article titled "Intimate partner and sexual violence research, scientific progress, scientific challenges, and gender." *Trauma, Violence & Abuse, 18*(2), 134–144. https://doi.org/10.1177/1524838015596962

Wong, T., & Hisashima, J. (2008). *Domestic violence exploratory study on the DVSI and SARA*. Hawaii State Department of Health Interagency Council on Intermediate Sanctions Technical Report #1. http://icis.hawaii.gov/wp-content/uploads/2013/07/SARA-DVSI-Exploratory-Study-Oct-2008.pdf

Wormith, J. S., Hogg, S., & Guzzo, L. (2012). The predictive validity of a general risk/needs assessment inventory on sexual offender recidivism and an exploration of the professional override. *Criminal Justice and Behavior, 39*(12), 1511–1538. https://doi.org/10.1177/0093854812455741

Wright, E. M. (2015). The relationship between social support and intimate partner violence in neighborhood context. *Crime and Delinquency, 61*(10), 1333–1359. https://doi.org/10.1177/0011128712466890

Wuerch, M. A., Giesbrecht, C. J., Price, J. A. B., Knutson, T., & Wach, F. (2017). Examining the relationship between intimate partner violence and concern for animal care and safekeeping. *Journal of Interpersonal Violence*. Advance online publication. https://doi.org/10.1177/0886260517700618

Xie, M., & Lynch, J. P. (2017). The effects of arrest, reporting to the police, and victim services on intimate partner violence. *Journal of Research in Crime and Delinquency, 54*(3), 338–378. https://doi.org/10.1177/0022427816678035

Yakubovich, A. R., Stöckl, H., Murray, J., Melendez-Torres, G. J., Steinert, J. I., Glavin, C. E. Y., & Humphreys, D. K. (2018). Risk and protective factors for intimate partner violence against women: Systematic review and meta-analyses of prospective-longitudinal studies. *American Journal of Public Health, 108*(7), e1–e11. https://doi.org/10.2105/AJPH.2018.304428

Zhang, D. C., Highhouse, S., Brooks, M. E., & Zhang, Y. (2018). Communicating the validity of structured job interviews with graphical visual aids. *International Journal of Selection and Assessment, 26*(2–4), 93–108. https://doi.org/10.1111/ijsa.12220

Zikmund-Fisher, B. J., Witteman, H. O., Dickson, M., Fuhrel-Forbis, A., Kahn, V. C., Exe, N. L., Valerio, M., Holtzman, L. G., Scherer, L. D., & Fagerlin, A. (2014). Blocks, ovals, or people? Icon type affects risk perceptions and recall of pictographs. *Medical Decision Making, 34*(4), 443–453. https://doi.org/10.1177/0272989X13511706

Index

A

B

S

T

About the Author

N. Zoe Hilton, PhD, is an associate professor of psychiatry at the University of Toronto, Ontario, Canada, and senior research scientist at the Waypoint Centre for Mental Health Care, Penetanguishene, Ontario, Canada. She is also a registered psychologist and a Fellow of the Canadian Psychological Association. She earned degrees from the University of Southampton, England; the University of Cambridge, England; and the University of Toronto. She has authored or coauthored more than 100 publications, primarily on violence risk assessment, risk communication, and other areas of forensic psychology. She received the 2010 Significant Contribution Award from the Canadian Psychological Association Criminal Justice Section for outstanding contributions to domestic violence risk assessment. For many years, she worked with the late Grant T. Harris, PhD, and Marnie E. Rice, PhD, especially and extensively on the development and validation of the Ontario Domestic Assault Risk Assessment (ODARA) and Domestic Violence Risk Appraisal Guide (DVRAG), tools that are the subject of Part II of this volume.